m55

Syria

THE ROUGH GUIDE

There are more than one hundred Rough Guide titles
covering destinations from Amsterdam to Zimbabwe

Forthcoming titles include
Bangkok • Central America • Chile • Japan

Rough Guide Reference Series
Classical Music • European Football • The Internet • Jazz
Opera • Reggae • Rock Music • World Music

Rough Guide Phrasebooks
Czech • Egyptian Arabic • French • German • Greek
Hindi & Urdu • Hungarian • Indonesian • Italian • Japanese
Mandarin Chinese • Mexican Spanish • Polish• Portuguese
Russian • Spanish • Swahili • Thai • Turkish • Vietnamese

Rough Guides on the Internet
www.roughguides.com

ROUGH GUIDE CREDITS

Text editor: Paul Gray
Series editor: Mark Ellingham
Editorial: Martin Dunford, Jonathan Buckley, Samantha Cook, Jo Mead, Kate Berens, Amanda Tomlin, Ann-Marie Shaw, Chris Schüler, Helena Smith, Judith Bamber, Kieran Falconer, Orla Duane, Olivia Eccleshall, Ruth Blackmore, Sophie Martin (UK); Andrew Rosenberg (US)
Production: Susanne Hillen, Andy Hilliard, Judy Pang, Link Hall, Helen Ostick, James Morris, Julia Bovis

Cartography: Melissa Flack, Maxine Burke, Nichola Goodliffe
Picture research: Eleanor Hill
Online editors: Alan Spicer, Kate Hands (UK); Geronimo Madrid (US)
Finance: John Fisher, Celia Crowley, Neeta Mistry
Marketing & Publicity: Richard Trillo, Simon Ca Niki Smith (UK); Jean-Marie Kelly, SoRelle Braun (
Administration: Tania Hummel, Alexander Mark R

ACKNOWLEDGEMENTS

The authors would like to thank the British–Arab Chamber of Commerce, London, for providing much valuable information; and the Meteorological Office, Bracknell, Berkshire.

Andrew: thanks to Peter Cheshire for his company on the long overland trek to Damascus through Eastern Europe and Turkey, and for his research into Aleppo eateries; Elaine Galloway and the EC 1997 cruise party, who put up with being stuck for a night in Tartous harbour with far greater forbearance than me, and without whom I might never have got to the Crac; and the folks back home in the Chilterns, who provided a quiet and leafy haven in which to finish and correct the manuscript.

Tim: thanks to all the numerous people across Syria whose friendliness and hospitality on a daily basis r researching the book so much pleasure; back home, thanks also to family and friends, in particular Huw, Darryl, Darren and Ant.

The editor would like to thank Alison Cowan and Nick Thomson for Basics research, Jennifer Speake proofreading; The Map Studio, Romsey, Hants and Maxine for cartography; Link, Helen, James and Jud for production.

PUBLISHING INFORMATION

This first edition published September 1998 by
Rough Guides Ltd, 62–70 Shorts Gardens,
London WC2H 9AB.
Distributed by the Penguin Group:
Penguin Books Ltd, 27 Wrights Lane, London W8 5TZ.
Penguin Books USA Inc., 375 Hudson Street, New York 10014, USA.
Penguin Books Australia Ltd, 487 Maroondah Highway, PO Box 257, Ringwood, Victoria 3134, Australia.
Penguin Books Canada Ltd, 10 Alcorn Avenue, Toronto, Ontario, Canada M4V 1E4.
Penguin Books (NZ) Ltd, 182–190 Wairau Road, Auckland 10, New Zealand.
Typeset in Linotron Univers and Century Old Style to an original design by Andrew Oliver.
Printed in England by Clays Ltd, St Ives PLC.
Illustrations in Part One and Part Three by Edward Briant.
Illustrations on p.1 and p.253 by Henry Iles.

© Andrew Beattie and Timothy Pepper 1998.
No part of this book may be reproduced in any form without permission from the publisher except for quotation of brief passages in reviews.
304pp – Includes index.
A catalogue record for this book is available from th British Library.
ISBN 1-85828-331-0

The publishers and authors have done their best to ensure the accuracy and currency of all the inform in *The Rough Guide to Syria*; however, they can ac no responsibility for any loss, injury, or inconvenie sustained by any traveller as a result of informatic advice contained in the guide.

Syria

THE ROUGH GUIDE

written and researched by

Andrew Beattie and Timothy Pepper

THE ROUGH GUIDES

THE ROUGH GUIDES

TRAVEL GUIDES • PHRASEBOOKS • MUSIC AND REFERENCE GUIDES

 We set out to do something different when the first Rough Guide was published in 1982. Mark Ellingham, just out of university, was travelling in Greece. He brought along the popular guides of the day, but found they were all lacking in some way. They were either strong on ruins and museums but went on for pages without mentioning a beach or taverna. Or they were so conscious of the need to save money that they lost sight of Greece's cultural and historical significance. Also, none of the books told him anything about Greece's contemporary life – its politics, its culture, its people, and how they lived.

So with no job in prospect, Mark decided to write his own guidebook, one that aimed to provide practical information that was second to none, detailing the best beaches and the hottest clubs and restaurants, while also giving hard-hitting accounts of every sight, both famous and obscure, and providing up-to-the-minute information on contemporary culture. It was a guide that encouraged independent travellers to find the best of Greece, and was a great success, getting shortlisted for the Thomas Cook travel guide award, and encouraging Mark, along with three friends, to expand the series.

The Rough Guide list grew rapidly and the letters flooded in, indicating a much broader readership than had been anticipated, but one which uniformly appreciated the Rough Guide mix of practical detail and humour, irreverence and enthusiasm. Things haven't changed. The same four friends who began the series are still the caretakers of the Rough Guide mission today: to provide the most reliable, up-to-date and entertaining information to independent-minded travellers of all ages, on all budgets.

We now publish a hundred titles and have offices in London and New York. The travel guides are written and researched by a dedicated team of more than a hundred authors, based in Britain, Europe, the USA and Australia. We have also created a unique series of phrasebooks to accompany the travel series, along with an acclaimed series of music guides, and a best-selling pocket guide to the Internet and World Wide Web. We also publish comprehensive travel information on our Web site:

www.roughguides.com

HELP US UPDATE

We've gone to a lot of effort to ensure that The Rough Guide to Syria is accurate and up to date. However, things change – places get "discovered", opening hours are notoriously fickle, restaurants and rooms raise prices or lower standards. If you feel we've got it wrong or left something out, we'd like to know, and if you can remember the address, the price, the time, the phone number, so much the better.

We'll credit all contributions, and send a copy of the next edition (or any other Rough Guide if you prefer) for the best letters. Please mark letters "Rough Guide Syria Update" and send to:
Rough Guides Ltd, 62–70 Shorts Gardens, London WC2H 9AB, or Rough Guides, 375 Hudson St, 9th Floor, New York, NY 10014.
Or send email to: *mail@roughguides.co.uk*
Online updates about this book can be found on Rough Guides' Web site at *www.roughguides.com*

THE AUTHORS

Andrew Beattie read geography at Oxford University, specializing in Middle Eastern geopolitics, and now teaches the subject at an independent school in London. He is the author or co-author of five books, including two plays for children, and has contributed articles on travel and history to *Contemporary Review* and *The International Dictionary of Historic Places*.

Tim Pepper has been travelling and writing ever since he left Oxford University with a degree in history. He has co-written books on Hungary, and the Czech and Slovak Republics, and besides the Middle East, his wanderings have taken him throughout Southern Africa, North and Central America, and Eastern Europe.

CONTENTS

Introduction x

PART THREE CONTEXTS 253

LIST OF MAPS

MAP SYMBOLS

━━	Railway	ⓘ	Tourist office
═══	Road	⊠	Post office
-----	Path	▲	Peak
────	Waterway	⌃⌃	Mountains
─ ─ ─	Chapter division boundary	✕	Airport
─ ─ ▪	International borders	★	Bus/taxi station
⊓⊓⊓⊓	Steps	◉	Accommodation
◆	Point of interest	▪	Restaurant
▥	Mosque/madrasa	▬	Building
♯	Castle	⊞	Church/monastery
∴	Ruins	☨	Church/monastery (regional maps)
⊞	Hospital	⊹	Cemetery
⚖	Souk	▨	Park
⊜	Bank/exchange booth	⊡	Beach

INTRODUCTION

Syria is one of the least visited, and least familiar, countries in the world. Jammed in between the vastly more popular tourist destinations of Turkey, Jordan and Israel, for many years it has been considered an unlikely destination by many travellers, scared off by a combination of safety worries, the yards of red tape that a visit required, a military government obsessed with internal security, and closed frontiers. Through much of the 1980s these fears were justified: Syria was cast as a supporter of international terrorism and broke off diplomatic relations with a number of Western countries, making it virtually impossible for many nationalities (including Britons and Americans) even to set foot there. But after President Assad voiced support for the allies during the Gulf War and helped to secure the release of the Beirut hostages, things started looking up as far as travellers were concerned; a steadily growing stream of Westerners have visited the country in the 1990s, drawn by the wealth of archeological remains, by the renowned hospitality of the people, and perhaps most of all by sheer curiosity.

Politically, modern Syria is a result of boundary drawing by the old colonial masters of the region, France and, to a lesser extent, Britain. The **French** took over in 1920, occupying the political vacuum left by the end of four hundred years of **Ottoman rule**, and separated their territory from British-administered Transjordan by drawing a ruler-straight line across the desert. During its 26-year rule, France did little for the country, governing it without the consent of the people and treating it largely as a barracks, and Syria approached its hard-won **independence** with an understandable lack of confidence: coup followed coup in the early 1950s, and then came the disastrous political union with Egypt, which broke up into a further period of political instability in the 1960s. Since 1971, however, the country has been ruled by a former airforce commander and Defence Minister **Hafez al-Assad**, the leader of a radical wing of the Ba'ath (Arab Socialist) party. Assad has treated dissent with bloody determination, killing thousands in the 1982 crackdown on the outlawed Muslim Brotherhood opposition group, but he has maintained power with unerring shrewdness, never letting his country lapse into the civil war and political anarchy that beset neighbouring Lebanon for much of the 1970s and 1980s.

Most Syrians are **Arabs**, though there is some degree of heterogenity – in Aleppo, for example, you'll find Armenian and Turkish speakers. The greatest concentration of non-Arabic speakers, however, is in the northeast, where **Kurdish** is spoken by those

---

TRANSLITERATION OF ARABIC WORDS

There's no standard system of transliterating Arabic into English. Many sounds in Arabic have no equivalent in English and any attempt to render them in English script is bound to be imprecise – you're certain to come across Arabic words and proper names in this book that don't match transliterations elsewhere. Place names are the biggest sources of confusion, varying from map to map and often from sign to sign, so where possible we've used the transliteration that's most common on the spot; in less clear instances, we've stuck to the most frequent national transliteration. The definite article "al" and its various elisions have been removed from most place names, except where it's common practice to keep it. World-renowned scholars have broken their heads over transliterating Arabic into English, yet it remains a complete dog's breakfast. The best way to deal with it is just to practise a little lateral thinking: if you want to go to Deir ez-Zur and you see a sign to Deir Aw Zawr, followed by one to Deir ez-Zor, you know you're heading in the right direction.

who dare – using the language has long been seen as a sign of dissent, particularly in the light of the Kurdish uprising in neighbouring Turkey. Syrians are divided more on religious than ethnic grounds: although the majority are followers of **Sunni Islam**, there is a large **Christian** minority (itself divided into a number of sects), plus a tiny number of Jews. President Assad himself is a follower of the **Alawite** religion, a curious branch of Islam followed in the mountains of the northwest, with the **Druze** and the **Shi'ites** making up the remainder of the non-Sunni Muslims.

Though a small country – about the size of Scotland – Syria's political isolation and high population growth reduce the amount and effectiveness of international aid, and the country is one of the poorest in the region, with huge disparities in the level of development. The rich, Europeanized urban elite of Aleppo and Damascus, most of whom have got where they are through government connections, live largely separate lives to the majority of the people. In the same cities, however, you'll find the familiar trappings of developing world poverty – shoe-shine boys out in force, begging, prostitution, and hawking of all kinds – while in the countryside agriculture is carried out using age-old techniques of irrigation, planting, harvesting and selling, with a proliferation of carts and working animals, and few modern machines. Many of the **Bedouin**, the traditional tent-dwelling nomads of the Middle East, have been forcibly resettled by the government in towns and cities, but some still roam the desert with their herds of goats and sheep, much of their lifestyle unchanged for centuries.

Despite the country's political isolation, its unhappy colonial past and its resentment towards the West for its perceived support of Israel, the reputation of Syrians for **hospitality** towards foreigners is well deserved, and it is this which makes the country such a rewarding place to travel in, particularly if you go independently and make an effort to stray from the cities and the most popular tourist spots. You can actually cause offence by rebutting any friendliness extended towards you, and the most casual meetings can often lead to an invitation to take tea at someone's home. Rarely do such offers of friendship come with strings attached, and in most cases the warmth of the welcome you'll receive is entirely genuine.

Where to go

With most road, rail and air routes into Syria leading to **Damascus**, it's not surprising that virtually all visitors to the country visit the capital – usually at the beginning of their stay. It's a disappointing, frustrating place in many ways, for despite its claim to be the oldest continuously inhabited settlement on earth, much of its rich historical legacy is smothered by almost defiantly ugly urban highways and half-built office blocks, and its oriental mystique often seems drowned in a sea of car horns and traffic fumes. But there's still plenty to see here, and once you get used to the noise, grime and heat of the place you can't fail to be overwhelmed by the fabulous Islamic monuments and the pungent, hectic souks of the Old City. If you tire of it, retreating to the hills – as Damascenes do – is easy, and forty minutes by road (or three hours by narrow-gauge train) will bring you to the clean, cool air of Bloudane and Zabadani, mountain resorts in the Anti-Lebanon range to the west of the city.

Beyond Damascus, Syria's landscape is crammed with a bewildering variety of archeological sites, reflecting the value that was placed on the region by a long list of warlike major powers, from Egyptians and Hittites, through Assyrians, Babylonians, Persians, Greeks and Romans, to the medieval Crusaders. The **Hauran**, a table-land of wheat fields and desert scrub between the capital and the Jordanian border, is characterized by outcrops of black volcanic rock which the Romans used to built the trading city of **Bosra**. One of the "big three" archeological sites in Syria, it's an absorbing place, surprisingly intact and with families inhabiting many of the shops and bath houses that still stand. The centrepiece is the fabulous theatre, its survival guaranteed by conversion to a defensive citadel by Arab occupiers. Many visit Bosra as a day-trip from the capital

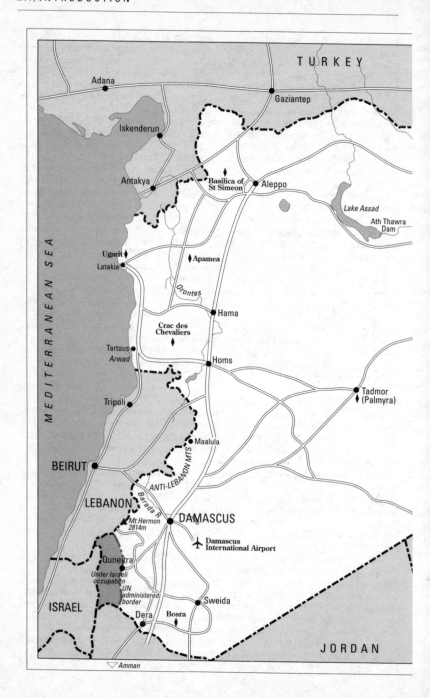

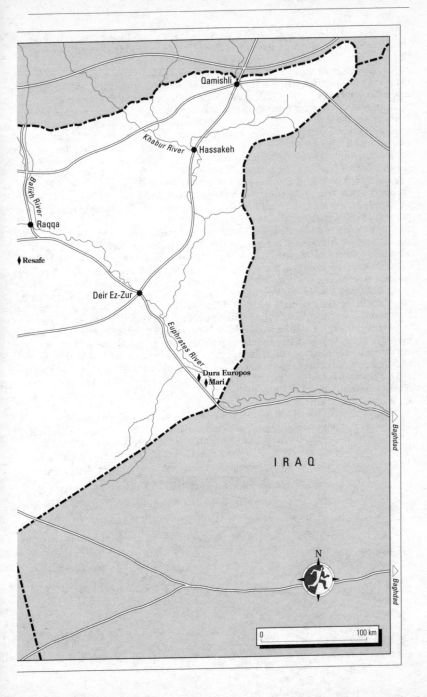

Qamishli

Khabur River

Hassakeh

Balikh River

Raqqa

Resafe

Deir Ez-Zur

Euphrates River

Dura Europos
Mari

I R A Q

Baghdad

Baghdad

N

0   100 km

and forget the rest of the region, but if you've got time on your hands, the Byzantine church at **Ezra** (thought to be the burial place of St George) and the Roman sites near **Sweida**, east of Bosra, would justify a longer foray.

The main highway north from Damascus to Aleppo passes through two very different towns on the **Orontes River: Homs** is a busy provincial town that's safe to ignore if you can, but **Hama** is delightful, boasting one of the most attractive town centres in Syria, where you can eat at riverside restaurants and watch the turning *noria*s, restored medieval waterwheels now set in manicured gardens. Hama is also the obvious base from which to see nearby **Apamea**, an expansive and fascinating Roman trading settlement which was one of the most westerly caravan halts on the long trek from the Mediterranean coast to China. It's dramatically set on a high desert ridge above the fertile Orontes valley, though its accessibility from Hama means that it's now one of the most touristed sites in the country. More off-beat destinations in the area include **Qalaat Burzey** beyond Apamea, a ruined castle accessible only by scrambling up a rocky hillside, and northeast from Hama, the Roman temple in the desert at **Isriya**, one of the remotest archeological sites in Syria.

The two main coastal settlements, **Tartous** and **Latakia**, don't have a lot to recommend them, nor has much of the coastline itself, a succession of rubbish-strewn beaches, military zones and industrial complexes. Both towns, however, make good bases for day-trips into the **mountains** that run parallel to the sea, where tiny villages and forested ravines are overlooked by a wealth of lofty ancient sites. Pre-eminent among them is the **Crac des Chevaliers**, built by the Crusaders and considered by T.E. Lawrence to be "the finest medieval castle in the world". If you don't have a car, however, you may find travelling in this area frustrating, as few buses link the isolated upland settlements; the Roman temple set high on a rocky hillside at **Hosn Suleiman** is particularly difficult to reach. Things get a bit easier further north, however: **Qalaat Saladin**, the spectacular defensive haunt of one of Islam's most famous commanders, and the ancient Bronze Age settlement of **Ugarit**, where one of the world's first alphabets was devised, are both easily reached from Latakia. Near the latter stretch Syria's best **beaches**, characterless private strands which you'll have to pay to use, but where at least the sea is clean and the sand litter-free.

Aleppo, the second city, is on the whole less hectic and more manageable than Damascus, and proves more appealing to most visitors. It's similarly a storehouse of fine early Islamic remains, and its souks, vaunted as the largest area of covered markets in the Middle East, are no less vibrant, but it's easy to escape the bustle in the

CLIMATE

Damascus

	J	F	M	A	M	J	J	A	S	O	N	D
Average minimum temperature (°C)	2	4	6	9	13	16	18	18	16	12	8	4
Average maximum temperature (°C)	12	14	18	24	29	33	36	37	33	27	19	13
Average no. of days with rain	7	6	2	3	1	0	0	0	2	2	5	5
Average monthly rainfall (mm)	43	43	8	13	3	0	0	0	18	10	41	41

Aleppo

	J	F	M	A	M	J	J	A	S	O	N	D
Average minimum temperature (°C)	1	3	4	9	13	17	21	21	16	12	7	3
Average maximum temperature (°C)	10	13	18	24	29	34	36	36	33	27	19	12
Average no. of days with rain	11	10	7	4	2	0	0	0	0	4	8	10
Average monthly rainfall (mm)	89	64	38	28	8	3	0	0	0	25	56	84

charming narrow lanes of the medieval Christian quarter. Surrounding Aleppo is the greatest concentration of historical sites in Syria: the so-called **Dead Cities**, Byzantine settlements abandoned to the desert during the seventh century, whose appeal today is their staggering degree of preservation. Most visitors to Syria see **Qalaat Semaan**, the church surrounding the pillar on which mystic St Simeon sat for forty years, but it's well worth taking time to travel out to other Dead Cities, particularly those around Maarat al-Numan, where some of the best-preserved remains lie in almost complete isolation.

The least-visited part of the country, the northeast, consists of flat plains cut through by the green swathe of farmland along the banks of the **Euphrates River**, which has always dominated the history and geography of this region. Of the two main riverside towns, **Raqqa** and **Deir-ez Zur**, the latter is much the more appealing, with a laid-back but distinctly Asiatic feel, and is the best spot to appreciate the languid river. The major historical sites around here are the remote, largely Roman settlements of **Resafe** and **Halebiye**, and the more ancient strongholds of **Mari** and **Dura Europus**, set on bleak ridges above the Euphrates east of Deir. **Qamishli**, the main town in the far northeast, has little to offer travellers except a risky back-door entry into Turkey, though it is the jumping-off point for the Arab bridge at **Ain Diwar** on the River Tigris, set amidst the most stunning scenery in the whole country.

Last but not least, there's no denying that **Palmyra** is probably Syria's most exciting destination. Although the ancient site has been somewhat blighted by tourism in recent years, the extraordinary spectacles of the sun setting over the Arab Castle and the wind blasting through 2000-year-old columns and tower-tombs will undoubtedly form some of your most vivid memories of Syria. Indeed, only four hours by road from Damascus, it's a good place to see last of all, spending two or three days ambling through the ruins before heading for home; and when you're travelling to and from Palmyra, you can't fail to be impressed by the **desert** itself – so expansive, empty and harsh as to be almost shocking.

When to go

As Syria receives comparatively few visitors, there is no particular tourist high season, so the weather is the main determinant of when is best to visit the country. With hot, dry summers and wet, cold winters, spring and autumn are the ideal times to visit.

Summers in Syria can get unbearably hot, particularly in the eastern desert, around Palmyra and Deir ez-Zur; in mid-afternoon in July and August it regularly reaches 40°C here and can climb even higher, although there's often a stiff breeze to moderate the temperature quite considerably, and the heat is dry rather than humid, which makes things more bearable. Damascus and Aleppo are slightly cooler during these months, but with no desert breezes and huge pollution problems, things can get wearying and unpleasant there, too. Summers on the coast and in the mountains are rather different: it's cool and cloudy in the hills, and hot and humid on the coast, and it occasionally rains in these areas – usually in the form of short, violent thunderstorms in the early evening or late afternoon. But the majority of the country experiences no rain and cloudless skies from June to September, and by early autumn is parched dry.

Winter, on the other hand, can be cold, wet and miserable. From December to February temperatures in Damascus and Aleppo rise little above 10°C, with rain, overcast skies and chilly evenings and nights the norm; very occasionally these cities grind to a halt after heavy snow. In the mountains you can be certain of snow and freezing temperatures during January and February, while biting winds in the east of the country will regularly bring night-time temperatures down below zero; winds blowing down from the high mountains of eastern Turkey can even bring a dusty smattering of snow to Palmyra. Tartous and Latakia on the coast can also be dispiritingly cold and wet in mid-winter, battered frequently by Mediterranean gales which can occur well into April.

GETTING THERE FROM BRITAIN AND IRELAND

The simplest way of getting to Syria from Britain and Ireland is to fly. Direct flights link London with Damascus almost daily, but it's not possible to fly direct from any other British cities or from Ireland. If you're daunted by the prospect of visiting Syria independently, you should consider hitching up with one of the upmarket archeological tours on offer. At the other end of the scale, the overland trip by train or bus from Britain across Europe and Turkey is relatively straightforward, making it possible to take in Syria as part of wider travels around the Mediterranean or the Middle East; if you qualify for one, an InterRail ticket will take you right up to the Syrian–Turkish border, within 40km of Aleppo.

FLIGHTS

There are **direct scheduled flights** between London and Damascus on either Syrianair or British Mediterranean Airways, an offshoot of British Airways (which handles all their booking arrangements). Both fly three times a week from Heathrow, either nonstop or with short stopovers in Munich (Syrianair) or Alexandria (BMed). Return fares on Syrianair are very reasonable, at £311 in low season, £351 in high season, which extends from July 1 to August 10 and from December 12 to 24. British Mediterranean Airways charges a fare of £402 throughout the year, for a stay of between 6 and 45 days.

Most other **European airlines** (see the box below) can sell you flights to Damascus, travelling via their home airport on the continent. Standards and prices vary enormously, from upmarket options such as Lufthansa and KLM to cheaper, less predictable airlines such as Malev Hungarian Airlines and Turkish Airlines. For stays

---

AIRLINES IN BRITAIN

Aeroflot, 70 Piccadilly, London W1V 9HH (☎0171/355 2233).

Air France, 10 Warwick St, 1st Floor, London W1R 5RA (☎0181/742 6600).

Austrian Airlines, 10 Wardour St, London W1V 4BJ (☎0171/434 7350).

British Airways, 156 Regent St, London W1R 5TA; 101–102 Cheapside, London EC2V 6DT; Victoria Place, Victoria Station, London SW1W 9SJ (☎0171/707 4747); 209 Union St, Aberdeen AB1 2BA; 146 New St, Birmingham B2 4HN; 66 New Broadmead, Bristol BS1 2DL; 32 Frederick St, Edinburgh EH2 2JR; 66 Gordon St, Glasgow G1 3RS; 19–21 St Mary's Gate, Market St, Manchester M1 1PU (all enquiries ☎0345/222111).

Egyptair, 296 Regent St, London W1R 6PH (☎0171/734 2395).

KLM Royal Dutch Airlines reservations ☎0990/750 900; ticket office at Terminal 4, Heathrow.

Lufthansa German Airlines, 7–8 Conduit St, London W1R 9TG, and Phoenix House, 78 St Vincent St, Glasgow G2 5UB (☎0345/737747).

Malev Hungarian Airlines, 10 Vigo St, London W1X 1AJ (☎0171/439 0577).

Olympic Airways, 11 Conduit St, London W1R 0LP (☎0171/409 3400).

Swissair, Swiss Centre, 10 Wardour St, London W1V 4BJ (☎0171/434 7300).

Syrianair, 27 Albemarle St, London W1X 3HF (☎0171/493 2851).

Turkish Airlines, 11–12 Hanover St, London W1R 9HF (☎0171/766 9300).

of between 6 and 35 days, the last-mentioned charges some of the cheapest prices going: £267 in the low season for a London–Damascus return ticket via Istanbul, rising to £340 between June 15 and August 15, with the attractive possibility of a stopover for a few days in Istanbul if you don't mind paying a little more. In summer you can also fly from Manchester with Turkish Airlines, at comparable fares. Malev Hungarian Airlines flies via Budapest from London for year-round fares of between £280 and £300 (obtainable only through its agents Danube Travel, 6 Conduit St, London W1R 9TG; ☎0171/493 0263).

It is much more expensive to enter Syria through **Aleppo**: you'll need to fly on BA or Lufthansa to Frankfurt (£136 return from London,

£146 from Manchester), then pick up a direct Syrianair flight on to Aleppo (£369). Direct Syrianair flights from Rome and Istanbul to Aleppo are also available, which may fit the bill if your travel plans are complex, though it would be a very pricey way of getting yourself to Syria; Syrianair's Cairo–Latakia and Kuwait–Deir-ez-Zur flights are even less likely to be useful.

Contacting a **flight discount agency** rather than the airline direct can reduce the amount you pay by a small amount, and with a bit of shopping around you'll probably get a fare to Damascus of around £270 with no time restrictions. **Student/youth travel specialists** such as Campus Travel and STA Travel offer seats sold on to them cheap by western and eastern European

---

DISCOUNT FLIGHT AGENTS IN BRITAIN

Campus Travel, 52 Grosvenor Gardens, London SW1W 0AG (☎0171/730 8111); 541 Bristol Rd, Selly Oak, Birmingham B29 6AU (☎0121/414 1848); 61 Ditchling Rd, Brighton BN1 4SD (☎01273/570226); 37–39 Queen's Rd, Clifton, Bristol BS8 1QE (☎0117/929 2494); 5 Emmanuel St, Cambridge CB1 1NE (☎01223/324283); 53 Forest Rd, Edinburgh EH1 2QP (☎0131/225 6111, telesales 668 3303); 122 George St, Glasgow G1 1RS (☎0141/553 1818); 166 Deansgate, Manchester M3 3FE (☎0161/833 2046, telesales 273 1721); 105–106 St Aldates, Oxford OX1 1DD (☎01865/242067). Student/youth travel specialists, with branches also in YHA shops and on university campuses all over Britain.

Council Travel, 28a Poland St, London W1V 3DB (☎0171/437 7767). Flights and student discounts.

Flightbookers, 177–178 Tottenham Court Rd, London W1P 0LX (☎0171/757 2444); Gatwick Airport, South Terminal, inside the British Rail station (☎01293/568300); 34 Argyle Arcade, off Buchanan Street, Glasgow G1 1RS (☎0141/204 1919). Low fares on an extensive offering of scheduled flights.

The London Flight Centre, 131 Earls Court Rd, London SW5 9RH (☎0171/244 6411); 47 Notting Hill Gate, London W11 3JS (☎0171/727 4290); Shop 33, The Broadway Centre, Hammersmith tube, London W6 9YE (☎0181/748 6777). Long-established agent dealing in discount flights.

North South Travel, Moulsham Mill Centre, Parkway, Chelmsford, Essex CM2 7PX

(☎01245/492882). Friendly, competitive travel agency, offering discounted fares worldwide; profits are used to support projects in the developing world, especially the promotion of sustainable tourism.

STA Travel, 86 Old Brompton Rd, London SW7 3LH; 117 Euston Rd, London NW1 2SX; 38 Store St, London WC1E 7BZ (☎0171/ 361 6262); 25 Queens Rd, Bristol BS8 1QE (☎0117/929 4399); 38 Sidney St, Cambridge CB2 3HX (☎01223/366966); 88 Vicar Lane, Leeds LS1 7JH (☎0113/244 9212); 75 Deansgate, Manchester M3 2BW (☎0161/834 0668); 36 George St, Oxford OX1 2OJ (☎01865/792800); and branches in Aberdeen, Birmingham, Canterbury, Cardiff, Coventry, Durham, Glasgow, Loughborough, Nottingham, Warwick and Sheffield. Worldwide specialists in low-cost flights and tours for students and under-26s, though other customers are welcome.

Trailfinders, 42–50 Earls Court Rd, London W8 6FT (☎0171/938 3366); 194 Kensington High St, London W8 7RG (☎0171/938 3939) ; 22–24 The Priory, Queensway, Birmingham B4 6BS (☎0121/236 1234); 48 Corn St, Bristol BS1 1HQ (☎0117/929 9000); 254–284 Sauchiehall St, Glasgow G2 3EH (☎0141/353 2224); 58 Deansgate, Manchester M3 2FF (☎0161/839 6969). One of the best-informed and most efficient agents for independent travellers.

The Travel Bug, 125A Gloucester Rd, London, SW7 4SF (☎0171/835 2000); 597 Cheetham Hill Rd, Manchester M8 5EJ (☎0161/721 4000). Large range of discounted tickets.

AIRLINES AND TRAVEL AGENTS IN IRELAND

AIRLINES

Aer Lingus Northern Ireland reservations ☎0645/737 747; 40–41 O'Connell St, Dublin 1, 13 St Stephen's Green, Dublin 2, and 12 Upper St George's St, Dun Laoghaire (centralized reservations at Dublin airport ☎01/705 3333); 2 Academy St, Cork (☎021/327 155); 136 O'Connell St, Limerick (☎061/474 239).

Air France, Second Floor, 29–30 Dawson St, Dublin 2, and at Dublin airport (☎01/844 5633).

Alitalia, 4–5 Dawson St, Dublin 2 (☎01/677 5171).

British Airways, 1 Fountain Centre, College St, Belfast BT1 6ET (☎0345/222 111). BA doesn't have a Dublin office; Aer Lingus acts as its agents (reservations ☎1800/626 747).

Lufthansa Reservations in the Republic ☎01/844 5544.

TRAVEL AGENTS

Apex Travel, 59 Dame St, Dublin 2 (☎01/671 5933).

Joe Walsh Tours, 34 Grafton St, Dublin 2 (☎01/671 8751); 69 Upper O'Connell St , Dublin 2 (☎01/872 2555); 8–11 Baggot St, Dublin 2 (☎01/676 3053); 117 St Patrick St, Cork (☎021/277 959).General budget fares agent.

Thomas Cook, 11 Donegall Place, Belfast (☎01232/242341); 118 Grafton St, Dublin 2 (☎01/677 1721). Package holiday and flight agent, with occasional discount offers.

Trailfinders, 4–5 Dawson St, Dublin 2 (☎01/677 7888). Competitive fares out of all Irish airports,

as well as deals on hotels, insurance, tours and car rental.

USIT, Fountain Centre, College St, Belfast BT1 6ET (☎01232/324073); 10–11 Market Parade, Patrick St, Cork (☎021/270 900); 33 Ferryquay St, Derry (☎01504/371888); 19 Aston Quay, Dublin 2 (☎01/602 1777 or 677 8117); Victoria Place, Eyre Square, Galway (☎091/565177); Central Buildings, O'Connell St, Limerick (☎061/415 064); 36–37 Georges St, Waterford (☎051/872 601). Student and youth specialists for flights and trains.

airlines, although you should be prepared for inconvenient travel times and long (possibly overnight) waits at the airport where you have to change planes. You might also want to look in publications such as *The Sunday Times*, and the Saturday editions of *The Guardian* and *The Independent*, as well as *Time Out* or *The Evening Standard* in London, through which you should be able to pick up similar deals. Discounts will never match those offered to Istanbul, and if you can't find a fare which matches your budget you might consider travelling there instead and continuing by surface routes. You could even pick up a **charter flight** on a UK airline such as Britannia or Monarch to Cyprus, southern Turkey or Egypt, and continue your journey from there by sea or land routes (see p.13 for details on reaching Syria from neighbouring countries).

There are no direct flights to Syria **from Ireland**, so you'll need connecting transport to London or a flight on a European airline from its continental hub to Damascus (see box above). British Airways, for example, quotes a return

Dublin–Damascus fare, with a change of plane in London, of IR£715. Flying with Aer Lingus and KLM via Amsterdam will cost much the same (IR£729).

PACKAGES AND INCLUSIVE TOURS

A number of specialist travel companies offer tours to Syria, often combined with visits to Jordan or Lebanon; look out for their box advertisements in the travel and classified sections of weekend broadsheets, and see the box on p.6. Most of these packages are based around visits to Damascus and Aleppo and tours of the main archeological sites, led by experienced British or Syrian academics. Such tours to Syria, however, are expensive compared with similar trips to Jordan or Egypt, and the choice on offer is rather limited. No British package tour operators seem to be interested in offering sun-seeking holidays to the Syrian Mediterranean, and there is nothing to suggest that they will in the foreseeable future.

SPECIALIST TOUR OPERATORS IN BRITAIN

Bales Tours, Junction Rd, Dorking, Surrey RH4 3HB (☎01306/885991). Twelve-day tour of Syria costs £1800; other tours of the region also available.

British Museum Tours, 46 Bloomsbury St, London WC1B 3QQ (☎0171/323 8895). Fifteen-day tour of the country for around £2000.

Cox and King's, St James Court, 45 Buckingham Gate, London SW1E 6AF (☎0171/873 5000). Offers an eight-day tour of Syria with guest lecturers; prices start at £1100.

Dragoman, 14 Camp Green, Debenham, Stowmarket IP14 6LA (☎01728/861133). Extended overland journeys in purpose-built expedition vehicles through Asia and Africa; includes Syria as part of journeys from the UK to Egypt and India.

Hayes & Jarvis, Hayes House, 152 King St, London W6 0QU (☎0181/748 5050). Offers a variety of tours of Syria (often coupled with Jordan/Lebanon).

Jasmin Tours, 53–55 Balham Hill, London SW12 9DR (☎0181/675 8886). A variety of tours on offer including some linked with Lebanon or Jordan; nine-day tour of Syria costs around £1000.

Martin Randall Travel, 10 Barley Mow Passage, London W4 4PH (☎0181/742 3355). Small-group archeological tours to Syria and other Middle Eastern destinations.

Swan Hellenic Cruises, 77 New Oxford St, London WC1A 1DS (☎0171/800 2200). Some cruises stop off at Tartous and/or Latakia, with tours of the Crac des Chevaliers and/or Palmyra on offer.

OVERLAND ROUTES

Travelling to Syria overland through Europe and Turkey only makes sense if you want to take in a number of other countries en route, but it remains an exciting and unusual option, giving you the opportunity of travelling through cities as diverse as Brussels, Paris, Vienna, Budapest, Sofia and Istanbul. If you're not taking your own vehicle, you can travel by bus or train (or more expensively a combination of both), and if you are certain that ferries are running, you could even complete the latter stages of the journey by sea from Greece or Cyprus to Beirut or Latakia (see p.14). If you're travelling out overland to Syria and intend to fly back, wait and buy your single airline ticket back to the UK in Damascus or Aleppo rather than before you set out – they're at least a third cheaper, and all Western airline offices in these cities will accept major credit cards.

BY TRAIN

By train the most obvious route from London to Aleppo is via Brussels, Frankfurt, Vienna, Budapest, Bucharest, Sofia and Istanbul; rail links between Turkey and Syria are discussed on p.13. This suggested itinerary purposely avoids the former Yugoslavia, parts of which at the time of writing are still fairly lawless and unpredictable for foreigners, with travellers reportedly being the frequent victims of robbery or assault. If you're British or Irish, the only visas you'll need are for Romania

and Turkey, and you can buy these at the land frontiers of both countries. Another, longer option would take you through Switzerland to Brindisi on the Italian Adriatic, where you can catch a ferry to Patras in Greece and travel to Istanbul via Athens and Thessaloniki. How long your journey takes obviously depends on how long you want to spend in each place, but count on a week as the absolute minimum – and take at least two weeks if you want to make this option worthwhile.

The cheapest way of doing the journey is to buy an **InterRail** pass, which allows the freedom of unlimited train travel in selected European countries for a month. If you're under 26 years of age, tickets are sold according to which zones you want to travel in; a ticket which gets you from Ostend to the Turkish–Syrian border covering all possible zones will cost £259. For those over 26, tickets are not sold zonally; you'll need to pay separately to get to the Belgian–German border at Aachen as these InterRail Plus tickets do not include Belgium, but after that you can get to the Turkish–Syrian border for £215 (ticket valid for 15 days) or £274 (one month). In the UK tickets can be bought at main British Rail stations or at travel agencies. Residence in Europe for at least six months will allow you to purchase an InterRail; if you don't have a European passport you may be asked to prove to the issuer that you've fulfilled this requirement.

Visitors from North America and Australasia can buy a **Eurail** pass, which gives a similar sort

TRAIN INFORMATION IN THE UK

British Rail, International Rail Centre, Victoria Station, London SW1V 1JY (European information line ☎0990/848 848).

Eurostar, EPS House, Waterloo Station, London SE1 8SE (reservations ☎0345/303030). Eurostar trains link London Waterloo directly with Brussels and Paris, and may be the first stage of your train journey to Syria.

Eurotrain, Campus Travel, 52 Grosvenor Gardens, London SW1W 0AG (☎0171/730 3402). Discounted return rail fares for under-26s on a number of European routes.

Le Shuttle, Customer Services Centre ☎0990/353535. Le Shuttle operates train services from Folkestone to Calais for car drivers and their passengers.

Wasteels, Victoria Station (by platform 2), London SW1V 1JY (☎0171/834 7066).

of deal to InterRail and may be useful if you intend to travel through Europe to reach Syria. The pass, which must be purchased before arrival in Europe, allows unlimited free first-class train travel in Austria, Belgium, Denmark, Finland, France, Germany, Greece, Hungary, the Republic of Ireland, Italy, Luxembourg, Netherlands, Norway, Portugal, Spain, Sweden and Switzerland. It costs US$538 for fifteen days, $698 for 21 days, $864 for one month, $1224 for two months and $1512 for three months. If you're under 26, you can save money with a Eurail Youthpass, which is valid for second-class travel and is available in fiteen-day (US$376), 21-day ($489), one-month ($605), two-month ($857) and three-month ($1059) increments. If you're travelling with one to four other companions, the joint Eurail Saverpass can knock about fifteen percent off the cost of the standard Eurail offerings. You stand a better chance of getting your money's worth out of a Eurail Flexipass, which is good for a certain number of travel days in a two-month period. This, too, comes in first-class and under-26 (second-class) versions: ten days cost

$634/$444; and fifteen days, $836/$585. Again, parties of two to five can save fifteen percent with the Eurail Saver Flexipass. Whichever Eurail pass you buy, it makes sense to travel to Istanbul via Switzerland, Italy and Greece, as eastern European countries are not covered by these passes; unfortunately, neither is Turkey, so you'll have to pay separately for tickets once you reach the Greek–Turkish border.

BY BUS

Travelling **by bus** to Syria is possible but it's difficult to see any advantages it has over trains. If you're determined to do it, you can journey from London to Aleppo in three stages. National Express Coaches (☎0990 808080) will sell you a ticket from London to Sofia (28hr, £105 one-way, with a change of buses in Frankfurt); from there you'll need to pick up one of the two or three weekly services to Istanbul (12hr). More imaginative, and inevitably more expensive, options between London and Istanbul might take you via Prague and/or Budapest. Bus links between Istanbul and Aleppo are discussed on p.13.

OUTLETS FOR DISCOUNT RAIL PASSES OUTSIDE THE UK

IRELAND
Continental Rail Desk, CIE Tours International, 35 Lower Abbey St, Dublin 1 (☎01/703 1888). InterRail agents.
NIR Travel, 28–30 Great Victoria Street Station, Belfast 2 (☎01232/230 671). InterRail agents.
USIT (see p.5 for addresses). InterRail agents.

NORTH AMERICA
Rail Europe, 226 Westchester Ave, White Plains, NY 10604 (☎1-800/438-7245 in USA; ☎1-

800/361-7245 in Canada). Official Eurail Pass agent in North America; also sells Europass, multinational passes and most single-country passes.

AUSTRALIA AND NEW ZEALAND
Thomas Cook Rail Direct, Level 8, 130 Pitt St, Sydney 2000 (☎1300/361 941); 96 Anzac Ave, Auckland 1 (☎09/263 7260).

There is currently no organized lift share agency in the UK. The best option is to consult the noticeboards of specialist travellers bookshops or put up your own notice; Nomad Books at 781 Fulham Rd, London SW6 5HA (☎0171/736 4000), has a particularly good noticeboard downstairs.

The travel magazine *Wanderlust* has a useful "Connections" page worth consulting for possible lift shares/travel companions; you can also advertise for free on this page (up to 35 words). Address mail to: Connection Wxxx, Wanderlust, PO Box 1832, Windsor, SL4 6YP.

BY CAR

It takes at least a week to **drive** from the UK to Syria, through Eastern Europe and Turkey. Some Germans and Italians do it, but few (if any) Brits attempt this potentially highly problematic journey. You'll need a *carnet de passage* to prove ownership of your vehicle, an international driving permit, and insurance and registration documents to complement the third-party insurance which must be purchased when you drive into Syria.

Some insurers may not give you cover for Syria, as they assume it is a "war zone". Most vehicles driven by locals are Japanese or Korean and spare parts for European models are difficult to find; in any case, bring along as many replacement parts as you are able to (including a gearbox), and consult motoring organizations back home for advice before you set out. Advice on repair shops in Aleppo and Damascus is included in the relevant Listings sections for each city; see also p.30.

GETTING THERE FROM THE US AND CANADA

There are no direct flights from the US or Canada to Syria, and currently the US Government has an embargo on Syrianair, which might otherwise be your most obvious choice. However, plenty of American,

Canadian and European airlines will get you to Damascus, with a change of planes in a European city (see box opposite). A wide range of archeologically slanted tours to Syria (and surrounding Middle Eastern countries) is offered by North American specialist operators, but most do not include transatlantic flights in the package.

If Syria is only one stop on a longer journey, you might want to consider buying a **Round-the-World** (RTW) ticket. Damascus is not on the set itineraries of RTW trips, but you may be able to customize one with agents like High Adventure or Air Brokers International (see box on p.10). One possible itinerary would be Los Angeles–London–overland to Athens–Cairo–Damascus–Cairo–Bombay–overland to Delhi–Bangkok–Jakarta–Denpasar–Los Angeles, at a cost starting at around US$1900.

The prices quoted below are for round-trip tickets, travelling midweek (where there's a difference in price) and exclude **taxes** (roughly $72 on flights from the US and CAN$70 from Canada).

SHOPPING FOR TICKETS

Barring special offers, the cheapest of the airlines' published fares is usually an **Apex** ticket, although this will carry certain restrictions: you will, most likely, have to book – and pay – up to 21 days before departure, spend at least seven days abroad (maximum stay three months), and you tend to get penalized if you change your schedule.

You can normally cut costs further by going through a **specialist flight agent** – either a **consolidator**, who buys up blocks of tickets from the airlines and sells them at a discount, or a **discount agent**, who in addition to dealing with discounted flights may also offer special student and youth fares and a range of other travel-related services such as travel insurance, car rentals, tours and the like. If you travel a lot, **discount travel clubs** are another option – the annual membership fee may be worth it for benefits like cut-price air tickets and car rental.

Don't automatically assume that tickets purchased through a travel specialist will be cheapest – once you get a quote, check with the airlines and you may turn up an even better deal. Be advised also that the pool of travel companies is swimming with sharks – exercise caution and *never* deal with a company that demands cash up front or refuses to accept payment by credit card.

FLIGHTS FROM THE US

Your most convenient option in terms of flying times will probably be Air France, via Paris (actual flying time to Damascus from New York approximately 12hr 15min; add on another 2hr from Chicago and 3hr from LA). At the time of writing, however, British Airways, in partnership with British Mediterranean, offers the cheapest published fares from the US to Damascus, with Lufthansa, Air France and KLM/Northwest close behind. The current APEX fares with British Airways are $1135 (low season)/$1235 (shoulder season)/$1435 (high season) from New York, $1285/$1385/$1585 from Chicago, and $1390/$1490/$1690 from LA.

Another option would be to fly to Jordan and make your way overland from there. At the time of writing, Northwest/KLM has very reasonable fares from New York to Amman of $613 (low)/ $793 (shoulder)/ $1219 (high), while EgyptAir has a special high-season LA–Amman fare of $1299.

FLIGHTS FROM CANADA

Excluding the possibility of special limited offers, an APEX ticket will be the cheapest way of flying to Syria from Canada. The current cost is around CAN$1930 (low season)/CAN$2125

AIRLINES IN THE US AND CANADA

Transatlantic flights are generally overnight, and the days listed below refer to the first leg of the journey; the Europe–Syria leg will be on the following day.

Air France (in US ☎1-800/237-2747; in Canada ☎1-800/667-2747). Flights from New York and Toronto on Sunday, Tuesday and Thursday, with connections in Paris.

Alitalia (☎1-800/223-5730). Flights from New York on Monday, Tuesday and Friday, with connections in Rome.

American Airlines (☎1-800/433-7300). Daily flights from most major North American cities via Europe.

British Airways (in US ☎1-800/247-9297; in Canada ☎1-800/668-1059). Flights via London from the US on Sunday and Friday with connections on British Mediterranean, and from Canada on Monday, Wednesday and Friday with connections on Syrianair.

Canadian Airlines (in Canada ☎1-800/665-1177; in US ☎1-800/426-7000). Daily flights via London or Rome from most major Canadian cities.

Continental Airlines (☎1-800/231-0856). Flights via Europe from most major US cities.

Delta Airlines (☎1-800/241-4141). Daily flights via European hub cities from most major US cities.

Egyptair (☎1-800/334-6787 or 212/315-0900). Flights from New York on Thursday, Friday and Sunday, with connections in Cairo.

Lufthansa (in US ☎1-800/645-3880; in Canada ☎1-800/563-5954). Flights from New York or Toronto on Monday, Wednesday and Saturday with connections in Frankfurt.

Northwest/KLM (in US ☎1-800/374-7747; in Canada ☎1-800/361-5073). Via Amsterdam, from several North American cities, on varying days of the week.

DISCOUNT AGENTS, CONSOLIDATORS AND SPECIALIST TOUR OPERATORS IN THE US AND CANADA

DISCOUNT AGENTS AND CONSOLIDATORS

Air Brokers International, 150 Post St, Suite 620, San Francisco, CA 94108 (☎1-800/883-3273 or 415/397-1383). Consolidator and specialist in RTW tickets.

Council Travel, 205 E 42nd St, New York, NY 10017 (☎1-800/226-8624), and branches in many other US cities. Nationwide US organization that mostly, but by no means exclusively, specializes in student travel.

High Adventure Travel, 353 Sacramento St, Suite 600, San Francisco, CA 94111 (☎1-800/350-0612 or 415/912-5600; www.highadv.com). Round-the-world ticket specialist, with a website featuring an interactive database that lets you build and price your own RTW itinerary.

New Frontiers/Nouvelles Frontières, 12 E 33rd St, New York, NY 10016 (☎1-800/366-6387 or 212/779-0600); 122 Rue St. Hubert, Montréal, H2L 3Y8 (☎514/526-6774); and other branches in LA, San Francisco and Québec City. French discount travel firm.

STA Travel, 10 Downing St, New York, NY 10014 (☎1-800/781-4040 or 212/627-3111), and other branches in the Los Angeles, San Francisco and Boston areas. Worldwide discount travel firm specializing in student/youth fares; also student IDs, travel insurance, car rental etc.

Travac, 989 6th Ave, New York NY 10018 (☎1-800/872-8800), plus an office in Orlando. Consolidator.

Travel Avenue, 10 S Riverside, Suite 1404, Chicago, IL 60606 (☎1-800/333-3335). Full-service travel agent that offers discounts in the form of rebates.

Travel CUTS, 187 College St, Toronto, ON M5T 1P7 (☎1-800/667-2887 or 416/979-2406), and other branches all over Canada. Organization specializing in student fares, IDs and other travel services.

Unitravel, 11737 Administration Drive, St Louis, MO 63146 (☎1-800/325-2222 or 314/569-0900). Consolidator.

SPECIALIST TOUR OPERATORS

Abercrombie & Kent (☎1-800/323-7308). Six-day tour around Syria for US$2375 (land only).

Adventure Center (☎1-800/227-8747). "Crusader Castles & Desert Cities" sixteen days in Syria and Jordan from $1555; "Exploring the Old Levant" fourteen days in Syria and Lebanon from $1175 (both land only).

Adventures Abroad (☎1-800/665-3998 or 604/303-1099). A range of tours offering Syria alone (two weeks from $3359, land/air), or combined with Jordan, Egypt, Yemen, the Gulf States etc.

Archeological Tours (☎212/986-3054). Sixteen-day tour in Jordan and Syria (with optional extension to Israel) led by an archeology professor and local guides. From $4450 (land/air).

Geographic Expeditions (☎415/922-0448). "The Sands of Araby" 22 days in Egypt, Jordan and Syria from $5290 (land only).

Himalayan Travel (☎1-800/225-2380). "Syrian Highlights" nine days from $995; "Syrian Adventure" fifteen days from $1095; "Journey through Jordan and Syria" fifteen days from $1695 (all land only).

Saga Road Scholar Tours (☎1-800/621-2151). Educational tours for 50-and-overs: "Syria – The Undiscovered Land" ten days from $2499, with optional three-day Jordan extension $2895 (land/air).

Wilderness Travel (☎1-800/368-2794 or 510/558-2488). "Lawrence's Arabia" seventeen days in Jordan and Syria from $2995 (land only).

(high season) from Toronto and Montréal, CAN$2200/CAN$2400 from Vancouver. The actual flying time to Damascus from Toronto and Montréal is approximately 11 hours 30 minutes; add on another three hours from Vancouver.

GETTING THERE FROM AUSTRALIA & NEW ZEALAND

Airlines or Thai Airways to cover various sectors. From Auckland, Air New Zealand flies to most Asian and European capital cities, where you can pick up services on to Damascus.

Given that you'll have to touch down anyway, it might be worth looking at some of the good-value **stopover** deals on offer with most of the Asian and Middle Eastern airlines. Flying with Royal Jordanian, for example, you can spend two nights (three days) in Amman for A$200, including transfers, accommodation and day-tours to Petra and Jerash or the Dead Sea.

FARES

There are no non-stop flights from Australasia to Syria, so your only option is to fly via Asia or Europe. The Middle Eastern and Asian airlines, plus Alitalia, tend to offer the best deals, but routings via Europe can result in a longer flight time. Flying from Australia, Gulf Air, Emirates and Egyptair offer some of the most direct routes, going via Singapore and Bahrain, Dubai or Cairo, respectively. Royal Jordanian and Kuwait Airways both team up with Ansett Australia, Qantas, Malaysian Airlines, Singapore

Whatever kind of ticket you're after, first call should be one of the **travel agents** listed in the box on p.12, which can fill you in on all the latest fares and any special offers. If you're a **student** or **under 26**, you may be able to undercut some of the prices given below; STA is a good place to start.

The fares quoted here are for travel during low or shoulder seasons; flying during high season (April–Aug & Dec) can add substantially to these prices. Flying **from Australia**, the least expensive return fares you're likely to find are around A$1699 from the eastern states, A$1755 from Western Australia. With code-share arrange-

---

AIRLINES IN AUSTRALIA AND NEW ZEALAND

Air New Zealand, 5 Elizabeth St, Sydney (☎13 2476); 139 Queen St, Auckland (☎09/357 3000).

Alitalia, 32 Bridge St, Sydney (☎02/9247 1308); 6/229 Queen St, Auckland (☎09/379 4457).

Ansett Australia, 19 Pitt St, Sydney (☎13 1767); 2/50 Grafton Rd, Auckland (☎09/796 409).

British Airways, 26/201 Kent St, Sydney (☎02/9258 3300); 154 Queen St, Auckland (☎09/356 8690).

Egyptair, 630 George St, Sydney (☎02/9267 6979).

Emirates, 456 Kent St, Sydney (☎02/9267 3955).

Gulf Air, 64 York St, Sydney (☎02/9321 9199).

Kuwait Airways, 15/31 Macquarie St, North Sydney (☎02/9264 8277).

Lauda Air, 11/143 Macquarie St, Sydney (☎02/9251 6155).

Malaysian Airlines, 16 Spring St, Sydney (☎13 2627); 12/12 Swanson St, Auckland (☎09/373 2741).

Qantas, 70 Hunter St, Sydney (☎13 1211); 154 Queen St, Auckland (☎09/357 8900 & 0800/808 767).

Royal Jordanian Airlines, 20/44 Market St, Sydney (☎02/9262 6133).

Singapore Airlines, 17 Bridge St, Sydney (☎13 1011); cnr Albert St & Fanshawe St, Auckland (☎09/379 3209).

Thai Airways, 75 Pitt St, Sydney (☎13 1960); 22 Fanshawe St, Auckland (☎09/377 3886).

Turkish Airlines, 16/388 George St, Sydney (☎02/9221 1711).

ments involving the ritzier airlines such as British Airways and Qantas you'll definitely be looking at fares in excess of A$2000. **From New Zealand**, fares start at NZ$2400, rising to NZ$2800 or more during high season.

RTW TICKETS

Given these fares and routings, **round-the-world tickets** that take in the Middle East are worth considering, especially if you have the time to make the most of some stopovers. Although few, if any, itineraries take in Damascus specifically, several offer a stop in Cairo, Istanbul or Rome, from where you can take a side-trip to Syria. Ultimately, your choice of route will depend on where else you want to visit, but starting from **Sydney**, you could fly to Hong Kong, Singapore, Cairo, and travel overland to London, before flying on to Chicago, Denver, Los Angeles and back to Sydney (from A$2239); or, starting from **Perth**, fly to Denpasar, Casablanca, Istanbul, Nairobi, Capetown, Johannesburg and back to Perth (from A$2299).

From **New Zealand**, a possible route would be Auckland to Los Angeles, Rome, London, Bangkok and Melbourne, before returning to Auckland, with fares starting from NZ$2499.

PACKAGES AND TOURS

Package deals from Australia and New Zealand are pretty flexible, and most specialist agents can do anything from booking a few nights' accommodation in Damascus for when you first arrive, to arranging a fully escorted tour.

Adventure World, for example, offer two nights' twin-share hotel accommodation, transfers and daily sightseeing for around A$432–453 per person. Most tour companies offer a range of itineraries that take in the major sights, many with the option of spending a few days in Egypt or Jordan as well. For example, Adventure World's eight-day tours of Syria, taking in Damascus, Aleppo, Palmyra and Krak des Chevaliers, start from A$2192, including all transport and accommodation and some meals, but not flights from Australia. Middle Eastern specialist Y'alla Tours can also make private tour arrangements in Syria, with prices starting at A$1176 for five days.

The more adventure-orientated operators such as The Imaginative Traveller offer small-group escorted tours ranging from nine days (from A$1150) to fifteen (from A$1980), with the option of adding on a four-day extension to Lebanon (A$830). Their no-frills tours aimed at budget travellers offer good value, especially for longer stays: a 22-day trip combining Syria and Jordan starts from A$1995. Again, all these prices exclude flights.

For **New Zealand travellers**, a nine-day tour of the major sights will set you back around NZ$1325, while itineraries including Jordan start from NZ$2280 for fifteen days (international flights not included).

FLIGHT AGENTS IN AUSTRALIA AND NEW ZEALAND

Anywhere Travel, 345 Anzac Parade, Kingsford, Sydney (☎02/9663 0411).

Brisbane Discount Travel, 260 Queen St, Brisbane (☎07/3229 9211).

Budget Travel, 16 Fort St, Auckland, plus branches around the city (☎09/366 0061 & 0800/808 040).

Destinations Unlimited, 3 Milford Rd, Auckland (☎09/373 4033).

Flight Centres Australia: 82 Elizabeth St, Sydney, plus branches nationwide (☎13 1600). New Zealand: 205 Queen St, Auckland (☎09/309 6171), plus branches nationwide.

Northern Gateway, 22 Cavenagh St, Darwin (☎08/8941 1394).

STA Travel Australia: 702 Harris St, Ultimo, Sydney; 256 Flinders St, Melbourne; other offices in state capitals and major universities (nearest branch ☎13 1776, fastfare telesales ☎1300/360 960). New Zealand: 10 High St, Auckland (☎09/309 0458, fastfare telesales ☎09/366 6673), plus branches in Wellington, Christchurch, Dunedin, Palmerston North, Hamilton and at major universities.

Thomas Cook Australia: 175 Pitt St, Sydney; 257 Collins St, Melbourne; plus branches in other state capitals (local branch ☎13 1771, Thomas Cook Direct telesales ☎1800/063 913). New Zealand: 96 Anzac Ave, Auckland (☎09/379 3920).

GETTING THERE FROM NEIGHBOURING COUNTRIES

If your travels include Turkey, Lebanon, Jordan, Cyprus or Egypt, moving on to Syria is fairly straightforward; travelling from Israel and Iraq to Syria is virtually impossible, however. Air services to Damascus from nearby Middle Eastern cities are relatively expensive (and surprisingly infrequent), and with rail services slow and irregular from Turkey and Jordan, you're likely to make all your border crossings by road.

FROM TURKEY

Among a number of **road** crossing points between Turkey and Syria, the one at **Bab al-Hawa** on the Antakya–Aleppo road is the most frequently used, and usually the most crowded. If you're driving, you're probably better off heading for the crossing at **Kassab** on the Antakya–Latakia road, probably the least busy of those along the western portion of the border.

There are many competing **bus** companies on the **Istanbul–Aleppo** route, with some selling through tickets to **Damascus** as well. If you shop around the firms at the huge Aksaray bus station in Istanbul (metro: Aksaray-Otogar) you'll find that most companies charge around US$25 for the 24-hour journey to Aleppo, and US$30 to Damascus, which takes another six hours. Agencies in downtown Istanbul often charge US$40 for the same journey, taking a fair cut of this fare themselves. Most buses are air-conditioned, though it might be a good idea to look at the vehicle before you

decide to part with your money. Count yourself very lucky if you don't end up having to change buses at least once, probably in Antakya. The arrival terminals in Aleppo and Damascus are very close to the centres of each city.

You can also cross by road between **Gaziantep** and Aleppo, although there is no real advantage to doing this. There's supposedly a daily bus linking the two centres; if this is more theory than reality, you'll need to take a taxi from Gaziantep or Killis (the town nearest the border) to the actual frontier post, and walk along the road across no-man's-land. On the other side you can get a taxi to Aleppo or to Izaz, from where you can continue by bus. If you do the whole thing by taxi from Gaziantep to Aleppo it will probably cost you around US$50.

The *Thomas Cook International Timetable* lists three weekly **trains** from Istanbul to Aleppo, but these trains exist mainly in the dreams of the timetablers, and don't bear much relation to reality. If you do get a through train, the journey time is a sedate 36 hours (at least), and you'll probably find it difficult to get a couchette (although they do exist). If you're on an InterRail pass, staff at Haydarpasa Station in Istanbul will sell you a ticket from the Turkish–Syrian border to Aleppo. If there's no through service to Aleppo, take a train from Istanbul to Adana or Gaziantep in southeastern Turkey, from where you can continue to Aleppo by road (from Adana via Antakya, from Gaziantep via Killis).

FROM LEBANON

Frequent buses run between **Beirut** and Damascus (4hr) and from **Tripoli** to Tartous (up to 3hr, depending on border delays) and Latakia (up to 4hr); Karnak, the Syrian government bus company, run daily services on these routes. Syrian visas are not available in Lebanon so buy one before you leave home. If you want to visit both countries, you might consider buying a multiple-entry Syrian visa; you can then pop in and out of Lebanon as you please, as Lebanese visas are available with a minimum of fuss at the border. There are at present no sailings along the coast between Beirut and Latakia.

FROM JORDAN

There's only one **road** crossing point between Syria and Jordan, just southwest of **Dera** (see p.100). Things can get quite congested here, with trucks lining the border approach roads for miles on either side, waiting to cross. The government **bus** companies of Syria and Jordan (Karnak and JETT, respectively) each run a daily service between Amman and Damascus, which takes anything up to seven hours and costs around US$5. In Amman, buses depart from the JETT international office on Al-Malek al-Hussein Street. Karnak also offers through tickets between Amman and Aleppo, though a change of bus in Damascus is likely. **Service taxis** between Amman and Damascus are faster, slightly more expensive and much more frequent. Crossing between Irbid (Jordan) and Dera by regular taxi is not difficult (see p.104).

Once a week, an extremely slow **train** travels the old Hedjaz rail line between Amman and Damascus, taking nine hours to complete the trip (5 hr if you just do the Amman–Dera portion). Tickets cost US$3 or less, and you'll finish up at the old Hedjaz Station, right in the centre of Damascus, which is the main advantage of entering the country this way. Trains are sometimes, but not always, hauled by the century-old steam locos which also work the line up from Damascus to Zabadani.

FROM EGYPT AND CYPRUS

Ferry services to Latakia from Alexandria (Egypt), Famagusta (Turkish Republic of North Cyprus) and Larnaca (Cyprus) have all operated in the past, but are currently in abeyance. There are daily **air services** between Damascus and Cairo, with services from Larnaca operating most days and a once-weekly service operated by Syrianair between Latakia and Cairo.

FROM IRAQ AND ISRAEL

Although it's possible to be in **Israel** and get within sight of the Syrian flag flying above Quneitra (see p.117), the main settlement in the UN-administered Syrian–Israeli border zone, there's no way of crossing the border here – in either direction. Until there's a major leap forward in the peace process the only viable route from Jerusalem to Damascus is via Palestine (formerly the West Bank) and Jordan. Crossing points between Syria and **Iraq** have been closed since the early 1980s, but in 1997 a small trade delegation travelled by road from Baghdad to Damascus, indicating a thaw in relations with Iraq and a possible loosening of border restrictions in the future.

VISAS AND RED TAPE

Most Syrian bureaucracy is frustratingly slow, but with a little patience and good humour you should find that obtaining visas (and extensions to visas) is straightforward enough. Syrian officials are usually polite, very apologetic about how patient you'll have to be, and will speak a modicum of English. However, government business with foreigners tends to be carried out in French rather than English, so if you have a smattering of the language you'll be marginally better off dealing with the paperwork than someone who hasn't.

VISAS

All visitors to Syria must hold a **passport** valid for at least six months beyond the proposed date of entry into the country. Virtually all nationalities must also obtain a **tourist visa** to gain entry to Syria.

Australians and New Zealanders can, in theory, obtain visas on arrival at Syrian border posts or airports, but to be on the safe side, it's best to get your visa before pitching up. Americans, Canadians and most European citizens (including British and Irish) should purchase visas before they leave home. It is possible to obtain a Syrian visa at consulates in Amman, Ankara or Cairo, but generally you'll need a "letter of recommendation" from your own embassy – costly and time-consuming to obtain – and you may face considerable delays to your application.

Syria maintains **consulates** in only a few countries of the world, and not in Australia,

SYRIAN CONSULATES ABROAD

UK, 8 Belgrave Square, London SW1 (☎0171/245 9012).
USA, 2215 Wyoming Avenue NW, Washington DC 20008 (☎202/232 6313).

Canada, Israel, Iraq, Ireland, the Netherlands, Scandinavian countries or New Zealand. Irish, Dutch and Scandinavian citizens can apply by post through the consulate in London, and Canadians, Australians and New Zealanders through the Washington consulate. You can't obtain a Syrian visa in Lebanon, so if you're planning to visit Lebanon from Syria you may want to consider a multiple-entry Syrian visa.

Obtaining visas through the consulates listed in the box is fairly unproblematic, whether by post (which takes about a week) or in person (which takes three days). If you plan to visit the embassy in person, phone ahead beforehand – the opening hours are sometimes rather bizarre. With your application, you may be asked to provide a letter from your employer on their headed paper, confirming the nature of your occupation. You will also be asked to state your religion, and you can assume that if you put "Jewish" your application will be refused. When returning the form, you'll also need to include a registered or recorded stamped addressed envelope, your passport, the required number of photos, and a postal or money order (not a personal cheque).

The **cost** will depend on the type of visa and your nationality. UK and Irish citizens pay UK£31.50/48 (single/multiple entry), and Canadians US$56/108. Americans (US$61), Australians (free) and New Zealanders (free) can only obtain single-entry visas. Single-entry visas are valid for fifteen days' stay, and multiple-entry visas are valid for use within six months; with both sorts of visa you'll need to get an extension (see below) if you stay more than fifteen consecutive days in the country.

VISAS AND ISRAEL

Evidence of a visit to **Israel** in your passport automatically disqualifies you from obtaining a Syrian visa, and will invalidate any visa you have already obtained. If you plan to include Israel and Syria in your Middle Eastern wanderings, then make sure you visit Syria first. Most nationalities don't need a visa for Israel and you'll get Israeli entrance and exit stamps on a separate slip of paper, but Egyptian stamps from border posts at Rafah or Tabah, or Jordanian stamps from the Allenby bridge, will indicate a visit to Israel, and Syrian embassy or border officials are adept at noticing them in your passport.

RED TAPE WITHIN SYRIA

On entering Syria, foreign visitors are given a **yellow card** which must be filled in; this is usually given to air passengers before they land. You need to look after this card carefully, as it must be presented when leaving the country; losing it will result in all sorts of hassle.

You need to keep your passport with you at all times when you're in Syria. Things aren't nearly as paranoid as they were in the 1980s, when random checks on foreigners by the police happened constantly, but you'll generally need to show your passport when using any form of public transport, and sometimes also when entering bus or train stations where the police are quite security-conscious; and of course you'll always need it to change money, collect mail and register at hotels. **Police checkpoints** on roads are common in the desert and the northeast, so have your passport handy when travelling by car or bus in these regions. As in most countries, it's wise to keep a separate photocopy of your passport in case you lose it – when your first port of call should be the nearest passport and immigration office. You'll need a special **permit** to visit Quneitra in the Golan Heights (see p.117) but otherwise you're free to travel where you want in the country, although you should be sensitive about travelling in border or military zones.

VISA EXTENSIONS

To stay in Syria longer than the fifteen days provided by a tourist visa requires a **visa extension**, lasting up to four weeks, which can only be granted in Syria on the fourteenth or fifteenth day of your visit. When buying an extension, you'll need to state your intended date of departure from Syria; only one extension will be granted per trip.

Extensions must be obtained at passport and immigration offices, which can be found in Damascus, Aleppo, Tartous, Latakia, Homs, Hama, Dera, Qamishli and Deir ez-Zur (their locations are shown on the maps of these towns in this book). These offices are usually open from 8am to 2pm, daily except Friday. Extensions can usually be given on the same day, but sometimes, especially in Damascus, you will be asked to return the next day to complete the procedures and pick up the extension permit.

Arranging the extension involves a great deal of waiting around and filling in forms, and all you end up with at the end of it are a few extra stamps in your passport and a slip of paper which is removed, along with your yellow card, when you leave the country. At least extensions are cheap, about US$2 for all nationalities, payable in Syrian currency; you'll either pay this in cash at the office, or be asked to buy a revenue stamp (used to indicate on paperwork that you have paid for a government service) for the amount from a designated booth outside the immigration office. You'll also need **passport photographs**, in black and white and colour; some passport offices (such as the one in Aleppo) require four photos, while others require fewer, perhaps two or three. To save trouble, it's best to bring out a number of these photos from home. Otherwise you'll find photographic shops in most cities, where you can get passport photos in a few hours; automatic photobooths do not exist.

CUSTOMS AND CURRENCY DECLARATIONS

In contrast to the visa and passport requirements, Syrian **customs** regulations are unlikely to trouble you. Import/export limits are 200 cigarettes and two bottles of spirits; no vegetable or olive oils, or meat products can be taken out of Syria. There's no need to declare possession of cameras or other equipment, although if you drive a car in you'll probably need to prove that you're the owner. You can import foreign **currency** up to a value of US$5000 without having to declare it; when you leave you can take S£2000 with you, although whether you'll be able to change it outside the country is another matter.

HEALTH AND INSURANCE

There are no mandatory inoculations required for entry to Syria, but you should have jabs against tetanus, typhoid and hepatitis A, in addition to a polio booster, before you leave home. If you're going to be travelling near the Euphrates in summer you should also take out a supply of anti-malaria pills, as an additional precaution.

HEALTH PROBLEMS AND LIKELY HAZARDS

Tap water is in theory safe to drink, being heavily chlorinated and (in restaurants) filtered, but with **bottled water** so cheap and plentiful you may not want to risk it, unless you're going to be travelling around the region for a long time – in which case your stomach will eventually get used to whatever foreign nasties are still present in the water. If you're avoiding the water, then you'll also want to stay off ice in your drinks, most ice cream, and salad vegetables which have been washed in water. **Milk and cream** should be avoided, as generally the products aren't pasteurized to the standards that your stomach will have got used to, although milk which is added to Western-style coffee is OK if it has been boiled.

You should definitely avoid contact with any **stagnant water** alongside the Euphrates and Orontes rivers. Although the risk is not so great as along the Nile, such water may harbour **bilharzia** (schistosomiasis) and other parasites which can enter your body through the skin (a sign of infection is blood in urine). Don't bathe in irrigation canals or the like, or walk barefoot on mud or grass wet with Orontes or Euphrates water; there's even a slight risk if you decide to go swimming in the main channels of these or other rivers.

COPING WITH THE HEAT AND DUST

Many health problems in Syria are caused by the excessive **heat** experienced during the summer. Sweat evaporates very quickly in the dry air, and it's easy to become **dehydrated** without realizing it; you should always maintain your fluid intake (at least three litres per day), and steer clear of too much caffeine or alcohol, which exacerbate dehydration. It does no harm to take a bit of **salt** with your food, as you lose a lot of body salts during perspiration. You should try to wear **loose-fitting clothes**, made preferably from cotton rather than synthetic fabrics, which will help to prevent **prickly heat**, an itchy rash caused by perspiration trapped within your skin.

Ideally, you should aim to start your day early and spend the afternoon resting, particularly in the east of the country where summer daytime temperatures above 40°C are common; and always try to stay out of direct sunlight, even if the only concession you make is wearing a hat. To avoid **sunburn**, bring out a good brand of suncream with you (unavailable in Syria) and keep as much of your skin covered as possible when you're out in the sun. **Fungal infections** such as athlete's foot or ringworm are caused by perspiration trapped within clothes, and can be treated by medicine available from pharmacists (and prevented by changing your clothes frequently). More serious are **heat stroke** and **heat exhaustion**, whose symptoms include fatigue, headaches, fever, vomiting or stomach cramps, moving on to an inability to sweat, a flushing of the skin and a rise in body temperature. Serious heat stroke can be fatal. Treatment for both ailments is to stay indoors and stay cool, preferably with wet towels wrapped around you to reduce body temperature. If you arrive in Syria direct from Europe, you should spend a few days getting acclimatized to the heat, and leave it a while before heading out to the desert – which can be like walking into an oven if you're not prepared for the extremes of temperature.

Dust and smog might affect your eyes and sinuses, particularly in summer when breezes constantly blow trapped city fumes into your face. In the desert, grit and dust can easily get into your eye with each fresh breath of wind; you might want to wear a scarf or similar to protect your **sinuses** which, like the eyes, can be irritated by dust carried in the wind. It makes sense to wear **sunglasses** outside, whatever the brightness; if you wear **contact lenses** you should seriously consider wearing glasses for a time.

DIGESTIVE INFECTIONS

Most travellers in Syria are unlikely to encounter any problems beyond bouts of **diarrhoea**, brought on through exhaustion or exposure to infected water or food. It's difficult to avoid dodgy food completely, but you can help yourself by avoiding all street food, dishes in restaurants which look as though they have been standing around for some time, and undercooked meat and fish dishes. Resting up for a few days, drinking only mineral water, sweetened tea or fruit juice, is the recommended remedy, getting rid of the bacteria by simply denying them sustenance; when you can manage to eat something, bread and plain boiled white rice are the best things to start off with. If you need to be on the move, however, you should have a supply of an anti-diarrhoea preparation with you such as Diocalm or the much stronger Lomotil or Immodium, which will block you up for a certain period but won't kill whatever's inside you making you ill. Whatever you do, you should ensure that you keep your fluid intake up to avoid dehydration – particularly dangerous during the summer. You might want to bring out with you a medical **rehydration preparation** to be taken should the need arise. Serious or stubborn cases of food poisoning may need a course of antibiotics, in which case you'll need to seek medical attention. If symptoms include severe fever, vomiting, stomach cramps, and/or blood present in stools, then you might have **dysentery** or **typhoid**, both of which need immediate medical attention. Dysentery comes in two forms – bacillary dysentery can be treated with antibiotics, but amoebic dysentery is harder to cure and may mean flying home.

Hepatitis A is easily picked up from infected food in Syria, and it makes a lot of sense to get inoculated against it before you set out. Symptoms include a darkening of urine and your skin turning yellow. If you've contracted it, you'll need to return home, as it can drag on for months.

ANIMAL HAZARDS

Snakes and **scorpions** often make their home among rocks and ruins, but they're generally nocturnal and will hide if people appear. Unwelcome attention from these beasts is very rare, but it makes sense not to turn over stones or poke your hand into dark crevices, for fear of what may be lurking there, and be very careful with shoes and clothes if you decide to camp out in the desert. Any bite from one of these creatures should receive immediate medical attention, and you should try to note the animal concerned in order to describe it to a doctor.

More likely hazards in the countryside are **dogs**: most Bedouin keep semi-wild, often extremely ferocious animals, which can dampen your appreciation of the Bedouin's famed hospitality, and in Bosra and other ancient sites you'll come across ordinary families living among the ruins, whose pets won't take kindly to you admiring the Roman stonework which happens to be their home. If you get bitten by a dog then get medical help immediately; first aid includes washing the wound with soap and water, and applying a bandage and antiseptic cream. As soon as possible you should begin a course of **anti-rabies treatment**, available free from Syrian state hospitals: all of them keep a stock of the French drug Verorab, which is given in the arm and not nearly as painful as the old stomach-injected shots. If you are bitten, or suffer an open wound, you might also be at risk from **tetanus** and should ask for a booster jab from a doctor, to supplement the preventative inoculation you should have had before leaving home.

Mosquitoes are present in many places in Syria, and you should bring your own flying insect repellents. In summer (May–Oct) around the Euphrates they can carry **malaria**: the risk is slight, and you should bring a course of anti-malarial pills (Chloroquine; available from pharmacies at home, but not in Syria). If you think you've got malaria, then hospitalization is essential as the disease is potentially fatal; symptoms include muscle soreness and fever, rising to bouts of serious fever and chill between four and eight days later. If you think mozzies in hotels might bother you, consider bringing a mosquito net out with you (never available in Syrian hotels). If you're really not keen on mosquitoes, or are heading for Egypt where they're much more of a problem, consider taking a course of vitamin B-12 tablets, which is supposed to make your blood unattractive to them.

HEALTH CLINICS AND INFORMATION FOR TRAVELLERS

BRITAIN

UK citizens might want to pick up the Department of Health's free publication *Health Advice for Travellers*, a comprehensive booklet available at the post office (or by calling the Health Literature Line on ☎0800/555777); it includes an application for Form E111, which UK residents must obtain to receive free emergency treatment in the European Economic Area – useful if you're travelling to Syria overland. The content of the booklet, which contains immunization advice, is constantly updated on pages 460–4 of CEEFAX.

British Airways Travel Clinic, 156 Regent St, London W1 7RA (Mon–Fri 9.30am–5.15pm, Sat 10am–4pm; ☎0171/439 9584), and in Flightbookers at 177 Tottenham Court Rd, London W1P 0LX (Mon–Fri 9.30am–6.30pm, Sat 10am–2pm; ☎0171/757 2504), walk-in service or by appointment. There are appointment-only branches at 101 Cheapside, London EC2 (☎0171/606 2977), and at the BA terminal in London's Victoria Station (☎0171/233 6661). BA also operates around forty regional clinics throughout the country (call ☎0171/831 5333 for the one nearest to you), plus airport locations at Gatwick and Heathrow.

Hospital for Tropical Diseases, St Pancras Hospital, 4 St Pancras Way, London NW1 0PE (☎0171/388 9600). Travel clinic and recorded message service (☎0839/337733; 49p per min) which gives advice on hygiene and illness prevention as well as listing appropriate immunizations.

MASTA (Medical Advisory Service for Travellers Abroad), London School of Hygiene and Tropical Medicine. Operates a pre-recorded 24-hour Travellers' Health Line (☎0891/224100; 50p per min), giving written information tailored to your journey by return of post.

IRELAND

Travel Medicine Services, PO Box 254, 16 College St, Belfast 1 (☎01232/315 220).

Tropical Medical Bureau, Grafton St Medical Centre, 34 Grafton St, Dublin 2 (☎01/671 9200).

Tropical Medical Bureau, Dun Laoghaire Medical Centre, 5 Northumberland Ave, Dun Laoghaire, Co. Dublin (☎01/280 4996, fax 280 5603; email tropical@iol.ie; Web site http:/www.iol.ie/-tmb/).

NORTH AMERICA

Canadian Society for International Health, 170 Laurier Ave W, Suite 902, Ottawa, ON K1P 5V5 (☎613/230-2654). Distributes a free pamphlet, "Health Information for Canadian Travellers", containing an extensive list of travel health centres in Canada.

Centers for Disease Control, 1600 Clifton Rd NE, Atlanta, GA 30333 (☎404/639-3311; www.cdc.gov/travel/travel.html). Publishes outbreak warnings, suggested inoculations, precautions and other background information for travellers. Web site is very useful.

Travel Medicine, 351 Pleasant St, Suite 312, Northampton, MA 01060 (☎1-800/872-8633). Sells first-aid kits, mosquito netting, water filters and other health-related travel products.

Travelers Medical Center, 31 Washington Square, New York, NY 10011 (☎212/982-1600). Consultation service on immunizations and treatment of diseases for people travelling to developing countries.

AUSTRALASIA

Travellers' Medical and Vaccination Centre, 7/428 George St, Sydney (☎02/9221 7133); 3/393 Little Bourke St, Melbourne (☎03/9602 5788); 6/29 Gilbert Place, Adelaide (☎08/8212 7522); 6/247 Adelaide St, Brisbane (☎07/3221 9066); 1 Mill St, Perth (☎08/9321 1977). Web site: http//:www.tmvc.com.au

Auckland Hospital, Park Rd, Grafton, Auckland (☎09/379 7440).

Finally, **flies** can be a real problem out in the desert, particularly around Palmyra. It's difficult to suggest any appropriate remedies for dealing with them beyond continually brushing them away from your skin; insect sprays (available locally) have some effect, but air conditioning is what really gets rid of them.

Bedbugs can be a problem in the cheapest hotels. The usual giveaway is tiny specks of blood on bed linen; treatment includes preparations easily obtainable from pharmacists, but prevention is better than cure – find another hotel. Other unwelcome features of cheap hotels are fleas, mites and giant cockroaches, all of which might result in skin irritation.

MEDICAL ATTENTION

Every small town has a **pharmacy** (called just that, if it has a sign in English), where you'll be able to obtain remedies for minor ailments such as diarrhoea, or bites and stings. Most medicines have details printed on them in English (at least with the barest information about what they're for), and many pharmacists speak English too. Pharmacists can dispense many medicines for which you'd need a prescription back home, and drugs are cheap. However, you should bring along with you a good supply of any medication you might need on a regular basis, as what you require (or its exact equivalent) may not be available in Syria.

In large towns you'll find doctors and dentists who are able to deal with **serious ailments**. Finding one is easy – they advertise in the way that shops or other services do – and most hotels (or your embassy) will be able to put you in contact with one quickly. Most doctors will have been trained in Europe and have a good working knowledge of English. Expect a consultation fee of around US$30–40, and remember to pick up a receipt for insurance purposes. If you are given an injection, insist that needles are taken out of the packet in front of you, and discarded afterwards; if you are in any doubt, then ask to buy a new syringe from a pharmacy (they're very cheap but you will need a prescription from a doctor).

Emergency hospital treatment is free of charge in Syrian state hospitals, but if you're able to it's always better to make a doctor, rather than a hospital, your first port of call. The **Shamy Diplomatic Hospital** in Damascus (address on p.89) is the only private hospital in the country, and its services are vastly better than anything offered by the state. If all else fails, then most medical insurance policies should cover the cost of an **emergency flight home**.

TRAVEL INSURANCE

Most people will find it essential to take out a good **travel insurance policy**, but you should check what levels of cover you may have from other sources. For example, **bank and credit cards** (particularly American Express) often have certain levels of medical or other insurance included, especially if you use them to pay for your trip. It can be quite comprehensive, anticipating anything from lost or stolen baggage and missed connections to charter companies going bankrupt; however, certain policies (notably in North America) only cover medical costs.

Note that very few insurers will arrange on-the-spot payments in the event of a major expense or loss; you will usually be reimbursed only after going home. In all case of loss or theft of goods, you will have to contact the local police to have a report made out so that your insurer can process the claim. If you plan to participate in water sports or do some hiking (unlikely in Syria), you may have to pay an extra premium; check carefully that any insurance policy you are considering will cover you in case of an accident.

BRITAIN AND IRELAND

If you have a good "all risks" **home insurance** policy it may well cover your possessions against loss or theft even when overseas, or you can extend cover through your household contents insurer. Many **private medical schemes** also cover you when abroad – make sure you know the procedure and the helpline number.

Most travel agents and tour operators will offer you dedicated **travel insurance** when you book your flight or holiday, and some will insist you take it. These policies are usually reasonable value, though as ever, you should check the small print. If you feel the cover is inadequate, or you want to compare prices, contact an insurance broker, bank or specialist insurance company.

Standard cover, costing from around £26 a month, should cover the cost of cancellation and curtailment of flights, medical expenses, travel delay, accident, missed departures, lost baggage, lost passport, personal liability and legal expenses. Good-value policies are issued by Campus Travel or STA (see p.4 for addresses); Columbus Travel Insurance, 17 Devonshire Square, London EC2M 4SQ (☎0171/375 0011); Worldwide, The Business Centre, 1–7 Commercial Rd, Tonbridge, Kent TN12 6YT (☎01732/773366); Endsleigh Insurance, Cranfield House, 97–107 Southampton Row, London WC1B 4AG (☎0171/436 4451); and Marcus Hearne & Co Ltd, 65–66 Shoreditch High Street, London E1 6JL (☎0171/739 3444).

Some insurance companies refuse to cover travellers over 65 (or stop at 69 or 74 years of age), and most that do charge hefty premiums. The best policies for **older travellers**, with no upper age limit, are offered by Age Concern (☎01883/346964).

Travel insurance for **Irish citizens** is best obtained through a travel specialist such as USIT (see p.5). Their policies cost from around IR£21 for six to ten days, IR£31 for one month. Discounts are offered to students of any age and anyone under 35.

US AND CANADA

Before buying a travel insurance policy, check that you're not already covered. **Canadian provincial health plans** typically provide some overseas medical coverage, although they are unlikely to pick up the full tab in the event of a mishap. Holders of official **student/teacher/youth cards** are entitled to accident coverage and hospital in-patient benefits – the annual membership is far less than the cost of comparable insurance. Students may also find that their **student health coverage** extends during the vacations and for one term beyond the date of last enrolment. **Homeowners' or renters' insurance** often covers theft or loss of documents, money and valuables while overseas.

After exhausting the possibilities above, you might want to consider **specialist travel insurance**. Most travel agents will arrange insurance at no extra charge, or you can call the following insurance companies direct: Access America (☎1-800/284-8300); Carefree Travel Insurance (☎1-800/323-3149); Desjardins Travel Insurance (Canada only; ☎1-800/463-7830); STA Travel Insurance (☎1-800/781-4040); Travel Assistance International (☎1-800/821-2828); Travel Guard (☎1-800/826-1300); Travel Insurance Services (☎1-800/937-1387). Policies vary: some are comprehensive while others cover only certain risks (accidents, illnesses, delayed or lost luggage, cancelled flights, etc). In particular, ask whether the policy pays medical costs up front or reimburses you later, and whether it provides for medical evacuation to your home country. For policies that include lost or stolen luggage, check exactly what is and isn't covered, and make sure the per-article limit will cover your most valuable possession. Most North American travel policies apply only to items lost, stolen or damaged while in the custody of an identifiable, responsible third party – hotel porter, airline, luggage consignment, etc. Even in these cases you will have to contact the local police within a certain time limit to have a complete report made out so that your insurer can process the claim.

The best **premiums** are usually to be had through student/youth travel agencies – STA policies, for example, come in two forms: with or without medical coverage. The current rates are $45/$35 (for up to 7 days); $60/$45 (8–15 days); $110/$85 (1 month); $140/$115 (45 days); $165/$135 (2 months); $50/$35 for each extra month.

AUSTRALIA AND NEW ZEALAND

Travel insurance, for periods ranging from a few weeks to a year or even longer, is available from most travel agents or direct from insurance companies such as Cover More, 9/32 Walker St, North Sydney (☎02/9202 8000 or 1800/251 881); and Ready Plan, 141 Walker St, Dandenong, Melbourne (☎03/9791 5077 or 1800/337 462), and 10/63 Albert St, Auckland (☎09/379 3208). A typical policy will cost A$100/NZ$110 for two weeks, A$170/NZ$190 for one month, A$250/NZ$275 for two months.

COSTS, MONEY AND BANKS

Once you've shelled out all the expense of getting there, Syria is a remarkably cheap country to travel in, and it's quite possible to exist on under UK£10/US$16 a day if you don't mind roughing it in terms of both food and accommodation. If you've come from Turkey, or especially from Jordan, you'll find that your cash stretches much further here than in those countries. Public transport, in particular, is dirt cheap. There's not much geographical variation in prices, although food and accommodation are a little more expensive in Damascus and Aleppo than elsewhere. Be warned, however, that there's a high rate of inflation which is steadily pushing prices up. The rate of exchange currently stands at just under seventy Syrian pounds to one pound sterling, and just over forty Syrian pounds to one US dollar.

COSTS

Accommodation varies from around UK£4/US$6.50 a night for a double room in a basic hotel to £150/$240 in Syria's most exclusive, business-oriented establishments. If you're on anything more than the most limited of budgets, you should bank on spending £15/$24 for a decent double room in a mid-range hotel, with prices rising perhaps to £20/$32 for a similar place in Damascus and Aleppo.

The price of a **meal** depends likewise on what you want; you can eat *felafel* and *shwarma* from street stalls or small eateries for as little as 50p/80c. A basic sit-down meal of meat (kebabs or chicken), chips, a side salad and a soft drink will rarely cost much more than £4/$6.50 in a local restaurant, but you'll pay more in the Western-style restaurants in Damascus or Aleppo, where a flash meal with wine or beer may cost double this. Locally produced **beer and wine** tends to be cheap, with a half-litre bottle of Al-Chark or Barada beer costing under £1/$1.60 in restaurants. European beers, however, sold mainly in hotels, are more expensive than back home. Local **soft drinks**, sold everywhere in small bottles, cost 15p/25c, but imported canned drinks (including 7-UP and Canada Dry) will cost twice that.

Transport costs are very inexpensive. Flying between Damascus and Aleppo, a distance of 370km, costs only £10/$16, and the same journey by Pullman bus costs just over £2/$3. The cost of a train ticket between these two cities is even less, at around £1.30/$2, with only a few pennies difference between first- and second-class fares. The cost of local buses and microbuses, which you'll use a lot if you don't have a car, is remarkably low. If you rent a car you'll pay about £29/$45 per day for a Peugeot 205 or similar. Petrol is cheap: around 30p/50c for a litre of "Super".

One of the biggest costs, which you can't do much to avoid, is the **entry charge** to museums and parts of some archeological sites. This is a fixed S£200 (UK£3/US$5), and it's the same whether you're gaining entry to the Crac des Chevaliers or some crummy local museum. If you're entitled to an **International Student Identification Card (ISIC)**, bring it along; in theory it should garner you a reduced entry charge of S£50, though in some places the officials won't understand what you're showing them and you'll have to cough up the normal price. You won't get anything off transport costs with an ISIC card.

BAKSHEESH

Baksheesh seems to make the Middle Eastern world go round, but things are much less frenetic in Syria than in Turkey or Egypt. The most obvious examples of *baksheesh* you'll encounter in Syria are tipping hotel and restaurant staff, paying drivers who give you lifts in rural areas and giving charitable alms to the poor. Waiters in any restaurant will expect you to round up the bill, perhaps to the nearest S£100, and if you're in even a moderately good hotel, you'll be expected to tip staff who clean your room or carry bags to it. It makes sense to have some small-value notes (or US one-dollar bills) to hand for this purpose. Unlike in Egypt and some other Asian countries, handing over money to speed along bureaucracy or to get yourself a seat on an otherwise crowded train or bus is not the done thing, and may cause offence or be misinterpreted.

You will encounter some **begging** on the street in cities, and in rural areas endless pestering (for money or pens) by small boys; the giving of **alms** to the needy is considered a natural act and a requirement of Islam, but how much to give and on what occasions is something only for individuals to decide. As a foreigner, it will always be assumed that you are rich, even if you think you aren't.

BARGAINING

In the **souks** of major towns you can bargain initially stated prices down by as much as half, and what you end up paying will be a balance between your own tenacity and how low a stallholder expects his profit margins to be. The banter associated with price discussion is all part of the shopping experience, and it takes skill, practice and determination to get what you want. Although it may seem rude, one way to get the price down is to express an interest in something and then walk away – and often you can do this several times over the same item at the same stall. Shopping in Syria is much less pressurized than in Egypt or Turkey, and you should not have much trouble persuading stallholders that you intend looking around for the best prices – which is, after all, what the locals do. The only other people with whom bargaining is appropriate are **taxi drivers**, especially if you want to be taken a fair distance out of town, and **hotel owners**, particularly if you intend to stay more than three days.

MONEY

The **currency** used in Syria is the **Syrian pound** (or *lira*), sometimes abbreviated to SP or LS (*Livre Syrien*), but more often shown as S£, which we have used throughout this guide. There are one hundred piastres, known as *qirsh*, to the pound, although you rarely deal with these as the pound is such a small unit of currency. **Coins** in circula-

tion are rare; most of the money is in the form of **notes**, some of which are so ragged as to be almost illegible (although you'll rarely have trouble getting them accepted). Details are printed on the notes in English and Arabic. There are coins for a quarter, half and 1 pound, and notes for 1, 5, 10, 25, 100 and 500 pounds. The S£500 notes are often too large a denomination to be accepted when you buy tickets or small purchases, although you will be given wads of them if you change a lot of money at one time.

CARRYING YOUR MONEY

Obtaining Syrian currency before you enter the country is difficult, but not impossible. Major travel agents at home such as Thomas Cook should be able to sell you Syrian pounds, so long as you give them sufficient notice. Otherwise, if you're entering the country via Jordan or Turkey, you'll be able to obtain some in banks (or on the black market) in those countries.

Given the time it takes to exchange travellers' cheques (see below), you'll probably want to bring at least some of your money in foreign notes. And this should be in the form of **US dollars** (preferably a variety of denominations), which act as the "unofficial" second currency in Syria. Often stallholders and taxi drivers will ask for payment in US dollars, and in all but the very cheapest hotels, prices are quoted in, and bills are expected to be settled in, US dollars (see p.33 for further details). Note that Australian and Canadian dollars, sterling and the major European currencies can also be exchanged at banks in Syria, but that Irish and New Zealand currencies cannot.

Credit cards can only be used in a very limited number of outlets, including some three- and all four- and five-star hotels, car rental outfits, international airline offices and a few souk stalls in Aleppo, Damascus and Palmyra which are used to seeing tourists. It is impossible to get cash advances on any type of credit card, unless you go through the Thomas Cook representative in Damascus (see p.89). Eurocheques aren't accepted anywhere, and there are no automated teller machines.

BANKS AND EXCHANGE

There is only one institution in Syria which changes money – the **Commercial Bank of Syria**. It's the only high-street bank, and also controls exchange booths in city centres and at airports and hotels. The Commercial Bank maintains branches in most large towns, though not all change foreign currency, and some will only change cash, but not travellers' cheques. The best currency to take is US dollars, and American Express seems to be the most recognized brand of cheque, though most brands are acceptable. The exchange rate is the same everywhere – don't bother to shop around. There are no **foreign banks** with branches in Syria; Thomas Cook and American Express have representatives in Damascus, but they can do little for you (see pp.88–89).

Opening hours vary slightly from branch to branch, but usually they open between 8am and 9am and close for the day at around 2pm. In the very largest centres, there may be a period of opening in the early evening, from 5pm to 7pm or 8pm. Banks are always closed on Fridays. **Exchange booths** in large cities are usually open long hours, perhaps 8am to 6pm, seven days a week, but often for the exchange of cash only.

Some banks (ludicrously) ask those who exchange **travellers' cheques** to show the **bank receipts** which are given at the time of purchase of the cheques, ignoring the fact that these are not meant to be kept with the cheques themselves. Although persuasion will normally win them round, it may be worth asking banks at home to give two separate receipts which prove the sale of the cheques. It can take an age to exchange travellers' cheques, particularly in out-of-the-way places where you'll need to go from office to office getting signatures on your paper-

work, so it's best to change as much as you dare at any one time. Keep all exchange receipts as you may be asked to show that you have changed money legally before making large purchases.

There is a strong **black market** in foreign currency, which can be used by Syrians to buy items which otherwise they would find unobtainable. In Damascus, Aleppo and other tourist spots you will find that stallholders, street hustlers, waiters and hotel staff will offer to change money for you, an illegal and risky practice for which caution and discretion are advised. You'll get a slightly enhanced rate of around fifty Syrian pounds for each US dollar, and the equivalent for other major currencies. Some black marketeers will even take travellers' cheques.

SENDING MONEY TO SYRIA

Having money wired from home is never convenient or cheap, and should be considered a last resort. Amex Moneygram and Western Union do not operate in Syria, so the only way of sending money from overseas is through banks. In the UK, for example, high-street banks will transfer money to most branches of the Commercial Bank of Syria; their Damascus branch no. 1 in Mouaweia St is probably the easiest place in the country to pick up money sent to you. The process costs about UK£14 (you may also have to pay a fee when the money is collected in Syria), and takes about three working days. In Syria the money can be collected in US dollars or Syrian pounds.

INFORMATION AND MAPS

The Syrian government does not maintain tourist offices abroad, although their embassies may be able to provide you with the most basic maps and glossy handouts. Information is a commodity in short supply (and constant demand) in Syria, and it's best to be as fully prepared as possible before you leave home, particularly as far as maps are concerned.

INFORMATION IN SYRIA

Major towns in Syria have **tourist offices**, which are generally open from 8am to about 2pm, daily except Friday; some also open up again in the early evening. There is usually someone who speaks English in the offices, but most of the time they have little information to hand. Indeed, probably the most useful thing these offices do is to distribute free maps, and you may well find that people working on the reception desks in hotels are just as good a source of information. The English-language newspaper the *Syria Times* (see p.36) gives a random and far from comprehensive listing of exhibitions, talks, films and theatre shows in Aleppo and Damascus. Most archeological site offices sell maps or information booklets about the sites, some of which are horrendously dated.

MAPS

The best fold-out **map** of Syria is *Road Map:Syria* published by the Austrian cartographers, Freytag-Berndt. It has an excellent road map of the coun-

try at 1:800,000 scale, plus detailed plans of Damascus, Aleppo and Palmyra. You can buy the map in Syria at English-language bookshops in Damascus (see p.89) and in bookshops in large luxury hotels throughout the country; it is also available from map stockists around the world (see box overleaf). The map of Syria published by Geoprojects (Beirut) is not nearly as accurate (or as widely available). The *Lonely Planet Travel Atlas* covering Jordan, Lebanon and Syria in book form may be worth obtaining before you leave home; the maps are accurate and detailed, but surprisingly there are no town or city plans.

Tourist offices in Syria give out a free map of the country, as well as a series of regional maps, which include local town plans and a certain amount of information in English, French or German (depending on which editions offices have in stock). It would be a good idea to visit the tourist office in Damascus first and stock up on these maps for the regions you will be travelling to, but use them with caution – they are often poorly printed and compiled.

USEFUL INTERNET SITES

British Foreign and Commonwealth Office
www.fco.gov.uk/reference/travel_advice/
Constantly updated advice for travellers.

UK Meterological Office
www.metro.govt.uk
Weather forecasts and links to other sites.

Cheap Flights
www.cheapflights.co.uk
A new way of finding flight deals plus links to other travel sites.

US State Department Travel Advisories
travel.state.gov/travel_warnings.html
Web site providing "consular information sheets" detailing the dangers of travelling in most countries of the world.

Syria on the Web
www.mysite.com/syria/yrll.html
Excellent list of Web sites relating to Syria, with everything from book reviews to travel and hotel information; updated monthly.

George Azar
www.awar.org
Azar is an American-Lebanese photojournalist,

MAP STOCKISTS AND MAIL ORDER SPECIALISTS

LONDON

Daunt Books, 83 Marylebone High St, W1M 3DE (☎0171/224 2295); 193 Haverstock Hill, NW3 4QL (☎0171/794 4006).

National Map Centre, 22–24 Caxton St, SW1H 0QU (☎0171/222 2466).

Stanfords, 12–14 Long Acre, WC2E 9LP (☎0171/836 1321); maps by mail or phone order are available on this number. Other branches in London are located within Campus Travel at 52 Grosvenor Gardens, SW1W 0AG (☎0171/730 1314), and within the British Airways offices at 156 Regent St, W1R 5TA (☎0171/434 4744).

The Travel Bookshop, 13–15 Blenheim Crescent, W11 2EE (☎0171/229 5260).

THE REST OF ENGLAND AND WALES

Austic's City Bookshop, 91 The Headrow, Leeds LS1 6OJ (☎0113/243 3099).

Heffers Map Shop, 3rd Floor, 19 Sidney St, Cambridge CB2 3HL (☎01223/568467).

Latitude, 34 The Broadway, Darkes Lane, Potters Bar, Herts EN6 2HW (☎01707/663090).

The Map Shop, 30a Belvoir St, Leicester LE1 6QH (☎0116/2471400).

The Map Shop, 15 High St, Upton-upon-Severn, Worcestershire WR8 0HJ (☎01684/593146).

Newcastle Map Centre, 55 Grey St, Newcastle upon Tyne NE1 6EF (☎0191/261 5622).

Stanfords, 29 Corn Street, Bristol BS1 1HT (☎0117/929 9966).

Whiteman's Bookshop, 7 Orange Grove, Bath BA1 1LP (☎01225/464029).

SCOTLAND

Aberdeen Map Shop, 74 Skene St, Aberdeen AB10 1QE (☎01224/637999).

John Smith and Sons, 57–61 St Vincent St, Glasgow G2 5TB (☎0141/221 7472).

James Thin Melvern's Bookshop, 29 Union St, Inverness IV1 1QA (☎01463/233500).

IRELAND

Easons Bookshop, 40 O'Connell St, Dublin 1 (☎01/873 3811).

Fred Hann's Bookshop, 27–29 Nassau St, Dublin 2 (☎01/677 1255).

Hodges Figgis Bookshop, 56–58 Dawson St, Dublin 2 (☎01/677 4754).

Waterstone's, Queens Bldg, 8 Royal Ave, Belfast BT1 1DA (☎01232/247 355); 7 Dawson St, Dublin 2 (☎01/679 1415); 69 Patrick St, Cork (☎021/276 522).

US

Adventurous Traveler Bookstore, PO Box 1468, Williston, VT 05495 (☎1-800/282-3963).

Book Passage, 51 Tamal Vista Blvd, Corte Madera, CA 94925 (☎415/927-0960).

The Complete Traveler Bookstore, 199 Madison Ave, New York, NY 10016 (☎212/685-9007).

Map Link, 30 S La Petera Lane, Unit #5, Santa Barbara, CA 93117 (☎805/692-6777).

The Map Store Inc., 1636 1st St, Washington DC 20006 (☎202/628-2608).

Phileas Fogg's Books & Maps, #87 Stanford Shopping Center, Palo Alto, CA 94304 (☎1-800/533-FOGG).

Rand McNally, 444 N Michigan Ave, Chicago, IL 60611 (☎312/321-1751); 150 E 52nd St, New York, NY 10022 (☎212/758-7488); 595 Market St, San Francisco, CA 94105 (☎415/777-3131); call ☎1-800/333-0136 (ext 2111) for other locations, or for maps by mail order.

Traveler's Bookstore, 22 W 52nd St, New York, NY 10019 (☎212/664-0995).

CANADA

Open Air Books and Maps, 25 Toronto St, Toronto, ON M5R 2C1 (☎416/363-0719).

Ulysses Travel Bookshop, 4176 St-Denis, Montréal (☎514/843-9447).

World Wide Books and Maps, 736 Granville St, Vancouver, BC V6Z 1E4 (☎604/687-3320).

AUSTRALIA AND NEW ZEALAND

Bowyangs, 372 Little Bourke St, Melbourne (☎03/9670 4383).

The Map Shop, 16a Peel St, Adelaide (☎08/8231 2033).

Perth Map Centre, 891 Hay St, Perth (☎08/9322 5733).

Specialty Maps, 58 Albert St, Auckland (☎09/307 2217).

Travel Bookshop, Shop 3, 175 Liverpool St, Sydney (☎02/9261 8200).

Worldwide Maps and Guides, 187 George St, Brisbane (☎07/3221 4330).

who has posted his photographs and stories relating to Syria on his Web site; esoteric quotes from the likes of Mark Twain and T.E. Lawrence are mixed in with photos of people and archeological sites, and background information relating to what you can see.

Tell Tuneinir

www. stlcc.cc.mo.us/fv/

Photos and information relating to this archeological dig in the northeast of Syria, including information on how to join in the excavations yourself.

The al-Mashriq server

www.hiof.no/almashriq

Travel, business and other information relating to the Levant, including plenty of links to other sites. Syria receives only a small amount of coverage compared to Lebanon.

GETTING AROUND

As rail services in Syria are very sparse, you're most likely to rely on buses, which come in all varieties from luxury, air-conditioned European-built vehicles to the ubiquitous cramped white microbuses that link most settlements on a regular basis. Syrianair provides a limited network of ultra-cheap domestic flights, which can be useful for the longer distances, even if you're on a relatively tight budget.

TRAINS

Trains are very cheap, but they're slower than buses, and not necessarily any more comfy, so it's difficult to see much advantage in using them. The only occasion when they might be preferable to road transport is for travelling between Damascus and northeastern towns such as Deir ez-Zur or Qamishli, which is a journey that can be done overnight.

Chemins de Fer Syriennes (CFS) operate all passenger rail services within Syria. The main **route** is Damascus–Homs–Hama–Aleppo–Deir ez-Zur–Qamishli, with a secondary route which runs from Homs along the coast through Tartous and Latakia and then through the mountains to Aleppo. Narrow-gauge routes run from Damascus up the Barada valley to Zabadani, and south to Dera and the Jordanian border, and on to Amman.

No **timetables** are published in Syria, and trains seem to run according to whim rather than to any sort of schedule. The only published source of information anywhere is the *Thomas Cook Overseas Timetable*, but even that is usually out of date. All this means that the only way of finding out the current situation is to ask at **railway booking offices** (there's one in the centre of many towns) or at stations themselves. In practice, there is generally one train a day on the Damascus–Homs–Hama–Aleppo route, but Latakia, Tartous and Qamishli may only be linked with Damascus once a week. There are usually two trains per week from Damascus to Zabadani, and two per week from Damascus to Dera, one of which continues to Amman.

All trains carry first-class accommodation (air-conditioned), and on the Damascus–Qamishli route first-class sleepers are available. Second class is not air-conditioned and there's slightly less leg room (there's no third class). To give you an idea of **fares**, a ticket for the six-hour journey from Damascus to Aleppo will cost S£60 in second class and S£85 in first; a sleeper on the Damascus–Qamishli route costs S£800.

BUSES

Given that the road network is much better developed than the rail, but that comparatively few Syrians own cars, it's not surprising that **bus transport** is by far the most convenient method of getting around. At the top end of the scale, inter-regional buses are inexpensive, frequent and comfortable, with competition between the various private **Pullman** firms – and the ailing state bus company, **Karnak** – ensuring a good deal for travellers. They cover all towns in Syria, and if you're in the country for any length of time you're likely to make considerable use of them. Some inter-regional routes are also covered by cheaper **microbuses**, but they're really too uncomfortable for any journey of a couple of hours or more; it's best to save them for shorter journeys, which they cover along with larger **local buses**.

Whatever form of road transport you're using, you will usually need to show your **passport** before you travel, and you should bear in mind that it is often considered offensive for men to sit next to lone women passengers – locals will often arrange their seating so that the possibility of this does not happen.

KARNAK AND PULLMAN BUSES

Karnak buses, coloured orange and white and air-conditioned, are operated by the government, and cover all the major centres in Syria, as well as linking Beirut and Amman with Damascus, and Tripoli with Tartous and Latakia. They tend to have their own designated bus stations in towns and cities, which are usually near the centre. Besides the bus stations, there are Karnak offices in the centres of most cities which will sell tickets and give information; it is normally advisable to buy tickets in advance.

For many years the staple means of long-distance bus travel in Syria, Karnak vehicles are beginning to look distinctly ancient in comparison with their snazzier **Pullman** competitors. These private bus operators – biggest of which are Damas Tour, Al-Ahliah and Qadmous – run Renault or other European-built luxury coaches on major routes, most of which start or finish in Damascus or Aleppo. Vehicles are air-conditioned and comfortable, but generally have pirated martial-arts videos or Egyptian TV comedies blaring away at the front. There's usually a conductor on the bus who keep passengers supplied with drinking water and boiled sweets at regular intervals. Pullman companies tend to have offices in town centres, as well as at the bus stations themselves, where you can get information and buy tickets, though services are so frequent that you'll rarely have to wait long to get a seat where you want to go. In the cities of Damascus, Aleppo and Homs, Pullman buses have a designated terminal some distance away from the town centre; in some small towns, Pullmans don't use a bus station at all, but pick up and drop off passengers outside the company office .

Pullman buses tend not to serve international routes, and if you're travelling in the northeast, or between Damascus and the Hauran, you're likely to find Karnak more convenient. In other areas, Pullman services usually leave Karnak standing in terms of frequency, comfort and reliability – though there's little difference in terms of the speed of your journey.

You'll pay slightly more on Pullman than on Karnak services. As a guide to **fares**, it costs S£150 for the five-hour journey between Damascus and Aleppo on a Pullman bus, S£100 with Karnak. Karnak and Pullman buses all run more or less to set schedules, but there are no published **timetables**.

MICROBUSES AND LOCAL BUSES

You see **microbuses** – white Mazda minivans known to locals as *meecro* – everywhere. They mostly serve smaller places, fanning out from towns into the surrounding countryside. Microbuses are owned and operated by their drivers and do not run to timetables. They simply leave when they are full, which means that you'll sometimes wait a long time before enough passengers turn up, and that the vehicle is usually full to bursting when it finally sets off. Services tend to be good in the morning, but thin in the afternoon and all day on Friday.

Unlike Karnak and Pullman buses, microbuses can be flagged down anywhere along their route. In large towns they operate out of designated **stations**; in Damascus and Aleppo there are several of these, covering different destinations. Some of these stations have ticket offices where you have to purchase a ticket for a numbered seat, paying in advance; otherwise you'll end up paying once you're on the bus, when (at the request of the driver) everyone passes their money to the front and states their destination, with the required change somehow getting back to the right people in the same way.

Local buses which link towns with surrounding villages are ancient affairs, often adorned inside and out by an incredible array of ornaments, stickers, photographs and decorations. Middle Eastern pop music screeching out of tinny speakers is a feature setting these larger buses apart from microbuses, which in terms of price and routings they resemble. People are set down and picked up anywhere along the route, making journeys rather slow, but it's a good way to meet the locals, especially in remote areas. Local buses tend to operate from microbus stations, but are a dying breed, gradually being replaced by their zappy white cousins.

Sometimes it's not clear whether you'll be catching a microbus or a large local bus when you buy a ticket for a particular journey. If you get the option, plump for the latter, as microbuses tend to be uncomfortable on long journeys – although some areas of the country (most notably, the northeast and the Hauran) are only covered by microbuses.

Fares on microbuses and local buses are very cheap: about S£20 for a forty-kilometre trip on the former, S£15 on the latter.

SERVICE TAXIS

Shared **service taxis** (called *servees* by locals) are an institution all over the Middle East, although you'll find that they're used much less in Syria than in Egypt or Jordan. Big, usually yellow, limousines (often American vehicles dating from the 1940s and 1950s), service taxis run set routes between centres but drop passengers off where they want at the end. They usually operate out of Karnak, Pullman or microbus stations, and are expensive but quite fast; you might find yourself paying up to S£500 per person for a trip from Damascus to Aleppo. You'll find them most useful on international routes (eg Damascus to Amman or Beirut); internally, they are really only used for travel on the Damascus–Homs–Hama–Aleppo road.

FLIGHTS

Syrianair operates air services between Damascus and Aleppo, Deir ez-Zur, Latakia and Qamishli; the two largest cities are linked by air two or three times a day, but flights to other centres are only weekly. **Fares** are cheap: S£600 Damascus–Aleppo, for example, and S£900 Damascus–Qamishli/Deir ez-Zur. Given the time

you'll take travelling from town centres to airports, however, air travel isn't actually much faster than the bus, unless you're heading for Deir ez-Zur or Qamishli.

Most towns have a Syrianair office, and in some places the airline runs a bus out to the airport, but mostly you'll have to use taxis. Planes use Damascus International Airport (there's no separate terminal for internal flights), and in the capital you'll find an office dealing solely with internal flights, up by the Central Bank building (see p.88).

DRIVING AND HITCHING

Driving in Syria (see also p.234) is not an experience for the faint-hearted or road-wary, with traffic often moving at dangerous speeds and obeying few of the laws of the road that you are used to back home. Hazards include ambling animals and pedestrians, horse-drawn vehicles moving much slower than the general flow of traffic, occasional flooding after heavy rain, and potholed roads which can result in sudden swerves or blow-outs, depending on how much warning you get about them.

You drive on the right, but beyond that **rules of the road** are subject to interpretation. Lane discipline is practically non-existent, and on the highways and arterial roads of Damascus drivers weave in and out of lanes constantly, horns blaring at all times. A single long blast of the horn usually means "get out of the way, I'm coming through", and the largest vehicle on the road at the time is the one who normally gets right of way. On the open road, overtaking is usually done regardless of what's coming the other way, and the flow of traffic is fast whatever the state of the road. At night, headlights are rarely used beyond a warning flash at another car approaching, and the same daytime hazards – children, animals, carts and potholes – are of course still there, only practically invisible.

On roads in the desert and the northeast you'll pass **police checkpoints**. You'll probably be asked to show your passport or driver's licence, but foreigners are usually treated with kid gloves. There's **signposting** in English on main roads, but it tends to be in Arabic only once you're into the backroads – especially in the mountains, where drivers with no knowledge of Arabic will experience some difficulty getting around.

The official **speed limits** are 60km per hour in built-up areas, 70km per hour on most open roads and 110km per hour on the main Damascus–Aleppo highway, which is a dual carriageway (although this doesn't stop shepherds crossing it with their flocks on occasions).

CAR RENTAL

Renting a car pays obvious dividends if you want to see a lot of the country fast, or, more particularly, if you want to reach historic sites which are not on public transport routes; the most obvious of these are the Dead Cities around Aleppo, and sites in the mountains accessible from Tartous or Latakia. If you don't want to drive yourself, then it's usually possible to hire a car with a driver.

In some places there are **small rental outfits** which charge very low rates, but they're only able to do this through offering no insurance policies. You're strongly advised not to touch these firms with a bargepole, and instead to pay more at **established firms** such as Europcar or Budget, whose vehicles can be booked from abroad. This is, in any case, a good idea if you're planning to rent a vehicle, since most companies will tell you thay haven't got anything immediately available if you turn up without a reservation. Not surprisingly, the greatest choice of rental outfits is in Damascus (see p.89). Elsewhere in the country the first place to look is one of the big luxury hotels; the Cham Palace chain has their own car rental arm, Chamcar, and Europcar and other companies operate through these and other hotels.

As a guide to **prices**, you'll probably pay as much as you would in Europe: Budget in Damascus, for example, charges US$45 a day, including insurance, for a small Daewoo, rising to US$68 for a Peugeot 405, and most other reliable firms charge about the same. Rental is always charged in dollars and, given the deposit that many firms expect you to pay, this is one of the few occasions in Syria where you'll probably have no option but to use your plastic for payment. Most firms insist that drivers are at least 21 years of age.

PETROL AND BREAKDOWNS

Petrol stations are reasonably common in large towns and along major highways, but in desert areas it always pays to keep your tank well topped up. The Freytag-Berndt map of Syria we've recommended on p.25 indicates the positions of filling stations. Fuel is extremely cheap: many cars run on diesel *(mazout)*, with regular petrol *(benzin)* slightly more expensive. **Oil filters** need to be checked and cleaned regularly to prevent dust from clogging the engine.

In Damascus and Aleppo there are plenty of **repair shops** (details in the "Listings" for each city), and elsewhere in the country you should be able to find a local garage with a competent mechanic. If you happen to have brought your own vehicle, it might be difficult to get it repaired as most Syrians drive Japanese and Korean cars, with European models comparatively rare.

HITCHING

In areas where there's minimal public transport – most particularly, in the mountains and around the Dead Cities – you may well resort to **hitching** at some time or other. Locals themselves hitch a lot in these out-of-the-way areas, and as a foreigner you quickly attract attention and are likely to be offered a lift somewhere without even asking for it first. Note, however, that drivers often

INTERNATIONAL CAR RENTAL AGENCIES			
BRITAIN		**AUSTRALIA**	
Avis	☎0990/900500	Avis	☎1800/225 533
Budget	☎0800/181181	Budget	☎13 2727
Europcar/InterRent	☎0345/222538		
		NEW ZEALAND	
IRELAND		Avis	☎09/526 2847
Avis: Northern Ireland	☎0990/900 500;	Budget	☎09/375 2222
the Republic	☎01/874 5844		
Budget: Northern Ireland	☎0800/181181;	**US & CANADA**	
the Republic	☎0800/973 159	Avis	☎1-800/331-1084
Europcar: Northern Ireland	☎0345/222525;	Budget	☎1-800/527-0700
the Republic	☎01/874 5844	Dollar	☎1-800/800-6000

want to be paid for their services, so it makes sense to agree a cost with them before you set out. In the desert, you're likely to be picked up by lorries (whose drivers will also want paying) or by one of the ubiquitous Bedouin pick-up trucks, some of which run "unofficial" bus routes between settlements, charging locals for the ride. In more densely settled areas (where there are more buses) you might find getting a lift is actually more difficult than in remoter regions, and if you try hitching on main roads you're much more likely to stop a passing microbus or local bus than a private vehicle. **Women** are advised not to hitch alone.

CITY TRANSPORT

All towns and cities have **taxis**, which are always coloured bright yellow; many are American cars from the 1940s and 1950s, which their drivers somehow manage to keep going despite the potholes and lack of spare parts. Most taxis have meters, although not all drivers who have them

use them, and more often than not you'll end up agreeing a price before you set off ; as a guide no ride within Damascus should cost more than S£100. Taxis are easy enough to hail in the street or to pick up at bus stations, but if your journey starts or finishes at one of the big hotels, you're almost asking for the fare to be inflated. In Aleppo there are also local **service taxis**, largely indistinguishable from normal taxis on the outside, which run set routes – essentially taxis operating as buses.

Syrian cities have **bus services** operated by two sorts of vehicle: lumbering, smoke-belching, jam-packed ancient buses and faster, smaller, newer microbuses. They're difficult to use as all destination signs and numbers are in Arabic (or are simply not displayed at all), and there are no route maps or timetables published or displayed anywhere; even bus stops can be hard to spot. For this reason, few foreigners use city buses or microbuses, but the city centres are usually compact enough to walk around in any case.

ACCOMMODATION

Finding a bed for the night at the price you want is generally no problem in Syria, and the only times when you might want to telephone in advance is if you are planning to arrive in Damascus or Aleppo late in the day. However, there are no youth hostels in Syria, and only a handful of fairly dreadful camp- sites, so you're left with no real option but hotels as far as accommodation goes. Tourist offices know nothing about local hotels, so it's likely to be a matter of shopping around once you've arrived in a town. Hotels come in all varieties from filthy, noisy, dirt-cheap hotels in city centres, where you will be certain to spend your night with a wide variety of insect life, up to huge five-star luxury places, including those of the Meridien and Sheraton chains.**

The government ranks hotels from one to five stars, with the most expensive receiving a five-star de luxe category all of their own. By law, hotels must display their prices at the reception desk, but in all bar the most expensive you'll probably be told that the rates shown are out of date. If you're planning to stay in four- and five- star places (price code ⑤ and above, according to our system), you should consider taking a package tour from your own country as you'll inevitably get much better rates in them. Lastly, bear in mind that you won't ever find a double room with one large bed in it – they always come with twin beds.

CHEAP HOTELS

The **cheap hotels** (one or two stars) charge about S£300 for a very basic single room, S£400 for a double. If you're a solo traveller and the hotel's fairly full you may end up sharing, but this is rare; more typically you'll be given a double room to yourself, and pay the single room price. Rooms are unlikely to have en-suite facilities, but will have a bed with a sheet or two provided, usually a fan, and perhaps a sink plumbed into the wall. Some of these places are unhygienic and chronically dirty, with bedbugs and roach-infested shared squat toilets; always look at your room before you decide to take it. In summer you'll want the window open, which will mean that street noise can be a real problem, so it makes sense to try to get a room at the back. In addition you should try to avoid hotels adjacent to mosques, unless you fancy being woken up by the dawn call to prayer from the *muezzin*. Hot water will generally be available in the evening and early morning. These hotels tend to be inadequately heated in winter, when it can get quite cold in Syria.

In Damascus and a few other large towns, you can get hold of beds for as little as S£100 in **dormitory accommodation** mostly used by itinerant workers – avoid it unless you're really desperate.

MID-RANGE HOTELS

Mid-range hotels (three stars; ③–⑤ on our price code system) usually cost around $15/25 for a single/double room, rising to $40/50 in Damascus and Aleppo. Facilities in these hotels will be en suite with hot water throughout the day, and you'll have efficient (but noisy) air conditioning and a TV; breakfast will be available in the more expensive of these places, as well as perhaps a telephone and minibar. Generally the mid-range establishments we've listed in the Guide are clean and friendly, with owners who speak a modicum of English and are often good sources of information about the local scene.

EXPENSIVE HOTELS

In Damascus, Aleppo and a few other touristed areas, **expensive hotels** are appearing which fill the wide gap between the mid-range and the luxury places. You'll typically pay anywhere between $50 and $90 per night (⑥) for accommodation, classified as three or four stars, which isn't really much superior to the mid-range hotels. Normally there'll be a bar or a restaurant, the TV will be hooked up to receive satellite services, rooms will be carpeted and there will be central air conditioning. Most of these hotels are modern but rather characterless, and are largely aimed at tour groups.

LUXURY HOTELS

International-standard **luxury hotels**, classified as four- or five-star and starting at $90 for a double, can be found in most large towns and tourist centres. Air-conditioned throughout, they tend to be oases of marble floors and shiny blandness. The less expensive of these places (price code ⑦ according to our system) have central air conditioning, a bar and more than one restaurant, and usually a pool, snack bar and a shop; rooms will have satellite TV, telephone, minibar and bath. Most of the Syrian-owned Cham Palace hotels come in this category. Band ⑧ hotels are confined mostly to Aleppo and Damascus, and usually provide all the above plus a nightclub, sporting and business facilities and a small-scale shopping arcade; they are the favourite haunts of visiting diplomats and moneyed business travellers from the Persian Gulf or Europe, and include hotels run by the Sheraton and Meridien international chains.

One of the advantages of the luxury hotels is that they can be **booked from abroad** in advance with some degree of certainty that your reservation will be honoured. For reservations at the Meridien hotels in Damascus and by the beach in Latakia, call ☎0171/439 1244 in the UK, ☎1-800/543-4300 in North America. For the Sheraton hotel in Damascus, call ☎0800/353535 in the UK, ☎1-800/3253535 in North America. The Cham Palace chain comprises several hotels in Damascus and others in Palmyra, Bosra, Hama, Safita (in the mountains near Tartous), Aleppo, Deir ez-Zur, and on the coast just north of Latakia (the Cote d'Azur de Cham resort, the only apartment complex in the country). International reservations are dealt with in Paris (☎01.42.99.87.00) and Washington DC (☎202/835-0099); their website, through which you can make reservations, is at www.chamhotels.com.

ACCOMMODATION PRICE CODES

In this book, all hotels have been categorized according to the **price codes** outlined below. They represent the minimum you can expect to pay for a **double room** in each hotel; note that prices do not tend to vary seasonally.

In categories ① and ② you'll pay in **Syrian pounds**, though hotel keepers are unlikely to object if you offer them **US dollars**; in ③ and ④ establishments you'll usually be asked for payment in dollars (cash) but a bit of persuasion will allow you to pay in Syrian pounds, depending on the whim of the owner – always check before you agree to take the room, and to be on the safe side carry a fair-sized stock of US dollars with you if you're going to be using these places a lot. All

establishments in category ⑤ and above will expect payment in dollars. Some places in band ④, and all in bands ⑤–⑧, will let you pay by **credit card** and **travellers' cheques**.

In category ④ places and above, **breakfast** will usually be included in the price you pay; you won't get a rebate if you choose not to have it. Breakfast will normally consist of coffee, bread with various spreads and fillings, and olives or other fruit. Some places in category ③ might provide an optional breakfast for around S£100. ① and ② hotels will never offer breakfast.

Bargaining is possible in ① and ② hotels, and in ③–⑤ establishments if you're planning to stay longer than three days.

① under S£300/US$7.50
② S£300–600/US$7.50–15
③ S£600–1000/US $15–25
④ S£1000–1400/US$25–35

⑤ US$35–50/S£1400–2000
⑥ US$50–90/S£2000–3600
⑦ US$90–130/S£3600–5200
⑧ US$130 and over/S£5200 and over

EATING AND DRINKING

Don't come to Syria looking for a varied and interesting cuisine. Syrian food is indistinguishable from what you'll find in the rest of the Arab world, and, especially if you're on a tight budget, you'll soon get tired of chicken, kebabs, *felafel, hummus* and salads which form the standard fare in most basic eateries. Even if you can afford to splash out now and again, chances are you'll end up

with a pale imitation of Western cooking (although it's difficult to go wrong with a pizza). Not surprisingly, Damascus and Aleppo are the centres with the most variety in terms of restaurants.

STREET SNACKS AND PASTRY SHOPS

If you're travelling on a budget – or you're just in a rush – you'll find that food purchased from **street vendors** is usually filling, tasty and extremely cheap but, as in other countries around the world, possibly suspect: if you have a meat dish, make sure that it's been thoroughly and recently cooked, and stay away from any stalls which don't look clean.

Felafel, hummus and *fuul* are the staple street snacks. Found all over the Middle East, **felafel** consists of deep-fried balls of chickpea paste with spices, served in a piece of unleavened bread (*khobz*) along with varying degrees of salad, pickled vegetables and yoghurt. The meaty equivalent of a *felafel* is a **shwarma**, filled with either spit-roasted chicken or lamb (layers of lamb or

A FOOD AND DRINK GLOSSARY

General

bayda	egg	*laban*	yoghurt
bayda masloo	boiled egg	*malh*	salt
filfil	pepper	*samak*	fish
jibna	cheese	*shorba*	soup
katchkaval	sheep's milk cheese	*sukkar*	sugar
khobz	bread	*zibda*	butter

Meat (*lahm*)

betelloo	beef	*kelaawi*	kidney
farooj	chicken	*kibda*	liver
felay	steak	*lahm danee*	lamb

Vegetables (*khadrawat/khodar*)

aesh elghorab	mushrooms	*kharoum*	cabbage
arnabeet	cauliflower	*khass*	lettuce
banadura	tomato	*khayar*	cucumber
basal	onion	*koosa*	courgette
batatis	potatoes/chips	*ruz*	rice
bedingan	aubergine	*salata*	salad
besilla	peas	*tum*	garlic
fasolya	green beans	*zatoon*	olives
gazar	carrot		

Fruit (*fawakih*)

aenab	grapes	*lamoon*	lemon
ananas	pineapple	*manga*	mango
batteekh	watermelon	*mishmish*	apricot
burtuqqal	orange	*moz*	banana
farowla	strawberry	*tamr*	date
goz	nuts	*teen*	fig
graybfroot	grapefruit	*toot*	raspberry
khokh	peach	*tufah*	apple
kommitra	pear		

Desserts

baqlawa	honey-soaked pastry, often filled with nuts	*isfinjiyya*	coconut slice
booza	ice cream	*mahalabiyya*	very sweet rice pudding, often with nuts
halawat al-jibna	syrup-topped doughy pastry filled with ice cream or cream cheese		

Drinks

aaseer fawakih	fruit juice	*haleeb*	milk
ahmar	wine	*miya*	water
ahwa	coffee	*miya atta abiyya*	mineral water
beera	beer	*shai*	tea
gazoza	soft drink		

mutton are piled onto a vertical spit and heated before a gas-heated grill, and as the outer layers cook they're sliced off). To make **hummus**, cooked and ground chickpeas are mixed with a paste made from sesame seeds (*tahina*), garlic and lemon; it's served as a side dish with main courses, or as a dressing for bread or *felafel*. **Fuul** is a paste made from fava beans, garlic and lemon, and is often served in oil.

Very sweet desserts, usually made from honey, syrup, pastry, cream and nuts in various combinations, are sold in **pastry shops** in every town. Many of these pastry shops double as sit-down places, and ice-cream parlours have sprung up in Damascus and Aleppo, which will also sell a variety of desserts and cakes.

RESTAURANTS

Sit-down eateries come in all varieties from greasy chicken-and-kebab joints to pricey affairs which, outside Damascus and Aleppo, are almost exclusively attached to hotels. Wherever you go, you'll get a glass of tap water, which should be safe to drink, and some unleavened bread put on your table.

You'll find **cheap restaurants** crammed together in the centres of all towns and cities, and in the smallest villages too. You'll soon discover, however, that they're all basically selling the same things, and your decision about where to eat will depend on which place looks the cleanest. With little to choose from, there are no menus available in these establishments (in any language). Since Islam proscribes the consumption of pork, and beef is very hard to come by, lamb kebab and chicken are the staple meats available, possibly supplemented by fish if you're by the sea. Usually, **chicken** is roasted on spits in large ovens and comes with onion and chillies (and occasionally olives), with side dishes of salad and *hummus*. For the **kebabs**, minced lamb pieces are pressed onto skewers and grilled over charcoal, and then served with similar side plates. **Chips** are also a popular side dish, available virtually everywhere. In the end you'll usually end up paying around S£250 for a meal of meat, side salad, chips and a soft drink; only a few cheap places serve alcohol.

In the larger or more touristy towns, you'll find **more expensive restaurants**, with a little more on offer and alcohol served (though usually limited to bottled beers). You might find a **menu** avail-

able in these places, but don't get your hopes up too early – usually most of what's written down isn't actually available. Widely available **stews**, however, generally served on rice (*ruz*), make a pleasant change from chicken and kebabs: *fasolya* is a green bean stew, *batanas* potato and *mulukiyyeh* spinach stew. Some restaurants will serve basic pasta such as spaghetti, although don't expect much to come with it apart from a meat-and-tomato-based side serving. **Desserts**, if there are any, will be of the sticky pastry or ice cream variety.

Self-explanatory **pizza and burger** joints, modelled on Western chains, have appeared in the main cities in recent years, while pricey restaurants in Aleppo and Damascus make an effort to serve more distinctively Arabic food. One of the particular gastronomic delights on offer is the Middle Eastern **mezze** (meaning "table"), basically a buffet consisting of about a dozen salads, grilled meat, fresh vegetables and lots of sweet pastries. A *mezze* can be a precursor to a main meal or a main meal in itself, and the point of it is that it's a shared experience, so people travelling alone – or even in pairs – are likely to be able to enjoy only a pale imitation. Some hotels catering to Western tastes offer an eat-all-you-want evening **buffet dinner**, consisting of cooked and cold meats, pasta, salads, with cakes or fruit as dessert. You'll also find Chinese, French and Italian restaurants in Aleppo and Damascus, but nowhere else.

DRINKS

Tap **water** in Syria is considered to be safe, though many people prefer to buy bottled spring water which is quite cheap and available everywhere, including the very cheapest restaurants and stalls. It's always as well to check the seal hasn't been broken, or you may be sold just plain old tap water. The most common brands are Boukein, bottled in the Barada Mountains west of Damascus, and Dreikish, which comes from the Anti-Lebanon Range near the Crac des Chevaliers.

TEA, COFFEE AND SOFT DRINKS

Tea (*shai*), drunk constantly by everyone, everywhere, is served in small glasses and you sweeten it yourself. **Coffee** (*ahwa*) is very dark, strong and usually sweet (*ziyada*); if you want less sugar ask for it *mazboota* (medium), if you want none, *saada* (plain). You rarely get more than a mouthful in your cup, but if you take a second swig you'll end up with what feels like a mouthful of silt. In the centre of many towns you'll find cavernous bars which dispense endless cups of tea and coffee to their clients (usually exclusively male) until well into the early hours. You'll get nothing in the way of food or other drinks at these places, but they're good for hanging out in, watching the locals discussing away an afternoon or playing cards or backgammon; a *nargileh* (hookah pipe) is always on hand to help the pace amble along. If you're missing Western-style coffee, head for any five-star hotel. You should always avoid **milk** as it's unpasteurized, containing bugs which Syrian stomachs are used to but which yours definitely won't be able to cope with; if you have milk with coffee, make sure it's been boiled first.

Soft drinks are very cheap. Locally produced brands of fizzy, garishly coloured lemon- and orange-flavour drinks come in tiny glass bottles which stallholders always want back. Cans of fizzy drinks produced by the Canada Dry company, including 7-UP and various orange and cola varieties, are available at inflated prices; at the time of writing, Syria was one of the few countries in the world where Coca-Cola and Pepsi were not on sale.

Fruit juice (*aaseer*) stalls can be identified by the string bags of fruit hanging out front; they produce thirst-quenching drinks by the glass, stallholders crushing the fruit in front of you. Popular varieties are grapefruit, lemon, orange, banana and watermelon, but beware of stalls which put tap water (or, more dangerously, milk) into drinks to dilute them.

WINE, BEER AND ARAQ

Some local **wines** are available, but most are best left alone if you place any value on the back of your throat; the rosé varieties are probably best. Wine is very cheap at liquor stalls but pricey if you have it in a restaurant (it's only the most expensive restaurants which serve it).

There are two local brews of **beer**, Barada from Damascus and Al-Chark from Aleppo. They taste about the same and can be quite thirst-quenching when cold (but quite sickly when warm). In the more expensive hotels and in Damascus imported beer is available, but it's expensive. The local liquor **araq** is similar to Greek *ouzo*, a clear strong aniseed concoction which packs quite a punch; it's meant to be drunk with a meal, not on its own, and it's worshipped by some as a cure for upset stomachs.

THE MEDIA

The Arab-language broadsheet and tabloid newspapers, read and bought avidly, are unlikely to interest you unless you read Arabic; closely written and poorly printed, with few photographs, the news that people read is heavily controlled by the government news agency, SANA – the Syrian Arab News Agency – which also supplies TV and radio news information.

ENGLISH-LANGUAGE NEWSPAPERS

The most reliable places to find **foreign newspapers** such as the *International Guardian* and the *International Herald Tribune* are the bookshops of the *Meridien*, *Sheraton* and *Cham Palace* hotels in Damascus, and in the English-language bookshops listed on p.89. Occasionally British newspapers such as *The Times* and *The Daily Telegraph* also turn up at these places too. Outside Damascus it is virtually impossible to get hold of any of these papers; in Aleppo and other tourist centres, check in the big hotels – if they have anything at all it will be very out of date.

Syria's **English-language newspaper**, the *Syria Times*, is supposed to be published daily but actually appears less often than this. Published under government control, its main purposes seem to be to rubbish Syria's enemies (Iraq and Israel, mainly) and provide information to Western readers as to how wonderful the government is. Much of the news is outrageously boring reports of trade and diplomatic summits, and coverage of foreign affairs is minimal. There is a good listings section, however, with details of films, exhibitions, lectures and museum opening times for Aleppo and

Damascus. The newspaper is available from some newsstands in Damascus and Aleppo, but again the big hotels are probably the best place to find it.

TV AND RADIO

There are two channels on terrestrial **Syrian television**, and many hotels have televisions which will receive them adequately. Channel 2 broadcasts news in English at 10pm every evening, a somewhat hysterical round of anti-Israel propaganda and fastidiously reported government business. Foreign news stories (particularly Northern Ireland) get a fair amount of coverage, but always in the second part of the bulletin. The weather forecast after the news is usually pretty accurate, and provides a nostalgic reminder of what weather reporting back home was like before forecasters developed charisma. Channel 2 also shows lots of English-language programmes – everything from recent BBC sitcoms to 1970s American cop shows – subtitled in Arabic with their original soundtrack left intact.

The largest international hotels have CNN and other **satellite channels** (including BBC World Service Television) piped into hotel bars and rooms. Homesick Americans and other news addicts can also watch CNN in the library of the American Cultural Centre in Damascus, where it is switched on permanently. Most TVs in the west and north of the country can receive, respectively, **Lebanese and Turkish television**, and in Aleppo you can usually pick up both. These channels show a more commercially oriented, Western-influenced diet of game shows, pop music and sports programmes, movies and American soaps.

The Syrian Broadcasting Service also broadcasts **radio** news and features in English and other foreign languages. Frequencies and broadcast times are given in the *Syria Times*. The BBC World Service, the most reliable source of news for any Syrian who can understand English, can be picked up on 1323kHz short wave or 227mHz medium wave; also try 720kHz and 417mHz.

POST AND TELEPHONES

Post and telephone services are operated by the same government department so, not surprisingly, usually share the same building in any large town – commonly labelled in the French style, PTT. Phone and post offices have been marked on the town maps

in this book, and are usually clearly indicated on published maps.

POSTAL SERVICES

The postal service is slow but generally reliable. Airmail **letters** take a week to reach the UK and anything up to a month to reach the US or Australia. It will speed up the delivery process if you get someone to write the name of the country on the envelope in Arabic. Mailboxes in the street are red and marked *boite aux lettres*, but it's usually better to send mail from **post offices**. In most places **opening hours** are 9am to 2pm daily except Friday, with seven-day opening and longer hours in Aleppo and Damascus. Private **courier firms** such as DHL have offices or agents in most large towns.

Sending a **parcel** abroad is a time-consuming business as the contents must be inspected before the parcel is wrapped in cotton, tagged, stamped and dispatched. It's best to go to one of the post offices in Aleppo or Damascus, where staff will do all the necessaries for you.

Receiving mail **poste restante** is a bit of a hit-and-miss affair, since post office workers often file letters wrongly – something addressed to Mr John Smith, for instance, might end up being filed under M, J or S. Ask officials to check carefully, and get senders to underline your surname. Poste restante mail is always held at the central post office of any town (unless specified otherwise), and you'll need your passport to pick up any mail sent this way. You'll probably be charged a small **holding fee** of S£10 or so.

TELEPHONE SERVICES

The Syrian telephone system is very gradually hauling itself into the modern world; improvements in international connections mean that phoning abroad is now probably easier and more reliable than placing internal calls.

INTERNATIONAL CALLS

International calls can be made from big hotels, who will normally put on a massive surcharge, or from telephone offices, which have limited opening hours but at least don't charge you the earth. At a telephone office, you will usually have to write down the number and give it to the clerk, who will then dial it and direct you to a booth where you can take the call; there is a minimum call time of three minutes, and you might have to wait anything up to two hours for a line to be made free. In a number of larger towns, plastic **phonecards** (S£900) are sold by post and telephone offices, for use in phones located inside or just outside these offices. You can't buy these phonecards anywhere else, and you can't really use them anywhere else, either. Instructions are pinned up in English inside the phone boxes. Connection is usually instantaneous, making cardphones by far the best way to call out of the country. Calls from telephone offices and cardphones to North America, the UK, Ireland and Australasia cost S£125 a minute. You can't make **reverse charge (collect) calls** from Syria.

INTERNAL CALLS

Placing **telephone calls within Syria** is less reliable than telephoning out of the country. Public coinbox telephones can only be used for **urban calls** (ie within that town), and take S£1 coins – another problem, since these small pieces rarely turn up in change. Lines from these phone boxes are notoriously unreliable.

To call **long distance** within Syria, you can go to a telephone office, and use the cardphones (see above) to dial direct, or book a call with one of the clerks. Alternatively, the older telephone offices have rows of public phone boxes inside and outside them, from where you can call other towns in Syria, with certain boxes hooked up to certain towns (and long lines of people waiting outside each of them). Internal telephone calls from hotels attract a much more reasonable surcharge than international calls, and this may be your best bet if you don't mind paying slightly more than you would at a telephone office.

FAXES, TELEXES AND TELEGRAMS

If the phone system lets you down, you could send a **fax**, **telex** or **telegram**. Fax machines were banned in Syria for security reasons until recently, but large hotels and phone offices are now slowly equipping themselves with them. You'll pay S£200 for the first page of a fax you send abroad from a phone office, and S£100 thereafter.

USEFUL TELEPHONE NUMBERS

To **telephone Syria from overseas**, dial your country's international access code, then 963 for Syria, the area code minus the initial zero, and then the subscriber number.

For **telephoning overseas from Syria**, the international operator is on ☎143/144. International dialling codes from Syria include:

Australia ☎0061	Ireland ☎00353	New Zealand ☎0064
USA and Canada ☎001	UK ☎0044	

PUBLIC HOLIDAYS AND BUSINESS HOURS

Public holidays and festivals are closely observed in Syria, though you probably won't see much in the way of festivities (most of it takes place behind closed doors). The situation is confused by the existence of both Muslim and Christian holidays, which rarely coincide, and often mean a day off for all. Furthermore, although the country works on the Gregorian (ie Western) calendar as far as business and government is concerned, the Hijra calendar dictates Islamic holidays. The most important festival to be aware of is Ramadan, when most Muslims (85 percent of Syrians) fast from sunrise to sunset for a month.

HOLIDAYS CONFORMING TO THE GREGORIAN CALENDAR

Government offices, banks, post offices and large companies are likely to be shut on New Year's Day (1 January), Revolution Day (8 March), Evacuation Day (17 April) and Christmas Day (25 December). Public transport (particularly microbuses) will operate less frequently on these days, although the country by no means closes down, and most shops and stalls operate as normal.

ISLAMIC HOLIDAYS

The **Islamic Hijra calendar** dates from the flight of Mohammed from Mecca in 622 AD, and years are designated AH – *Anno Hegirae*. Thus the Islamic year which begins in mid-April 1998 is AH 1419. Each year consists of twelve months, but is eleven days shorter than a Western year. **Islamic holidays** in the coming years are listed in the box, but note that the precise dates depend on sightings of the moon, so are known only a short time in advance. Holidays celebrated include the first day of the Islamic New Year (*Ras al-Sana*), the birthday of the Prophet Mohammed (*Mulid al-Nabi*), the small feast at the end of Ramadan (*Eid al-Fitr* or *Eid as-Sagheer*), and the Big Feast (*Eid al Adhah*), which celebrates the willingness of Abraham to sacrifice his son to God. You will find that Islamic holidays are followed much more strictly than the Gregorian-based holidays – although Christian-run businesses stay open as normal.

FORTHCOMING ISLAMIC HOLIDAYS

The following dates are approximate and depend on sightings of the moon. In the UK, exact details are available from the Arab-British Chamber of Commerce (☎0171/235 4363).

	Ramadan begins	*Eid al-Fitr*	*Eid al Adhah*	*Ras al-Sana*	*Mulid al-Nabi*
1998	20 Dec	–	–	–	–
1999	10 Dec	19 Jan	27 March	18 April	28 June
2000	1 Dec	9 Jan and 31 Dec	17 March	8 April	18 June
2001	21 Nov	21 Dec	7 March	29 March	8 June
2002	–	–	26 Feb	19 March	29 May

RAMADAN

Ramadan is the ninth month of the Islamic calendar and commemorates the revelation of the Koran to Mohammed. Devout Muslims avoid sex all month, and must fast during daylight hours, letting nothing pass their lips; even smoking is frowned upon. Business hours are much shorter during Ramadan, and many restaurants and shops do not open in daylight hours. However, when restaurants open after sunset, the big evening meal – *iftar* – is a lively occasion, enjoyed by many who have fasted during the day.

Not all Syrians are Muslims, and not all Muslims comply fully with Ramadan. Non-Muslim foreigners are not expected to follow suit, but smoking or eating in public during Ramadan may cause offence, and you should be sensitive to local feeling. Ramadan affects life out in small villages and towns much more than in the big cities, where a lot of things carry on as normal. Most problematic to travellers is the curtailment of public transport during Ramadan, particularly microbuses and local buses.

OPENING TIMES AND BUSINESS HOURS

Most government offices and banks are open from 8am to 2pm every day except Fridays and public holidays. Shops and other offices usually open during these times in the morning, and then again between 4pm and 7pm. On Fridays and holidays, most restaurants stay open, and in cities a few traders operate limited opening hours. All these hours are reduced during Ramadan (see above). In Christian quarters of Aleppo and other cities, things go on as normal on Fridays and shut down on Sundays.

However, these business hours, as well as public transport times (if they are even published), should be taken with a pinch of salt, and the museum and site opening times detailed in this book should be treated only as a rough indication of what actually happens; often things only open or start running when the official or driver concerned decides to turn up. Patience is something that travellers should bring to Syria in copious amounts.

MONUMENTS, MUSEUMS AND RELIGIOUS SITES

You'll be charged S£200 to look round most monuments and museums – from the Crac des Chevaliers and Palmyra's Temple of Bel to the murkiest local museum or dusty ruin; on top of that, many places charge extra for the right to take photos or use a video camera. In some places you'll get a reduction in admission charge if you can present an ISIC card (see p.22). Although you may begrudge shelling out S£200 to see what turns out to be a few glass cases, a fan and a custodian, remember that many sites, including most of Palmyra and Bosra, the Dead Cities and other desert sites, are open for you to wander round at any time and are completely free of charge.

GUIDES

You'll have to look around quite carefully if you want an official, government-registered **guide**. Tourist offices, large hotels and travel agencies

(in that order) are the best places to hire one; you shouldn't count on them being available on the spot (as they are at many Egyptian or Turkish ruins), except at Palmyra, Bosra and Apamea. Most other ruins will be virtually deserted, and your most likely guides will be local children begging you to let them show you around, so that they can practise their English and earn a little *baksheesh*.

In towns and cities you may be approached by young men who offer to show you around as **unofficial guides** – again, usually with a view to practising their English more than anything else. Many people you meet this way are unemployed teachers or lecturers, though they might turn out to be official guides touting for work independently if there aren't any tour groups around at that time. Whether you take them up on their offers is of course up to you, but agree on a price before you do so and never pay more than you feel is right. Often these people don't actually want any money and genuinely want to help and meet foreigners; even if you don't want to be shown around they will help you in whatever way you ask, such as pointing out which bus to take or helping you bargain with a taxi driver. Such encounters rarely come with hidden "strings attached" and can lead to invitations to a guide's home later in the day, so (on either side) they make for a good way of meeting people.

MUSEUMS AND ANCIENT MONUMENTS

Syria's ancient sites and monuments are maintained by the **Syrian Antiquities Department**. Those few which have a custodian are usually open daily. None require any special permits to allow you to visit them, and if you want to scramble over a *tell* to see what's there in the way of excavations, then there's nothing to stop you doing just that. In some places you can see pieces of pottery and the like lying all over the place, but you should remember that removing anything in the way of artefacts from any site is illegal.

Museums are mostly drab affairs, consisting of haphazard and poorly labelled (or just unlabelled) cases of artefacts. Most of the good stuff has been moved from provincial museums to the two main archeological collections in **Damascus** and **Aleppo**, but in **Sweida** in the south and **Deir ez-Zur** on the Euphrates, you'll be pleasantly surprised by the quality of the collections displayed in their new museums. All museums tend to shut on Tuesdays (official opening times are detailed throughout the guide).

MOSQUES, CHURCHES AND MONASTERIES

All **mosques** are open to non-Muslim visitors, although you should try to avoid visiting at prayer time, especially the main service of the week at noon on Fridays. No one is ever likely to object to your presence in any mosque, although only two – the Umayyad Mosque in Damascus and the Great Mosque in Aleppo – are classified as ancient monuments and so are used to seeing tourists.

Always take your **shoes** off at the entrance to a mosque; there should be no difficulty in leaving them there while you look round. Bare shoulders, shorts and short skirts may cause offence, and women may be required to wear a headscarf. Most mosques are surprisingly relaxed places, with groups of people getting on with whatever they want – worshipping, sleeping, sightseeing or talking. Attached to many mosques are **madrasas**, religious schools which sometimes boast fine architecture dating from Ottoman times. A few have been mentioned in the text, but unfortunately almost all of them are locked most of the time.

Syria abounds in Christian **churches and monasteries**. Churches are almost always locked, even those in the centre of Aleppo. Only St George's Monastery, near the Crac des Chevaliers, is used to seeing tourists; other monasteries are secluded, working religious houses which don't welcome casual visitors. Most of the same dress codes are applicable to churches as to mosques, though you won't have to take off your shoes.

TROUBLE AND THE POLICE

Syria is a remarkably safe country to travel in, with surprisingly little petty crime, cities which remain safe after dark and, despite a bus station bombing in 1996, next to nothing in the way of terrorism. Police are everywhere, in particular the feared secret police service, the Mukhabarat; however, beyond passport and other security checks few tourists will ever have cause to come into contact with them or their uniformed counterparts, who make up a variety of civilian and military police forces. If you do have dealings with the police, expect civility and courtesy from them, though few officers speak English – and anticipate a lot of paperwork.

EMERGENCY NUMBERS
Ambulance ☎110
Police ☎112
Fire ☎113
Traffic police ☎115

PETTY CRIME

In Syria, **pickpocketing** and other types of theft are nowhere near the problem that they are in Turkey or Egypt. Nevertheless, it always makes sense to hang onto your things carefully in a crowded bus or a queue, and to keep valuables – including your passport, which you must carry around with you at all times – in a moneybelt around your waist or a pouch under your shirt. Casual **theft from hotels** is also unlikely, but given the poor security of both rooms and reception desks (which are often unstaffed and have no lockable storage areas), it makes sense to leave nothing to chance and to always carry your valuables with you. If you're **driving**, it's best to ensure that nothing valuable is visible in your car when you leave it.

Petty crime can take the form of **overcharging** by stallholders or taxi drivers (though sometimes this can amount to no more than a misunderstanding). You should be cautious over money and prices, particularly during your first few days in the country, to avoid being caught off guard by the odd dishonest trader; but remember that most Syrians are unfailingly honest and courteous, and you shouldn't let a cautious outlook spoil your trip, or be tempted to read anything sinister into the genuine offers of hospitality you receive.

TERRORISM

In recent years tourists in Egypt, Turkey and Israel have been caught in the crossfire – or been the intended target – of extremist terrorists, but Syria has remained largely unblemished in this respect. The bombing of a Damascus bus station in 1996 was blamed on a Lebanese group, and remains an isolated incident; all the same, bus and train stations are security-conscious places, and you are likely to have your bags and passport checked when you enter them, with security at Damascus Airport likewise very tight.

The only potentially unsafe area in Syria is the northeast, which, though quiet at the time of writing, is occasionally at risk of absorbing some of the Kurdish separatist troubles from over the border in Turkey. For an update on the latest situation, you might want to ask the advice of your embassy in Damascus, or contact the government advice lines in the UK (☎0171/270 1500) or the US (☎202/647-5255) or their Web sites (see p.25). The area on the Turkish side of the border here is definitely a no-go area for Westerners at the moment.

THE POLICE

You'll probably initially be shocked by the armed police and army presence on the streets of towns and along roads in the countryside, but Syria has a strong tradition of maintaining tight internal security, backed up by compulsory conscription into the armed forces. The interest the police will take in you as a traveller, however, is minimal, unless you're suspected of espionage, other anti-government activity or having anything to do with drugs.

One of the most obvious police units is the **traffic police**, blessed with the almost impossible task of controlling traffic in larger cities, who will stop cars for pedestrians to cross at intervals. The **municipal police** handle crimes like theft, and you'll need to contact them first in an emergency; there's a police station in even the smallest town. Flashily dressed **security police**, the sharp-suited gentlemen in designer shades, are there to guard embassies and other important buildings in Damascus and Aleppo and shouldn't give you any trouble. There's no specific tourist police force.

The **Mukhabarat** is the internal Syrian secret police force, responsible to the Ministry of the Interior for passing on information relating to suspected anti-government activity. Although things are much more relaxed than they were in the 1980s, it is unwise to get into a conversation about politics with any Syrian, lest you say something you shouldn't and find that it's a secret policeman you're talking to rather than the ordinary citizen you thought it was. Likewise, don't discuss Syrian politics or mention Assad when talking with travelling companions in public spaces: this is a country where the walls have ears.

DIPLOMATIC MISSIONS IN SYRIA

If you find yourself in trouble, contact your **embassy** in Damascus (see p.89); the UK also maintains a **consulate** in Aleppo (see p.198). Diplomatic missions can advise on legal matters and help to replace lost or stolen passports, but will not be much help to you if you've been arrested, particularly if it's on narcotics charges (drug smuggling carries the death penalty in Syria). They won't lend you any money if you've run out or had it stolen, but as a last resort they'll get you back home – somehow.

CULTURAL ATTITUDES AND BEHAVIOUR

Many Syrians speak English and French and, in a country where tourism is still very limited, it is often they who will make the first move in establishing contact with foreign visitors – if only to try out their languages or talk to you about football. Single women excepted, you will very rarely encounter an approach which carries suspicious motives, and many such instances will result in invitations to a Syrian's home.

You should, however, be aware of certain aspects of etiquette which might cause offence. In the rare cases when offers of goods or services are made over-persistently, you should rebut them with a polite refusal rather than rude or aggressive behaviour: most Syrians take "no" as an answer the first time, which might come as something of a surprise if you've travelled elsewhere in the Middle East. It's also important to be aware of acceptable standards of **dress**: Islam requires modesty, and shorts (worn by men or women) and shirts which do not cover the shoulders will invite comment and looks, at the very least. If you are not appropriately dressed, you won't be allowed into mosques or churches, and you may inadvertently offend people, particularly out in remote regions.

Male travellers should be aware of conventions on **public transport** by which women do not end up sitting with men they don't know. Sometimes this seems unavoidable, but often a group of women will reposition themselves so that it doesn't happen; in any case you should always be sensitive to each situation and respond if adverse comments are made. You should also be careful when **photographing people**: men and boys make willing and easy subjects, but women and girls will often slink into the background when they see a camera. Finally, if you are invited into someone's home, remember that it is customary to take off your shoes before going inside, that it is considered offensive to sit with the soles of your feet pointing at someone, and that you shouldn't handle food with your left hand.

WOMEN TRAVELLERS

Many single women travelling in Syria will unfortunately receive some sort of unwelcome attention from men they encounter. Such behaviour can be partly put down to ill-founded perceptions of Western women stemming from their portrayal in imported TV programmes and films, and also the traditional inferior status of women in Arab and Islamic eyes. Looks, comments in garbled English or mumbled Arabic, staring or groping are all part of the problem, and seem an ingrained part of the Middle Eastern male psyche rather than anything which is deliberately provocative or malevolent. For this reason, decisive action on your part to any unwelcome attention is likely both to end it and to elicit sympathy from others, shaming the perpetrator into swiftly melting away: *sibnee le wadi* (don't touch me) is one response which is likely to have the desired effect. Remember that for a man to grope a Syrian woman would be considered illegal and immoral, and there is no reason at all why the same shouldn't apply to you.

It's possible for women travellers to make life easier for themselves in a number of ways: try to avoid crowded places (unless you're with a male friend or partner), ignore comments that are thrown your way if you are able to, and avoid eye contact with young males unless you know them well. All too easily, casual friendliness on your part might be mistaken as a come-on by Syrian males. Try to sit with Syrian women on public transport, and wearing a wedding ring, whether or not you're married, will lend you a greater mark of respectability in the eyes of Syrian men. Walking confidently and looking as if you know where you're going will often stymie adverse attention; remember that downtown Aleppo and Damascus are haunted by prostitutes after dark, and walking there alone at that time would definitely not be a good idea. Coffee bars and cinemas tend to be male-dominated places where women are likely to feel uncomfortable or, even worse, assumed to be on the lookout for male company.

Most importantly of all, women travellers should be careful that their **dress** does not cause offence or unwanted attention: bare shoulders, upper arms, thighs and cleavage will definitely send out the wrong signals, and loose, opaque clothing is advised for daily wear (the private beach resorts near Latakia are perhaps the only places where this advice doesn't hold).

WORK AND STUDY

Finding work in Syria is difficult, and your options are really limited to teaching in Damascus or working on archeological digs elsewhere in the country. It's best to arrange employment back home before you leave for Syria; work and residence permits will be sorted out for you by your employers after you start. If you're after the sort of casual work that you can pick up in resort towns elsewhere in the Mediterranean, forget it. Opportunities for study are similarly limited, restricted essentially to learning Arabic.

TEACHING

The British Council in Damascus (at the north end of Al-Jalaa Street; ☎011/333 8436) and the American Language Center (PO Box 29, Rawda Circle; ☎011/332 7236), are just about the only two places in the country where you might find work **teaching English as a foreign language**. The first doesn't encourage casual work-seekers, and most teaching posts are filled by the British Council, 10 Spring Gardens, London SW1 2BN (☎0171/930 8466), who will interview you there before deciding whether to offer you a place. You can specify that you want to teach in Damascus – which might work to your advantage, since it isn't the most popular location to be posted. Either way, you'll need a TEFL certificate and relevant experience. Once you've got a job, the British Council will arrange your flights and living accommodation.

Casual work is easier to come by at the American Language Center, which is always in

need of teachers. If there's a post available and you're a native speaker of English, it's just possible that they'll employ you on the spot; a TEFL certificate, proven linguistic ability, teaching experience and a good university degree will all improve your chances. Rates start at S£400 per hour but climb rapidly according to experience.

There's a remote possibility of teaching or private tutoring at the language faculty of Damascus or other universities, but you'll need contacts to be able to do this; you might want to enquire through your embassy, through the bodies described above, or even through Arabic departments of Western universities.

ARCHEOLOGICAL DIGS

Unless you're a trained archeologist, your chances of getting work on a dig in Syria are slim, to say the least; far more opportunities exist in Jordan, Israel and Turkey, where digs coordinated by Western universities are always in progress. Nevertheless, if you're determined, you could try contacting the Archeological Institute of America (AIA, 656 Beacon St, 4th floor, Boston MA 02215-2010; ☎617/353 9361): they produce an annual booklet listing current digs in the Middle East and other parts of the world which may require voluntary workers, entitled *Archeological Fieldwork Opportunities Bulletin* (US$16; published by Kendal-Hunt, 4050 Westmark Drive, Dubuque, Iowa 52002; ☎319 589 1000).

STUDYING

Opportunities for study are limited to following a **course in Arabic**. The place to do this, if you already have a grounding in the subject, is the Arabic Teaching Institute for Foreigners, Jadet al-Shafei No. 3, PO Box 9340, Damascus (☎011/222 1538). A six-month course, with teaching in Arabic, costs about US$500, with classes held for three hours each morning. If you are a beginner, you might want to try asking expats at the American or British cultural centres, who should be able to put you in touch with one-to-one language tutors. The Institut Français runs Arabic courses for beginners, intermediate and advanced students, but teaching is in French, of course. Lessons take place in the evenings and courses run for about three months.

DIRECTORY

ADDRESSES Many Syrian streets simply do not have names, and those that do usually indicate them only in Arabic; only in larger centres will you find street signs in English. Sometimes, if a building is on an unnamed street, the nearest named street is given as the address, with attendant confusion over the exact location of the place.

BRING a hat, sunglasses and suncream in summer; warm clothes and wind- and waterproof jacket in winter; a universal plug – many sinks and baths don't have one; a water container; a torch – many out-of-the-way places are poorly lit at night; travel alarm clock for early trains and buses; and to get yourself up to enjoy the coolest part of the day in summer; earplugs to cut out the street noise in cheap hotels; a walkman, to cut out the blaring pop music in buses (or just to take refuge from your travelling companions for a while); a Swiss army penknife; a small sewing kit for emergency repairs; and a sleeping bag, if you're travelling in winter and planning to stay in cheap hotels, where heating is often inadequate. Note that many medical items, including contact lens accessories, tampons and contraceptives, are difficult to get hold of, at least in familiar brands – it's best to bring your own from home. For a **basic medical kit**, you'd probably want to include bandages, antiseptic cream or liquid, cotton wool, tweezers, a thermometer, paracetamol or aspirin, emergency diarrhoea treatment and rehydration sachets, insect repellents and treatment for insect bites, and vitamin tablets, to make up for a potentially poor diet whilst you're out on the road. It's easy to make this up before you leave, or to purchase ready prepared – a more expensive option, but one that is likely to include a supply of clean syringes.

CHILDREN Kids are certainly welcomed in Syria, which is blessed with having one of the world's highest birth rates. Hotel rooms with three or four beds are easy to find, and you'll get discounts for children on most forms of public transport. Powdered milk and baby food is readily available, but disposable nappies are hard to come by. You might want to avoid visiting the country in the depths of winter or summer, when the weather can make travel with kids very wearing; you need to be especially careful over things like high temperature and intense sunlight, which can affect children more severely than adults. Other things to be wary of are the busy traffic, which has a tendency to hoot rather than slow down if there's something in the way, and archeological sites, where unexpected holes, crumbling walls and unstable columns are rarely indicated or fenced off, making them less of the kids' adventure playground than they might initially seem. If you're travelling without children you'll often be asked whether you have any – carrying photographs of them is a great way of initiating conversations.

DEPARTURE TAX S£200 payable on all international flights out of the country.

DISABLED TRAVELLERS Syria makes little provision for travellers with disabilities. There are no ramps to help you negotiate crossing the road, public transport (particularly buses and microbuses) is not adapted for disabled travellers, and ruins and archeological sites will be very difficult to get around in the most part. For advice in **Britain and Ireland**, try the following organizations: RADAR (Royal Association for Disability and Rehabilitation), 12 City Forum, 250 City Rd, London EC1V 8AF (☎0171/250 3222; Minicom ☎0171/250 4119) , who produce a guide giving advice about long-haul travel in alternate years; Tripscope, The Courtyard, Evelyn Rd, London W4 5JL (☎0181/994 9294, fax 994 3618), who provide a national telephone information service offering free advice on international travel for those with a mobility problem; Disability Action Group, 2 Annadale Ave, Belfast BT7 3JH (☎01232/491

011); and the Irish Wheelchair Association, Blackheath Drive, Clontarf, Dublin 3 (☎01/833 8241, fax 833 3873; email: *iwa@iol*). In the **US and Canada**: Directions Unlimited, 720 N Bedford Rd, Bedford Hills, NY 10507 (☎914/241-1700), a travel agency specializing in custom tours for people with disabilities; Mobility International USA, PO Box 10767, Eugene, OR 97440 (Voice and TDD: ☎541/343-1284), which provides information and referral services, access guides, tours and exchange programmes, for an annual membership of $25 (includes quarterly newsletter); Society for the Advancement of Travel for the Handicapped (SATH), 347 5th Ave, Suite 610, New York, NY 10016 (☎212/447-7284; www.sit-travel.com), a non-profit travel-industry referral service that passes queries on to its members as appropriate; Travel Information Service (☎215/456-9600), a telephone-only information and referral service; and Twin Peaks Press, Box 129, Vancouver, WA 98666 (☎360/694-2462 or 1-800/637-2256), publisher of the *Directory of Travel Agencies for the Disabled*, *Travel for the Disabled*, the *Directory of Accessible Van Rentals* and *Wheelchair Vagabond*. In **Australia and New Zealand**: ACROD (Australian Council for Rehabilitation of the Disabled), PO Box 60, Curtin, ACT 2605 (☎02/6282 4333); and the Disabled Persons Assembly, 173–175 Victoria St, Wellington (☎04/811 9100).

ELECTRICITY The current used is 220 volts, 50 cycles, out of double round-pin sockets. British appliances need a 3-to-2 plug adaptor; North American ones need an adaptor and a transformer too (except for dual-voltage shavers). Lengthy power cuts were common in the late 1980s, and although the situation has calmed down in recent years, supply can sometimes be erratic. Most hotels and businesses have to resort to their own generators (fired up with an extraordinary din) at least once a week or so.

EMERGENCIES Ambulance ☎110; police ☎112; fire ☎113; traffic police ☎115.

FILM AND PHOTOGRAPHY You can buy Western brands of print film (particularly Fuji products) in the centres of most large towns, and there are 24-hour film developing outfits in Damascus and Aleppo. Camera shops, which are easy to find in the largest centres, will sell you a camera, but you'll probably find it difficult to get your model repaired, or even to obtain new batteries for it. It's wiser to bring all photographic needs out with you, including any slide film, which is impossible to buy in Syria. Be careful of getting dust in the shutter mechanism, a sure way to foul up your camera and ensure that you have no photographic record of your trip.

Regarding what you point your camera at, never take photographs of police or military installations, or of strategically sensitive things like bridges, railways stations, airports, dams or guarded public buildings. Men and children are usually willing to be photographed, and may even get offended if you've got a camera with you but don't use them as a subject; women will normally deliberately steer clear of you if you're taking pictures.

GAY AND LESBIAN TRAVELLERS With homosexuality illegal and punishable by at least imprisonment, Syria is not an easy place for gay and lesbian travellers – although Robert Tewdwr Moss, in his book *Cleopatra's Wedding Present* (see p.269), provides a recent, readable account of a gay man's solo travels in the country. It may be worth consulting the *Spartacus Gay Guide*, which even lists some possible cruising areas in Damascus, or a series of publications by Ferrari, PO Box 37887, Phoenix, AZ 85069, US (☎1-800/962-2912 or 602/863-2408): *Ferrari Gay Travel A to Z*, a worldwide gay and lesbian guide; *Inn Places*, a worldwide accommodation guide; *Men's Travel in Your Pocket* and *Women's Travel in Your Pocket*; and the quarterly *Ferrari Travel Report*.

LAUNDRY There are no laundrettes in Syria. All hotels will wash guests' clothes for them, although the turn-around time might be anything from twelve hours to three days (in the cheapest places). Expect to pay about S£30 per item.

LEFT LUGGAGE There are no left luggage facilities anywhere in Syria.

TIME Two hours ahead of GMT in winter; daylight saving time is observed between the last weekend in March and the last in October, when Syria is three hours ahead of GMT.

TOILETS You'll occasionally find public toilets next to mosques, usually filthy and of the squat-hole variety. In cheap hotels you'll also find this style, with a floor-level tap supplied for washing yourself off. Toilet paper is rarely provided, and if you carry your own you shouldn't throw it down the hole – use the small bin provided. In mid-range hotels and more expensive restaurants you'll find Western-style toilets.

CHAPTER ONE

DAMASCUS AND AROUND

With a justifiable claim to being the oldest settlement on earth and a huge number of beckoning historical sights, **DAMASCUS**, known to Syrians as *Dimashq* or sometimes *Ash-Sham* (which literally translates as "Southern Syria"), is likely to be on every traveller's itinerary in Syria. Even if you wanted to, it would be hard to avoid the place: nearly all roads and railways in the country lead there, and its international airport is by far the most convenient point of entry into Syria from abroad. On many counts, however, the city is likely to disappoint. Modern Damascus is a chaotic and largely charmless jumble of building sites, flyovers and industrial zones, with pitifully few areas of open space in which to seek respite from the remorseless din of the traffic (and, in summer, relief from the wearying heat). If you have just come from Lebanon or Turkey you'll find little to tempt you in the city's restaurants, bars and nightclubs, and if you intend to shop in the souks you'll find the hawkers much more persistent and aggravating here than anywhere else in Syria. With its bewildering public transport system and confusing layout, you may initially feel that Damascus is worth only a short amount of your time before you push on to somewhere else less hectic and more easily manageable.

Yet these are only first impressions. Peel away the frantic modernity and forget some of the more disastrous aspects of postwar city planning, and a more complex picture emerges. The contrasts which you can see all over Syria – between the developed and developing world, Christianity and Islam, Europe and Asia – are accentuated in Damascus as in no other city. On the streets, modern Mercedes compete for road space with horse-drawn wagons laden with goods destined for the souks. Assorted donkeys, tractor-engined three-wheelers, bicycles and vintage American yellow taxis are all thrown in for good measure, making crossing the road a triumph in itself and ensuring that the job of the hard-pressed traffic police is never dull. Men in chinos and shades smoke *nargileh*s in coffee bars while women veiled in black from head to toe happily walk the streets with children whose junior fashions would not look remarkable in London or Paris. The clamour of tongues in the markets includes Arabic, Turkish, Farsi (Persian) and European languages, haggling over anything from goats' heads (freshly severed) to clothes from Benetton. Some of the architecture in the Old City is quite dazzling, and a deliberately unhurried wander beyond the more immediately touristy areas will reveal a secretive, fascinating world. Take time to dig beneath the surface and, like a vast *tell*, Damascus reveals much more than a casual preliminary glance might suggest.

In fact, as an archeological site Damascus has yet to be investigated to its full depths. Most of Roman and pre-Roman Damascus still lies buried beneath the

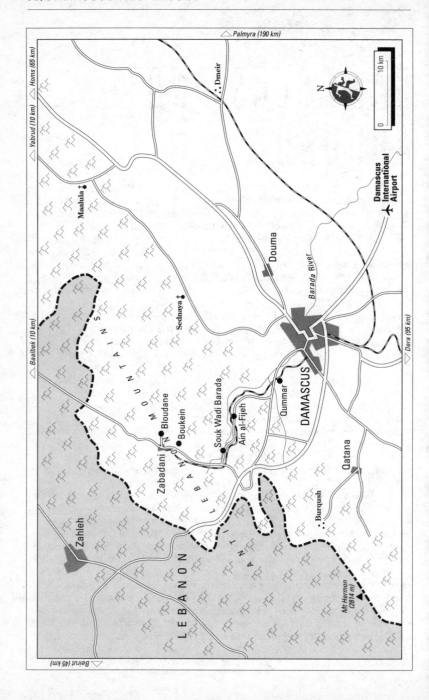

streets of the Old City, and the principal attractions for visitors are the reminders of the fine Islamic heritage which date from the era of the first Arab conquests. In the **Old City**, your priorities will be the stunning **Umayyad Mosque**, **Straight Street** and the **khans**, **madrasas** and hectic **souks** that stand between them. Of the Damascus museums, the archeological collections of the **National Museum**, in the **New City**, far outshine what you can see in those devoted to the army and epigraphy. When you've done with looking around the centre, you shouldn't ignore the attractions of the outer districts, most notably **Salihiye**, whose ageing mosques, mausoleums and madrasas line the narrow streets on the lower slopes of **Mount Qassioun**. The mountain's summit, providing magnificent views over the city and the desert beyond, allows you to appreciate the oasis-like nature of the capital's location. On the opposite side of the city from Qassioun, the **Saida Zeinab Mosque** is an important site of Shia Islamic worship, an unusually striking modern building that is much frequented by visiting Iranian pilgrims.

Within day-trip range to the west and north of Damascus rises the fine, barren countryside of the **Anti-Lebanon Range**, the mountain borderlands where Israel, Syria and Lebanon meet which have been fiercely contested for over thirty years. On warm summer days, Damascenes head by road or narrow-gauge rail line to the mountain resorts of **Bloudane** and **Zabadani**, near the source of the Barada River, for clean air, cool temperatures and fine views. If you're still in the mood for history and sightseeing, two pockets of Christianity to the north of the capital also make an easy and rewarding day-trip: the busy pilgrimage town of **Sednaya**, and the tiny, picturesque village of **Maalula**, one of the few places in the world where Aramaic, the language of Christ, is still spoken. Further afield, many of the places described in Chapter Two can be seen on day-trips from Damascus, with **Bosra** under ninety minutes away by direct bus. Even the **Crac des Chevaliers** (see p.152) can be visited on a long, but not impossibly long, jaunt from Damascus, although Palmyra is too far to be visited comfortably from the capital in a day.

Some history

Whether or not Damascus is, in fact, the oldest continuously inhabited settlement on earth is much disputed; Jericho and Aleppo are also claimants to the title. What is clear is that all three settlements, and many others in the Fertile Crescent (see p.121), were founded around 4000 BC when humans first adopted settled farming practices rather than wandering around hunting and gathering. Damascus owes its existence to the **Barada River**, now little more than a putrid ditch running in a series of concrete culverts through the New City, but once a vital source of fresh water whose headwaters are situated high in the Anti-Lebanon Range.

The city is first mentioned in written records dating from around 2500 BC found at Ebla and Mari. Such is the difficulty of digging up the streets of old Damascus to reveal its archeology that most of the city's earliest history has been pieced together from ancient records found in locations as distant as Turkey and Egypt. It is clear from these that Damascus and its surroundings formed a city state – but never one of any great importance – during Amorite, Aramean, Assyrian and Persian occupation of Syria, and in 332 BC even **Alexander the Great** largely ignored the city, leaving it in the hands of one of his generals before he himself pushed on. But it was under his chosen ruler, **Parmenion**, that Damascus was systematically planned for the first time, with a grid pattern of streets which included Straight Street, mentioned in the Bible (Acts 9:11) and still the principal artery of the Old City.

Although the **Romans** ruled their province of Syria from Antioch (Antakya in Turkey), Damascus assumed a certain degree of political importance during the seven centuries of Roman-Byzantine rule which began in 64 BC. They endowed the city with proper walls and gates, and built baths and temples, most notably refounding the former Aramean temple to Hadad to honour one of their own gods, Jupiter. At the time of the Christianization of the empire in the fourth century AD, the building was re-dedicated as a cathedral to St John the Baptist, whose head was entombed within; in 636 the city was overwhelmed by Arab tribes and became the capital of the **Umayyad Empire**, under whose rule the building was once again reconstructed, this time as the Umayyad or Great Mosque.

In the ensuing centuries Damascus lost ground as an Arab and Islamic centre, control over the city being exerted from Baghdad and later Cairo. The capture of Jerusalem during the First Crusade led to an influx of Jewish and Christian refugees, and to the subsequent growth of the Salihiye District. But it wasn't until 1260 and the start of **Mameluke** rule that the city once again assumed a political and cultural eminence. The Mameluke Sultan Baibars spent most of his time here, and Damascus soon became an imperial centre second only to Cairo in importance.

Under the **Ottomans**, who ruled the city between 1516 and 1918, the fortunes of Damascus suffered under a succession of largely capricious and self-serving governors. In the last few decades of their rule the rumbling conflict between Druze and Christians in Lebanon spilled over into rioting and a massacre of Christians in Damascus in 1860. It was during the Ottoman era, too, that the city became an important stop on the pilgrimage routes from Constantinople to Mecca. At the turn of the twentieth century, a tram network was constructed and rail links established across the mountains to Beirut and into Arabia via Amman – the latter, known as the Hedjaz Railway, to ferry pilgrims on the *hadj* to Mecca and Medina.

The Allied victory in World War I resulted in **French control** of the city in 1920, after a brief Syrian administration lasting barely a year. This tantalizing glimpse of self-rule combined with the deep unpopularity of the French administration led to concerted resistance activities, and an uprising in 1925 was put down by a French bombardment of areas of the city that had fallen into rebel hands. The French finally left in 1946, after another major outbreak of civil unrest in 1945, and on the foundation of the modern Syrian state Damascus was the obvious choice for the capital – and the city at last assumed autonomous control of its own affairs, arguably for the first time since the seventh century.

After Ba'athist political victories in the early 1960s, and the stability brought by the **Assad regime**, Soviet-funded **industrial investment** took off, and suburbs expanded into the desert to the east and north of the city. Construction – both of industrial plants and of apartment buildings for their workers to live in – still continues apace, with precious little concern for the city's visual environment or air quality. Major problems familiar to many cities in the developing world, such as smog, high levels of ozone and carbon monoxide, and a lack of open space, are allowed to continue unchecked; future prospects for tackling them seem as bleak as the surroundings which the urban planners have chosen to create.

Orientation, arrival, city transport and information

The central area of Damascus encompasses a number of contrasting districts, which broadly fit into two areas, the Old City and the New City. The centre is not particularly compact, but most distances are walkable without any real problems, and unless you are heading out to suburban districts you are unlikely to feel the need to use public transport. At the heart of the **New City**, and of every visitor's mental map of the capital, is **Martyrs' Square**, marked *Al-Shouhada* on most maps but known to locals as *Plas Marjeh*. Traffic-clogged and unremarkable, this is a point of reference rather than a place to see, with one of the main highways out of the city – Shoukry al-Qouwatly Street, which leads into Fayez Mansur, the road to Beirut – joining at its northern corner. Yousef al-Azmeh Street runs from its northern edge up to **Yousef al-Azmeh Square**, a busy junction which is the second orientation point within the New City. It is around these two squares that you will find most of the city's banks, airline offices, restaurants and mid-range hotels. From Yousef al-Azmeh Square, the road you are likely to use most is Salihiye Street, which runs in a northwesterly direction into the largely pedestrianized central shopping area; another road, Maisaloun Street, runs west towards the **diplomatic quarter**, which occupies the lower, gentler slopes of **Mount Qassioun**. Qassioun's rocky summit plateau and military installations are a useful orientation point from most parts of the city. The **Salihiye District** lies to the east of the diplomatic quarter, its mosques and narrow streets hugging the contours of the increasingly precipitous slopes of the mountain.

Shoukry al-Qouwatly Street runs due west from Martyrs' Square to **Al-Umawyeen Square**, an expansive roundabout beyond which lies the campus of Damascus University. Between the two squares, on the south side of the road, you will find the **National Museum** and trade fair grounds which now include two theatres; close to the museum and within walking distance of the centre are the **Karnak and service taxi stations**, as well as the **local bus and microbus depot**. The screech of traffic along the carriageways of Shoukry al-Qouwatly Street (don't even think about trying to cross this stretch) and the stench of the Barada running alongside render this a particularly unappealing area of the city.

The area to the immediate south and west of Martyrs' Square is a jumble of streets lined with small eateries and stalls, the floors above given over to cheap hotels. In this relentlessly busy and lively area your main point of reference will be the **Hedjaz Station**, with the main post and telephone offices close by. The major artery of **An-Naser Street** runs between the station and the formidable bulk of the **Citadel**, which stands at the entrance to the souks and the **Old City**. Walking along under the wrought-iron roof of the **Hamidiye Souk** will bring you to the **Umayyad Mosque**, which lies at the heart of ancient Damascus amidst a dense network of covered markets. Heading south you'll soon hit **Straight Street** which will bring you to the Christian monuments (and some good restaurants) at the eastern end of the Old City.

Beyond these central districts you need to negotiate the ever-expanding residential sprawl, dissected by numerous fast urban motorways, to reach far-flung bus and microbus depots and distant points of interest such as the **Saida Zeinab Mosque** on the southern outskirts.

Arrival

Damascus International Airport is the main gateway into Syria. Located 35km to the southeast of the city, it's a shabby place, with one terminal handling both internal and international flights – and be warned that immigration formalities can be very slow. Once through the final passport checks you will find **exchange facilities** (open 24hr), a Europcar desk (no point in turning up here without a

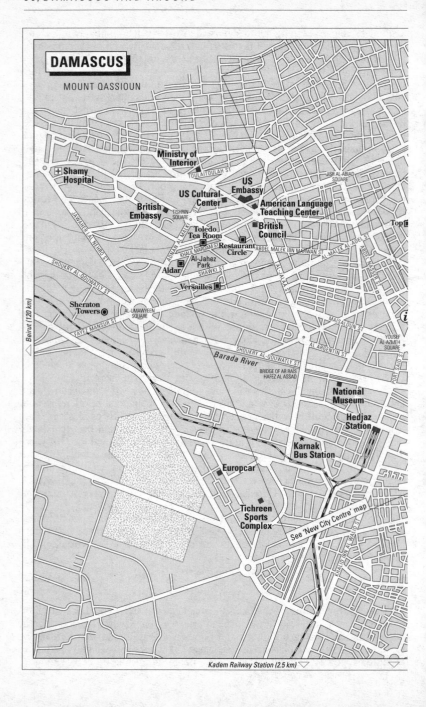

DAMASCUS

MOUNT QASSIOUN

Beirut (120 km)

Shamy Hospital

Ministry of Interior
TOULAITOULAH ST

JISR AL-ABIAD SQUARE

US Embassy

US Cultural Center

British Embassy
TISHRIN SQUARE

American Language Teaching Center

Top

Toledo Tea Room

British Council

Restaurant Circle

KHALIL MARDAM ST

ABDEL MALEK IBN MARWAN ST

AL-MALEK AL-ADEL ST

Al-Jahez Park

Aldar

SHAWKI ST

Versailles

JAWAHER AL NEHRO ST

SHOUKRY AL-QOUWATLY ST

ADNAN AL MALKI

AL JALA ST

Sheraton Towers

AL-UMAWYEEN SQUARE

YAYEZ MANSUR ST

MAISALOUN ST

YOUSEF AL-AZMEH SQUARE

SHOUKRY AL-QOUWATLY ST

AL ARGENTIN ST

Barada River

BRIDGE OF AR RAÏS
HAFEZ AL ASSAD

National Museum

Hedjaz Station

Karnak Bus Station

Europcar

See 'New City Centre' map

Tichreen Sports Complex

KHALID IBN AL WALID ST

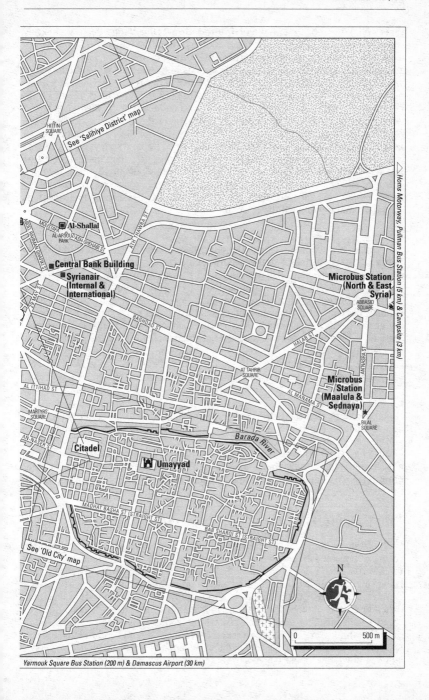

reservation – see p.30) and an **accommodation office** which deals exclusively with the various five-star hotels in the country. Note that when you fly out of this airport on international flights there's a S£200 **departure tax** to pay.

Ignore the private taxi and limousine offices in the arrivals hall (which charge you anything up to $25 to get you into the centre of town), and use instead the airport bus or one of the normal city taxis. The **bus** leaves every thirty minutes from next to the terminal building (turn right as you come out of the main doors) and costs S£10 for the 35-minute journey to the downtown terminal outside the *Kairouan Hotel* on Al-Ittihad Street, a block northwest of Martyrs' Square (pay on board). The bus doesn't run between midnight and 5.30am, so if your flight lands in Damascus in the middle of the night you will have no option but to take a **taxi** into town. These congregate at all hours immediately outside the main terminal entrance and can cost as little as S£100 with hard bargaining, but are more likely to set you back S£300; at night the drivers may well take advantage of their monopoly and try to push the price up.

By train

Of Damascus's two train stations the one you are less likely to use is the central **Hedjaz Station**, terminus of the narrow-gauge trains from Amman via Dera and Ezra, and from Zabadani. The station is a short walk away from the main areas of cheap and mid-range hotels. Mainline services from Qamishli, Aleppo, Homs, Hama and the coast use **Kadem Station**, located right out in the southwestern suburbs of Damascus; a free microbus provided by the rail company meets arriving and departing trains, and will drop you (or pick you up) outside the Hedjaz Station. If by any chance the bus doesn't materialize, there are plenty of city microbuses buzzing into the centre of town along the busy highway outside Kadem Station – just flag one of them down, and check that it's heading for *Plas Marjeh* or the central depot by the National Museum.

By bus

If you arrive in Damascus **by bus**, you'll be deposited at one of at least seven depots which are spread around the city; where you end up depends on where you've come from and what kind of bus you're on – see "Travel Details" at the end of this chapter for a full run-down. Only the Karnak and International bus depots are central enough to be within walking distance of Martyrs' Square; arriving at other terminals will mean catching a taxi or, if you're brave, a local microbus into the centre (see below).

City transport

With distances in the centre of town easily walkable, you'll probably only need to resort to taxis or city buses and microbuses to reach the suburban bus depots, the few outlying sights or the airport. Trying to use the crowded white-and-blue **buses** and the smaller but ubiquitous white **microbuses** can be very frustrating. Both display their route numbers in Arabic only, there are no route maps published or displayed anywhere, and no information at bus stops (in any language) about which buses to take. Don't try asking at the tourist office, either – staff there will think you bizarre for even considering using a bus and will just tell you to hop in a taxi. In general, people wait at designated stops for the larger buses, and flag down microbuses anywhere in the street, but if you want to give it a go, the best place to start fathoming out the situation is the **city bus and microbus depot**, situated underneath the flyover immediately west of the National Museum, about ten minutes' walk away from Martyrs' Square. There you can ask (and keep asking) and eventually you will get on the bus you want. Fares are very cheap – you'll never pay more than S£10 for a cross-town journey.

Fortunately, **taxis** are cheap too. You should insist that the driver uses the meter, but it's also sensible to discuss what the price is going to be before you start off, in case the driver tries to tell you that the meter is wrong, prices are out-of-date or some such, when you reach your destination. It shouldn't cost more than S£100 to travel into town from even the most far-flung suburban bus station, and most journeys around town will cost a lot less. Taxis are yellow and buzz around looking for trade at all hours of the day; just flag one down in the street. If you take one from or to an international hotel you're almost asking for the fare to be hiked up considerably, and possibly for it to be demanded in US dollars.

Information

The city's two **tourist offices** claim to be open 24 hours, seven days a week, but may be closed at odd periods if they're short of staff. The main one is on 29 May Street, just up from Yousef al-Azmeh Square, with a smaller branch reached through a side entrance of the Ministry of Tourism building on Shoukry al-Qouwatly Street. The staff in both are friendly but, apart from their free maps of Damascus and other regions of Syria, they will have little information to impart to you.

The best **map** of Damascus, far outstripping the tourist office freebie in terms of scale and quality of cartography, is on the reverse side of the locally published Avicenne map of Syria. Costing S£250 and available in all the English-language bookshops listed on p.89, it shows the locations, addresses and phone numbers of embassies, banks, hotels, government buildings and hospitals, but is probably only worth investing in if you plan to stay more than a few days in the capital.

Accommodation

Virtually all **hotels** in Damascus are situated within ten minutes' walk of Martyrs' Square; they range from noisy, dirty, cockroach-infested dosshouses costing S£100 or less a night to five-star luxury in internationally owned chains such as the *Meridien*, where prices start at over $100 and head for the sky. Once prices break past the S£1000/$25 threshold in Damascus, you'll be expected to pay in US dollars, although a bit of friendly persuasion should change the mind of all but the most

---

ACCOMMODATION PRICE CODES

In this book, all hotels have been categorized according to the **price codes** outlined below. They represent the minimum you can expect to pay for a **double room** in each hotel; for further details, see p.31.

① under S£300/US$7.50

② S£300–600/US$7.50–15

③ S£600–1000/US$15–25

④ S£1000–1400/US$25–35

⑤ US$35–50/S£1400–2000

⑥ US$50–90/S£2000–3600

⑦ US$90–130/S£3600–5200

⑧ US$130 and over/S£5200 and over

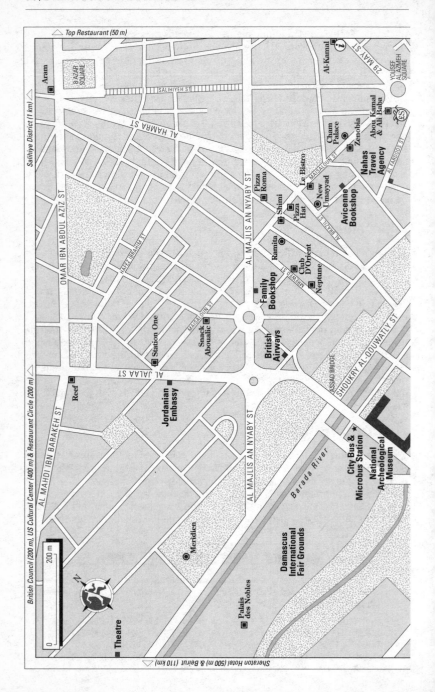

Top Restaurant (50 m)

Aram

8 AZAR SQUARE

SALIHIYEH ST

AL HAMRA ST

Salihiye District (1 km)

OMAR IBN ABDUL AZIZ ST

HAFEZ IBRAHIM ST

AL MAJLIS AN NYABY ST

MAISALOUN ST

Station One

Snack Aboualic

MAISALOUN ST

Family Bookshop

Ramita

AL BRAHIS ST

Shimi

Pizza Roma

Le Bistro

New Umayyad

Avicenne Bookshop

Pizza Hat

Club D'Orient

IS CHAMTIR

Neptune

British Airways

AL JALAA ST

Reef

AL MAHDI IBN BARAKEH ST

British Council (200 m), US Cultural Center (200 m) & Restaurant Circle (200 m)

Jordanian Embassy

Meridien

Palais des Nobles

Theatre

Sheraton Hotel (500 m) & Beirut (110 km)

AL MAJLIS AN NYABY ST

Barada River

ASSAD BRIDGE

SHOUKRY AL-QOUWATLY ST

City Bus & Microbus Station

National Archeological Museum

Damascus International Fair Grounds

Al-Kamal

29 MAY ST

YOUSEF AL AZMEH SQUARE

Cham Palace

Zenobia

Abou Kamal & Ali Baba

Nahas Travel Agency

AL FARDOSS ST

N

200 m

0

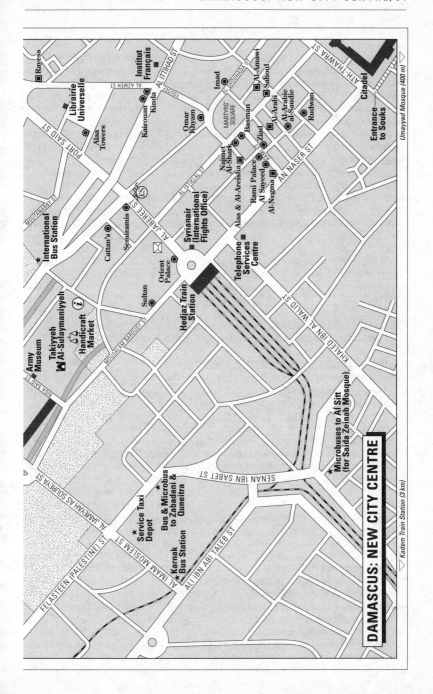

DAMASCUS: NEW CITY CENTRE

Umayyad Mosque (400 m)

Kadem Train Station (3 km)

Citadel

Entrance to Souks

Rayess

Librairie Universelle

Institut Français

AL AZMEH ST

AL ITTIHAD ST

YOUSSEF AL AZMEH ST

AL SHOUHADA ST

ATH-THAWRA ST

Imad

Al-Amawi

Safhoul

Alaa Towers

Kairouan

Kinda

Omar Khyam

MARTYRS' SQUARE

Basman

Al-Arabie
al-Saudie

Al-Arabi

Rudwan

PORT SAID ST

AL ISTIKLAL ST

Najmet
Al-Shark

Ziad

Rami Palace

AN NASER ST

MOUTANAABY ST

AL JABREE ST

Semiramis

Syrianair
(International
Flights Office)

Alaa & Al-Areisha

Al Sayeed

Al-Negma

International
Bus Station

Cattan's

Telephone
Services
Centre

Orient
Palace

KHALED IBN AL WALID ST

Sultan

Hedjaz Train
Station

Army
Museum

Takiyyeh
Al-Sulaymaniyyeh

Handicraft
Market

RIDA SAID ST

MOUSALAM BAROUDY ST

Microbuses to Al Sitt
(for Saida Zeinab Mosque)

SENAN IBN SABET ST

AL JAMEYAH AS SOUREYA ST

Service Taxi
Depot

Bus & Microbus
to Zabadani &
Quneitra

Karnak
Bus Station

FELASTEEN (PALESTINE) ST

AL IMAM MOSLEM ST

ALI IBN ABI TALEB ST

grumpy receptionist. A lot of hotels above this threshold, and all top-quality ones, will let you pay by credit card.

Generally there should be no problem at all finding a place to stay, but booking ahead is advisable if you're arriving in Damascus late in the day in summer and you want somewhere decent. All hotels have a receptionist who speaks at least a modicum of English, and who will (usually grudgingly) show you a room before you decide to stay. Conveniently, hotels of a similar quality tend to cluster together in the same area, making room-hunting relatively easy, even if you're lugging a heavy pack around. The **cheapest** cram the area between Martyrs' Square and the Citadel (with the notable exception of the *Ramita* to the north of the square), with **mid-range hotels** clustering around the Hedjaz Station (where the *Sultan* stands out) and the triangle formed by Yousef al-Azmeh, Port Said and Al-Ittihad streets. Syrian-owned **top-class hotels** such as the *Cham Palace* can be found in the centre of town, with more recently built, internationally managed chains relegated to the outskirts.

The only alternative to hotels is Syria's one and only **campsite**, *Damascus Camping*, situated just off the Homs motorway (from where it's clearly signposted) 4km north of the centre. It's a small, scrubby site, really a courtyard rather than a field, but there is hot water, and toilet and cooking facilities are available. You'll pay S£300 per person per day, which is hardly worth it considering the inconvenience of getting in and out of the centre; it's much more popular with campervan owners than with those pitching tents.

If you're after an apartment to **rent long-term**, the first place to look is probably the noticeboard at the American Language Center (see p.45 for address); after that, head for the accommodation rental agencies around the diplomatic quarter, such as Al-Chark Flat Rental on Al-Jalaa Street (☎011/333 752).

South and southeast of Martyrs' Square

Packed into the area between Martyrs' Square and the Citadel, 250m to the southeast, are dozens of **cheap hotels**, all of them occupying the upper storeys of buildings which house stalls, workshops, eateries and offices at ground level. It's a noisy, lively area, bounded by An-Naser Street, Ath-Thawra Street, Rami Street and Al-Istiklal Street, full of tiny lanes along which traders gather from well before dawn, selling caged birds, live chickens and all manner of meats and fresh carcasses. None of this is particularly conducive to a good night's sleep but staying here ensures contact with a constantly changing community of travellers, and you're undeniably in the centre of things, with the souks, the National Museum, the Umayyad Mosque, the Hedjaz Station and all the major banks and offices under fifteen minutes away on foot.

There's actually very little to distinguish the hotels in this area, and your choice is most likely to depend on cleanliness rather than any other factors. Most charge a similar sort of price (between S£300 and S£500), under the pressure of fierce competition. If you bargain, or even if you make your apologies and leave because you don't fancy what's on offer, you may find that you can reduce prices by S£100 or even more. Typically, you enter these hotels through a narrow ground-floor entrance which leads to a lift and a shuddery journey up to the first or second floor, where you'll find reception. The reception area will usually double as a communal room, with a constantly blaring TV and furniture in various states of collapse spread about. The bedrooms will be spread across two or three floors; some will come with a squat toilet, some will have just a wash basin, with communal facilities down the hall; most will have a fan and a window. Remember that you'll probably want to keep the window open throughout the night, so if they've got a room which overlooks a quiet back alley, take it. Beds are usually supplied with a minimum of bedding; if there are specks of blood on sheets, or on the walls, then it's a sure sign of bedbugs. If you don't like the look of a particular room, the owners will usually show you another one which (for whatever reason) they consider to be superior. In most of these hotels you'll find that hot water is available intermittently – usually early morning and late evening.

The cheap hotels described below (in categories ① and ②) have been listed either because they're slightly cleaner or more accommodating than the norm, or because you would be well advised to steer clear of them. The other places listed fall into category ③ or ④, and should display appropriately enhanced standards of cleanliness, comfort and facilities.

Al-Arabie al-Saudie, off An-Naser St (☎011/221 5151). Singles and doubles available in a perfectly acceptable budget place, which is cleaner and quieter than many others. ②.

Basman, Rami St (☎011/221 8003). A very reasonably priced mid-range hotel, with air-con and fans in all rooms. ④.

Imad, Al-Shouhada St, just off Martyrs' Square (☎011/231 4225). Slightly dingy, high-ceilinged rooms with TV, air con and fan. Rather cramped and a little overpriced, with street noise a problem unless you get a room at the back. ④.

Najmet al-Shark, southwestern corner of Martyrs' Square (☎011/222 9139). A good option at this budget, noisy but undeniably at the heart of things, overlooking a major traffic intersection on the square. ②.

Omar Khyam, Martyrs' Square (☎011/231 2666). Old mandate-era hotel in a good position overlooking the square. The shabby, dark rooms have definitely seen better days, though here and there you can see traces of the former opulence showing through. ⑤.

Rami Palace, Rami St (☎011/221 9971 or 221 9972). Acceptable and good-value mid-range hotel, offering single and double rooms, with or without shower. If you can afford a move up the price categories, this is definitely a good place to head for – it's cleaner, quieter and much more bearable than the cheapies which line both sides of this street. ③.

Rudwan, off An-Naser St (☎011/222 1654). Clean rooms with shared showers in one of the better cheapies, located on one of the quieter streets in the district; the slightly higher price (at the upper end of this price category) reflects this. ②.

Al-Sayeed, Rami St (no phone). Scruffy hotel with grumpy staff in a tall building with no lifts. Dingier and dirtier than most, and overlooking one of the noisiest streets in the district. Avoid. ②.

Ziad, Rami St (no phone). Unquestionably the cheapest bed in Damascus, and you get what you pay for: a cramped, stuffy and filthy dosshouse approached along cavernous, workshop-lined corridors, which sleeps 3–4 per room; a dreadful place, which you should only stay in if you're absolutely desperate. ①.

West of Martyrs' Square

Hotels located between Martyrs' Square, the Hedjaz Station and the National Museum are quiet and central, but generally pricier than those to the south and southeast of the square.

Cattan's, Shoukry al-Qouwatly St (☎011/221 5785 or 221 2514). Good mid-range hotel which fills up quickly. ⑤.

New Semiramis, Al-Jaberee St (☎011/221 3813). Ghastly exterior fashioned from green and mauve tiles which give it the appearance of an enormous bathroom. Inside, all of it renovated in 1995, guests can enjoy a restaurant, nightclub with live music, fitness room and shops. ⑧.

Orient Palace, opposite Hedjaz Station (☎011/223 1351, fax 221 1512). Dating back to colonial mandate times, and sharing with the train station an oddly melancholic charm. Plush foyer gives way to spacious if dim and shabby rooms, with TV, fridge and air con throughout. Price includes breakfast. ⑤.

Sultan, Mousalam Baroudy St (☎011/222 5768 or 221 6910). The best mid-range option in Damascus, a small, friendly and justly popular hotel just up from the Hedjaz Station, with clean air-con rooms with fans. There's a travellers' noticeboard and a library for guests. Get there early or ring in advance. ④.

North of Martyrs' Square

North of Martyrs' Square is a modern, soulless area of the New City, though it's very central. Most of the mid-range hotels here occupy modern high-rise buildings in the triangle formed by Yousef al-Azmeh Street, Port Said Street and Al-Ittihad Street; for your money you'll get clean carpeted rooms with en-suite facilities, air conditioning, TV, fridge and minibar. As with the cheapies on the other side of Martyrs' Square, there's not much to choose between each hotel; the exceptions are the luxurious *Cham Palace* and *New Umayyad* and the down-at-heel *Ramita*, a small hotel that's marooned far away from its sibling cheapies.

Alaa Towers, west end of Al-Ittihad St (☎011/231 7739). Small, overpriced hotel with rather cramped rooms. If full it may direct you to one of its other five branches in the city. ⑥.

Cham Palace, Maisaloun St (☎011/223 2300, fax 221 2398). Modern hotel whose rather brutal dark-brick exterior is something of a city-centre landmark, and whose atrium is a virtual forest of ornamental plants. Plush rooms and suites, with fitness centre, sauna, squash courts, shops, several bars and a roof-top swimming pool. Among its many eating places are the only Chinese and revolving restaurants in Syria. This is the most expensive central hotel, and the best of three *Cham Palace* hotels in the city. ⑧.

Kairouan, Al-Ittihad St (☎011/231 3338, fax 231 3343). Good rooms, all with TV and fridge, but lousy service and breakfast. ⑥.

Kinda, Al-Ittihad St (☎011/231 9760, fax 231 7438). Fairly ordinary, modern hotel popular with tour groups. ⑤.

New Umayyad, Al-Brazil St (☎011/221 7700 or 223 5500, fax 221 3516). Luxury hotel where the quality of the rooms does not quite live up to the impressively grand foyer. Lower standards of service, but more character, a friendlier welcome and cheaper prices than the other luxury spots listed here. ⑦.

Ramita Hotel, off Maisaloun St (☎011/221 6507). Mercifully quiet, basic and very small hotel, with OK rooms and shared bathrooms. ①.

Away from the centre: luxury hotels

With the exception of the *Semiramis* and the *Cham Palace*, the biggies are located outside the city centre and tend to be populated mainly by Western and Gulf Arab business travellers.

Le Meridien, Noussair St (☎011/373 8730, fax 371 8661). Recently done up and now extremely smart hotel, with several snack bars, restaurants, an outdoor pool and a business centre, plus the Oasis Bar on the ground floor, with an English-style pub (serving draught beer). It takes about 15min to walk to Martyrs' Square. ⑧.

Sheraton Towers, Al-Umawyeen Square (☎011/373 4630, fax 211 3737). High-rise hotel set amidst its own gardens on a roundabout 3km from the city centre along the Beirut road. Shops, restaurants and business facilities, and a big outdoor pool. Rooms rated according to what they call "luxury" – basically, size. ⑧.

The Old City

So much of its fabric has been preserved and rehashed over the centuries that the **Old City** is more a place for wandering and absorbing than for seeking out specific sights. There is one obvious highlight, the **Umayyad Mosque**, one of the most famous monuments of Islam, but it is in the labyrinthine lanes of the **souks** that you will probably spend most of your time; these fascinating, vibrant bazaars may offer travellers their best opportunity in Syria for souvenir hunting but their principal function is still to provide locals with their daily needs. Most of the Old City remains residential, and some of the grander historic homes are open to visitors; foremost

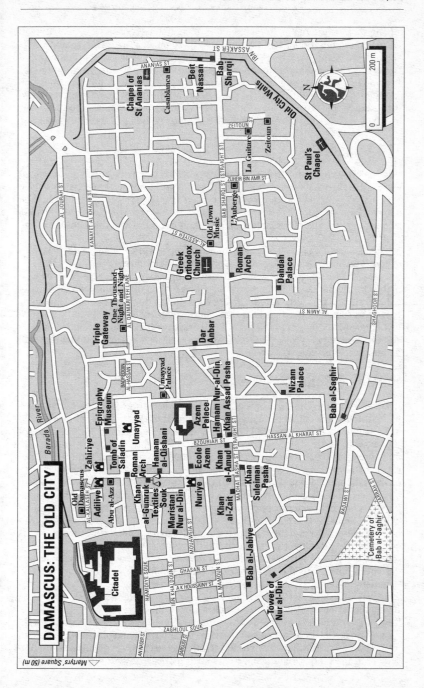

DAMASCUS: THE OLD CITY

among them is the **Azem Palace**, built in the eighteenth century by an Ottoman governor, though the museum within devoted to popular arts and tradition is disappointing. **Straight Street** has been the main east–west thoroughfare of Damascus since Hellenistic times and was known to St Paul, whose stay in the city is commemorated by a couple of still-revered monuments. A full day would be enough to see the highlights of the route described below, two days would be more than enough to take in the lot – though a lot depends on how much time you want to spend investigating the souks and narrow alleys of the Old City for yourself.

The Citadel

You can't help but notice this huge building which stands right outside the main entrance to the souks and the Old City. Formidably intact and protected by twelve surviving towers the **Citadel** was only retired as a prison in 1985, and since then substantial restoration has been taking place; it is not yet possible to visit the interior, though you may be able to gain a peek at the courtyard through one of the (usually guarded) entrances.

This has been a military site since at least Roman times though little is known of the Roman or Byzantine fortifications, and what you see today largely dates from the thirteenth century when Damascus became a key centre of resistance to the Crusaders. Badly damaged during a fierce Mongol siege in 1400 the Citadel fell into neglect and, although the Turks used the building as a military base, their repairs were half-hearted; in 1912 Baedeker even reported that it was "shortly to be demolished", though in the event the Turkish empire was dismantled instead and the building survived. The solidity of the exterior walls suggest that they will be here for some time to come.

Hamidiye Souk

Upon entering the Old City through the cavernous **Hamidiye Souk** to the south of the Citadel, you can immediately feel the weight of Damascus's history; indeed in Roman times this street would have led to the western facade of the Temple of Jupiter, at the heart of the ancient settlement. It's slightly surprising therefore to find out that the Hamidiye Souk only came into its present form in the 1870s, the result of an urban renewal programme by the city's governor Rashid Nasha Pasha, who almost doubled the width of the street, built a couple of storeys of shops and offices on either side and put a corrugated iron roof on top. Huge paintings of a benign-looking president hang every 100m or so from the vast roofing which is regularly pierced with holes creating an attractive star-like effect. The holes were put there deliberately in the 1870s to let sunlight in, though locals claim that they owe their presence to the French bombardment of the mid-1920s – the entire Hariqa quarter immediately to the south of the Hamidiye Souk was destroyed during this thoughtless act of military vandalism.

Initially the shops are quite tourist-orientated with a great variety of copperware, woodwork, carpets, swords, musical instruments, kafirs and gold souvenirs. Invitations to change money or to look inside a shop are most persistent here, though after a firm but polite refusal you won't get hassled; of course if you do want to do some shopping there's no harm in taking up a no-obligation invitation for a cup of tea. Hawkers are numerous, mainly small boys or invalids, though they tend to sell quite mundane items such as pens or socks or the inevitable packs of Marlboro. Pretty soon the souk turns into a regular clothes market, with only occasional "Oriental Goods" stalls, announcing their cosmopolitanism with stickers that proclaim their ability to handle Mastercard, Visa and American Express. Smaller lanes branch off from the main concourse, stalls here selling anything from beach balls and sunglasses to spatulas and Smarties.

Maristan Nur al-Din

Leaving the souk to the south you can make a short but compelling diversion to the **Maristan Nur al-Din**, founded in 1154 with ransom money collected by the Muslim commander Nur al-Din from the Crusaders. The hospital remained in use until the turn of the twentieth century, and what you see today largely dates from restorations in 1283 and the eighteenth century. The place now serves as an instantly forgettable **museum of medical history** (daily except Fri 8am–2pm; S£100) – it's more the building itself that you're paying to see with its cool courtyard and richly decorated *iwan*s (open reception areas off the courtyard). The larger *iwan* opposite the entrance was used for consultations and teaching purposes but the more intimate one on the south side has the more attractive decoration; note particularly the vines and grapes that adorn its white marble *mihrab*.

The Umayyad Mosque

Undoubtedly one of early Islam's most magnificent monuments, the **Umayyad Mosque** (daily 9am–5pm, closed Fri 12.30–2pm; S£10, including admission to the Tomb of Saladin) stands on a site which has been held sacred for at least three millennia, its chameleonic biography reflecting the monumental shifts in the history of the city. The compound of the Roman **Temple of Jupiter** would have stretched from the grand triumphal arch and arcade at the eastern end of the Hamidiye Souk right over to the monumental gate that lies half-buried beneath street level, some 120m beyond the eastern gate of the present-day mosque. Within this huge enclo-

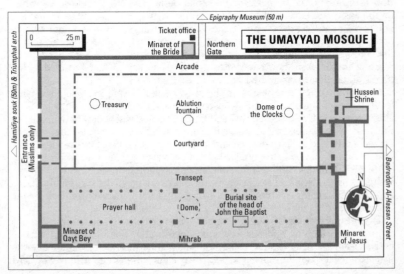

sure would have been an inner compound corresponding to the dimensions of the mosque today. In the late fourth century AD the temple was converted into a church dedicated to **St John the Baptist**, thought to cover roughly the same area as today's prayer hall. When the Arabs took Damascus in 636 the Christian population was initially allowed to continue worshipping here, though in the early eighth century Caliph al-Walid negotiated with the Christian community the ceding of the site in return for permanent rights to four other church sites in the city (including that of the present-day Greek Orthodox church).

Hired Byzantine architects and craftsmen constructed essentially what you see today between 708 and 715; it is said that the building work cost a total of four hundred chests of dinars and that eighteen camels were required just to transport the expense sheets. This was the first mosque in Syria to feature minarets, a *mihrab*, a *minbar* and ablution fountains, all now standard features, and it became the prototype for numerous other monumental constructions built under the Umayyads, including those at Aleppo and Hama and even the Great Mosque of Cordoba in Spain, constructed in 786. A number of disasters both natural and man-made have over the centuries conspired to diminish the building's original splendour, the most serious of which was a major fire in 1893 which destroyed much of the prayer hall.

The courtyard and minarets

The tourist entrance to the mosque is through its northern gate, the **Bab al-Amara**, where you can see the remains of the arcade that once connected the outer and inner walls of the Roman structure. Men and women wearing shorts will be given a black robe to wear at the ticket office. From here you enter the marble-floored **courtyard** facing the magnificent facade of the prayer hall; on the right is a small octagonal building elevated on eight recycled Classical columns which used to function as the **treasury**, its beautiful mosaics thought to date from a thirteenth-century restoration. In the centre of the courtyard the modern **ablution fountain** is said to mark the mid-point between Istanbul and Mecca, while on the eastern side is another domed pavilion, dating to the eighteenth century, popularly known as the **Dome of the Clocks** because it was used until 1958 to house the mosque's clock collection. Shi'ite pilgrims tend to gather in this part of the courtyard because in a room off the eastern arcade is the legendary burial place of the head of their revered leader Hussein, son of Ali, who died at the hands of the Umayyads at the Battle of Kerbala in 680.

Most of the original **mosaics** on the prayer hall and arcaded walls have been lost in a succession of fires and reconstructions over the centuries, but what is on show today is still an awe-inspiring sight, glistening ostentatiously in the sun. For the best appreciation of the surviving original work look under the western arcade, under the western portico and in the darker sections of the transept, midway along the facade of the prayer hall. In accordance with Muslim prohibition there are no representations of people or animals in the mosaics, which depict a lush, rolling landscape of orchards, fields and rivers populated by grand palaces and fantastical cities – a remarkable evocation of the Paradise promised by the Koran to the righteous.

The **Minaret of the Bride** rises above the northern arcade, a ninth-century structure to which an upper storey was added in the twelfth century. Its name derives from the story of a merchant, whose daughter married the Caliph after he had provided lead for the minaret's roof. The late fifteenth-century **Minaret of Qayt**

Bey, named after the Mameluke sultan responsible for its construction, rises from the southwest corner of the prayer hall, while at its southeastern corner is the **Minaret of Jesus**, built in 1247 on the site of an Umayyad structure. It is traditionally believed by Muslims that Jesus will descend from heaven via this minaret to lead the final conflict against the Anti-Christ just before the Last Judgement.

The prayer hall

You enter the **prayer hall** by one of the doors at either end, removing your shoes first. The interior is actually rather plain with the carpeting slightly threadbare, and it's really the sheer scale which impresses. The building essentially follows the plan of the destroyed Roman triple-aisled basilica and is unusually wide because the church altar was at the eastern end, but the *mihrab* had to be placed in the middle of the south wall, to reorientate the building in the direction of Mecca. The present dome crowning the north–south transept dates from 1893, and in fact there is little here that predates the great fire, though you can still see the exquisite wood panelling of the transept ceiling on the courtyard side and fragments of eleventh-century mosaic work on the north wall. A lavish marble monument commemorates the legendary burial site of the **head of John the Baptist**, who is revered by Muslims as a precursor of Christ; again this dates from after 1893, the former wooden mausoleum having been consumed in the flames. During the construction of the mosque in the early eighth century it is said that workmen came upon a small Christian crypt containing a basket with the head inside.

North of the mosque

Exiting the mosque by its northern doorway, turn left and you'll soon pass the **Epigraphy Museum** (daily except Tues 8am–2pm; S£100), where you can view, in the dim light, a collection of illuminated manuscripts and inscriptions on stone, metal and glass, thoughtfully labelled in English. The collection occupies a *madrasa* dating from 1420, which displays some beautiful marble and pearl-shell mosaics.

The red-domed building a little further up the street houses the **Tomb of Saladin** (daily 10am–5pm; S£10, including admission to the Umayyad Mosque), the military genius who united the Muslim world against the Crusaders. It's a select location even if the building is not so impressive, and perhaps its understatedness is appropriate for such an unassuming man. Inside there are two sarcophagi: the rotted walnut one is original, the marble one next to it appeared in the late nineteenth century. Kaiser Wilhelm II of Germany, passing this way in 1898, had the whole chamber restored, so keen was he to pay his respects to the great Arab military leader and to cement a Turkish alliance.

Madrasa Zahiriye and Madrasa Adiliye

Continue westwards along the street from Saladin's Tomb, then take the first turn-off to your right, which will bring you to two buildings standing opposite each other with impressive doorways. On your right is the **Madrasa Zahiriye** whose entrance, wonderfully carved with cascading shells and arches and inset with three marble bands of finely worked inscriptions, is a small masterpiece. The building is today a library but it also contains the **tomb of Baibars**, the Mameluke Sultan who virtually rid the Middle East of the Crusaders and who died in Damascus in 1277. You may have to ask someone to open the domed tomb chamber, which stands to your right as you enter the courtyard and also contains the tomb of one of Baibars' sons.

SALADIN

Saladin ranks as one of not only Islam's but the world's most brilliant military leaders; he was the great unifier of western Asia against the Crusaders and yet was revered by the Franks for both his military skill and his sense of honour.

At the end of the eleventh century the Crusaders entered a politically fractured land, a chaotic mess of independent city states, and within a few decades the whole of the eastern Mediterranean coast was under Frankish control. The first ruler to offer any form of unified Muslim resistance to the invading armies was Saladin's uncle **Nur al-Din**, the Zengid regent who united Aleppo and Damascus. Having been raised at Nur al-Din's court, Saladin made his military reputation by thwarting Crusader interest in Egypt during the 1160s; the Zengids became the new ruling force in Egypt, and Saladin became the effective ruler.

In 1174 Nur al-Din died leaving only an eleven-year-old son as heir, and Saladin deftly moved into the obvious vacuum, not through the might of the sword but largely through the power of his purse. His only major opposition to unifying the Muslim world came from the Zengids in Aleppo, and over the next ten years Saladin waged small-scale wars against them and the Crusaders. It was not until 1186 when the Zengids finally capitulated that Saladin was ready to engage the Franks in a full-scale campaign. On a boiling-hot July day in 1187 30,000 knights were caught by surprise at **Hattin** on their way to relieve the Muslim siege of Tiberius and were defeated by Saladin's army. After the battle, Crusader garrisons toppled one by one until in October **Jerusalem** was finally recaptured; the peaceful evacuation of the Christian population was in marked contrast to the slaughter that had accompanied the Crusaders' entry into the city 88 years previously.

Saladin's decision to abandon the siege of Tyre at this point was later to prove costly, as it became the rallying point for the **Third Crusade**, support for which arrived in large numbers in 1189. In 1191 further armies arrived under the command of King Philip of France and King Richard of England, the "Lionheart". The Crusaders immediately seized much of the coastline but were far too weak to attempt to penetrate inland. In September 1192 Richard, anxious to return home and realizing Jerusalem could not be taken easily, agreed to a treaty, honoured by Saladin, which gave the Franks the right to visit Christian shrines in the holy city.

Constant campaigning had by this time taken its toll on Saladin, who entered a rapid decline and, on March 4, 1193, at the age of 54, died in Damascus. An austere man, Saladin died without personal wealth, but his achievements were monumental, both in military and political terms. Much of his success came about not simply by force of arms but by the strength of his personality; many chronicles, both Muslim and Christian, testified to his sense of honour and justice, and Ibn Shaddad, his friend and biographer, wrote: "I have heard people say that they would like to ransom those dear to them with their own lives, but this has usually been a figure of speech, except on the day of his death. For I know that had our sacrifice been accepted, I and others would have given our lives for him." Yet Saladin's unification of Muslim territory was never institutionalized, and, in the absence of any able successor, much of his work was lost within decades of his death in squabbles and divisions.

Both tombs are plain marble affairs but the interior mosaic decoration in the chamber is exquisite, echoing that of the Umayyad Mosque.

Opposite this building is the **Madrasa Adiliye**, dating from the early thirteenth century. Its honeycomb-style entrance is impressive, though rather overshadowed by the portal opposite. Under the large dome in the near left corner of the courtyard stands the tomb of Al-Adil Saif al-Din, Saladin's brother who became Sultan of Syria and Egypt in 1200 and who was largely responsible for the reconstruction of the Damascus citadel in the early thirteenth century.

The south and east walls of the mosque

Heading south from the Madrasa Adiliye will bring you to the square along the western facade of the Umayyad Mosque. From here you can either continue south through the souks to Straight Street (see below), or you can complete your appreciation of the mosque with a walk around its southern walls. About 30m along is the southern entrance, the **Bab al-Ziyadeh**; the mosque's windows are so high up along here because the Roman wall at this point was left substantially intact. A little further along, partially obscured by an electricity sub-station building, is a **Roman doorway**, the original southern entrance to the Temple of Jupiter's inner compound, which was walled up when the prayer hall was built. With heavy irony, a Greek inscription over the blocked doorway, adapted from Psalm 145, reads "Your kingdom, Christ, is an everlasting kingdom, and your dominion endures throughout all generations".

Gold tends to dominate the souk at this point, more for the benefit of tourists from the Arab world than Westerners. As you walk further along the southern wall of the mosque a number of **woodwork** shops appear, many of them also serving as workshops where you can watch the vendor practise his trade. This is the best place to look for an inlaid chess or backgammon board and pieces, though anything from stools to cutting boards and spoons are on sale here.

At the corner turn along the east wall up to the mosque's eastern gate, the **Bab al-Nawfarah**. This was the principal entrance to the inner compound of the Roman temple, and would have been approached from the east along a colonnaded "sacred way", which ascended a broad flight of stairs to a columned porch projecting from the triple portal. If you walk 100m along Badreddin al-Hassan Street, the avenue that follows the line of the sacred way, you'll come to the half-buried triple gateway that would have marked the eastern entrance to the temple's outer compound. Beyond lie the twisting streets of the old Christian quarter, though by this stage the traditional cafés by the mosque's eastern gate might prove a greater temptation than moving on.

Through the souks to Straight Street

If you return now to the remains of the triumphal arch at the end of the Hamidiye Souk, you can turn south along a narrow textiles souk, the Souk al-Haiyatin, which runs all the way down to Straight Street. About 50m along here to your right you'll come across the **Khan al-Gumruk**, a seventeenth-century customs house in the form of an L-shaped hall topped with six domes, where duties would have been imposed. A few metres further on to your left is the sixteenth-century Hamam al-Qishani, once the changing room of a public bath (you can still see tiled panels above the doorway), now simply part of the souk. Another 50m south brings you to a crossroads of sorts; to the left is the way to the Azem Palace but it's worth continuing straight ahead for another 10m to look at the Madrasa Nuriye on your right which houses the **tomb of Nur al-Din**, one of the great military rulers of the Middle Ages and predecessor to Saladin (see p.170). The relatively plain tomb can be viewed from the souk through a grill just next to a water fountain.

Along the street leading to the Azem Palace, you'll come across a late eighteenth-century *madrasa* which now serves as a wonderfully musty antiques shop called the **Ecole Azem**. Here you are free to browse without hassle collectibles such as inlaid wood, swords and goldware in evocative surroundings – essentially a small courtyard arranged around a fountain. Continuing eastwards you'll soon be in the heart of the **perfume souk** which sells everything from well-known Western brands to odd-looking potions in unlabelled jars which you'll need a bit of help identifying: most stalls bear lists in English of the various aromas on offer.

Azem Palace

Through the perfume souk you'll come to a small, relatively peaceful square and the entrance to the **Azem Palace** (*Beit Azem*), which today houses the **Museum of Popular Arts and Tradition** (daily except Tues 8.30am–4pm, closed Fri 12.30–2.30pm; S£200). Built between 1749 and 1752 by the Ottoman governor of Damascus, Assad Pasha al-Azem, the palace's most notable feature is its central courtyard which, with a cool pond and shady citrus trees, offers seductive respite from the bustle of the souk outside. Red arrows and a few basic signs in French guide you on a tour of sorts of the rooms, which are adorned with a series of costumed wax dummies engaged in various crafts and activities, illustrating the original function of each room. The principal quarters, consist of a schoolroom, drawing rooms, a library and a room set up as a marriage chamber. Continuing clockwise will bring you to the small entrance to the bath complex: after a large, domed room for changing and relaxing, a succession of warm and hot rooms lead to a central steam room, behind which is a cleansing room with two massage chambers. Beyond this is the main reception hall with a fountain in the centre of its beautiful marble floor. The final section of the complex consists of the private quarters, which were badly ruined by fire in 1925 though they have undergone some restoration.

Souk al-Bazuriye

The broad street on the left as you exit the Azem Palace, which leads to Straight Street, is the spices and confectionery souk, the **Souk al-Bazuriye**. About 30m along on the left stands **Hamam Nur al-Din**, which was founded in the twelfth century, but was used as a soap factory in the early years of this century, before being pristinely restored and reverting to its original function as a bath-house (men only; daily 8am–11pm; S£280 for bath and massage). Even if you don't want to use the facilities it's worth a peek in to see the gleaming white, Ottoman domed chamber; a series of photos in the hall gives some idea of the reconstruction process.

To your left , another 40m on and only a short distance before Straight Street, is undoubtedly the finest of the Damascene khans, the **Khan Assad Pasha**, built in 1752 by the same Ottoman governor who built the Azem Palace. Unfortunately the place is undergoing some major reconstruction (there are plans to turn it into some form of tourist bazaar or possibly a hotel), so all you'll be able to take in of the grand interior is a glimpse through the door – if it's unlocked and if there's no one stopping you. In complete contrast opposite the entrance is the less impressive, rather dilapidated **Khan al-Amud**, which has been in continuous use as a warehouse since the seventeenth century and is still clogged with goods to be sold in the souks.

Straight Street

Since Hellenistic times **Straight Street** (the ancient *Via Recta*, now Madhat Basha Street and Bab Sharqi Street) has been the main east–west thoroughfare of Damascus. It was the Greeks who reorientated the city on a grid pattern based on rectangles 45m by 100m, and today's seemingly random streets and alleys still concur at many points with this ancient layout. Straight Street itself, however, was laid on top of an existing thoroughfare which dodged around existing buildings and low hills so it has never fully lived up to its name. As part of their civic programme the Romans broadened Straight Street, lining it with columns; at that time it would have been some four times wider than at present, but over the centuries buildings have encroached onto the street and in places today there is barely enough room for pedestrians to walk along either side. The cell-like shops along Straight Street purvey anything from fruit and meat to cassettes and washing-up powder – there's little discernible order to it, though towards Bab Sharqi the pace is certainly much less hectic, and tourist-orientated antique shops proliferate.

Coming from the Souk al-Bazuriye, most of Straight Street stretches off to the east (left), but there are a couple of khans west along the street which might be worth a quick detour. After about 50m in this direction on your left you'll see the striped entrance to the early eighteenth-century **Khan Suleiman Pasha**. Its upper gallery is still intact, but the twin-domed roof which once covered the courtyard has long since collapsed. Another 50m westwards along Straight Street, on the opposite side of the road, stands the late sixteenth-century **Khan al-Zait**, once the depot for the olive oil trade and today one of the more pleasant of the surviving khans, with an attractive tree-shaded open courtyard.

Nizam Palace and Dar Anbar

A short way east of the Souk al-Bazuriye you can detour south off Straight Street to the **Nizam Palace** (*Beit Nizam*), its exact location trumpeted in English along its blank facade. This eighteenth-century Ottoman dwelling was the residence of the British consul for part of the nineteenth century, and inside are three attractive courtyards with intricately decorated *iwan*s. It's a quiet, restful place though some hustlers sitting around may demand *baksheesh* for a mini-tour. Another good example is the **Dar Anbar**, further east along Straight Street and then north into

---

TRADITIONAL DAMASCENE HOUSES

The uncompromising blank facades of most old Damascene houses, pressed hard against one another in the Old City and designed to preserve privacy, give little sense of the often spacious dwellings to be found within. Traditionally the living quarters are arranged around one or more **courtyards**, typically with a **fountain** in the middle (supplied by spring water) and a clutch of citrus trees. Another typical feature is an **iwan**, an area open to the courtyard set into the side of the building and sheltered by its roof, which would be a place for relaxing and for receiving and entertaining guests. Most of the houses are built on two levels; in the past the family would have lived on the warmer upper storey during the winter while in the summer they retreated to the cooler ground floor. A few of the plusher and better-preserved examples are accessible to visitors, though without specific opening times (the doors tend to be left open in the mornings except Fridays); all of them are just a short walk off Straight Street.

the back lanes, which manages to combine opulence with a cool austerity. Built in 1867 as the residence of a wealthy Turkish merchant, in 1920 the building became the first secondary school in Syria; it is now a government-owned administrative building, though no one seems to mind you taking a quick look around.

From the Roman arch to Bab Sharqi

The third-century **Roman arch** which stands as a small but notable landmark on Straight Street, a little way to the east of the turning to Dar Anbar, once stood at the crossroads with the main north–south intersecting axis, though by the end of the nineteenth century it was lying completely buried and forgotten beneath the surface of the street. It was accidentally discovered by workmen during the French Mandate, excavated and re-erected. Beyond here the northeastern segment of the Old City comprises the traditional **Christian quarter**, with a large, modern **Greek Orthodox church** just to the north of the arch. A Christian church is said to have stood on this spot since Byzantine times; during the 1860 massacre of the Christian population by the Druze (see p.109), three hundred people who were seeking refuge were consumed by flames when the church was burned down.

The southeastern part of the Old City was the **Jewish quarter**, until Assad "invited" the remaining Jews of Syria to leave the country in the early 1990s. The lane that leads south just before the arch takes you via a signposted route to the **Dahdah Palace**, a grandly atmospheric example of eighteenth-century Syrian domestic architecture with a shady courtyard and intimate *iwan*. If the door is shut press on the doorbell, though the warmth of the reception can vary dramatically.

Back on Straight Street the remaining stretch to the east tends to be slightly less hectic with the route dominated by antique shops and smart restaurants; there's also a small drinks store on the street which will serve a cheap beer if thirst gets the better of you. Finally you arrive at the disappointingly plain eastern gate of the Old City, **Bab Sharqi**. Dating to the second century, though it underwent restoration during the French Mandate, it's the oldest existing monument in Damascus and the only Roman gate to preserve its original form – a triple gateway, the central one designed for wheeled traffic and the ones either side for pedestrians.

On the trail of St Paul

To reach the **Chapel of St Ananias**, formerly a house where St Paul the apostle was reputedly given shelter by Ananias after his famously blinding conversion, take the narrow lane that leads north just before the Bab Sharqi for about 150m. On the way you'll pass another grand Damascene residence (signed in English on the wall), **Beit Nassan**, featuring a finely decorated arcaded courtyard set around a fountain. The chapel (daily except Tues 9am–1pm & 4–7pm) is located below ground level, entered via a stairway at the corner of a courtyard. The small, dank interior has a suitably reverential air, disturbed only by the steady stream of Western tourists. Although the attribution of the house to Ananias can neither be proved nor disproved, there is scientific evidence to suggest that the building is indeed contemporary with the events described in the Bible.

To continue on the trail of St Paul, retrace your steps and exit the Old City by Bab Sharqi, then turn right and walk for about 400m along the city walls until you come to **St Paul's Chapel**. This simple twentieth-century chapel built into the walls is said to mark the spot where Paul was lowered in a basket to flee the city, after learning that his evangelizing in the synagogues had provoked a plot by the Jews to kill him. To gain entry to the chapel you have to walk through the break in the wall next to it; once inside you'll notice that the shrine incorporates the remains of a fairly unremarkable fourteenth-century Arab gateway, the Bab Kaysan.

The New City

The desire to turn Damascus around from a colonial backwater to a modern Middle Eastern capital has rendered much of the **New City** an aesthetic disaster area. You'll definitely want to see the **National Museum** and probably the charming **Takkiyeh Mosque** next door, but with traffic screeching along busy radial roads and the chaotic construction work all over, the central area of the New City is not a pleasant place to wander.

To escape the chaos, head for the summit of **Mount Qassioun**, which provides the most stunning views over the city, or the **Salihiye District**, an area of narrow lanes lined with mosques and madrasas on Qassioun's lower slopes, which was first colonized in early medieval times as a wealthy overspill settlement from Damascus. To the south of the city, the **Saida Zeinab Mosque** is one of the most striking modern buildings in Damascus, a riot of gleaming colours and white-washed arcades.

Martyrs' Square and the Hedjaz Station

It's no use pretending that **Martyrs' Square** (*Plas Marjeh*) is anything other than a traffic interchange with a grandiose name (the said martyrs were 21 Arab nationalists who were hanged on May 6, 1916 for their part in the Arab Revolt against Ottoman rule). Photographic prints of the square taken a century ago (which you'll see hanging on the walls of many hotels and restaurants) show a rather elegant open space, with horse-drawn trams gathering outside the post office, and a small garden, ideal for the evening family stroll, in the centre of the square. Time has not been kind. The post office has moved a few blocks away, and the centre of the square is now a scrubby little area of shrubs marooned inside the continuous circle of moving traffic. The long-blocked fountains and ornamental bridges across the putrid Barada River just give the place an extra underlining of pathos. But taking any of the streets heading east from the square towards the Citadel will plunge you into the noisiest, liveliest part of the New City – an overspill from the souks, with tiny foodstalls with fresh carcasses hanging outside, metal workshops which stretch into dark recesses, and chickens clucking away at each other in cages by the roadside, waiting to be sold. There's nothing specific to see, but a wander through this tightly packed network of streets and alleyways is an absorbing experience.

One building you shouldn't miss in this part of Damascus is the **Hedjaz Station**, a short walk away up Rami Street from the square and then right along busy An-Naser Street. It was built by the Turks in the early twentieth century for the pilgrimage rail route to Mecca and Medina, but now only the grandiose entrance hall hints at the station's once-vital role. The station becomes noisy and crowded when infrequent trains roll up, but at other times a **bar** serving cheap beer in an elegantly restored Ottoman carriage on the main platform provides a haven from the noise and bustle in this part of the city and at least prevents the place from becoming a forgotten colonial relic; some of the abandoned wagons on the grassy sidings look as if they haven't been moved since mandate days.

The Takiyyeh as-Sulaymaniyyeh complex

The main reason for following **Shoukry al-Qouwatly Street** to the west is to reach the National Museum, but just before you get there you'll find a small clutch of interesting sights along Rida Said Street. The first and most obvious is the **Takiyyeh as-Sulaymaniyyeh Mosque**, part of an Ottoman complex which includes the Army Museum and the Handicraft Market.

The mosque was built in 1553 by **Sinan**, the greatest architect of the Ottoman era, whose most noted buildings in Istanbul (such as the Suleimaniye Mosque) are on a far more grandiose scale than this gracious, understated construction. Unfortunately this modest building is rather lost next to the hulk of the National Museum and its intimacy drowned by the traffic screaming along the adjacent main road, but once inside it's still possible to appreciate the calmness of the gardens and courtyard, cooled by a fountain and shaded by trees. Having been commissioned by the Sultan himself, Suleiman the Magnificent, Sinan set out to honour his master by designing a mosque which included both Turkish and Arab elements, thus reflecting Damascus's role as a vital stopping place on the pilgrimage from Istanbul to Mecca: the domed prayer hall, the slim minarets and the delicate sense of proportion are typically Turkish, whereas the alternating layers of black and white stonework forming the entrance arch follow more local styles.

Unfortunately this is as much of the mosque as many people will see, as the prayer hall is often locked (except during services) and you'll have to find the keeper to get inside. It's worth persevering, as the walls inside are adorned with brightly painted tiles which are beautifully complemented by the coloured glasswork in the windows beneath the dome. Note also the sense of space that Sinan imparted to the interior by supporting the dome on arches which emerge from the wall, rather than on columns which would have interrupted the interior proportions.

The name of the mosque derives from the building next door, which was originally a **tekke** (a monastery for whirling dervishes) before it was converted into a khan for travelling pilgrims. Now the fighter planes and big guns outside, all looking rather the worse for wear, identify the building as the **Army Museum** (daily except Tues 8am–2pm; S£5), which is often full of bored conscripts on their day off, being dragged round by their commanding officers to look dutifully at fairly mundane collections of weapons and armour. Recent episodes of Syrian military history, such as the wars fought against Israel in 1967 and 1973, are explained with unashamed bias; more honest and more interesting are displays relating to the former Syrian-Soviet space programme, which came to an end as Syrian foreign affairs shifted more towards the West during the 1990s and the Soviet space programme began to run out of money.

East of the museum and mosque the **Handicraft Market** (*Artisanat*) is a small area where traditional goods are made and sold on traders' premises. Everything from carpet-weaving and glassblowing to shoe and chessboard manufacturing can be seen in action, and souvenir hunting is much more straightforward here than in the souks. Part of the market is set round the shady courtyard of the **Selimiye Madrasa**, built by Suleiman the Magnificent's successor, Sultan Selim II; weaving workshops and the like now occupy the cells where Islamic scholars once taught their students, but you can still see the high-domed prayer hall which opens off one side of the courtyard.

The National Museum

Housed in a purpose-built complex around a shady courtyard on Shoukry al-Qouwatly Street, the **National Museum** shelters the bulk of artefacts unearthed from archeological sites in Syria over the past century and a half (daily except Tues 9am–6pm, closed Fri 12.30–2pm; S£200). In size and scope it is not a patch on similar museums in Ankara and Cairo, but it's definitely worth spending a good couple of hours or more wandering around its dimly lit galleries. It is probably best, if your itinerary will allow, to make the museum one of the last, rather than one of the first, things you see on a visit to Syria, to gain a better perspective on the ancient sites around the country that you have visited. If you only have time for the highlights, you should head for the synagogue built in Dura Europos in the second century AD and transported to the museum piece by piece, looking

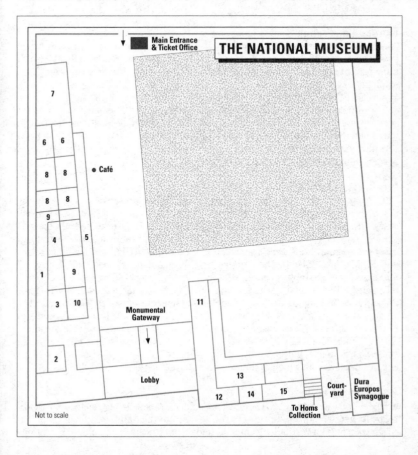

in along the way on the archives from Ugarit which gave the world its first alphabet, the beautifully fashioned manuscripts and jewellery from the Byzantine era and the stonework and silk and cotton textiles from Palmyra, unearthed only this century after being wonderfully preserved in the desert sands.

There's a drily comprehensive **guidebook** on sale at the ticket office if you want to know more than what's given here, and investing in this or tagging along with a guided tour group is a good idea – many of the exhibits are poorly labelled, mostly in French and Arabic, only occasionally in English and sometimes not at all. Most rooms are arranged by area or site although there is also a broad organization of exhibits into three eras – pre-Classical, Classical and Early Byzantine, and Arab-Islamic – all of which can give you a somewhat confused historical perspective if you look round the whole museum. The **room numbering** shown on our map and used in the text does not refer to any numbering system you'll find in the museum itself, but reflects the easiest way to get around the museum without too much backtracking. Once you're done with looking round, the shady **café** fronting the garden is a good place to cool off (the museum is not air-conditioned and can get hot and stuffy).

Entrance and lobby

One of the most striking aspects of the museum is the **monumental gateway**, which looms up at you as you cross the sculpture-strewn garden and through which you must pass to get inside the museum buildings. Once these two huge semicylindrical stone pillars formed the front entrance to Qasr al-Heir al-Gharbi, a seventh-century Umayyad palace in the remote desert between Homs and Palmyra. The honey-coloured pillars are carved with geometric designs, but the whole effect is rather crudely grandiose – you can only imagine that the gateway must have looked so much better in its original setting. Once inside the **lobby** you can read (in English) several comprehensive, but readable and well-illustrated, accounts of the periods of Syrian history covered by the artefacts in the museum.

Pre-Classical galleries

The majority of the exhibits from pre-Classical times are displayed (mostly unlabelled) in a long gallery (**1**) which stretches part of the length of the west wall of the museum, but three indiviudal rooms are given over to finds from specific sites in northern Syria. Heading right from the lobby, you'll come to the first and most interesting, the **Ugarit** room (**2**). Here the tiny gold-plated statuette of the god El, his hand raised in benign greeting, is astonishingly beautiful, and you'll find cases of stone tablets carved with probably the world's first alphabet, invented around 1400 BC by Ugarit merchants to record trading details (see p.167). To the right of the long gallery, which contains artefacts from a bewildering number of sites and eras, are rooms (**3** and **4**) devoted to the early Bronze Age sites of **Mari** and **Ebla**, which flourished around 2500 BC. There is little to grab the attention in either room, although the reconstructed tomb containing fifteen human skeletons is gruesome enough; assorted animal remains, weaponry, jewellery and ceramics are also included in the open sarcophagus.

Arab-Islamic galleries

It's best now to return to the lobby to gain entrance to the section on **Arab-Islamic art**, which roughly covers the seventh to the eighteenth centuries. You reach it through a vestibule devoted to finds from **Raqqa**, a city on the Euphrates which flourished in early medieval times (see p.216); the principal exhibit here, given a case all to itself, is a twelfth-century mounted horseman, believed to have been fashioned in Chinese Turkestan. The long gallery beyond it to the right (**5**), displaying mostly coins and seals from Abbasid to Mameluke times, is fairly unexciting, although the weaponry from the early Middle Ages at the far end – notably some beautiful Damascene swords – gives a good insight into the perfunctorily grisly violence of the times.

At the end of the long gallery you should turn left to find carved wooden items spanning all centuries from the thirteenth to eighteenth (**6**). The most striking piece is an ornate sarcophagus (1250), whose original faded colours still cling to the wood determinedly; close by is a prayer niche (1798), fashioned from beautifully carved cedarwood. Beyond this gallery you can see a reconstructed room (**7**) from the **Azem Palace** in the Old City (see p.72), whose marble floor and timber panelling give a good sense of the former opulence of this eighteenth-century residence. Heading back in the general direction of the main lobby, through rooms which line the western wall of the museum, you can admire beautiful Korans and other early medieval Islamic manuscripts (**8**), before you come upon the medieval ceramics (**9**), with their intricate designs and colours intact. Beyond them, in a room (**10**) sandwiched between the long gallery and the Mari collections, you can see stonework from the same era, including a touchingly fashioned child's tomb dating from 1350. From here you can get back into the Raqqa room and head through the main lobby to the museum's east wing.

Classical and Early Byzantine galleries

The east wing is the most interesting and most carefully laid out of the three sections. The first room (**11**) contains mostly stonework from various sites in the **Hauran**, although the most striking exhibit is an extraordinary mosaic from Latakia which depicts the River Orontes as a god. In the centre of the room there's a magnificent Roman sarcophagus dating from the third century AD, boasting a representation of its incumbent lounging across the top as if his tomb were a stone-carved chaise longue.

Beyond the Hauran room, against the back wall of the museum, is a room (**12**) devoted to exquisite textiles unearthed from the tower tombs in **Palmyra**. Used mostly to wrap the bodies of the dead, all the pieces were fashioned around eighteen hundred years ago and owe their high quality of preservation to the dry atmosphere and the absence of light in the tombs. The linens and wools were locally derived, but the dyes were Indian and the silks came from China – an indication of just how far-flung Palmyra's trading partners were.

Beyond the textiles you'll find a collection of Roman sarcophagi and other preserved stonework from Palmyra (**13**), and displays of early Christian icons and triptychs, many featuring St George and the dragon (**14** and **15**).

The Homs Collection and the Hypogeum of Yarhai

The steps leading up from room 15 bring you to the **Homs Collection**, a valuable hoard of coins and jewels from Roman and pre-Roman times which were uncovered from the area around Homs in central Syria. Some of the coinage depicts such noted figures as Alexander the Great, who passed this way in 332 BC, and Philip the Arab, Roman emperor from 244 to 249 AD who was born in Shahba, about 90km south of Damascus. Unfortunately, the stairs are usually roped off, and if you want to see the collection you must ask the curator in the main lobby;

depending on staffing levels in the museum and the mood of the curator, some-one may be available to take you up there. Don't bother asking on a Friday, when there is only a skeleton staff present and the museum director (who has to give his permission for the room to be opened) doesn't come in.

Taking the stairs down from room 15 will bring you to the cool, dank **Hypogeum of Yarhai**, an underground tomb fashioned from the characteristic pale yellow stone of the Syrian desert, which was moved here from the Valley of the Tombs in Palmyra. As was customary, the whole tomb was given over to mem-bers of one family (the Yarhais), their mortal remains set into stone vaults with a bust of the deceased incumbent placed outside (the women are depicted veiled to represent death). The tomb has its own *triclinium* (dining hall) where funeral banquets would have been eaten.

The Dura Europos Synagogue

A doorway from room 15 brings you for an instant into a colonnaded courtyard and glaring sunshine, before you plunge into the sunken, rather musty atmos-phere of the reconstructed **Dura Europos Synagogue**. The settlement from which the synagogue comes was established around 290 BC as a fortress town on the Euphrates in northeastern Syria (see p.226). The building itself, which can be dated (in the form you see it) to 245 AD, was hailed as a major archeological find when it was unearthed accidentally by the British army in 1920; other finds from Dura finished up in the Louvre and at Yale University, but the extraordinary syn-agogue stayed in Syria, and was moved piece by piece in the 1930s to this spe-cially constructed wing of the museum.

The intimacy of the building is offset by the grandiose execution of its **wall paintings**, which the sand and dust had kept intact for so many centuries, their original colours still vibrant and the intentions of the artists still breathtakingly clear. What is so interesting about the paintings – aside from the fact that they have survived at all – is that they depict the human form, something expressly for-bidden in the Talmud. Among other subjects, the paintings depict the crossing of the Red Sea by the Israelites, the First Temple in Jerusalem and, above the niche where the Torah scrolls were kept, Abraham sacrificing a ram (caught in the near-by thicket) instead of his son. The preservation of this building – it's by far the museum's most important feature – is all the more remarkable when you consid-er the recent fate of Syria's Jewish population and their places of worship; made scapegoats by Assad for the perceived wrongdoings of the state of Israel, the last Syrian Jews were "invited" to leave the country in the early 1990s, which rendered redundant the few remaining Damascus synagogues.

The Salihiye District

Not to be confused with the modern shopping precinct of the same name in the heart of the New City, the old **Salihiye District** is centred on Madaress Assad ad-Deen Lane, some 2km north of the Old City walls, on the lower slopes of Mount Qassioun. Many of the district's thirteenth-century madrasas, mosques and mau-soleums are only open irregularly or have been adapted for modern-day purpos-es, but a wander through its evocative, winding lanes, crowded with bustling veg-etable stalls, can still be heartily recommended.

It's best to begin at the busy traffic intersection called Jisr al-Abiad Square, on the north side of which stands the **Madrasa Maridaniye**, dating originally to

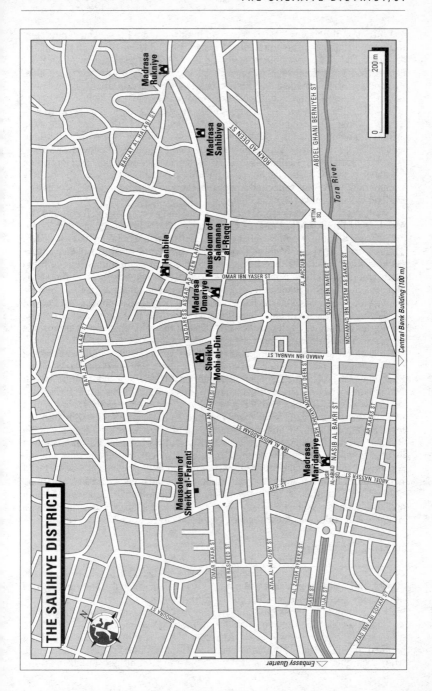

THE SALIHIYE DISTRICT

1213 (though the minaret was erected two hundred years later). The name refers to its benefactor, a Turkish princess who had the ill fortune to die on pilgrimage to Mecca and so was not able to be buried in the building she endowed; look out especially for the fine wood carving above the doorway on the northern side. From here walk north up Afif Street, passing several crumbling mausoleums before reaching **Madaress Assad ad-Deen Lane**. Turning right, you'll pass, after about 30m on your right, the recently restored, though permanently padlocked, Mausoleum of Sheikh al-Faranti, who died in 1224; immediately after is a primary school, a former madrasa, whose simple minaret is the only surviving example from the thirteenth century in Damascus. Another 10m on to your right is a thirteenth-century madrasa, whose pretty, copper-coloured, honeycombed doorway is worth particular attention. At this point the street starts to narrow considerably and busy stalls make progress slow – though the noise, smells and frenetic market activity are absorbing.

About another 200m down Madaress Assad ad-Deen Lane you'll come to the **Mosque of Sheikh Mohi al-Din**, containing the burial chamber of the celebrated Sufi poet and philosopher who died in 1240 (the actual building dates to 1518). Though born in Spain, Mohi al-Din lived in this street most of his life, having decided the district had the cleanest air after stringing up four pieces of fresh lamb around the city and monitoring their decay (a practice some might say is still alive and well). His intimate, still-revered burial chamber can be reached via the stairway in the courtyard. The second tomb here used to house the body of the Algerian patriot Abd al-Kader al-Jazairi, who lived in exile in Damascus following his resistance to the French conquest of the mid-nineteenth century; his corpse was returned to Algiers following independence.

Walk on for another 70m, keeping left at the V-intersection, until you reach a small street ascending to your left. A short way up here is the **Hanbila Mosque**, built between 1202 and 1213. From the exterior it barely looks like a mosque but the minaret gives it away; the courtyard incorporates six recycled Classical columns, while in the prayer hall is a very fine *minbar* dating to 1207. Now return to and cross Madaress Assad ad-Deen Lane, continuing downhill for 50m; over the fence to your left lie the ruins of the **Madrasa Omariye**, the oldest building in the Salihiye quarter whose origins go back to the exodus of Muslims from Jerusalem in 1099 following its capture by the Crusaders. You can just about work out the remains of some student cells grouped around two litter-strewn courtyards. From here you can return to complete your walk down Madaress Assad ad-Deen Lane, passing on the way the early thirteenth-century Mausoleum of Salamana al-Raqqi and the Madrasa Sahibiye – built between 1233 and 1245 and now in use as a school – and ending up at the recently rebuilt Madrasa Rukniye.

Mount Qassioun

Overlooking Damascus to the northwest is **Mount Qassioun**, whose summit is strewn with a variety of transmission towers and military installations, making it an obvious point of orientation when you're in (or approaching) the city. It is not possible to get right to the top, but the perimeter road which runs around the summit leads past a collection of shabby cafés and drinking places, from whose terraces there are very good views over Damascus. Those who are supposed to have climbed this hill include Abraham, Jesus and Mary, and the Prophet Mohammed, who, according to legend, looked down from the summit and proclaimed that

Damascus was a "paradise on earth"; indeed according to Arab folklore the mountain will be spared from the chaos and havoc of the Day of Judgement, which may be worth bearing in mind if you're staying in the city at the time.

Although it's possible to scramble down the slope from the cafés to the Salihiye District, trying to do this in reverse is a bad idea, and with no public transport the only sensible option for getting here is to take a taxi from the centre of town. Come up in the afternoon when the sun is behind you, leaving the slopes in shadow but casting brilliant light directly across the roofs and streets of the New City.

Saida Zeinab Mosque

Out in the southeastern suburbs, 8km from the city centre and close to the road which runs out to the airport, is the **Saida Zeinab Mosque**, where one of the granddaughters of the Prophet Mohammed is buried in a beautiful modern mausoleum. To get there by public transport, pick up a **city microbus** from the northeastern end of Ibn al-Abbas Street, 600m west of Martyrs' Square, to the al Sitt suburban microbus station in southern Damascus, where you'll need to change onto another city microbus for the ride to the mosque. You'll probably find on both journeys that people will guess where you're going and help you accordingly; the microbus fares should not come to more than S£20. Alternatively, a **taxi** can cost you up to S£300 one way, an expensive option since taxi drivers are unlikely to get a fare back into town; you'll need to agree on the fare before you set off – drivers will be reluctant to use the meter, telling you it's only for journeys within the city limits – so bargain hard (something like S£200 would be a fair price).

Zeinab's brother was Hussein, who was slaughtered by the Umayyads at the Battle of Kerbala (southern Iraq) in 680 (she herself was taken into captivity in Damascus), during a complex series of events which split Islam into its two major factions: Shi'a Muslims, who predominate in Iran, follow the succession from Hussein and his father Ali, while Syria and most Arab countries have a pronounced Sunni majority, who reject the successors of Ali. Many Shi'a Muslims come from Iran to visit this shrine, which was constructed with money donated for the purpose by their revolutionary Shi'ite government – an act which cemented further political ties between Damascus and Tehran.

Once at the mosque, you'll find that non-Muslims are not allowed into the **central sanctuary**, where Zeinab's tomb lies behind silver railings which are kissed with touching reverence by the Shi'ite faithful. However, anyone can look around the main **courtyard**, which is flanked by shady cloisters and overlooked by the dazzling mosaics which adorn the minarets and onion domes.

Eating and drinking

In comparison with the rest of Syria there is a relatively good choice of eating places in Damascus, so if you're only in the city for a short while, make the most of it. With its fairly constant stream of tourist and business visitors, the city's **restaurant** scene ranges from street stalls which will sell you a filling, cheap meal of *shwarma* or roast chicken, right through to Chinese, Mexican and Italian restaurants, situated mostly in the Old City or in the big hotels. All except the cheapest places sell alcohol; if it's a **bar** you're after, the choice is slimmer, limited largely to places that are geared specifically towards Western visitors.

Restaurants

Numerous restaurants around the city will serve inexpensive **Syrian** fare of kebab or chicken with salad, *hummus* or chips, and it's hard to differentiate between them. For a little more choice look for a **Western** menu and a small increase in price and quality, or failing that head for one of the numerous **pizza** joints. For a **snack**, there are dozens of *felafel* places, particularly around Martyrs' Square – too numerous to mention and most of them don't have names, anyway – and a number of decent Western-style fast-food choices in the New City. Also listed below are a couple of places in the New City where you can get ice cream or cakes for **dessert**.

Most **hotels** have attached restaurants which, generally speaking, are unremarkable places. However, the *Sheraton* can offer a very good Italian place called *Luigi's*, while the *Cham Palace* boasts the country's only Chinese restaurant and also its only revolving restaurant (on the fifteenth floor). Not to be outdone the *Meridien* boasts Tex-Mex specialities at *L'Hacienda* and a 1930s-style restaurant with singers and dancers and international cuisine. The Alaa Towers chain also has decent restaurants in four of its hotels; the one on Ath-Thawra Street overlooks the Old City, and there's also a good panoramic view over the city from the tenth floor of the al-Basha Street branch.

The restaurants in the listings below have been categorized as cheap (under S£200 for a main meal), moderate (S£200–400) or expensive (over S£400).

The Old City

The Old City is by far the most atmospheric place to eat, remaining lively until well into the evening. However, some of the restaurants here are pricey, tourist-oriented affairs, where the Western-style muzak and the displays of dancing – usually wild, intrusive, though good-natured performances by some whirling dervishes, wheeled out to amuse the foreigners – may not be to everyone's taste.

Abu al-Azz, in the shoe souk, just north of the triumphal arch in the Hamidiye Souk. Regular Syrian cuisine in a surprisingly bright and roomy interior; occasional live band and whirling dervishes. Cheap.

L'Auberge, Zuheir bin Amr St, just off Straight St halfway between the Roman arch and Bab Sharqi. Excellent pizzas served in a pleasantly intimate interior. Cheap.

Casablanca, Ananias St. Classy place, serving a delicious Western selection, with a rotund pianist in the evening – very busy after 9pm. Disconcertingly, no prices on the menu. Moderate.

La Guitare, Zeitoun St, south off Straight St 100m before Bab Sharqi. Good Italian food; in summer you can eat on the rooftop terrace. Live music in the evenings. Moderate.

Old Damascus, Al-Kallaseh St, near the Citadel. Standard Syrian fare in good clean surroundings with friendly staff. Cheap.

Old Town Music Restaurant, Al-Assiyeh St, off Straight St near the Roman arch. Good Western food and a pianist in the evenings. Moderate.

One Thousand Night And Night, Al-Qaimariyeh St, 150m east of the Umayyad Mosque. Decent but slightly overpriced Middle Eastern food. Music and whirling dervishes in the evenings. Moderate.

Umayyad Palace, signposted off the southeastern corner of the Umayyad Mosque. Pricey joint aimed directly at the tourist trade with its heavily atmospheric Arab decor and traditional Arab buffet. Quite good food though, if you don't mind the imposition of the inevitable whirling dervishes. Moderate.

Zeitoun, Zeitoun St, signposted beyond *La Guitare*. Slightly superior Syrian eaterie with a pleasant courtyard and modestly priced beer. Cheap.

Around Martyrs' Square

This busy part of the New City, where most of the hotels are situated, has a surprisingly poor choice of restaurants. Most of the eateries here are simply cheap places to fill up in and don't serve beer.

Alaa, off the southwest corner of Martyrs' Square. Clean, mirror-strewn eaterie offering standard chicken-and-kebab fare. Cheap.

Al-Amawi, Al-Istiklal St. Predictable food in spruce surroundings with a friendly atmosphere; breakfast available. Cheap.

Al-Arabi, off the southeast corner of Martyrs' Square. This is actually two restaurants, of which the one further up the pedestrianized street is slightly more sassy. Unsurprising Middle Eastern menu, but it's popular with tourists and backpackers. Cheap.

Al-Areisha, next door to the *Alaa*. Bright sit-down option serving the old Syrian favourites. Cheap.

Al-Negma, Rami St. Very popular with locals, and there's an English menu outside for perusal, though you'll find nothing out of the ordinary on it; decent breakfasts available. Cheap.

Sahoul, Al-Istiklal St. Agreeably clean establishment with very friendly service and a predictable menu in English. Enticing selection of afters on display. Cheap.

Around Yousef al-Azmeh Square

Maisaloun St, where there are a number of good choices to suit all tastes and pockets, tends to be the busiest part of the New City at night, as young people patronize its numerous cake shops and ice-cream parlours.

Abou Kamal, first-floor restaurant on Yousef al-Azmeh Square. A class above the ordinary with a healthy and popular selection of tasty Middle Eastern and Western-style dishes. Cheap.

Ali Baba, in the basement underneath the *Abou Kamal* on Yousef al-Azmeh Square. Intricately decorated wood panelling and hanging lanterns provide an atmospheric setting for some pleasing Middle Eastern and European eats. Cheap.

Club D'Orient, Mrewed St. Glitzy five-star establishment for the well-to-do, with a very good reputation. If you're looking for a blowout, this is the place to come. Expensive.

Al-Kamal, 29 May St. Bright spot serving a good basic Western menu, with a Parisian café-style overspill onto the pavement. Meticulous service but slightly over-enthusiastic air conditioning. Cheap.

Le Bistro, Maisaloun St, corner of Al-Brazil St. Part of the *New Umayyad Hotel* and expensive for what you get, though there's a good snack menu for those watching the cash. The place also serves as a bar. The Italian restaurant next door seems permanently shut. Moderate.

Neptune, Mrewed St. Cheerful little place with a small terrace and English menu posted outside. Serves a decent selection of Western foods from chicken kiev to spaghetti, but no beer. Cheap.

Pizza Hat, Maisaloun St, near the Franciscan church. Very popular pizzeria that also does a brisk trade in ice cream. Cheap.

Pizza Roma, just off Maisaloun St, opposite *Pizza Hat*. Good deep-pan pizzas that are very popular with tourists. Cheap.

Rayess, Yousef al-Azmeh St. Mountain lakes and golden beaches form the unlikely pictorial backdrop to your kebab and chips here. The food isn't special but there's a likeable provincial air to the place and they're more than happy if you just want to sit and drink beer. Cheap.

Shimi Patisserie, Maisaloun St. Family-orientated coffee and cake shop, popular with the locals. Cheap.

Snack Aboualic, just off Maisaloun St beyond the Dar es Salam school. Very friendly and good sit-down Western fast-food joint with takeaway service available. Cheap.

Station One, Maisaloun St, near the corner of Al-Jalaa St. Very enjoyable Western food, with the option of a special *plat du jour*, served in a classy ambience – though curiously no beer. It also has a fast-food takeaway section. Moderate.

Zenobia, Maisaloun St, on the first floor of the desolate shopping complex opposite the *Cham*. Dingy location for a five-star establishment, but with a good menu of tasty international cuisine. Expensive.

Salihiye shopping precinct

This is where Damascenes go to do their shopping, and it's not the most fertile hunting ground for good food, though one or two places stand out.

Aram, north side of 8 Azar Square. The rooftop location is the only real draw here, not that there's much to look over. Middle Eastern food. Cheap.

Reef, Al-Jalaa St, corner of Omar ibn Abdul Aziz St. Highly recommended, good-value menu of Eastern and Western grub with the odd Japanese speciality thrown in for good measure. Moderate.

Al-Shallal, Moustafa ash-Shehabi St, opposite Al-Arsouzi Park. Good Middle Eastern cuisine but slightly out of the way. Cheap.

Top, at the roundabout where Abdel Rahman Ghafiki St and Al-Malek al-Adel St meet. One of the brightest and best pizza/fast-food places, tucked away under ground level. Cheap.

Restaurant Circle and the diplomatic quarter

At the heart of the most affluent part of Damascus, Restaurant Circle, off Abdel Malek ibn Marwan St, is a small green around which are a number of establishments of varying quality and price.

Aldar, off Khalil Mardam St, by Aj-Jahez Park. Coffee shop with a limited menu of pizza, hamburger and steak. Takeaway available. Cheap.

La Chaumiere, Restaurant Circle. Selection of Arab and Western dishes with a good reputation for its seafood and *mezze*. Moderate.

Le Chevalier, Restaurant Circle. Overpriced French menu (in French, and no prices either) catering mainly for diplomats; a good choice of fish. Expensive.

Joy, Restaurant Circle. Varied menu, including recommended *mezze*. Pianist in the evenings. Expensive.

Pizza Bundukie, Restaurant Circle. Recommended pizzas in a friendly, laid-back atmosphere. Cheap.

Toledo Tea Room, Khalil Mardam St. Coffee, beer and ice cream, in a select location with vehemently red decor. Good place to chill out. Cheap.

Vendome, Restaurant Circle. Decent choice of Eastern and Western dishes, and you can sit either inside or out. Moderate.

Versailles, on the semicircular green off Shawki St. Excellent European food. Moderate.

Palais des Nobles

This strange place on the south side of Shoukry al-Qouwatly Street near the Al-Umawyeen roundabout was built as an upmarket cultural complex of sorts, with a few restaurants, some function rooms and a couple of theatres. There's a reasonably good cheap outdoor pizzeria called the *Pizza Pino* which does a good thin-crust version, though the only company you're likely to have here are the stray cats. Indoors choose between an expensive Middle Eastern restaurant with an S£880 flat fee (excluding drink), and à la carte in a similarly expensive French restaurant, which is set in a mock garden installed inside something which is supposed to resemble the palace at Versailles. The place only really gets busy during the International Trade Fair (the last two weeks of August), whose grounds are next door.

Cafés and bars

Hubble-bubble cafés proliferate around Damascus; the best ones to head for are those by the eastern gate of the Umayyad Mosque, the *Ash-Sham* and the *Al-Nofara*. The latter even has a story-teller in the early evenings, a tradition common before the arrival of radio and television. In the New City there are a couple of less atmospheric *nargileh* spots on Moutanabby Street: the one on the corner of Port Said Street is good for an early morning coffee, while the other much larger establishment gets busy in the evenings. For a more **Western-style** ambience and coffee, head for *Le Terrace* on the top floor of *Le Piano Bar* on Ananias St in the Old City, or to one of the international hotels.

Although many restaurants are generally happy for you to sit and drink beer into the evening after your meal, or indeed in place of a meal (though the bill may well be upped by thirty percent if no food is eaten), proper **drinking holes** are scarce. Your best bet is probably the bar at the Hedjaz Station, which serves cheap beer (S£50) inside the restored Ottoman train carriage permanently parked there (see p.75). The *Karnik*, off Martyrs' Square next to the *Siyaha Hotel*, is populated mainly by holidaying Arabs come to loosen up, but it may be useful in that most restaurants around Martyrs' Square are dry and it doesn't shut until around 1am. *Le Piano Bar* on Ananias Street in the Old City (closes 2am) is a popular and lively place with MTV on the telly, spirited karaoke in the evenings and even a sign above the door indicating when the place is full, though at S£140 for a Barada this is an expensive place for a tipple. In theory couples only are admitted, but if you turn up before the place has filled you should be OK. Of course, all the more expensive hotels have bars selling imported European beer; the *Sheraton* even has a "genuine" English pub with red letter- and phone boxes, and draught bitter (open until 2am).

Nightlife and entertainment

Although its restaurants and few bars stay open until the early hours, Damascus is not the place to go looking for a night out, and by Egyptian, Israeli or Lebanese standards the nightlife is very quiet. **Nightclubs** are rather sordid affairs, featuring floor shows for boozy visitors, and definitely not a place where single women would feel comfortable. Shows tend to be cabaret acts, featuring belly-dancing and the like, which you sit and watch at a table with a drink and maybe some snack food – there's no Western nightclub-style dancing or live music on offer. The flashing neon, tatty decor and sycophantically attentive service may hold a certain kitsch fascination, if nothing else. Western-style **discos** are sometimes staged by the big hotels, but if they don't like the look of you they might tell you they're only for guests; Eastern European prostitutes tend to hang around the doors at closing time. The **theatre** or **cinema** may provide a more engaging diversion, but it's difficult to find out what's on; most of the time you'll just have to turn up at venues yourself to ask.

Nightclubs

Generally these places charge admission and seem to be open from about 9pm for drinks, with the floor show beginning a couple of hours later.

Juhara, Port Said St. Take the steps up to the entrance from a passageway leading off the street. Waiter service makes for a classier ambience than other venues. S£300.

Moulin Rouge, 29 May St. Pictures of fat cabaret singers and "glitzy" dancers by the entrance may put you off this one. Aloof staff, lurid green decor. 11pm start. S£400.

Semiramis, Salihiye St. Dingy, sweaty place on the street running northwest from Yousef al-Azmeh Square. Simply follow the neon into a subterranean world of sleaze (S£450). The *Casa,* a very similar place but with a more limited range of drinks, is next door (S£250).

Super N.C., Al-Jaberee St. A decent variety of drinks on offer, with a programme of dancing and cabaret in more tasteful surroundings than other places listed here. Credit cards taken. S£450.

Al-Wassim, 29 May St. Enticingly sleazy-looking premises with attractive goldfish in the foyer and unattractive bouncer on the door. Early 10pm kick-off for the cabaret. S£350.

Cinema and theatre

There are dingy, threadbare **cinemas** all around Martyrs' Square: wander around for ten minutes and you'll encounter half-a-dozen, all showing the same Kung-Fu/Jackie Chan pap; ticket prices are around S£25. The best cinema in Damascus by far is in the *Cham Palace* (separate entrance on Maisaloun St), which shows many English-language films (subtitled in French and Arabic) in pleasant surroundings, with good-quality sound and projection; here tickets cost up to S£100. All the city's **cultural centres** (see p.89 for addresses) show films on a regular basis. As for **theatres**, there are two at the western end of Shoukry al-Qouwatly Street, near the *Sheraton,* which put on plays and concerts staged by touring Arab pop singers.

Listings

Airlines Most airlines maintain offices in the New City, between the Hedjaz Station and Yousef al-Azmeh Square. On Maisaloun St opposite the *Cham Palace* are Lufthansa (☎011/221 9513); Austrian Airlines (☎011/223 6001); Pakistan International (☎011/221 1581); Gulf Air (☎011/224 4203); and Iran Air (☎011/222 6431). LOT Polish Airlines (☎011/221 3441) and Balkan Bulgarian Airlines (☎011/221 7112) face each other across Yousef al-Azmeh Square, and on Fardoos St, a block south, you'll find Malev Hungarian Airlines (☎011/222 7944), CSA Czech Airlines (☎011/222 5804) and KLM (☎011/221 3395). Aeroflot (☎011/442 7956) and Royal Jordanian (☎011/442 8112) face each other on 29 May St. Air France (☎011/221 8580) is in the *Semiramis Hotel* building on Al-Jaberee St. British Airways (☎011/331 0000), also representing British Mediterranean Airways (the Damascus route operator) and Qantas, is on Argentina St by the north end of the flyover. Nahas Travel and Tourism on Fardoos St (☎011/223 2000) represents a number of airlines which do not fly into Damascus, including TWA and Air Canada. Syrianair has a number of offices: their international office is opposite the Hedjaz Station, with another office by the Central Bank (Baghdad St) which deals with internal and international flights (☎011/223 2154 for both offices).

Airport bus Half-hourly departures daily 5.30am–midnight from outside the *Kairouan Hotel* on Al-Ittihad St; journey time 35min, S£10.

American Express Their agent, offering very limited Amex services, is the Kaeou Shaar Group located in the Sudan Airlines office on the road linking Fardoos St and Al-Moutanabby St (☎011/221 7813); the address is PO Box 1373, Damascus. It is not possible to obtain cash using your card, nor can you buy travellers' cheques; they will hold post for you, though.

Arabic language courses Try the French cultural centre (see below), or the Arabic Teaching Institute for Foreigners, Villat Sharkiyah, Mezzeh, Jadet al-Shafei No. 3, PO Box 9340, Damascus (☎011/222 1538). For further information, see p.45.

Banks Convenient branches of the Commercial Bank of Syria are on Yousef al-Azmeh Square and on Al-Jaberee St, by the pedestrian footbridge. Both are open daily except Fri

8.30am–12.30pm, and will change cash and travellers' cheques. The booth outside the Yousef al-Azmeh Square branch is open 8.30am–7pm daily except Fri, but only changes cash. If you get stuck, head for the branches at the *Sheraton* or *Meridien* hotels, which open on Fridays and in the afternoons, and don't mind changing money for non-guests (cash or travellers' cheques). The branch at the airport stays open daily 24hr and changes cash and travellers' cheques.

Bookshops Damascus abounds in bookstores, but the only English books you'll find on sale in most of them are dictionaries and computer manuals. Bookshops in the *Meridien*, *Sheraton* and *Cham Palace* hotels stock novels, guidebooks, newspapers, maps and postcards. Specialist bookshops include Avicenne, just off Maisaloun St, on a road running between *New Umayyad* and *Fardoss Tower* hotels (daily except Fri 9am–2pm & 4.30–8.30pm), which sells English and French novels (with plenty of Penguins and Picadors), guidebooks, children's books, periodicals and newspapers. The Family Bookshop, on An-Majlis an-Nyaby St, just west of the Franciscan church and Dar es Salam school, has an excellent selection of English fiction, including stacks of Penguins; also periodicals and newspapers. On Yousef al-Azmeh St is the Librarie Universelle where you'll find a limited choice of American, French and English paperbacks, both fiction and non-fiction.

Camera shops Try Carmen Photo on the pedestrian mall opposite the People's Assembly on Salihiye St, or Pluto Photo Services on Maisaloun St, up past the *Cham Palace Hotel*. Both do developing and printing and sell new cameras, and can advise you on camera repair.

Car rental Europcar maintains offices at the airport and at big hotels; their downtown office is on Musab Ibn Uner St (☎011/212 0624). Other major firms are Budget, Felasteen St (☎011/212 2220); Avis, Al-Rawabi Co., Othman bin Affan St (☎011/223 0880); and Chamcar at the *Cham Palace Hotel* (☎011/223 2300). Most require several days' notice before they can have a car ready for you.

Car repairs A number of car repair shops specializing in European models cluster around the Pullman station in northern Damascus, close to (and signposted from) the main Damascus–Homs motorway.

Thomas Cook Represented by Nahas Travel on Fardoos St (daily 8am–7pm). They can get Thomas Cook to send them money, which you then pay for with a Visa card – the only way of using a credit card to withdraw cash in Syria. The process takes a couple of hours.

Cultural centres The British Council is at the north end of Al-Jalaa St (☎011/33 8436); the American Cultural Center (☎011/333 8443) is just off Al-Mansour St, in a leafy villa-lined street just up from the US embassy. Both show films (look at the noticeboards inside to see what's on), and the American Cultural Center has a library (S£100 non-borrowing membership, S£500 borrowing), where you can sit and read *Newsweek* or watch CNN to your heart's content. The Institut Français is opposite the *Alaa Towers Hotel* in a short street leading east off Yousef al-Azmeh St, and the Goethe Institut can be found just off Maisaloun St; both put on films and concerts, but are closed July and August.

Dentists Emergency treatment is available at the Shamy Diplomatic Hospital (see "Hospitals"); for less urgent treatment, ask your embassy for a list of recommended dentists.

Embassies Australia, Faraby St, 6km west of city centre off the Beirut road (☎011/666 4317); Britain, Mohammad Kourd Ali St (☎011/371 2561); Canada, 4km west of city centre on the Beirut road (☎011/611 4000); Jordan, Al-Jalaa St (☎011/333 4642); Netherlands, Al-Mansour St (☎011/333 6871); Norway, Adnan Malki St (☎011/333 7114); Sweden, Shakib Arsalan St (☎011/332 7261); US, Al-Mansour St (☎011/333 2315). New Zealand and the Irish Republic do not maintain embassies in Syria and their citizens should enquire at the British embassy if they need consular assistance. Most embassies are open from 8am to 2pm and are closed Fri & Sat, plus Syrian public holidays and national public holidays of the country concerned.

Emergencies Police ☎112, ambulance ☎110, fire ☎113, traffic police ☎115.

Hospitals The main hospital for foreigners is the Shamy Diplomatic Hospital on Jawaher al-Nahro St, northwest of the city centre. Here you will be assured of prompt and excellent service from English-speaking medics; a consultation with a doctor will cost you $25 (you can pay in Syrian pounds).

Opticians Two good opticians face each other across the small street running off Salihiye St by the People's Assembly.

Pharmacy The best in Damascus is the Kanawati Principale on Yousef al-Azmeh Square.

Phones and faxes Public coin-operated phones will only connect you with numbers in Damascus. The big new Telephone Services Centre (daily 8am–10pm) is by the Hedjaz Station on An-Naser St. Phonecards are available here and there are two cardphone booths along the road heading away from the Hedjaz Station, on the right. Alternatively, make a timed call from the centre and pay when you're done. You can also send a fax from here – S£200 for the first page, S£100 for each further page, to Europe, North America or Australasia.

Post office The central post office is on Al-Jaberee St (Mon–Thurs, Sat & Sun 8am–7pm, Fri 8am–1pm). For parcels, use the other entrance around the corner. The poste restante counter is on the far left as you enter the main hall; it's the only one in Damascus, so your letters shouldn't get lost. If you're an Amex customer, you can have mail sent to their office (see above).

Swimming pools The *Cham Palace*, *Meridien* and *Sheraton* hotels will let non-guests use their outdoor pools for around S£500. There's a huge public indoor pool (part of the Tichreen Sports Complex) on Musab ibn Umer St, which you can use for S£50.

Travel agencies Most are on Port Said St, Yousef al-Azmeh St and the small alleyways linking them. Services include airline bookings and car rental, but don't expect to find any youth, discount or student-orientated agencies.

West of Damascus

Although the **Barada River** as it flows through Damascus is nowadays little more than a rubbish-strewn ditch, it is an ancient and fabled river, celebrated in II Kings 5 as having curative properties superior even to the rivers of Israel. If the marsh near Damascus Airport into which the river drains makes for something of an ignominious lower end, its source region, in the **Anti-Lebanon mountains** northwest of the capital, is altogether more inspiring. The landscape around the Barada headwaters is wild and barren, consisting in the main of rocky mountain ridges broken by narrow valleys forged by tributaries of the Barada. **Burqush** sits atop one of these ridges, a remote Byzantine and Roman site where the remains of a sixth-century basilica are set in stunning scenery. Easier to get to are **Zabadani** and **Bloudane**, two bland resort towns linked to the capital by narrow-gauge rail line, where there's nothing much to do except savour the clean air and relaxed atmosphere.

Zabadani and Bloudane

Zabadani, 45km northwest of Damascus, and its higher neighbour Bloudane are shamelessly summer-orientated resorts where Syrians and foreign visitors come simply to cool off; there's nothing specific to see, and in the cooler months there's not a lot of point coming here. In truth, half the fun of visiting the area is travelling on the rickety train which makes the twice-weekly journey up from the capital; if that's something which doesn't appeal, or if the train isn't running, then you probably won't find an excursion here worthwhile.

Of the two resorts, **ZABADANI** is larger and busier, the terminus of the narrow-gauge trains but actually a fairly dull place, its shops full of tourist kitsch and its restaurants blaring Western pop music at full volume. If you've made it all the way up here, it's better to continue on to **BLOUDANE**, a smaller, quieter resort accessible on a steep, winding seven-kilometre road from Zabadani; microbuses congregate by the train station. One of the springs in Bloudane provides the water bottled as Boukein, the most widespread mineral-water brand available in Syria. The air is fantastically clean up here, and the views (far superior to those in Zabadani) encompass the whole of the upper Barada valley, as far as the Beka Valley across the border in Lebanon. If you have some spare cash, you can quite happily spend it on a drink or meal in the *Grand Hotel*, whose outdoor terrace restaurant is probably the best situated of any in Syria.

Souk Wadi Barada

The route the train takes up to Zabadani goes through **SOUK WADI BARADA**, a fairly ordinary, though picturesquely situated town where some minor ruin-spotting is possible. Immediately north of the settlement the rail line and road pass through a tunnel and a steep gorge, on whose upper slopes you can see (from a vehicle or the train) remains of Roman rock-cut burial caves (accessible by a bit of tricky scrambling) and a cutting, dug into a terrace on the mountainside, which once carried the Roman road from Baalbek to Damascus. Remains are scant, the road having been washed away on many occasions by the floods which it was supposedly constructed to avoid, and really there is very little to see here. The Romans knew Souk Wadi Barada as **Abilia**, after Abel, supposedly murdered here by Cain and buried on a summit to the west at a spot now marked by a Druze holy place; the buildings in the modern town utilize pieces of Roman masonry left over from ancient Abilia, of which nothing now remains. Microbuses up to Zabadani and Bloudane don't pass through here, so it's only worth considering stopping off here if you're travelling by car; if that's the case, you should use the route via Dummar to reach Zabadani, which will take you through Souk Wadi Barada and the gorge.

Practicalities

The narrow-gauge **rail line** is served by a train sardonically nicknamed "The Zabadani Flyer", which operates occasionally (currently only on Fridays, Tuesdays and public holidays; S£30 one-way) from the Hedjaz Station in the centre of Damascus. Hauled by century-old steam engines built in Switzerland, the train, when it runs, takes three hours to struggle up to Zabadani, jammed with families laden with food for their day out. The first part of the journey is along tracks laid tramline-style through the streets of Damascus, with the train hair-raisingly competing for space with the usual jumble of trucks, horse-drawn carts and perpetually hooting taxis and private cars. Beyond the city limits the line hugs the valley side, coping with steep rock outcrops and narrow gullies by a bewildering succession of bridges, tunnels and cuttings; so infrequent are the trains that locals use the tracks as a parking lot for their cars and trucks, and passengers are roped in at regular intervals to move offending vehicles if their owners fail to respond to the train's fierce whistling. With only one service there and back on operating days (currently leaving Damascus around 8am and returning from Zabadani at 2pm), there's no possibility of breaking your journey at Souk Wadi Barada, and not a great deal of time to look round Bloudane or Zabadani – unless you take a microbus back, much later in the day. The line continues beyond Zabadani to Beirut, and may be reopened one day, although the track suffered from bombing during the Lebanese civil war and is still in a far from usable state.

Duller, faster and more frequent are the **microbuses** (S£20; 1hr) which depart for the resorts from the bus station at the eastern end of Felasteen Street in

Damascus, a ten-minute walk south of the National Museum; microbuses serving Bloudane do not pass through Zabadani, which is actually no bad thing. The quickest route **by road** is to take the motorway towards Beirut (signposted from the centre of Damascus), turning off to Zabadani shortly before the Lebanese border; if you're driving up to the resorts – by whatever route – then you might want to investigate one of the many small **restaurants** which have sprung up along the roadside, attractively situated on the valley slopes and good for a drink or cheap meal.

Most people head up this way for no more than a day-trip, but if you're considering the possibility of staying over, you can certainly pass over the claims of drab Zabadani in favour of its loftier neighbour. The first two **hotels** you come to in **Bloudane** face each other across an open square. The *Akel* is a characterless, modern place with a grumpy owner, but the rooms are decent (☎013/228604; ④). The *Grand* is a much classier hotel, with tennis courts, an open-air swimming pool and a restaurant with fabulous views across the valley (☎013/227551; ⑦). A five-minute walk up the main road from these hotels is the much cheaper *Al-Sahl al-Akhdar*, a small place with a genial owner and some balcony rooms with a view (☎013/238526; ②).

Burqush

The border between Syria and Lebanon, to the west of Damascus, is a sensitive area, so travel in the region is hampered by military activity, road blocks and the presence of numerous no-go areas. The most obvious place to head for is **Burqush**, the site of fairly scant Roman and Byzantine ruins within 5km of the border, beyond the town of **QATANA** which itself is 26km west of Damascus. There are plenty of microbuses and buses from Damascus out to Qatana (use the depot next to the Karnak bus station in the city centre), and it's perfectly possible to drive there from the capital (use the Quneitra turning off the main Beirut road), but once there things become difficult. You'll need to arrange a taxi in the town to get you any further, as local drivers will be best placed to negotiate military road blocks and cope with the complete lack of signposting; at any point in your journey you might find yourself joined by a soldier as an escort. Burqush is situated well away from metalled roads and can only be reached by a thirty-minute walk up a steep hill from a farm track.

The main focus of the site is a ruined sixth-century **Byzantine basilica**, built above a narrow ridge of mountainside, flattened off to form a plateau – it's difficult to fathom how anyone got the enormous blocks used to build the three-aisled structure up here. The basilica was built on the podium of a former Roman temple, thought to date from the first century AD, and itself constructed on a site used for religious purposes for at least four hundred years prior to that. On all sides there are more blocks, some jumbled around like bizarre geological outcrops, others recognizably the outlines of buildings: the most obvious of these, 100m to the north of the basilica, form the base of the semicircular apse of another former Roman temple. The superb views from the basilica encompass the desolate border region on the lower slopes of Mount Hermon.

Northeast of Damascus

If you've arrived in Syria by air and have seen nothing of the country bar the bustling souks and choked streets of Damascus, you may well be ready for a jaunt out to the small, historic towns to the northeast of the capital. Two of these, **Sednaya** and **Maalula**, are Christian enclaves up in the Anti-Lebanon mountains, the former a popular pilgrimage centre dominated by a large convent, the latter a much more characterful town, huddled dramatically beneath an escarpment and famed for its use of Aramaic, the language spoken by Jesus. **Dmeir** is a former Roman settlement out in the desert on the road to Palmyra, which grew up on the intersection of two major caravan routes, its main attraction being a brilliantly pre-served temple.

Each of the three towns is an easy day-trip from Damascus. Sednaya can be reached in forty minutes by a frequent **microbus** service from the Bilal Square station in Damascus. Microbuses to Maalula from the same station are less fre-quent, and the journey takes just under an hour. No buses cover the 25km between Sednaya and Maalula, so to combine the two in one visit, you'd need to hire a microbus or taxi for around S£300. Microbuses to Dmeir from the depot on Abbasid Square in Damascus take just under an hour. If you get stuck, there are a couple of cheap **hotels** signposted in the centre of Sednaya, and in Maalula the four-star Safir (☎012/770250; ⑦) designed to cater for tour groups, but there are no hotels in Dmeir.

Sednaya

High in the barren hills 27km north of Damascus lies the small Christian settle-ment of **SEDNAYA**, crowned by the castle-like **Convent of Our Lady**. A steady flow of chattering pilgrims is drawn to the convent by its miracle-working image of the Virgin, said to have been painted from life by St Luke for whom, it seems, Mary was an habitual sitter. Legend further has it that the convent is situated on the spot where Noah planted the first vine after the Flood, and indeed the town still produces its own sickly-sweet wine, though it's not particularly recommend-ed. The convent was established in 547 when, during his wars with the Persians, Justinian and his army were encamped here, and it's no surprise to learn that a miracle has become attached to its foundation, too. The story goes that while he was out hunting a deer the emperor was suddenly overwhelmed by a bright light; the deer then changed into a woman dressed in white who commanded him to build a church and convent on the site, and this he did, installing his sister as the first mother superior.

It's not known when the icon of the Virgin was brought here, but a succession of miracles associated with St Luke's handiwork during the Middle Ages turned the place into the most popular pilgrimage centre in the Middle East after Jerusalem. According to *The Voyage of Sir John Maundevile*, the most widely read travel guide to these parts in the fourteenth century, the icon turned to flesh on a regular basis and a nearby river used only to flow on Saturdays. With such an astonishing press it's hardly surprising that not all visitors were impressed by what they found. Henry Maundrell, writing in 1697, remarked with horror that the convent was "possessed by twenty Greek monks and forty nuns who seem to live promiscuously together, without order or separation", although he did com-ment favourably on the "most excellent" local wine. Today the Greek Orthodox Church runs the place, having wrested control from the Greek Catholics some two hundred years ago.

The convent **complex** itself is rather maze-like, with stairways winding all over the vine-covered courtyards leading eventually up to the roof and some splendid views over the town and down onto the arid plain below. Chock-full of icons dating from as far back as the fifth century, the centrepiece **Chapel of the Virgin** is usually very busy, particularly on the main pilgrimage day, September 8. The reputation of the icon has had the curious effect of attracting a large number of Muslims to the shrine, particularly on Fridays, and the chapel is about as touristy a place as you'll find anywhere in Syria.

Most of Sednaya's twenty **other churches** are modern buildings, though between the convent and the microbus station is a small, square Roman construction which has been converted into a church dedicated to St Peter. Particularly striking is its refurbished door, constructed by placing a slab of stone in the old doorway and cutting a smaller hole out of it to ensure that worshippers would have to bow upon entering. In the escarpment opposite the town are a number of **caves** used by the early Christians, though you would need to arrange for a guide from the convent to get inside them. About 2km to the north of the town along a rough road is the **Convent of St Thomas**, another converted Roman monument, with a great view and a large grotto, thought to have served either as a burial chamber or possibly a meeting place for priests.

Maalula

Nestled in a harsh landscape 58km away from the Damascene city bustle, **MAALULA** is probably the most enchanting town in Syria, its attractive pastel-coloured houses climbing the slopes of a dramatic escarpment. Yet besides its striking location, Maalula is also famed as an extraordinary pocket of Christianity, for not only is this small settlement packed with tiny churches, as well as a large monastery, but this is also one of the very few places in the world where **Aramaic** is still spoken.

The Monastery of St Tekla

The Damascus **microbus** usually drops off at the small roundabout in the centre of town; from here take the right fork as it winds up the hill to the **Monastery of St Tekla**. Tekla was reputedly a follower of St Paul and one of the first Christian martyrs: the story goes that upon conversion to the new faith she broke off her engagement in order to be able to devote herself to God, but her fiancé out of revenge had her flogged and then sentenced to death by burning. Tekla was, however, saved by a thunderstorm, managing to escape and eventually finding sanctuary in a cave here where she is said to be buried.

Whether Tekla even existed or not is open to serious question, and even if she did a more popular legend has her buried in Silifke in Turkey. The monastery itself is uncompromisingly modern but its snug location under the cliff is impressive. Inside the complex you can climb up and see Tekla's reputed **grotto**, where sacred water trickles from the ceiling, said to be a cure for flatulence.

Beyond the monastery

Walk on beyond the monastery and you'll soon find yourself in a narrow gorge, said to have been formed miraculously: whilst fleeing from the pagans, Tekla prayed for help, and the mountain which barred her passage split, letting her through. Where the gorge ends turn left up and beyond the incongruous four-star *Safir Hotel* to the Greek Catholic monastery. Inside, you'll find the **Church of St**

Sergius, an intimate early fourth-century structure, containing icons dating to the thirteenth century. Its unusual early Christian altar has a seven-centimetre rim around it, which reflects the traditional form of a pagan altar – this would have been used to prevent the loss of blood during sacrifice.

Cut into the hillside beyond this are a number of litter-strewn **caves** thought to have been used in the Stone Age, and known to have been in use, whether for living, worship or burial, in the first few centuries AD. Follow the road back on down to the village and the roundabout from where you can pick up a microbus back to Damascus; on the way you pass some more caves cut into the opposing rock face, some of which may be accessed by dodgy-looking ladders.

Dmeir

DMEIR is a dusty, inconsequential sort of place today, but during the Roman period it was an important fortified post standing at the crossroads of the Homs–Palmyra and Damascus–Resafe caravan routes. One remarkable remnant survives from this period, the **Temple of Zeus Hypsistos**, still intact up to roof level. The temple is in the centre of town, just beyond the main crossroads to your right, standing in a hole some five metres deep; it's usually kept locked but ask around for the key.

Numerous inscriptions survive on the monument, one of which dates it to 245 AD; carved portraits in relief in the interior may be of Philip the Arab, the emperor at the time, and his wife. The discovery of an altar (now in Paris) dedicated to the Semitic sky god Baal-Shamin suggests that this site was used earlier by the Nabateans, in the first century AD. The temple later served as a Christian church and then as an Arab fortress, and indeed the locals sometimes refer to it as the *qalaat*.

A couple of kilometres east of Dmeir, by the side of the main road and right next to an air-force base, are the scant remains of a late second-century **Roman military camp**. There's precious little of substance to see apart from a few crumbling walls and a lot of fallen masonry, but it's a small detour if you have your own transport.

travel details

BUSES AND MICROBUSES

Buses and microbuses use different terminals in the city according to vehicle type and destinations served. The Karnak and International bus terminals are a ten-minute walk away from Martyrs' Square; to get to the other depots, you'll need to use a taxi, or take a microbus from the city depot by the National Museum.

Microbuses and local buses

Most **microbuses heading north and east** depart from the depot on Abbasid Square, marked on maps and generally known as *Abbasayeen*, 3km east of the city centre. Though uncomfortable over long distances, this is the cheapest way to travel if you're looking to save every pound. The highest fare you'll pay is about S£180 to Qamishli (9–10hr), while Aleppo costs S£80 (6hr) and the more bearable hop to Homs S£40 (2hr 30min). Other destinations served include Deir ez-Zur (7–8hr), Dmeir (1hr), Hama (3hr), Latakia (6hr) and Tartous (4hr). A small depot on An-Nasera Street by Bilal Square, south of the Abbasid Stadium in east Damascus, handles microbuses out to Maalula (55min) and Sednaya (40min).

Nearly all **microbuses heading south** use the depot next to Yarmouk Square; destinations served include Dera, Ezra, Shahba and Sweida (all 1hr–1hr 30min; for Bosra, see below). Clattery old buses also operate from this depot out to the same destinations, taking slightly longer and costing slightly less.

Microbuses heading west to Bloudane, Zabadani (both 1hr) and other destinations such as Qatana (1hr) in the mountains west of Damascus use the microbus station next to the Karnak bus station, a couple of hundred metres south of the National Museum and walkable from the city centre. Buses and microbuses to Bosra (2hr) and Quneitra (1hr) also depart from here, though you'll have to get a permit to go to the latter destination (see p.117).

Karnak buses

Government-run **Karnak buses** leave from the dedicated station on Al-Imam Muslim Street, south of the National Museum, and walkable from the centre. Karnak has an information line (☎011/212 2499) and an office in the centre on Port Said St (daily except Fri 8am–1pm), but you can't buy tickets there and staff give consistently unreliable information. As a comparison the fare to Aleppo is S£110 and to Homs S£50.

Destinations include: Aleppo (4 daily; 5hr); Amman (4 daily; 4hr); Beirut (5 daily; 4hr); Dera (1 daily; 1hr 30min); Hama (4 daily; 2hr 30min); Homs (6 daily; 2hr); Latakia (1 daily; 5hr); Palmyra (1 daily; 4hr); Safita (1 daily; 3hr); Sweida (1 daily; 1hr 30min); Tartous (1 daily; 3hr 30min).

Pullman buses

Private **Pullman bus** operators running to destinations within Syria operate from a huge, recently built garage on the northern edge of Damascus, just off the Homs motorway, a good 5km or so from the centre. A few of the operators have offices in the centre of town: Al-Aliah are always reliable and have an outlet on Felasteen St; Damas Tour has an office in the city microbus terminal next to the National Museum. Most destinations in Syria are covered; sample fares are S£160 to Aleppo (5hr), S£80 to Homs (2hr) and S£350 to Qamishli (9hr).

International buses

The **International Bus Station** is the most central of all the depots, at the western end of the Shoukry al-Qouwatly Street flyover, on the north side of the dual carriageway; it's actually a collection of offices advertising the services of competing operators, which makes it easy to shop around for what you want. This is the place to go to pick up top-of-the-range, air-conditioned private coaches for journeys into Turkey, Lebanon, Jordan, Egypt and Saudi Arabia (though note that Karnak buses also serve Amman and Beirut from their own depot).

SERVICE TAXIS

Service taxis, seating up to six people, use a depot adjacent to the Karnak Bus terminal, 300m south of the National Museum. Destinations served in Syria include Aleppo (5hr; S£500 per person), Hama (3hr; S£300) and Homs (2hr; S£250), but with good bus transport to these places, you're unlikely to feel the need to use them. Service taxis are much more useful for travelling out of Syria, as they regularly serve Amman (5hr; S£500), Beirut (3hr; S£400) and other major centres in northern Jordan and in Lebanon.

TRAINS

Chemins de Fer Syriennes (CFS) operate mainline **trains** out of **Kadem Station** in southwest Damascus to Aleppo (6hr) via Homs and Hama, Tartous (5hr) and Latakia (7hr), and Qamishli (15–16hr) via Deir ez-Zur. Services do not bear much relation to what is advertised in the *Thomas Cook Overseas Timetable* and you should enquire at the booking office in the Hedjaz Station in central Damascus for details of current services (usually one train a day to Aleppo, one a week to the other destinations). The Qamishli service is overnight and carries first-class sleepers (S£800). CFS operates a free bus out to Kadem Station from the Hedjaz Station, timed to leave before major departures.

CFS also operate a twice-weekly train from the **Hedjaz Station** south to Ezra (2hr) and Dera (4hr); one of these services carries on to Amman (9hr). Trains to Zabadani operate from the same station twice a week (3hr).

DOMESTIC FLIGHTS

Syrianair operates **flights** from Damascus International Airport to Aleppo (2–3 daily), Deir ez-Zur (2 weekly), Latakia (1 weekly) and Qamishli (3 weekly); all flight times are under ninety minutes. See p.88 for details of Damascus booking offices and the airport bus.

CHAPTER TWO

THE HAURAN AND THE GOLAN HEIGHTS

R oads running south from Damascus pass at first through fertile agricultural country, across plains of wheat where nothing interrupts the flat horizon apart from huge grain silos. A speciality of the region is watermelon, sold along the roadside off wooden tables groaning with the weight of the huge fruits. Gradually, however, the countryside becomes desolate and barren, as fruit farms and fertile cropfields give way to some of the starkest and emptiest desert in Syria.

This is the **Hauran**, an area of rough steppe and grassland interspersed with strange basalt formations, which stretches across the border into Jordan. It was from these black rocks that the Romans built their desert garrison and trading settlement at **Bosra** which, with its well-preserved streets and magnificent theatre, is by far most important attraction of the region. With fast, easy connections linking Bosra with Damascus, it's quite possible to see nowhere else in the Hauran and still come away satisfied. However, the other, less accessible sights in the region are attractive for their very remoteness, and would justify a longer stay. On the way to **Dera**, the only place where it's possible to cross the **Jordanian border**, you'll find a Byzantine church at **Ezra**, the supposed burial place of St George. **Sweida**, northeast of Bosra and rather cut off from the rest of the Hauran, is a good place to head for if you're looking for somewhere more unusual, with an outstanding **museum** and some interesting ruins to visit nearby at **Qanawat** and **Shahba**.

Shepherds, traders and cultivators have formed the backbone of traditional life in the Hauran, which has led a largely quiet life through peaceful occupation by the Greeks, Nabateans, Romans, Byzantines and Arabs. The major interruption to the peace came with the **Battle of Yarmouk River**, fought in 636 AD near Dera, which marked the end of Byzantine rule in Syria and the introduction of Islam to

ACCOMMODATION PRICE CODES

In this book, all hotels have been categorized according to the **price codes** outlined below. They represent the minimum you can expect to pay for a **double room** in each hotel; for further details, see p.31.

① under S£300/US$7.50
② S£300–600/US$7.50–15
③ S£600–1000/US$15–25
④ S£1000–1400/US$25–35

⑤ US$35–50/S£1400–2000
⑥ US$50–90/S£2000–3600
⑦ US$90–130/S£3600–5200
⑧ US$130 and over/S£5200 and over

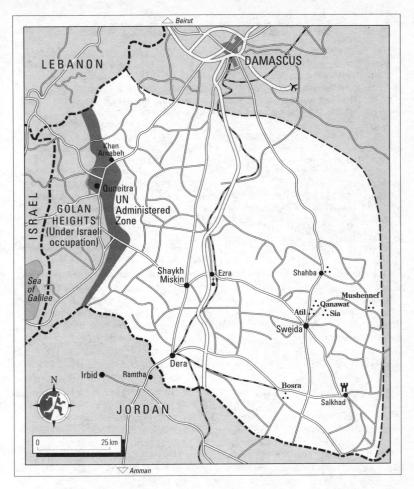

the country by the new Arab rulers who invaded from the south. Since then, nothing of any great historical note has occurred here, unlike the **Golan Heights**, the mountainous area southwest of Damascus which has been the focus of fierce dispute for over thirty years. In the demilitarized zone here, it's possible to make an unusual and unforgettable visit to the ghost town of **Quneitra**, razed by Israeli soldiers in 1973.

The southwestern Hauran

A fast highway and breathtakingly slow rail line head south of Damascus to **Dera**, 104km away, but only a detour to the Byzantine church at **Ezra**, reached after some 75km of monotonous travelling, might tempt you off the train or

THE BATTLE OF YARMOUK RIVER

The **Battle of Yarmouk River**, signalling the end of over six hundred years of Roman/Byzantine rule in the Middle East, is one of the most important events in Syrian, and indeed Arab, history. The beginnings of the Arab triumph go back to 629 when a band of three thousand raided the town of Mutah at the southern end of the Dead Sea. What appeared at the time to be just another Bedouin raid turned out to be the first shot in a war that would not end until Byzantium finally surrendered in 1453. In 630 Mohammed personally led a successful expedition to the oasis of Tabuk, and subsequent negotiations saw the capitulation of a number of towns stretching into southern Syria. After Mohammed's death, the Arabs under the first Caliph Abu-Bakr undertook a full-scale invasion of Syria, which culminated in 636 at Yarmouk River. The Byzantine forces were manoeuvred into a tight position between the Yarmouk and its tributary the Ruqqad and, with the Ruqqad bridge controlled by the Arabs, the Byzantine eastern line of communication was cut and victory sealed. Most of the defeated army was slaughtered and Emperor Heraclius declared, "Farewell, O Syria, and what an excellent country this is for the enemy."

road. Indeed, there's really not much reason to stop in Dera, aside from using it as a base from which to tackle the border crossing to Jordan at Ramtha (crossing the border at Sama is not possible, despite appearances to the contrary on many maps) or to visit Bosra; your fellow travellers will mostly be frustrated truckies, whose vehicles line the sides of the road running up to the busy frontier post.

Ezra

Despite being a bit of a drag to get to, the Byzantine church at **EZRA** is an unusual sight that's worth a short detour. If you're driving, simply leave the highway at the junction for Ezra, and you'll find yourself in the town almost immediately. There are frequent **microbuses** from the south bus station in Damascus, and the journey only takes an hour, making this a feasible day-trip from the capital. Trains from Damascus to Dera also pass through Ezra, but with only two services a week it's not much of an alternative. Microbuses also connect Ezra with Sweida (30min) and Dera (change at Shayk Miskin, total journey time 45min).

Ezra itself is a dusty, ugly place, centred around a crossroads (where buses and microbuses stop) and overlooked by a huge grain silo, visible for miles around across the flat countryside. Its extraordinary **Church of St George** (*Mar Georgis*), the purported resting place of St George, who is much venerated by Middle Eastern Christians, is located 3km from the centre in the northern suburbs – take a taxi from the crossroads. The church is usually kept locked, but if you stand around looking lost for long enough someone will alert the keeper of the key, who lives nearby, to the fact that there is a visitor.

The building is one of the oldest churches in Syria, its survival accountable to the fact that it was solidly fortified to protect the town's minority Christians in times of religious persecution. The inscription over the middle portal of the western entrance, which dates the church to 515 AD, remarks that in the place "where once idols were sacrificed to, there are now choirs of angels". The dome is modern, but the rest of the church has remained largely unaltered since Byzantine times. The interior arches, the unusual shape – an octagon within a square – and the dark stone give the place an intimate, sombre feel. In a side chapel, the tomb of St George is well looked after by the Greek Orthodox community which still worships here. Despite its remote location, the church is visited by a fair number of the pious and the curious, most of whom diligently record their names in an absorbingly polyglottal visitors' book.

THE LEGEND OF ST GEORGE

What little is known about the man who became the patron saint of England – a place of which he had probably never heard – is submerged in myth and legend. George was probably a soldier; he was martyred at Diospolis (now Lod in central Israel) in around 303 AD, during the persecutions of the early Christians in Palestine instigated by the Roman emperor Diocletian. A cult surrounding him grew up and became widespread in Palestine and Syria, and later in Europe, in the centuries following his death. Stories of his deeds have been around in England since at least the early eighth century, when he was mentioned in the writings of the Venerable Bede, the first English historian. In 1098 he was said to have been seen aiding the Crusaders at the Battle of Antioch, with the result that many of the soldiers returning to Europe popularized further his cult. Richard I placed himself and his crusading army under the protection of the saint in 1191, and two centuries later – at least according to the histories on which Shakespeare drew – Henry V, speaking to his soldiers at the Battle of Agincourt, again invoked George as the patron of the English army.

The most famous myth surrounding St George was translated and published for the first time in the **Golden Legend** by the English printer William Caxton in the fifteenth century. The story centred around a fire-breathing dragon, whom the terrified citizens of a country tried to appease through the offering of a girl – the daughter of the king – as a sacrifice. George intervened and fought the dragon, reducing the beast to tame captivity, and telling the relieved citizens that if they accepted Christianitiy he would rid them of the monster. The king and people agreed; George baptized fifteen thousand men and then killed the dragon. He accepted no reward but asked the king to maintain churches in his country, and to show compassion to the poor.

George did not become **patron saint of England** until Edward III (1327–77) made him the patron of the newly founded Order of the Garter; in 1348 Pope Benedict XIV ratified him as Protector of the Kingdom of England. Yet he was a much-venerated figure all over medieval Europe, and Venice, Genoa, Portugal and Catalonia also regarded George as their patron. There are still churches dedicated to him in Venice, Rome, Verona and Istanbul, and many other churches and cathedrals include a portrayal of his story in stained glass or on murals. After the Reformation his popularity declined in continental Europe but remained solid in England. Indeed, a much later legend records that he once visited England, coming from the west through the part of the Irish Sea which is now known as St George's Channel – a set of events which is about as likely as him taming the dragon.

Dera

There's next to nothing to see in **DERA**, but if you've got time to kill you may want to head for the remnants of the town's ancient past. Attractions – such as they are – include a fairly unremarkable thirteenth-century Ayyubid **mosque**, opposite which are the pitiful, litter-strewn remains of a Roman **amphitheatre**, whose only distinguishing features are the flies. To get to these places, which lie 2km south of the centre, head south on the Jordan highway, then take the road veering off it to the left before the river, following this up the hill and beyond until

LAWRENCE OF ARABIA AND THE "DERA INCIDENT"

T.E. Lawrence served out World War I as an adviser to Emir Feisal, the ruler of Mecca, guiding the Arab forces in their disruptive guerrilla tactics against the Turks. The rail terminus of **Dera** was a prime target for such activities, standing as it did between Damascus, and therefore Constantinople, and Amman, and therefore Jerusalem and Medina. Accordingly, in November 1917 Lawrence went on a dangerous reconaissance mission to Dera to determine with what ease the town itself might be taken. Of what happened next, we cannot be entirely certain as he told the story in so many versions and couched it in such coy terms. According to *The Seven Pillars of Wisdom*, Lawrence was wandering through the streets when he was apprehended by a Turkish officer and taken to see the governor of the town. After successfully repelling the governor's sexual advances, Lawrence was severely kicked and beaten and then tied to a bench and whipped. When subsequently he was left alone in a room, he managed to escape through a window.

Richard Meinertzhagen, however, a fellow intelligence officer and friend, insisted that Lawrence confided in him that he had been stripped and bound and sodomized by the governor and his servants, but had chosen not to reveal this in his book because it was too "degrading". This version has recently been corroborated by an unpublished early version of the manuscript for *The Seven Pillars of Wisdom* that has come to light. Lawrence's handwritten notes explicitly and movingly talk of a multiple rape by four Turkish soldiers and the traumatic effect it had on him: "I was feeling very ill, as though some part of me had gone dead that night in Dera leaving me maimed, imperfect, only half myself . . . probably it had been the breaking of the spirit by that frenzied nerve-shattering pain which had degraded me to beast level when it made me grovel to it; and which had journeyed with me since, a fascination and terror and morbid desire, lascivious and vicious perhaps, but like the striving of a moth towards a flame." This shattering experience awoke in Lawrence a need for violent sexual experiences, which he satisfied after the war by hiring young men to beat him.

On a political note, the recently uncovered manuscript also emphasizes the duality of Lawrence's position: helping the Arabs to overthrow Turkish domination but knowing as a British agent that it was destined to be replaced with rule by the allied powers. It was a position that confirmed Lawrence as an outsider on both sides. When the British army's advance into Syria began in September 1918, Lawrence was given the task of helping destroy the lines into the Dera terminus to prevent the arrival of Turkish reinforcements. This he successfully completed, and the Turks fled from the town making its capture a formality. The British army then proceeded onto Damascus alongside the Arabs and an Australian force, and Lawrence's role was at an end. At the peace conferences the English promises to the Arabs concerning the creation of an independent Arab state were duly revealed to be empty, and the mandates were imposed.

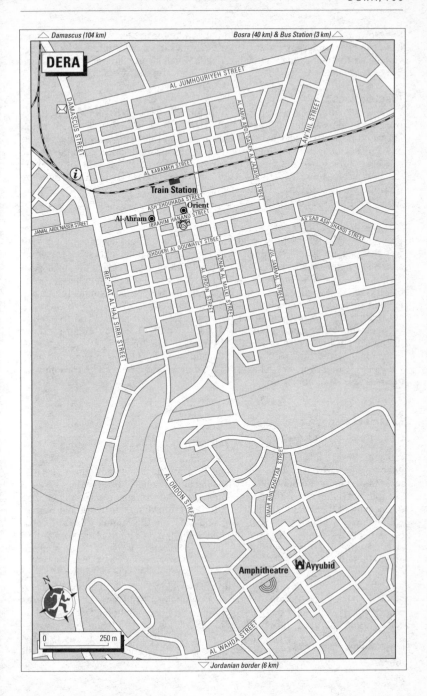

△ *Damascus (104 km)* | *Bosra (40 km) & Bus Station (3 km)* △

DERA

AL JUMHOURIYEH STREET

DAMASCUS STREET

AL AMIR ABDUL QADER AL JAZAIR STREET

AN-NIL STREET

AL KARAMEH STREET

Train Station

ASH'SHOUHADA STREET

Orient

Al-Ahram ⊙

IBRAHIM HANANO STREET

AS'SAD ASH SHARQI STREET

JAMAL ABDUL NASER STREET

SHOUKRI AL QOUWATLY STREET

ADNAN AL MALKI STREET

JUL JAMMA'IL STREET

RIF-AAT AL HAJ SIRRI STREET

AL ORDON STREET

AL ORDON STREET

OMAR BIN L-KHATTAB STREET

Amphitheatre 🏛 **Ayyubid**

N

0   250 m

AL WAHDA STREET

▽ *Jordanian border (6 km)*

the mosque appears on your left. Probably a better bet for wasting some time, however, is a wander around the town's central **railway station** for a look at the vintage steam trains and Ottoman carriages which stand marooned on discarded lines.

Practicalities

Dera is something of a transport hub for this part of Syria, with frequent **microbus** connections to Bosra (45min) and Damascus (1hr 30min). **Karnak** operates one service a day between Damascus and Dera (1hr 30min), and numerous **Pullman** buses also ply the route. The bus station is a three-kilometre taxi ride east of the town centre on the main road to Bosra. If you want to try something different, there's a twice-weekly **train** service on the narrow-gauge line from the Hedjaz Station in Damascus; it takes four hours to cover the distance, but at least the station in Dera is centrally located, one block north of the main street.

By far the best **hotel** in town is the dollar-priced *Orient* (☎015/222430; ④), on Ibrahim Hanano Street in the centre of town, which offers spotless rooms with TVs that pick up an entertaining blend of Syrian, Jordanian and Israeli transmissions. The hotel's **restaurant** is the best bet for a sit-down meal in the town. Also on this street is the *Al-Ahram* (☎015/221791; ③) which offers a number of rooms of varying quality; check what you're getting before you book in, as the crusty linen in some of the rooms looks decidely unenticing.

Crossing the **Syrian-Jordanian border** is easy: service taxis run frequently between the bus stations in Dera and Ramtha (S£170), or you might consider hitching from the centre of Dera – the road to the border is well signposted. Unfortunately you can't pick up any Damascus–Amman buses in Dera, but once you get to Ramtha you can get a bus to Irbid or Mafraq, from where travelling on to Amman is straightforward.

Bosra

Most visitors to Syria tend to write off **BOSRA** as Palmyra's poor relation. This is a pity, for though it lacks the latter's grandeur and epic desert setting, it can boast not only impressive Nabatean and Roman remains but also some of the oldest and most important monuments of the Christian and Islamic faiths in Syria. The local black basalt out of which the town is built gives it a striking visual presence, and the density of the stone has allowed it to last astonishingly well: the old Roman bath complex still boasts its roof, shops on the main thoroughfare are still capable of being used today, and the first jolting sight of the huge black Roman theatre, brilliantly preserved within an Ayyubid fortification, is one of the most memorable in Syria.

Bosra is also remarkable in that, like many of the ruined towns of the Hauran, it is still inhabited today. Many of the shapeless modern dwellings have been made from the ruins of Roman ones, so as you take a stroll down the *cardo maximus* you may encounter gaggles of children on their way home from school or eager young antique-sellers ready to invite you for a cup of tea in their premises off the ancient street. The only part of Bosra which you have to pay to enter is the citadel and theatre complex; the rest of the site is free and open at all times.

Some history

Bosra's grid pattern of streets is thought to have been laid out in Hellenistic times, though the irregular layout of the eastern half of the city suggests it may have assimilated an earlier settlement. What is clear, however, is that the town remained unimportant until the first century BC, when King Aretas III incorporated it into the Nabatean kingdom. Thereafter the town prospered, and in 70 AD the Nabateans transfered their capital from Petra to Bosra as a result of its greater commercial potential. After the Nabatean kingdom was conquered by the Romans in 106, Bosra was made capital of the province of Arabia, and the area around Bosra became a major centre for the production of corn. The town benefited greatly from the trade of the Via Trajana, the Roman road that linked Damascus to Aqaba, and was ambitiously expanded during the late second century; its prosperity was such that it even began minting its own coinage during the reign of the emperor Philip the Arab.

During the Christian era Bosra became the seat of an archbishopric, entailing the construction of a major cathedral in the sixth century. It was in Bosra that the prophet Mohammed, then a caravan leader, first learnt of Christianity from the Nestorian priest Bahira, and in 632 AD Bosra became the first Byzantine city to fall during the opening phase of the Arab expansion – a number of early mosques were built here, and Bahira's house became a revered Muslim site.

Bosra remained an important town both for caravan traffic and as a stopping point on the pilgrimage to Mecca, but its fortunes slowly declined as the region became increasingly politically unstable. The town was attacked at least twice by Frankish armies during the long Crusader struggles, it suffered great damage during the disputes between Cairo and Damascus in the thirteenth century, and it was devastated by a Mongol invading force in 1260. The caravan and pilgrimage routes were subsequently moved west, where things were safer; by the mid-nineteenth century the town had only a minimal population, allowing the resettlement here of a large number of Druze from Lebanon.

The citadel and theatre

The centrepiece and highlight of the ancient site, Bosra's **citadel and theatre** complex (daily: summer 10am–6pm; winter 9am–4pm; S£200) combines one of the most remarkably preserved amphitheatres in the Roman world with one of the finest examples of Arab military architecture in Syria. It's a brutal, intrusive building, constructed with defence rather than grace in mind, but no less impressive because of this.

Dated on stylistic grounds to the late second century, the theatre was first fortified by the Umayyads in the latter part of the eleventh century, though by far the greater part of the work was done by the Ayyubids in response to the Crusader threat of the early thirteenth century. A number of Arab buildings including a palace and mosque were built within the citadel (indeed the Swiss adventurer Burkhardt passing this way in 1810 didn't even realize there was a theatre inside), which were removed during the reconstruction programme of 1947 to 1970. The earth and sand that had filled most of the lower part of the theatre had done a remarkable job in preservation, so most of the reconstruction effort was directed at the stage area and the upper rows of seats; there are some 37 tiers in all, making this one of the largest theatres in the Roman world, with capacity for six thousand seated and standing room for a further three thousand.

The upper ramparts of the Ayyubid fortifications house an unexciting **folklore museum** and one of two cafés at the site, while on the terrace are a collection of Roman carved remains whose lack of subtlety only conveys the difficulty of carving in the dense black basalt. Visible from the ramparts in the fields by the *Cham Palace Hotel* is the outline of a **hippodrome** where chariot races would have taken place, thought to have had a seating capacity in the region of thirty thousand.

Along the cardo maximus to the western gate

The substantial remains of the Roman **bath complex** on the north side of the citadel, which would have been one of the city's main social institutions, are too dangerous to enter at the moment for fear that its mortar roof will collapse. The baths' northern entrance faces the main east–west axis of the town, the **cardo maximus**, once resplendent with colonnades and recently excavated down to its

Roman level. Some of the column stumps remain but most have been recycled into other buildings over the centuries; it is likely that most of Bosra's roads would have featured such colonnades, used to shade the pavement and their shoppers. You can still do some shopping here yourself as several enterprising young businessmen have taken over premises along the eastern stretch of the street in order to sell souvenirs.

Across the *cardo maximus* from the baths is the now largely blank Roman **marketplace**, the four tall columns at its near corner signifying the remains of a **nymphaeum** or public water fountain, built sometime in the second century. On the opposite side of the north–south street from this are the fragmentary remains of a **kalybe**, a pre-Christian open-air shrine in which statuary would have been displayed; one striking column remains but most of the stonework has been rearranged over the centuries. You can now head west down the main axis to the substantial **monumental arch** built in the early third century in honour of the Third Cyrenaica Legion, the Arabian province's principal military force, which had been garrisoned in Bosra since 123 AD. Though partially reconstructed in Arab times, its typical Roman design comprises a high central arch flanked by two smaller ones.

To your right some 50m beyond the arch is a large, cool underground warehouse, called a **cryptoporticus**, used to store products before their export and only rediscovered in 1968; the horizontal slits in the south wall were designed to admit light and air (the entrance is at its western end). The next major cross street from here was once marked by a tetrapylon, though today only traces of it can be made out. Head now from here to the well-preserved **western gate**, a fine monument that would once have been adorned with statuary; the Roman road underneath still provides excellent service today. The **walls** stretching either side are not in such a good state of preservation, much of the stonework having been used in the fortification of the theatre. Only the blocks that were too immense to be carted off remain – these may well predate even the Romans, being characteristic of urban fortifications in Syria in the second century BC.

Christian and Islamic Bosra

Head now back to the *cryptoporticus* but take the road north from here up to the tiny **Mosque al-Khider**, named after a local Muslim saint; most of the present-day structure dates from an 1133 reconstruction of an earlier mosque, built near the spring that supplied the town with fresh water. From here you can head east to the **Mosque of Umar**, built on the site of a pagan temple and thought to date to the beginning of the eighth century. Despite some reconstruction in the twelfth and thirteenth centuries, it is a rare example of a mosque from the earliest days of Islam which preserves its original form. Getting a look inside will depend more on luck than anything else as the mosque is only open for prayers, but what you will find if you're fortunate is a roofed courtyard surrounded on two sides by double arcades and on a third by the prayer hall. The minaret is Umayyad in origin, though was heavily rebuilt during the thirteenth century.

Beyond the Mosque of Umar is a recently restored Mameluke bath complex, the **Hamam Manjak**, late fourteenth century in origin and thus one of the last major buildings to go up before the town settled into its near-terminal decline. It's an interesting illustration of Bosra's role in catering for the pilgrimage trade to Mecca. The building is usually shut unless there's a tour group being shown around, but you can walk round to the back of the complex for a view over the bath chambers, set behind a reception area that once would have sported an expansive dome. About 100m east of the bath complex you'll come to the third-century Roman **basilica**, a well-preserved rectangular building originally constructed for civic use, then converted for Christian worship in the fourth century, and said to be the place where the monk Bahira met the prophet Mohammed. About 250m along the tarmac road heading northeast from here is the recently restored **Mabrak Mosque**, the western section of which dates to 1136 and features a *mihrab* said to mark the spot where the camel carrying the first copy of the Koran to Syria knelt to rest; the mosque subsequently became an important centre of learning.

South of the basilica and souvenir stalls are the remains of an early sixth-century **cathedral**. Though little remains today, this is an important building in the history of Christian architecture, as it was one of the first churches to be constructed with a circular dome over a square base. The idea had been used in secular buildings before, but its translation to Christian usage was a southern Syrian idea. The emperor Justinian used it as a model for cathedrals in Constantinople and Ravenna which are still standing, and it's also a direct ancestor of the Dome of the Rock in Jerusalem, built some two hundred years later. Behind the cathedral can be seen, meshed into some modern dwellings, the remains of a **bishop's palace**, while almost opposite is the **Fatima Mosque**, parts of which have been dated back to the eleventh century.

The eastern end of the cardo maximus

From the cathedral, it's easy to work your way round to the early second-century **Nabatean arch** at the eastern end of the *cardo maximus*, which is thought to have formed the entrance to a palace. Just to the south are the remains of a large two-storeyed dwelling constructed around a courtyard, which may have been the Roman **governor's residence**. A little to the south again lies a huge **cistern** measuring some 120m by 150m by 8m deep, one of the largest water storage facilities in the Roman East, which is today a popular swimming hole with the local boys, despite its slimy-green complexion. The lack of major rivers or natural springs in the Hauran necessitated the use of open tanks like this, even up until the early part of this century: Gertrude Bell passing this way in 1905 remarked that "the traveller may consider himself fortunate if he be not asked to drink a liquid in which he has seen the mules and camels wallowing". The **Mosque of Abu al-Feda**, a thirteenth-century construction restored in the 1980s, stands next to the cistern.

Practicalities

Given the lack of decent cheap accommodation in Bosra or nearby Dera, most budget travellers visit on a day-trip **from Damascus**. A direct **bus** to Bosra departs every two hours from the microbus station on Felasteen Street in the capital, dropping off two hours later – and picking up – on the main square on the east side of the citadel and theatre complex; the last bus back is at 8pm. Until the late afternoon there are frequent **microbuses from Dera** to Bosra, which arrive at and depart from the south side of the huge cistern. There are no buses between Bosra and Sweida; a taxi between the two won't cost less than S£400.

THE DRUZE

The Druze are a small but strongly cohesive religious sect, whose history and survival are remarkable. The key figure in their story is **Caliph Al-Hakim bi-Amr Allah** (996–1021) of the Shi'ite Fatimid dynasty of Egypt, who in the early part of his reign was notorious for his persecution of Jews and Christians – including the destruction of an estimated thirty thousand churches in the Holy Land, one of the sparks for the First Crusade. However, in 1016 the Caliph allowed himself to be proclaimed divine by his follower **Mohammed ad-Darazi** – from whom the sect derives its name – and in a remarkable change of heart restored religious freedom to Christians and Jews. He went on to institute his own name in place of Allah in mosque services, and prohibited Muslims from going on pilgrimage to Mecca. Whilst his subjects rose against the Caliph in uproar, ad-Darazi fled to Lebanon and founded the sect. Half of Cairo burned down in the ensuing chaos as Al-Hakim invoked the spirits of Adam and Solomon and carried out a policy of mass executions. In 1021, the Caliph disappeared without explanation while out one night observing the stars. While it's likely that he was assassinated, the Druze believe that Al-Hakim did not die but only disappeared, and will one day return to initiate a golden age. It is probable that a number of sects that grew up around the time shared this belief, but only the Druze have survived.

As to the Druzes' other beliefs, only a small number of initiates have full access to the **hikmah**, the Druze doctrines, and only they participate fully in their religious services. Outsiders are kept very much in the dark, both within and without the Druze community. Whether the Druze are even Muslims is debatable as their beliefs diverge at many different points: they reject much of Islamic law, their holy day is a Thursday and they believe in reincarnation. Conversion either to or from the religion is not permitted, nor is marriage outside their religion. In the late nineteenth century the Druze retreated to the Hauran following clashes with the Maronite Christian population in Lebanon, which culminated in the massacre of Christians in Damascus in 1860. During the mandate era French attempts to break down traditional Druze hierarchy and to impose their own administrative order provoked an uprising, assisted by Syrian nationalists, which spread to Damascus. It was only when the French resorted to bombarding both the capital and Sweida that the revolt was quelled.

Today there are an estimated 600,000 Druze, living mainly in southern Lebanon, but also in Syria and Israel. Their striking blue eyes and occasional blonde hair have led some to believe that they must have been descended from the Crusaders, though in fact their sect began about seventy years after the First Crusade. Their costume is also distinctive: the women wear tall conical headdresses and long, brightly coloured skirts, while the older men sport white turbans and emphatic moustaches.

Every odd-numbered year a **festival** of concerts and drama is held in the amphitheatre during the last two weeks of September. A **train** service connects Bosra with Dera and Damascus at this time – ask at the Hedjaz Station in Damascus for details.

There is only one **hotel** in Bosra, the *Cham Palace* (☎015/790488; ⑦), a couple of hundred metres south of the citadel. Luxuries include full air conditioning, several bars and restaurants, and a swimming pool, but the place seems to be rather overpriced on the back of its monopoly. If you have a sleeping bag it may be possible to stay inside the citadel for S£150 (though not during the Bosra Festival).

The southeastern Hauran: Sweida and around

In the southeast of the Hauran are a clutch of interesting ancient sites, grouped around the largest town and only viable base in the region, **Sweida**. The Roman remains at **Shahba** (which could be visited on route to Sweida from Damascus) and **Qanawat** are the most obvious draws, but all of the sites here are much less frequented than Bosra or even Ezra, and Sweida itself, despite its fine museum, doesn't give the impression of being used to seeing many tourists. However, for those with time on their hands who want to get off the beaten track, this is a good area to spend a couple of days exploring.

Sweida

SWEIDA, 106km south of Damascus, is a largely charmless provincial town, centred around a main square (Hafez al-Assad Square) of banal concrete, with a big army presence and little to recommend it save its **museum**. The town has a long history but most of the evidence for this was lost during the first decade of the twentieth century, when its ancient remains were used by Ottoman troops to build a barracks; the ruins of the temple, basilica, mosque and town gate described by Baedaeker in 1876 have now all gone. After checking in to a hotel, you'll want to look round the museum before heading out to Qanawat or Shahba, the two principal attractions nearby. Don't bother with the **tourist office**, by the main bus station on Hafez al-Assad Street, as they're polite but quite useless.

The museum

The **museum** (daily except Tues 9am–6pm; S£200) is an incongruously huge modern building on the northeast side of town, a kilometre or so from the centre on An'Nahda Street. Opened in November 1991, under the auspices of the French Archeological Institute and partly funded by the French oil multinational Total, it houses an impressive and well-laid-out collection, covering the history of the Hauran from the Stone Age to the early Arab occupation. Labelling is unusually excellent, so you should have no trouble finding your way around the numerous examples of early weaponry, finely decorated ceramics and black basalt Roman statuary.

Most interesting of all the museum's artefacts is the set of well-preserved **mosaics** from Shahba. The most famous – and one of the largest – is entitled *Artemis is Surprised whilst Bathing* and dates from the middle of the third century AD. Surrounded by magnificently portrayed garlands of fruit and foliage, it shows the naked goddess Artemis, bejewelled and attended by four nymphs, being surprised by the huntsman Actaeon, whose head emerges from the shrubbery in the top left-hand corner. The poignancy of the story lies in the fact that Artemis was obliged to turn Actaeon into a stag – then devoured by his own hounds – because the gods could not allow themselves to be seen without permission.

Practicalities

Microbuses from Damascus (south station), many of them travelling via Shahba, take just over ninety minutes to reach Sweida, pulling in at the bus station on Hafez al-Assad Street at the northern edge of town. Pullman bus compa-

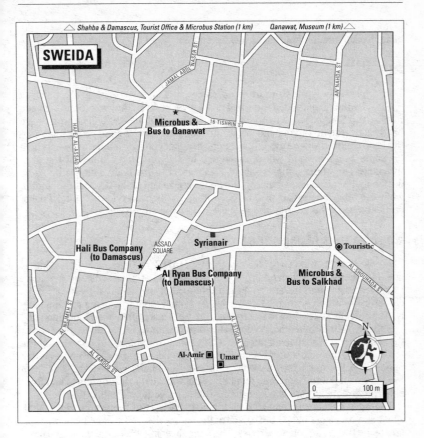

Shahba & Damascus, Tourist Office & Microbus Station (1 km)   Qanawat, Museum (1 km)

SWEIDA

JAMAL ABDUL NASSER ST
AN NAHDA ST

★ Microbus &
Bus to Qanawat   16 TISHRIN ST

HAFEZ AL-ASSAD ST

Hali Bus Company
(to Damascus) ■   ASSAD
SQUARE   ■ Syrianair   ◉ Touristic

Al Ryan Bus Company
(to Damascus)   Microbus &
Bus to Salkhad   AL-SHOUHADA ST

AL NEIMEH ST

AL ISTIQLAL ST

AL FAROSS ST

Al-Amir ■   ■ Umar

N

0   100 m

nies, whose offices in Sweida are grouped around Hafez al-Assad Square, offer frequent and slightly quicker services into the evening. There are also microbus connections **from Ezra**, 44km to the northwest along a good road, if you fancy breaking your journey from Damascus to visit the church of St George (see p.100). For those with a car, Sweida could be used as a base from which to visit Bosra, 35km south; you can't get there by bus, but taxi drivers in the town are prepared to make the trip for around S£400.

Plans are afoot to build a new luxury **hotel** in Sweida, but for the moment the choice of accommodation in town is grim. The *Touristic* on Al-Shouhada Street (☎016/221012; ④) has a forlorn air of incompetence about it – door handles come off in your hand, shower taps unscrew completely and light bulbs die with an emphatic bang rather than a whimper. The only other option is the nearby *Rawdat al-Jabal* (①), an uncompromisingly spartan budget establishment.

You're much better off as far as **restaurants** go, the pick of the crop being the bright and clean *Al-Amir* which serves very tasty Arabic food at very affordable prices. The service is exceptional for Syria – the waiters even refrain from smoking when serving – and the all-year Christmas decorations can only serve to heighten the cheerfulness of the ambience. The *Umar* opposite offers an adequate Syrian menu in more typically lax surroundings.

Atil

Two remarkably intact **Roman temples** can be found just 6km to the north of Sweida, by the main road in the small dusty town of **ATIL**. Any microbus between Sweida and Shahba will let you off at the north end of the settlement; from there head eastwards up the hill and ask around for the exact location of the temples – the local children will be more than happy to adopt you for an hour or so in return for some *baksheesh* and will probably try to sell you some lumps of Classical masonry. The small temples, about 200m apart, were both built to the same design in the mid-second century; the better-preserved of the two is free-standing while the other forms part of someone's house – the owner doesn't mind a polite request to view the interior and may even offer you coffee and grapes.

Shahba and Mushennef

The only Roman "new town" built in Syria, **SHAHBA**, 20km north of Sweida, is one of the most important architectural legacies of their rule in the East. Designed in a rough square on a rigid grid plan, it was founded by locally born emperor Philip the Arab in 244, possibly as a monument to himself and his family. At his death in 249, however, only half the walled area had been built upon and Shahba had only a token population. The town retains a remarkable proportion of the original walls, roads and public buildings that were built, but only during the last century has it been substantially repopulated with Druze from Lebanon. Situated on the main road that links the two, Shahba is easily accessible from Sweida (20min) and Damascus (south bus station; 1hr); **microbuses** to and from either are frequent until late afternoon. There are no hotels in Shahba.

The main cluster of ruins is to be found 100m west of the present-day roundabout and transport hub at the centre of the site, which was formally the intersection of the two main Roman arteries. The street heading west from the roundabout still retains its Roman basalt **paving stones**; after about 50m you will pass a flight of steps leading up to four tall **columns** which once formed the portico of a temple but which now form the rather impressive entrance to somebody's house. Continuing west, you'll find yourself in the **forum**, its dusty, littered basalt paving reminiscent of a school playground; at the far end is a **kalybe**, a shrine that would probably have displayed statues of Philip the Arab's ancestors, some of whom he proclaimed gods during Rome's thousandth-anniversary celebrations in 248.

Behind and to the right of the *kalybe* stand the confused remains of a **palace**, though the modern dwellings that have been incorporated into it make exploration difficult. On the forum's south side is a minimally decorated but well-preserved **temple**, thought to have been erected in honour of Philip's father, an Arab chief; in the early years of the twentieth century this building was functioning as the local school. A twee nine-rowed **theatre** stands just beyond this; again decoration is minimal, probably because of the difficulty of carving into the dense local basalt.

It's best to return from here to the roundabout and head south. Soon on your left you'll come across the substantial and slightly daunting remains of the Roman **baths**, far larger than a town of Shahba's size could justify and a project which was never completed. You can just about make out the remains of an aqueduct leading

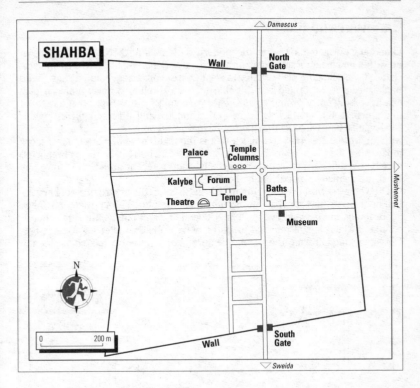

off behind the complex. Down the street running alongside the baths is a **museum** (daily except Tues 8am–2pm; S£200), containing some early fourth-century **mosaics**, helpfully labelled in English, which were found in a private house here. These are some of the best examples of the form to be found in Syria and form a worthy complement to the mosaics in the Sweida museum. One in particular stands out, a delicate, poignant portrayal of Orpheus entrancing a group of animals with his lyre.

Mushennef

In the middle of the reclusive town of **MUSHENNEF** is a finely decorated second-century Roman **temple**, located on the edge of a small artificial lake where the winter rains would have been collected, and now incorporated into an amalgam of modern dwellings. Not as rewarding as a visit to Shahba or Qanawat, though a good complement to both, a trip here is recommended principally for those with their own transport. Ask around for a look inside the temple, where the stubby basalt roofing beams, used as there was little wood available in the region, are especially notable; a pugnacious old woman living nearby has the key, and at the end of the visit she tends to point to her chest, moan a lot and shout "doctor, doctor" at you – this is not an invitation to call an ambulance but rather a request for *baksheesh*, which would be in order.

The road east from Qanawat to Mushennef is too poor for buses to run, so the only way to get here by public transport is from Shahba, 25km to the northwest: **buses** leave from the eastern exit of the main roundabout. Be warned that services back to Shahba are infrequent, and virtually non-existent after midday.

Qanawat and Sia

Like many towns in the region, the modern settlement of **QANAWAT** has grown up within an ancient Roman one, providing a disorientating mesh of past and present. It's a fascinating place simply to wander around: ancient columns have been haphazardly incorporated into humble modern dwellings, noisy children play amongst jumbled ruins and goats shelter peacefully by stonework that has stood undisturbed for centuries. During the fourth and fifth centuries, when Christianity flourished in the Hauran, Qanawat became the seat of a bishopric, with an impressive church complex that is the main focus of interest for visitors today. After the town fell to the Arabs, decline set in; by 1810 Burkhardt reported only two families living in this "ruined city", but in recent decades the town has been substantially repopulated by Druze.

The Qanawat **bus** leaves from 16 Tishrin Street in the centre of Sweida every half-hour or so (last bus back to Sweida at about 4pm). The journey only takes about fifteen minutes, and you will be dropped off right outside the main church complex, which is still referred to as the **seraya** (palace) after its original, pre-Christian function from the second century AD. The *seraya* has been recently

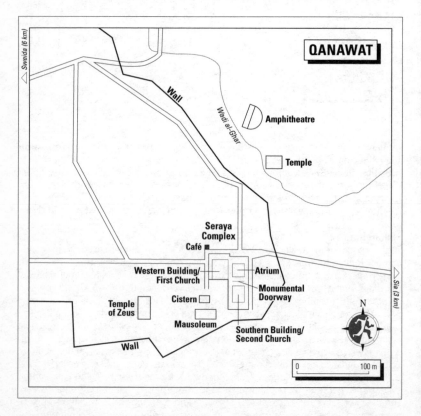

fenced so ask at the nearby café for the key; entry is via the western building, which, in the fourth or fifth century, was enterprisingly reorientated east–west, from the original north–south, to serve as a church. You can still make out the remains of the columned portico marking the original northern entrance while inside, an altar was placed at the eastern end and a wall constucted across the three semi-circular niches at the southern end. Originally built as one, the atrium and southern building were bisected by a three-doorwayed wall in the fourth or fifth century, with the area to the south being converted into a second church. East–west reorientation here was achieved by placing a raised semicircular platform against the eastern wall, which would have been used to frame a bishop's throne; on the ground before it is a large bowl, possibly used for baptisms.

Taking the road that heads north from the *seraya* will bring you sharply down to the Wadi al-Ghar, where it is just about possible to cross the trickling stream without getting your feet wet. You'll find here a curious and highly photogenic water-filled building, probably a **temple**, whilst nearby is a dinky **amphitheatre** built into the hillside. To the west of the *seraya* lies a huge underground **cistern** and the substantial remains of a **mausoleum**, and 50m to the south of this are the pitifully scant, but none the less expansive, remains of a second-century **temple of Zeus**.

Sia

According to the 1876 edition of *Baedeker's Guide to Syria and Palestine* the **Nabatean temple complex** at **SIA** was one of the most "interesting in the Hauran, resembling in style the Herodian Temple at Jerusalem". Unfortunately this magnificently preserved edifice was almost completely dismantled (along with a similarly dated temple in Sweida) by Turkish soldiers during the first decade of the twentieth century, and its masonry used to construct a barracks. For anyone with the imaginative powers required to make much sense of the place, Sia is a three-kilometre walk or hitch southeast from Qanawat (there are no buses); from the *seraya* complex follow the road (Roman in parts) that heads past a tower fragment. The ruins are on a small hill, and are partly incorporated into a farmyard. Two terraced courtyards can be made out, each preceded by a jumble of masonry signifying a gateway; at the end of the second courtyard would have stood the Temple of Baal-Shamin, dating from 37–32 BC.

Salkhad

The early thirteenth-century **castle** that tops the volcanic cone above the otherwise unremarkable town of **SALKHAD** was constructed by the Ayyubids to aid in the defence of Damascus while the Crusaders were occupying Jerusalem. It's an obvious fifteen-minute walk from the centre of the town up to the castle, but as it's situated in a military zone be prepared to answer the calls of any uniformed personnel and to show your passport. No photographs are allowed but you are free to wander at will through the labyrinth of subterranean vaults, containing two huge cisterns that still hold vast quantities of water; a torch would be useful to appreciate their full dimensions.

Buses from Sweida leave every thirty minutes or so from opposite the *Touristic Hotel* and drop you off in Salkhad town centre after 45 minutes. There are no buses between Bosra and Salkhad, but taxis will cover the ground for around S£250.

The Golan Heights

For over thirty years, the **Golan Heights** (*Al-Jawlan*) have rarely been far from the Middle Eastern headlines. This area of southwestern Syria was occupied by Israel

THE POLITICS OF THE GOLAN HEIGHTS

Before the **Six Day War**, the borders of Syria stretched as far west as the eastern shore of the Sea of Galilee (Lake Tiberias), encompassing the **Golan Heights** which stand to the east and north of the Sea. In a region virtually starved of fresh water, much of the Heights' strategic importance stems from the fact that the **River Jordan**, which waters a large part of Israel, rises there.

In May 1967 Israel began massing troops by its border with Syria, in reply to sporadic Syrian guerrilla attacks on settlements in the Golan–Galilee region. Support was immediately forthcoming from Syria's old ally, President Nasser of Egypt, who ordered the Straits of Tiran, at the entrance to the Red Sea, to be closed to Israeli shipping, effectively closing the Israeli port of Eilat. Jordan and Egypt then signed a mutual defence pact, which prompted Israel into taking pre-emptive military action against all its adversaries: in a pre-dawn raid on June 5 the Israelis wiped out the Egyptian Air Force on the ground, and within six days were in control of Egyptian, Jordanian and Syrian territory – Gaza and the Sinai Peninsula, the West Bank (including East Jerusalem) and the Golan Heights, respectively. The United Nations negotiated a ceasefire on June 11, and on September 22 passed **Resolution 242**, which called for Israeli withdrawal from all the territories it had occupied, and for all countries of the Middle East to live in peace with their neighbours within recognized boundaries. Syria refused to accept the resolution as it required Syrian recognition of the right of the state of Israel to exist, but this hasn't stopped it continuously quoting UN calls for Israeli withdrawal from the Golan as justification for its stance over the territory. Israel has refused to withdraw on the grounds that its pre-1967 boundaries were not secure.

In October 1973, Syria and Egypt launched a surprise attack on Israel to try to regain their lost territory. The resulting **Yom Kippur War** lingered on for months; there was fighting in the Golan until the following May, but very little ground was made by either side. The US Secretary of State, Henry Kissinger, shuttled backwards and forwards between Jerusalem and Damascus arranging a shaky truce between the two countries. This resulted in a few small territorial gains for Syria, and the establishment of the complex **buffer zone**, administered by the United Nations, to separate the two countries' armies. Israel gave up some of its post-1967 territory to create the zone, but not before its troops had razed the town of **Quneitra** to the ground in a gratuitous act of defiance.

In 1978 talks held under American auspices at **Camp David** resulted in the Egyptian government signing a full peace with Israel, incurring the wrath of the entire Arab world (and the loss of President Sadat to an assassin's bullet in 1981), but ensuring that the Sinai Peninsula was returned to Egyptian control. No such movements towards peace were made in the Golan, however, and in 1981 Israel formally annexed part of the Heights and began establishing **Jewish settlements** there. Jordan remained technically at war with Israel until peace was signed (again as a result of US mediation) in October 1994, as a result of which Israel returned a number of areas in the West Bank to Jordanian control. However, with both Jerusalem and Damascus retaining positions which are inflexible to the point of intransigence, no such progress seems possible on the similar problem of the Golan.

in 1967 during the Six Day War, and is now at the centre of the "land for peace" option being pursued by the American government, as it encourages Syria to withdraw its claims on the Heights. The Syrian position has always remained firm – no peace until the Golan returns to Syria – but with a similar hard-line stance being adopted by Israeli premier Benjamin Netanyahu, and with increasing insurgence and tension in the West Bank, any deal involving the area looks unlikely in the short term. Most of the Golan Heights remains firmly part of Israeli territory, and the only part of the area which can be visited from Syria is the town of **Quneitra**, which is in the demilitarized buffer zone supervised by the United Nations.

Practicalities

To get a **permit** to let you into Quneitra take your passport to the Ministry of the Interior (daily except Fri 8am–2pm), next to the Kuwaiti embassy on Toulaitoulah Street in Damascus. You only have to deal with the man in the booth outside the building and the whole process takes no more than ten minutes. The pass is valid for one day, and you'll be asked when you want to go. **Buses** towards Quneitra depart from Felasteen Street. Make sure the driver knows where you want to go and has seen your permit; he may take you to a UN–Syrian checkpoint just beyond the town of **Khan Arnabeh** or simply drop you off at Khan Arnabeh, from where you would have to pick up another bus to the checkpoint. Once you are in the hands of the Syrian army at the checkpoint they will take your permit and organize a **military escort**. This may be in the form of a walking tour, or you might be asked if you want to appropriate a bus to take you around (S£200 would be an appropriate sum to pay the driver). **Photographs** are permitted, but not of UN personnel or installations.

Quneitra

Of all the places you visit in Syria, the ghost town of **QUNEITRA** will probably have the most shocking emotional impact. Before the Israelis handed back Quneitra in 1973, they removed the entire population of 37,000 and razed the town to the ground – a phrase which has become a commonplace, but which gains a startling immediacy when viewed face to face. The first sight of the flattened houses on the outskirts of the town is the most dramatic; many of the unscathed roofs simply lie on top of a mass of rubble, leaving the impression of a building that has imploded. You will then probably be taken to the hospital by your military escort, its smashed interior strewn with broken tiles and riddled with bullet holes. Similar scenes of destruction are then repeated at the town's desecrated church and mosque, at the broken husk of the local cinema and in the empty cells along the main shopping street.

Oddly enough there is a working **restaurant** in the town, situated right next to the barbed wire that signals the end of Syrian-controlled land; to go with your meal or drinks the owner can offer a pair of binoculars for a view of the Israeli camp on the hill opposite. Noise always seems to follow you in Syria, yet here in the midst of its most politically vexed region, an uneasy silence hangs over the green and pleasant rolling landscape. At the town's final Syrian checkpoint, a little further on, you can just about make out the "Welcome to Israel" signs about 100m away across no-man's land. Heading back, you can pause at the town **museum**, which has got nothing to do with recent history but is rather a collection of bits and bobs largely dating from the Byzantine period, incongruously providing relief from the devastation in the rest of the town.

travel details

Trains
Damascus to: Amman (1 weekly; 9hr); Dera (2 weekly; 4hr); Ezra (2 weekly; 2hr).

Local buses and microbuses
Dera, frequent services to: Bosra (45min); Damascus (1hr 30min); Shayk Miskin (30min).
Ezra, frequent services to: Damascus (1hr); Shayk Miskin (15min); Sweida (30min).
Sweida, frequent services to: Atil (10min); Damascus (1hr 30min); Ezra (30min); Qanawat (15min); Salkhad (45min); Shahba (20min).

Karnak buses
Damascus to: Dera (1 daily; 1hr 30min); Sweida (1 daily; 1hr 30min).

Pullman buses
Damascus, frequent services to: Bosra (2hr); Dera (1hr 30min); Sweida (1hr 30min).

CHAPTER THREE

THE ORONTES VALLEY

Bounded by the mountains and forests of the coastal strip to the west and the parched desert expanse to the east, the **Orontes Valley** is a popular destination for travellers wanting to see something of provincial Syria on their way from Damascus to Aleppo or the coast. Getting around is fairly straightforward, though you'll have to hire your own transport to reach the more out-of-the-way sites, and within a small geographical area history and the terrain have conspired to throw up plenty of contrasts: Roman ruins lost in the desert, crumbling medieval castles, bustling towns with busy souks and dramatic but peaceful countryside along the banks of the **Orontes River**.

The Orontes dominates the region, though you will come across it only infrequently. Rising in the Lebanese mountains near Baalbek, the river enters Lake Qatinnah, first dammed in the second millennium BC and now providing the region with drinking water, before flowing through the outskirts of the industrial city of **Homs**, Syria's third largest city and a natural focus for travellers, if only because the main traffic arteries in the region seem to lead there. Further north, **Hama** is altogether more agreeable, with its reasonably intact old quarter and shady riverside parks and restaurants from where you can watch the *noria*s, the ancient, groaning waterwheels which have been turned by the water of the Orontes for centuries.

Beyond Hama the river enters the plain of the **Ghab**, a marshy, verdant area bordered by arid plains and shimmering hills. Here the course of the river is rather indistinct, its sluggish flow causing it to divide into many channels and stagnant reed beds, but the intensively cultivated Ghab is one of the most productive farming regions in Syria. Beyond the Ghab the Orontes follows a more definite course as it flows north, entering Turkey near Jish Shughur; it then makes an abrupt turn westwards, passing through Antakya before emptying into the Mediterranean.

The immediate region around Homs offers little of interest, but there are plenty of places worth seeing in the Ghab and in its mountain and desert fringes. Obvious destinations around Hama include the spectacular Roman ruins of **Apamea**, the Assassin fortress at **Misyaf** and the extravagant Byzantine desert palace at **Qasr ibn Warden**, beyond which lies the well-preserved Roman temple of **Isriya**, emerging from the parched plains in fantastic isolation.

ACCOMMODATION PRICE CODES

In this book, all hotels have been categorized according to the **price codes** outlined below. They represent the minimum you can expect to pay for a **double room** in each hotel; for further details, see p.31.

① under S£300/US$7.50
② S£300–600/US$7.50–15
③ S£600–1000/US$15–25
④ S£1000–1400/US$25–35

⑤ US$35–50/S£1400–2000
⑥ US$50–90/S£2000–3600
⑦ US$90–130/S£3600–5200
⑧ US$130 and over/S£5200 and over

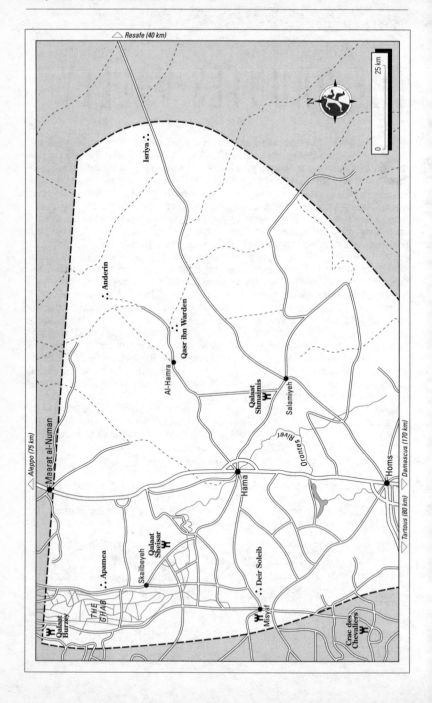

THE ORONTES RIVER AND THE FERTILE CRESCENT

Almost all the historical sites in this region owe their settlement to the **Orontes River**, which in Arabic is called **Nahr al-Assi**, the "rebel river", because unusually it runs from south to north. Its agricultural value has ensured that the region has been both densely settled and frequently fought over. The Crusaders built the Crac des Chevaliers to guard the main route running between the coast and the Orontes, while at Tell Nebi Mend (Kadesh), a Bronze Age fortress city by the river, the Egyptian Pharoah Ramses II fought a major battle against the Hittites around 1285 BC over control of the valley and Syria.

In biblical times, the Orontes, along with the Jordan, formed the western part of the so-called **Fertile Crescent**, a term popularized by American Orientalist James Henry Breasted. It refers to the watered and settled arc stretching from Jerusalem to the head of the Persian Gulf, with the Tigris and Euphrates forming the eastern section. It was here that some of the world's earliest forms of human settlement originated, with some village sites dated to around 8000 BC, and here that the seminal ancient states of Babylonia, Assyria and Phoenicia grew up.

In more recent times, Syrian abstraction of water from the Orontes has drawn complaints from the Turkish government, mindful of the necessity of keeping the fertile farmland of the Hatay (around Antakya) well watered. However, the fact that the Hatay is regarded by the Damascus government as part of Syria has meant that these grumblings have been largely ignored, especially as the Syrians accuse the Turks of abstracting more than their fair share from the Euphrates before it enters Syrian territory.

Homs

The modern housing developments and building sites which surround **HOMS** provide an ungainly but appropriate introduction: there's virtually nothing left of the city's ancient past, and the centre adds up to little more than a succession of busy traffic intersections, low-rise office buildings and a workaday souk. Syria's third city, Homs is ugly without being unpleasant, and busy without the big-city stress of Damascus or the confusing sprawl of parts of Aleppo. Its university, one of only four in the country, is a specialist engineering foundation, whose large student population gives Homs a more lively air than other towns in the region. The compactness of its centre, with most of the hotels, shops and public services clustering around Qouwatli Street, means that orientation is easy and, though there is very little to see in the city itself, Homs would make a convenient base to travel out to Crac des Chevaliers (see p.152) and possibly Palmyra (see p.236) before pushing north to the more obvious attractions of Hama.

Some history

Homs has been an important trading centre since ancient times, when its wealth challenged even that of Palmyra, the next great caravan halt on the long trek east. Known as **Emesa** during the Roman period, the city was ruled by a dynasty of priest-kings, guardians of a black stone representing the sun god that resided within the **Great Temple of Bel**. In 187 AD **Julia Domna**, daughter of the priest-king, married the local Roman commander Septimius Severus, who became emperor six years later. Under his patronage the city was ambitiously expanded;

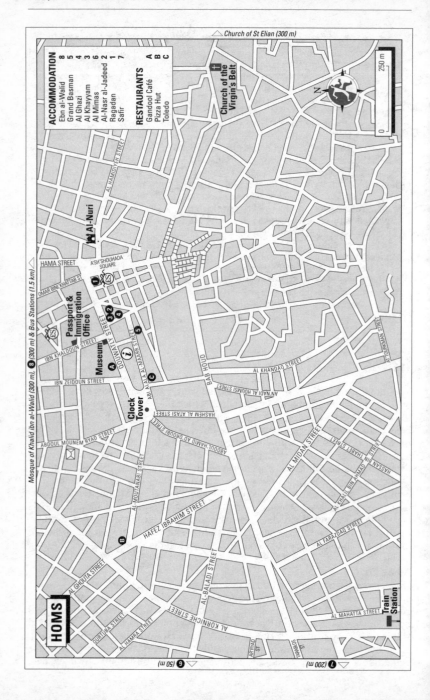

HOMS

Church of St Elian (300 m)

ACCOMMODATION
Ebn al-Walid   8
Grand Basman   5
Al Ghazi   4
Al Khayyam   3
Al Mimas   6
Al-Nasr al-Jadeed   2
Ragadan   1
Safir   7

RESTAURANTS
Gandool Café   A
Pizza Hut   B
Toledo   C

Church of the
Virgin's Belt

Al-Nuri

HAMA STREET

A'SH'SHOUHADA
SQUARE

Passport &
Immigration
Office

OMAR BINI KHATTAB ST

AL HAMIDIYEH STREET

IBN KHALDOUN STREET

Museum

IBN ZEIDOUN STREET

DOUWALY STREET

ABI ALA'A AL-MAARR STREET

Clock
Tower

ABDOUL MOUNEM RYAD STREET

HASHEM AL-ATASI STREET

BAB HOUD

AN NADI AL HOUMSI STREET

AL KHANDAQ STREET

ABDOUL HAMID AD DROUBI STREET

AL-MOUTANABI STREET

HAFEZ IBRAHIM STREET

AL MIDAN STREET

AT-TOURMAN STREET

HASSAN BIN THABET STREET

AL GHOUTA STREET

QURTUBA STREET

AL HAMRA STREET

AL KORNICHE STREET

AL-BALADI STREET

AL FARAZDAQ STREET

AL KHALIL BIN AHMAD STREET

AL MAHATTA STREET

Train
Station

ARFIAD ST

THARABUS ST

Mosque of Khalid ibn al-Walid (300 m), 300 m) & Bus Stations (1.5 km)

Museum 300 m) & Bus Stations

250 m

0

the Great Temple was completely rebuilt and came to rival the magnificent edifices at Baalbek and Palmyra.

Under Julia Domna's grandson **Elagabalus**, who was proclaimed Emperor Marcus Antoninus in Emesa at the age of fourteen in 218, the town was raised to the status of a metropolis. The black stone was removed from the Great Temple and taken to Rome, where the sun-worshipping cult took hold. Elagabalus' reign, however, was characterized by all manner of excess and depravity and was murderously cut short by the praetorian guard in 222. The black stone was sent back home, although Emperor Aurelian gave the cult official status in Rome later that century, when he credited the stone with aiding his victory over the Palmyrene princess Zenobia – he had prayed to the black stone at Emesa on his way to confront her.

The cult of Bel survived in Emesa until the fifth century, but by that time **Christianity** had begun to take a strong hold. Christian catacombs dating from between the third and seventh centuries have been found under houses in the old quarter of the city – though they cannot be visited for fear of collapse – and the most noteworthy remnants of Homs's ancient past are two churches. Otherwise, Homs is an unapologetically modern city: industrially, it's the most important in Syria, boasting the country's largest oil refinery and standing at the heart of its vital phosphate industry.

Arrival and information

As usual, the **train and bus stations** are towards the outskirts of town. If you arrive by train, a city taxi is the easiest way to cover the 1.5km into the centre, although the distance is walkable. The Karnak and microbus stations are next to each other over a kilometre north of Qouwatli Street, with the Pullman bus station 500m beyond these. If you're coming in on a microbus from the south (along the Damascus road), you'll probably be dropped off in the centre of town; otherwise, catch a taxi to the centre (S£50 maximum), or hop on a city microbus heading south towards the souk.

At the small **tourist office** (daily except Fri: summer 8am–2pm & 5–9pm; winter 8am–2pm & 4–8pm) in the park off Qouwatli Street, the staff are very friendly and can provide you with a few glossy brochures and a free map, but little practical information.

Accommodation

Most of the city's **hotels** are gathered either on or very near Qouwatli Street. The best of the **cheapies** is the *Al-Nasr al-Jadeed* in an old building on Qouwatli Street (☎031/227 423; ②, S£50 hot shower), where rooms are clean and the friendly owner speaks good English. Paying extra for a double here (if there are no singles left) is a better alternative for lone travellers than a night spent in either of the two hotels around the block: the relentlessly filthy *Al-Khayyam* (☎031/223 959; ①) only has doubles anyway, while the *Al-Ghazi* (☎031/222 160; ①, S£35 hot shower) next door at least has hot water available (if enough notice is given), though the rooms without windows are best avoided. A number of cheap and grotty hotels congregate near the mosque of Khalid ibn al-Walid, the pick of the bunch – though that's not saying much – being the *Ebn Al-Walid* (☎031/223 953; ①) on Kinana Street, off Hama Street, which features functional but bare rooms with en-suite bath.

Moving **upmarket** into the dollar category, the *Grand Basman* (☎031/235 700; ③), located in a small shopping arcade off Abi Alala al-Maarr Street, has acceptably clean if soulless rooms with bath, while the *Hotel Raghdan* (☎031/225 211; ③), on Qouwatli Street near the entrance to the souks, offers slightly grubbier rooms for slightly more money. If you want something better, try the hotel on the first floor of the octagonal Karnak bus terminal building (☎031/233 099; ④), which is very spruce and usually completely empty. The *Al-Mimas* (☎031/220 224; ⑤), somewhat lost on Al-Baladi Street over in the west of town, is overpriced though the rooms are agreeably clean. Anyone booked on a package tour will probably find themselves having to put up with the luxuries of the *Safir* (☎031/412 400, fax 433 420; ⑦), situated outside the town centre near the train station. All rooms have air conditioning, TV, radio and minibar; the tennis courts and enticing swimming pool are for the use of residents only.

The City

There is little trace of the Great Temple of Bel left today, and the walls and city gates of the ancient city were largely demolished during the Ottoman period; the citadel is now no more than a mound. After you've seen the very modern **Mosque of Khalid ibn al-Walid** and two semi-interesting **churches** – one of which, **St Elian**, is claimed to contain the oldest surviving frescoes in Syria – there's not much to do beyond drifting amongst the crowds of the souks and main shopping areas. Homs does boast a city **museum** (daily except Tues 9am–6pm; S£200), at the clocktower end of Qouwatli Street, opposite the tourist office, but it's a dingy place that seems in a permanent state of upheaval. If you do decide to venture inside, prepare yourself for a series of boring, ill-defined exhibits, some of which are unlabelled even in Arabic. At the end of your tour the curator may try to sell you some "antiques", an attempt to boost his undoubtedly meagre income; you'll be a prime target since you'll be the only visitor.

The mosques

Walking north for 300m from the crossroads outside the souk, you reach the city's only edifice of any real note, the **Mosque of Khalid ibn al-Walid**, which sits in a well-manicured and watered park, its bright tin roof glinting in the sun. The mosque dates from the last days of Turkish rule in Syria (1908–13) but incorporates into its architecture the ancient Syrian style of alternating bands of white and black stone. The spacious interior contains the mausoleum of Khalid ibn al-Walid who led the Arab forces at the Battle of Yarmouk River in 636, a confrontation which overturned nearly six hundred years of Roman rule in Syria (see p.100). The surrounding park, one of the few peaceful spots in the city, is a good place to find a shady tree, eat ice cream and people-watch. The only other important mosque in Homs is the **Great Mosque of Al-Nuri**, situated in the drab souk. The building itself is unremarkable, but it stands on the site of the Great Temple of Bel, of which all that remains are a few blocks of Roman masonry littering the courtyard.

The churches

Four hundred metres east of the Great Mosque of Al-Nuri is the most important Christian monument in Homs, the **Church of the Virgin's Belt** (*Kaneesat Um Zumaar*), named after a piece of cloth said to have belonged to the Virgin Mary that was found underneath the altar during a 1953 renovation. The belt is kept in a showcase in a special room and is a surprisingly unedifying item – you'll linger when looking at it simply because the warden has taken the effort to unlock the room for you. The church interior cosily resembles that of a modern English parish church, complete with cheap iconography, insubstantial wooden pews and gently peeling paintwork; indeed the present structure only dates from the nineteenth century, although it is claimed that this has been a site of Christian worship since 59 AD.

The same backroad that leads to the Church of the Virgin's Belt will bring you, 300m further east, to the **Church of St Elian** (*Kaneesat Mar Elian*); usually the only way to get inside is to rattle for attention on the gate enclosing the building. The church is dedicated to the son of a Roman officer who was martyred at the hands of his own father in 284 for refusing to renounce Christianity, and indeed is said to have been founded in 432 on the very site of the martyrdom, with Elian's remains placed in a sarcophagus in the crypt. A major renovation of the church in 1970 led to the discovery of some colourful **murals** of Christ, Mary, the

---

THE BATTLE OF KADESH

The **Battle of Kadesh** was the culmination of a trial of strength between the **Hittites**, based in central Turkey, and the **Egyptians**, under Ramses II, determined to restore Syria to their empire. The two armies met in combat around 1285 BC outside the city of Kadesh, the first major battle in history of which we know the sequence of events. The Hittites were waiting unseen to the east of the city, attacking unexpectedly when the bemused Egyptians attempted to enter Kadesh from the south. With magnificent fortitude Ramses collected together a division and drove at the weakest point of the Hittite line, stalling the advance and allowing his escape. This action was commemorated by Ramses on many monuments throughout Egypt as a victory, but the evidence of a surviving Hittite treaty with the city of Aleppo and a number of Hittite seals found at Ugarit suggests that Syria remained in the Hittite sphere of influence in the decades following the battle.

To archeologists, however, the Battle of Kadesh has a far wider significance in that it played a major role in the detective story which revealed the importance, indeed the very existence of the Hittite empire. Ramses II had broadcast his "victory" at Kadesh over a people he called the Hatti, but nothing connected these people to the Hittites, known only through a couple of unforthcoming Old Testament references and considered something of an enigma. In 1812 the famous Swiss explorer Jan Lewis Burckhardt noticed a number of inscribed basalt stones inside a house in the souk, but it was not until Sir Richard Burton stumbled upon what came to be known as the **Hama stones** in 1871 that they became the object of academic scrutiny. In the following decade connections were made between the stones and similar inscriptions, also undeciphered, found at various sites in Turkey, leading to the conjecture that a vast empire at one time must have filled much of Turkey and Syria. The final piece of the jigsaw fell into place with the discovery of the **Hittite royal archives** at Bogazkoy in central Turkey in 1906. These included a number of tablets written in decipherable Babylonian cuneiform, which not only identified Bogazkoy as the ancient capital of the Hittite empire, but also revealed a Hittite copy of a peace treaty made with the Egyptians which matched exactly Ramses' treaty with the Hatti after the Battle of Kadesh.

The site of ancient Kadesh is at **Tell Nebi Mend**, 30km southwest of Homs. You can get a direct microbus from the city, but there's precious little to see save a large mound with a few modern dwellings on top, and a lot of scrawny goats.

prophets and the apostles which had been brilliantly preserved under a layer of plaster in the crypt. These date back at least as far as the twelfth century and, if the claims of some experts are to be believed, possibly as far as the sixth century – making them the oldest surviving church paintings in Syria. The rest of the church is covered with more recent, and quite garish, paintings depicting the life of St Elian.

Eating and drinking

The numerous cheap eateries around Qouwatli Street will satisfy anyone seeking a snack, but actual **restaurants** are pretty thin on the ground. The *Toledo* on Abi Alala al-Maarr Street serves up the usual fare of kebab or chicken with chips and beer for a reasonable S£200. It's a fairly casual place, with waiters who tend to blow the tables clean rather than wipe them, and you can just sit there and drink if you want. At the end of Al-Moutanabbi Street you'll find the good-value *Pizza Hut*, which serves very filling pizzas for between S£75 and S£200, and has menus in English. The railway station has an ambitiously large restaurant, complete with cloakrooms, which offers cheap food and beer, but it's a bit out of the way and is usually unnervingly devoid of patrons (and indeed trains). The restaurant on the first floor of the octagonal Karnak bus terminal, though a little tatty and unused to serving in the daytime, is a much better bet for a sit-down meal. The *Safir Hotel* also has a couple of restaurants, which sell overpriced fare of an international flavour. The biggest of the city's **cafés** is the outdoor *Gandool* on the north side of Qouwatli Street; no food or beer is served, but it's a good place to chill out and watch endless games of backgammon.

Listings

Airline Syrianair has an office on Ibn Khaldoun St, north of the immigration office.

Bookshop The *Safir Hotel* has the only useful shop with English-language books.

Bus departures Neither Karnak nor the Pullman companies have offices in the centre of town, so on departure you'll have to make way out to one of the bus stations (see p.123). Departures are frequent to Aleppo, Crac des Chevaliers and Damascus, and it's not usually necessary to book ahead, though you may want to check in advance about departures to Palmyra.

Camera shops Numerous choices along either Al-Moutanabbi St or Abi Alala al-Maarr St for film, processing and cameras. A convenient photographer's shop for visa extensions is Photo Artin on Ibn Khaldoun St, by the immigration office.

Car rental The *Safir Hotel* has a Mercedes available for rental but only with a driver; examples of return fares (including waiting time) are $36 to the Crac des Chevaliers and $68 to Palmyra. Universal on Ibn Khaldoun St (☎031/468666) is a Europcar agent; English is spoken here but cars are not always available.

Exchange Change cash and travellers' cheques at the branch of the Commercial Bank of Syria just off Ibn Khaldoun St (daily except Fri 8am–12.30pm). Cash only may be changed at a booth a block south of the eastern end of Qouwatli St (daily except Fri 8am–8pm).

Immigration office Located on the third floor of a multipurpose building on Ibn Khaldoun St (daily except Fri 8am–2pm).

Pharmacies Try Modern Pharmacy on Al-Moutanabbi St or City Pharmacy on Abi Alala al-Maarr St.

Post and phones Main post and telephone services are provided in the post office on Abdul Mounem Ryad St (daily except Fri 8am–4.30pm).

Service taxis Departures from outside the *Al-Khayyam Hotel* on Qouwatli St; destinations include Aleppo, Damascus and Hama and (in Lebanon) Beirut and Tripoli.

Travel agents Universal and Al-Borg, both on Ibn Khaldoun St, deal with most of the major airlines. The *Al-Mimas Hotel* on Al-Baladi St has a travel agency attached which books flights and organizes local tours.

Hama

With its pleasant riverside parks and groaning *noria*s turned by the waters of the Orontes, **HAMA** boasts one of the most relaxed and picturesque city centres in Syria. To some the place may seem too much of a well-oiled museum piece – it's usually busy with coach parties photographing themselves beside the carefully restored water-wheels before heading off back to the air-conditioned luxury of the *Apamee Cham Palace* – but there is no denying that the city has charm, and with so many other sights in its immediate surroundings bypassing it simply because everyone else seems to go there would be churlish. However, beyond the obvious attractions of its carefully manicured gardens, there are other less inviting aspects of Hama which soon become apparent. Like Homs, Hama has grown exponentially during the last few decades, and its suburbs, which sprawl in every direction from the centre, are as shabby and as uninviting as any in Syria. Despite the massive building programme, evidence still remains, in the form of shell-pocked buildings and bullet-scarred walls, of the 1982 **Hama Massacre**, a brutal government suppression of a local uprising which represents the worst atrocity perpetrated by the Assad regime in Syria.

Hama's provincial air reflects a **history** spent away from the political spotlight and the major foreign trade routes. Evidence of human settlement here dates back to around 1100 BC when the small kingdom of **Hamath** was ruled from the citadel hill. During the Seleucid era the town, renamed **Epiphania**, became an administrative centre,of minor importance, a function which continued through the Roman and Byzantine eras. Because of its location Hama suffered badly in the disputes between Damascus and Aleppo during the eleventh and twelfth centuries but emerged to gentle prosperity in the Ayyubid period, through Ottoman times and up to the present. For many centuries the city has been a centre of **Sunni Muslim orthodoxy**, and there is a much greater feeling of conservatism here than anywhere else in Syria, with many women wearing traditional black veils, covering their heads completely.

Arrival and information

If you arrive by **train** you should be able to pick up a local bus to the corner of Sadik Avenue and Qouwatli Avenue in the centre of town, though ask the driver as not all buses from the station end up there. The **bus stations** for microbuses and local buses are opposite one another on Al-Mourabet Street, a ten-minute walk – or short bus ride – southwest of the junction of Sadik and Qouwatli. Pullman buses will drop you in the very centre of town at their company offices, most of which are near Sadik Avenue. All the main things to see in Hama are within walking distance of each other and the main hotels, so you are unlikely to need city transport unless you're going out to the train station.

There's a small **tourist office** (daily except Fri 8am–2pm) in the gardens in the centre of town. As usual, they try their best but the staff haven't really got that much to say and on occasions can be downright misleading; hotels are probably a better source of information.

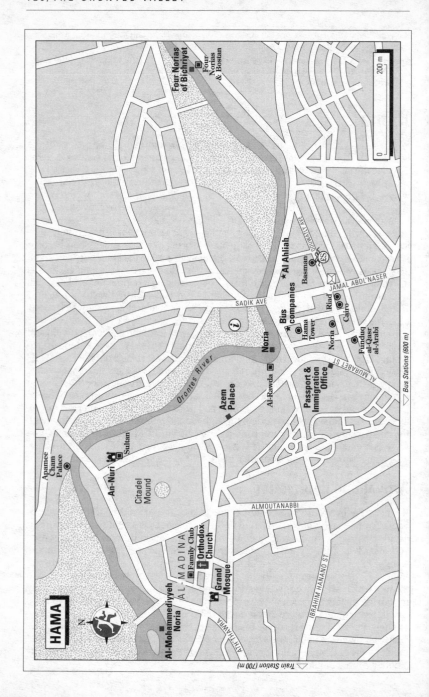

HAMA

Four Norias of Bichriyat
Four Norias & Bostan

Al Ahliah ★
Basman
DOUWATLY AVE
JAMAL ABDL'NASER
SADIK AVE
Bus companies
Hama Tower ★
Riad
Cairo
Noria
Funduq al-Qasr al-Arabi
AL MURABET ST
Noria
Passport & Immigration Office
Al-Rawda
Orontes River
Azem Palace
Sultan
An-Nuri
Apamee Cham Palace
Citadel Mound
ALMOUTANABBI
AL-MADINA
Family Club
Orthodox Church
Grand Mosque
IBRAHIM HANANO ST
AT-THAWRA
Al-Mohammediyyeh Noria

200 m
0

▷ Bus Stations (600 m)

▷ Train Station (700 m)

THE HAMA MASSACRE

Peaceful and mildly proserous though it may be today, in 1982 Hama witnessed the savage quelling of a civilian revolt by the Syrian army which resulted in the deaths of anything between 5000 and 25,000 people. What became known as the **Hama Massacre** has never been any great secret inside or outside Syria, and although few in the country are willing to talk about it, everybody knows it happened; it was, after all, intended as a warning that any dissent against the established order would be met swiftly with cruel violence.

In the late 1970s opposition to the Assad regime was mounting on many fronts, with widespread calls for democratic reform of the corrupt, Alawite-dominated government. Basic human rights were being violated by the secret police, and the military intervention in Lebanon was proving unpopular with the army and the intellectual community, as well as with the general populace, the arrival of Lebanese refugees deepening the existing housing crisis. The most active opposition came from the fundamentalist **Muslim Brotherhood** who wanted to replace the regime with a system based on Sunni orthodoxy. During the late 1970s and early 1980s the Brotherhood launched a series of terrorist attacks in the main cities and even made an unsuccessful attempt on Assad's life; the regime reacted with mass arrests and a series of summary executions. On the outskirts of Hama, one of the strongholds of the Brotherhood, guerrillas ambushed a security checkpoint on April 21, 1981. The government responded three days later by shooting dead an estimated 350 men, completely at random, leaving their bodies in the streets.

On February 2, 1982, sensing an embryonic revolt, special army units were sent into Hama to arrest members of the Brotherhood and confiscate guns. However when the soldiers entered the Barudi quarter of the old city they found armed members of the Brotherhood ready to meet them. The Brotherhood won the first round of fighting, and the call went up from microphones on the city's minarets for a *Jihad*, or holy war, to be waged against Assad. In the ensuing uprising, about a hundred policemen and party officials were killed, guns and ammunition were seized from the local police headquarters and the old city was barricaded. The Syrian army responded quickly and with massive force: up to thirty thousand men were brought into Hama from all over Syria, commanded by Rifaat Assad, the president's brother, and artillery units bombarded the city. The Brotherhood fought back strongly, but on February 22 Rifaat was able to claim victory for the government and promptly flattened the city centre, with thousands of bodies simply being discarded underneath the rubble. An estimated third of Hama's centre was destroyed, leaving some seventy thousand people homeless. (That is why much of the city today looks so modern; in the area where the *Apamee Cham Palace* now stands, for example, there used to be an ancient *noria* and a cluster of domed houses with projecting verandas overlooking the river.)

The Hama Massacre resulted in the immediate annihilation of an extremist terrorist organization, which in fact had little widespread support. But, by such a swift, brutal show of force – and by the widespread human rights violations which characterized the ensuing national state of emergency – Assad succeeded in silencing the wider opposition and ultimately secured the future of his regime as one of the most stable in the Middle East.

Accommodation

One of the reasons travellers have a tendency to linger in Hama is the city's very good selection of **hotels**. The *Cairo* (☎033/237 206, fax 511 715; ②) and the *Riad* (☎033/239 512; ②), next to each other on Qouwatli Avenue, are two of the best budget options in Syria: both are quite disarmingly clean and offer a variety of rooms with constant hot water and the options of en-suite bathrooms and satellite TV. In addition both hotels are very useful sources of information, giving out free maps and organizing tours. In summer for S£100 you can sleep on the roof of the *Cairo*, the owner of which also runs the similarly spotless and even plusher *Noria* opposite (☎ & fax 033/511 715; ④), aimed more at tour groups. An extremely basic budget hotel called the *Funduq al-Qasr al-Arabi al-Kabir* (②) just off Qouwtli Avenue is recommended only if everywhere else is full up.

A recent addition to the Hama hotel scene, and suffering slight teething problems, is the *Hama Tower* (③), located a block north of the *Noria*, which has clean but fairly bare rooms and polite, if slightly muddled, staff. However, it's certainly a better place than the *Basman* (☎033/224 838; ③) at the eastern end of Qouwtli Avenue; rooms here come with bath, TV and balcony, but the place has a run-down, seedy air to it. Five-star luxuries are offered at the *Apamee Cham Palace* (☎033/227 429, fax 233 195; ⑦), including tennis courts and a swimming pool, plus a variety of bars and restaurants.

The City

Greatly restored and unusually litter-free, the **gardens** stretching north of the city centre along the east side of the Orontes are the easiest place to see the *noria*s in action, and as such are the most obvious attraction in Hama. Immediately to the west of here, across the river, are the quieter streets of the **old city**, at the centre of which is the **Azem Palace**, the governor's residence in Ottoman times. It's now an excellent **museum** of Hama and the surrounding region, the exhibits often taking second place to the resplendent rooms and crumbling courtyards. Although it saw some of the fiercest fighting during the 1982 uprising, the prosperous Al-Madina quarter around the **Great Mosque** is worth exploring, too. West and east from the city centre, along the Orontes, are more *noria*s, and you could do a lot worse than allow yourself to finish up (and cool off) at the **Four Norias of Bichriyat**, where some of the tallest wheels grind away next to a couple of terraced waterside restaurants.

Along the Orontes

The thing which will probably surprise you most about the **norias** is the noise they make: a whining, almost mournful groan as the wheel turns in its central support. Out in the countryside you can often hear a *noria* before you see it, and in the central **gardens** of Hama that run up towards the *Apamee Cham Palace Hotel*, the sound is constant and relentless. The wooden wheels here, up to 20m in diameter, date from Mameluke and early Ottoman times and were built to supply water to places near the Orontes (the machines were first developed in Byzantine times, but no evidence of these early wheels remains). The water would be scooped up from the river, and deposited at the top end of a narrow aqueduct built adjacent to the wheel. The aqueduct, supported by elegant stone arches and built on a downward gradient, would then take the water off to nearby mosques and public buildings; out in the countryside the same principle was used for the irrigation of fields, using much more complex aqueducts. Most of the aqueducts have gone now, but the wheels in the central gardens still turn, and the cafés and restaurants in the surrounding area of parkland are pleasantly cooled by their spray. During the evenings well-to-do families are drawn here on their evening stroll – something akin to the Italian *passegiata*.

A ten-minute stroll east of the city centre will bring you to the most impressive set of wheels, known as the **Four Norias of Bichriyat**. Local kids swim in the river here, riding up on the wheels and then spectacularly jumping off the stone supports at the top. On the south bank are two decent restaurants (see p.132), from whose shady terraces you can observe all this mad activity whilst sipping a cool beer or two.

The old city

Immediately to the west of the river, as it makes an abrupt turn northwards in the centre of town, is the **old city**. Its narrow streets, shady and deserted on hot afternoons, are a good place for aimless ambling and offer occasional glimpses of life going on behind barred windows or inside gated courtyards – everything from raucous family arguments to private gatherings of men smoking *nargilehs*. The main sight here is the **Azem Palace** (*Beit al-Azem*; daily except Tues 9am–6pm; S£200), the expansive and beautiful former residence of an Ottoman governor of Hama, Assad Pasha al-Azem, who ruled the city up until 1742 when he assumed a similar office in Damascus (see p.72). The building itself is a draw, although many parts are rather ramshackle and recovering from the events of 1982; those rooms which survived the crossfire, or which have been restored, give a good impression of the extravagant lifestyle led by Ottoman overlords of Syria in the eighteenth century.

To the right of the main entrance you'll find the **haremlek** (the private quarters of the ruler), left much as the last Ottoman governor would have known it, with dark wooden panelling and delicate inlay work giving a feeling both of opulence and intimacy. Most of the rest of the palace is now given over to a rather haphazard **museum**, some rooms displaying historical artefacts from Roman and other times, others left bare or with enough finery intact to indicate further the lavish lifestyle of the Pasha. In one of the rooms leading off the courtyard are displayed finds unearthed from the citadel and from around the Orontes Valley; by far the most interesting is a very well-preserved **mosaic** found in a village near Homs and thought to have once decorated the floor of a Roman dining room. Unusually, the mosaic portrays an appealingly intimate domestic scene, rather than a religious or mythical story. The figures are shown playing musical instruments (the whole group is conducted by the woman on the left playing the cymbals), and historians have been able to use the illustration as a valuable source of information about music in Roman times; the organ, for example, is operated by children (dressed as Eros) working a bellows.

Heading upstairs you'll come to the **Royal Hall**, a bare but still rather grand room where the Pasha had his sleeping quarters. Adjacent to the upstairs courtyard is a series of unedifying rooms where costumes and rituals from local life are displayed by bemused-looking mannequins.

The **An-Nuri Mosque** to the north of the palace was built in the late twelfth century by Saladin's uncle, Nur al-Din, under whose command Muslim forces gained important victories against Crusader outposts in the mountains west of Hama. It's an intimate building, shady and secretive like many small mosques, with a striking minaret comprising bands of alternating yellow limestone and black basalt. Very close by are more **norias**, one of which can be observed from the *Sultan Restaurant* (see p.132), reached by a tunnel very close to the mosque.

The Al-Madina quarter

Few visitors seem to venture away from the carefully tended flowerbeds of the main parks and the peeling decay of the old city into **Al-Madina**, but there are a couple of things worth seeing amid the modern roads and well-heeled apartment buildings. Northwest of the An-Nuri Mosque you'll find the site of the **citadel** which is today no more than a mound. Excavated in parts by Danish archeologists, the site yielded evidence of occupation dating back to Neolithic times, but currently there is nothing more than a carefully landscaped picnic area here, popular with families on Fridays.

Three hundred metres to the west are the two buildings that have traditionally formed the religious centre of the town. Founded in the eighth century by the Umayyads on a site previously occupied by a Byzantine basilica and various pagan temples, the **Great Mosque** (*Jamia al-Umawi*) reflects the old basilica plan: its prayer hall has three aisles, and the domes on top were built in the form of a cross. However, the mosque was destroyed during the 1982 uprising and, nearly two decades later, its reconstruction is still not complete. To the northeast of the mosque stands the **Orthodox church**, grand and modern – and usually closed. Back on the river banks are two more *noria*s, one of which, the **Al-Mohammediyyeh Noria**, is the largest in Hama. Don't bother with the footbridge adjacent to the wheel, which leads across into some fairly uninteresting parkland on the north bank of the river.

Eating and drinking

It's very easy to eat well and cheaply in Hama, though there is little variety on offer – your choice of **restaurant** is going to be determined more by surroundings than by what's on the menu. Look out for the town's **speciality**: available in most of its restaurants and in any number of cake shops along Qouwatli Avenue, it's called *halawat al-jibn*, a sort of sugary rice pudding made from cheese, honey and syrup and often served with ice cream as a topping.

The *Four Norias* and the *Bostan* are two similar and generally quiet restaurants situated next door to one another by the Four Norias of Bichriyat; both will provide regular Syrian fare and a beer for around S£200, to the eerie accompaniment of the groaning waterwheels. Also in fine surroundings, overlooking the *noria*s in the centre of town, is the *Al Rawda*, which has pleasant views of the river and gardens, slightly offhand staff and reasonably priced food – about S£200 for a meal and drink (no beer). The similarly priced *Sultan* by the An-Nuri Mosque offers diners the opportunity to sit right next to a *noria*, watching its unceasing rotation through glass panes, but overall it's a drab little place and doesn't serve beer. A much brighter spot, and only a little bit more expensive, is the *Family Club* near the Great Mosque; in the evenings locals often just come here to chill out over a soft drink. The very cheap restaurant in the old train station on Abdul Mounem Riyad Street offers occasional live music and gets very busy on Fridays when there is much consumption of *arak* and impromptu dancing between 3pm and 8pm. However, the building itself is not as evocative as it might sound, its innards having simply been ripped out and replaced with tables.

Aside from these, there are numerous cheap eateries serving kebab and chicken on or around Qouwatli Avenue; for a cheap pizza or hamburger you could always try the café next door to the Al-Aliah office in the town centre. Alternatively, if feeling flush, you could venture into one of the restaurants at the

Apamee Cham Palace Hotel; its terrace is very popular with affluent locals on a Friday night, when there is sometimes a singer.

Listings

Banks The Commercial Bank of Syria on Qouwatli Ave will change cash and travellers' cheques (daily except Fri 8am–2pm & 5–8pm).

Bookshop The *Apamee Cham Palace Hotel* has the only decent selection of English-language books.

Bus companies The Karnak office in the *Cafeteria Afamia*, overlooking the main *noria*s in the centre of town, has services to Homs, Damascus and Aleppo. Next door is the Qadmous company which serves Homs, Damascus, Aleppo, Latakia and Tartous; next to this in turn is Al-Nawras which, in addition to the five towns served by Qadmous, runs buses to Qamishli and Raqqa. Al-Ahliah is located 100m east down the same road and has frequent services to Aleppo, Damascus, Homs, Latakia, Raqqa and Tartous.

Car rental The branch of Chamcar in the *Apamee Cham Palace Hotel* is the only option, or you might consider renting a car with driver (see "Tours" below).

Immigration office Hidden away on the third floor of a building on Al Murabbet St in the centre of town (daily except Fri 8am–1pm); look for a sign in English, "passports".

Post office A large, modern building on Qouwatli Ave (corner of Sadik Ave), which also offers telephone services (daily except Fri 8am–4.30pm).

Service taxis Departures to Aleppo, Damascus and Homs from outside the microbus station.

Tours The *Noria*, *Cairo* and *Riad* hotels all have drivers available to run to any itinerary you want, certainly worth considering for the desert sites of Qasr ibn Warden and Isriya (see pp.140–1) or a tour of some of the nearby Dead Cities (see p.208) where public transport is unreliable. Prices are reasonable: around $50 for a whole day depending on where you want to go, how long you want to stay there and how many of you there are.

Around Hama

As soon as you leave the built-up limits of Hama, the **desert** begins. You get the same jam-packed minibuses and lunatic truckies careering along the desert highways as you do everywhere else in the country, but the difference in this part of Syria is the scenery: the desert here, unlike the pancake flatness of the eastern and central desert, is rocky and hilly, and venturing out into it is an absorbing experience itself – never mind the wealth of archeological sites that can be reached from Hama.

Hama is a fairly good transport hub, and the sites described in this section are all reachable on day-trips – which is fortunate, since there are no hotels available at any of them. The most popular excursion is to the Roman ruins at **Apamea**, where extensively unearthed remains of the streets, buildings and fortifications of this former desert trading centre make for a full day's visit – though bear in mind that the bus service back to Hama is thin from mid-afternoon. Other ideas for excursions **west of Hama** include a number of ruined castles, the most interesting and accessible of which is at **Misyaf**, while nearby **Deir Soleib** offers a couple of remarkable ruined Byzantine churches.

East of Hama there is less of note to visit – and far fewer people looking around what sights there are. Two roads head out across the desert plains: one southeast to Salamiyeh via another impressive castle **Qalaat Shmaimis**, the other northeast to the flamboyant Byzantine palace at **Qasr ibn Warden** and the ruinous Byzantine settlement of **Anderin**. East again is the Roman temple at **Isriya**, possibly the remotest tourist sight in Syria. Microbuses head out along the Salamiyeh road passing Qalaat Shmaimis, but for the other sites you'll need to arrange some kind of transport, probably from Hama.

In the villages alongside these desert roads to the east of Hama, you're bound to notice the proliferation of traditional **"beehive" houses**, built of mud and straw, which have their origins in the round houses of the Neolithic period found in the region. If you want to investigate further, the *Cairo* and *Noria* hotels in Hama organize tours which allow beehive residents to entertain you with some tea and *laban* (a drink made of water, milk and fruit). The first thing you're aware of coming into one of these distinctive dwellings is the coolness inside, and the apparently incongruous presence of electric lighting and appliances. The people you'll meet are generally as friendly as language barriers will allow; as head of the household the father will dominate conversation with any visitors, whilst the children scamper in and out and the mother maintains an equilibrium between the two.

Another option for a day-trip, not covered in this chapter, would be the **Dead Cities** around Maarat al-Numan (see p.208), located halfway between Hama and Aleppo and conveniently approached from either centre.

Apamea

Most visitors to Hama – in fact, most visitors to Syria – make it to **APAMEA**, and although the tour buses which start pitching up here from mid-morning onwards detract somewhat from the excitement of its desolate location, it's still well worth the effort of seeing the place, even if you have only a passing interest in things Roman. Like Palmyra, Apamea was a **desert trading post** on the long trek from the Mediterranean to Central Asia, and the remains, well preserved by the dryness of the climate, form one of the most important archeological sites in the Middle East. Several eras of history threaten to sweep you off your tired feet here: the site is essentially Roman, with important additions from the Byzantine era, but the citadel dates from early medieval times, and in **Qalaat Mudiq**, the modern settlement stretching along the dusty main road which takes its name from the citadel, there is even an Ottoman *caravanserai* (now the site museum).

Some history

Apamea was founded around 300 BC by **Seleucus**, ruler of northern Syria and Mesopotamia following the death of Alexander the Great, and named after his Persian wife. During the Seleucid period the town became an important trading post, linking Latakia with Palmyra and eventually Persia and the Asian interior. After conquest by the **Romans** in 64 BC Apamea became an important garrison town and was dramatically rebuilt, its population expanding to about 500,000, of whom an estimated 380,000 were slaves. A huge rebuilding programme had to be undertaken following an earthquake in 115 AD, so the famous colonnaded main street as you see it today dates only to around 180 AD. Apamea's fortunes declined with the end of Byzantine rule, but it re-emerged into brief prominence in the early twelfth century when it was occupied by the **Crusaders**. However, after further **earthquakes** in 1157 and 1170 almost completely destroyed the town, the population moved to and refortified the old Roman acropolis on the hill overlooking the valley. During Ottoman times, this village within the walls, Qalaat Mudiq, became an important stopover point on the pilgrimage route from Istanbul to Mecca.

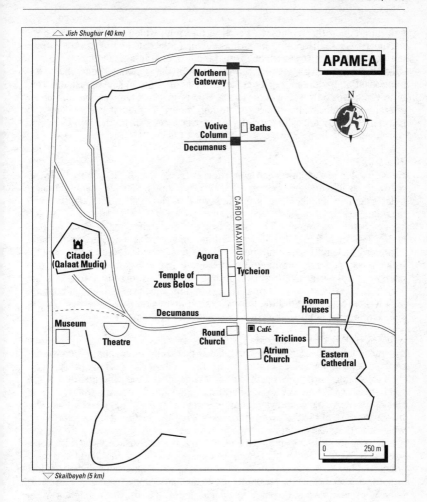

Practicalities

From Hama take a **microbus** northwest to Skailbeyeh (45km), where you'll have to change onto another microbus to complete the journey (9km north); remember to ask for **Afamia**, the local name, rather than Apamea, the Roman name which has stuck among English speakers. Total journey time should be no longer than an hour, but note that buses tend to dry up around 4pm, and anyone travelling here on a Friday should prepare for longer waiting times. About 25km out of Hama, buses to Skailbeyeh pass by **Qalaat Sheisar**, a badly ruined Arab castle once used as a base to mount attacks against the Crusaders stationed at Apamea; it's hardly essential viewing but an easy break in the journey.

The bus from Skailbeyeh will drop you outside the museum, from where a track runs past the entrance to the citadel, and close to the amphitheatre, up to the main site. If you're coming **by car or taxi**, it's best to drive on beyond the museum, taking the well-marked road to the right, which heads up around the northern edge of the citadel and brings you up to the café by the *cardo maximus*, the long, columned street which formed the heart of the Roman city.

In summer Apamea gets so scorchingly hot that looking round the site is unpleasant at any time other than early to mid-morning or late afternoon. This, however, leaves only a short time to see what is, in fact, a huge and absorbing set of archeological remains (there are no hotels here to make it easier). The only place on the site itself selling **drinks** is the overpriced café on the *cardo maximus* so remember to bring water with you.

The site

Head first for the whitewashed **café** right in the centre of the site by the *cardo maximus*, as it's the best place to get your bearings. The tarmac leading up here follows the line of a decumanus, one of several roads which intersected the *cardo maximus* at right angles – part of the Hellenistic grid pattern of streets bequeathed to the Romans. The long line of columns that form the *cardo maximus* is the site's most immediate draw, with the remains of several interesting buildings along its length. The churches and Byzantine cathedral south and east of the café are very ruinous, but the Roman houses along the road to the east are better preserved and easier to appreciate, despite – or because of – their smaller scale. Finally, there's the decrepit Roman theatre and the medieval citadel, both of them on a lavish scale but with little to recommend them save the fine views over the site, and the plain of the Ghab, from the entrance to the latter.

NORTH ALONG THE CARDO MAXIMUS
The most obvious feature of the site today is the **cardo maximus**, which was the main street and showpiece of Roman Apamea, built to show off the prosperity of the city. Aligned precisely north–south, it runs longer than the main thoroughfares in either Damascus or Palmyra, its high, fluted columns, mostly reconstructed during this century, striding energetically across the desert. Following the earthquake of 115 the *cardo maximus* was rebuilt starting from the north end, where the Classical sobriety of the columns contrasts vividly with a freer, more ornate style towards the southern end, which was reconstructed several decades later. The empty consoles projecting from many of the columns would have once supported busts of eminent citizens, but most of these have long since been lost, destroyed or carted off to museums in Aleppo and Damascus, though some can be seen in the museum beneath the citadel. In many of the paving stones on the street, the ruts made by chariot wheels can still be seen, while beyond the columns, where there once stood elegant doorways, there are now just vacant openings taking you into weed-strewn areas of rubble.

Strolling north along the *cardo maximus* from the café, the first remains you come to, on the left, are of the **agora**, the long, narrow marketplace, not all of which has been excavated, which runs for 150m beside the main street. Over the hill beyond this are the scant remains of the **Temple of Zeus Belos**, which was dismantled in 384 as Christianity took hold in the Roman Empire. Back on the main drag you can see on the east side of the street a series of columns with spiral fluting, the directions of the spiral on one column alternating with that on the next, a technique unique to Apamea. Their elegance forms a suitable counterpoint to the grandiose facade of the **tycheion** opposite, where Tyche, the protecting goddess of the city, was worshipped.

About 600m north of the Temple of the Tyche stands the single most striking feature of the *cardo maximus*, a **votive column** which once marked the intersection with a decumanus. Heavily restored and reconstructed, the column is little more than an ostentatious showpiece, architecturally useless but intended as a grandiose and permanent monument to the city's power and wealth. On your right, 150m beyond the column, are the **baths**, built in 117 AD by Emperor Trajan but now rather the worse for wear. No restoration has gone on here, so it's possible to appreciate only the scale of the original building but not its layout, which would have comprised two large halls for the warm and cold baths. At the end of the *cardo maximus* is a second-century **northern gateway** under which would have passed the road to Antioch, now in Turkey but in Roman times the seat of the provincial government of Syria. Of the 6km of city **walls**, which were refortified by the emperor Justinian during the sixth century, this is the best-preserved section – though that isn't saying a great deal.

THE SOUTHERN END OF THE CARDO MAXIMUS

Immediately south and east of the café building are large areas of ruins, mostly fallen stones from churches and civic buildings which are now hard to distinguish. Closest to the café are the scant remains of the foundations of a **round church**, dating to the sixth century. The jumbled collection of masonry opposite marks the **atrium church**, of similar dating, dedicated to SS Cosmas and Damian, twin brothers who worked as healers without charging fees; one of their services was a process called incubation, whereby a sick person could spend the night in their church in the hope that they would be cured by their dreams.

East over the brow of a low hill, yet more fallen stonework on the right marks the vast site of the **eastern cathedral**, which also dates mostly from around the sixth century. The remains of the walls reach 4m in height, and you can just about appreciate something of the cathedral's layout: the building was entered by steps from the decumanus, and the floor of the narthex, the entrance hall which spanned the width of the church, can still be seen. On the west side of the cathedral, the *triclinos* consisted of eighty rooms arranged around a courtyard, which points to its possible use as a governor's residence; on the southeast side, a series of rooms was used for baptisms and other ceremonies. Some of the most intricately decorated stonework and mosaics that were found in these two sets of buildings can be seen in the site museum.

Less monumental than the cathedral are the remains to the north of **Roman houses**, excavated since 1973. You can still make out the main courtyards, lined with columns, which would once have also had central fountains, benches in the cool arcades and marble paving. The intimate scale of the buildings here makes them one of the most interesting parts of the whole site, although they seem to be overlooked by most visitors.

THE THEATRE AND CITADEL

Located behind modern houses between the *cardo maximus* and the main road, the **theatre** probably dates from the late second century AD and would have been one of the largest in the Roman world. It was certainly the largest in Syria, with a stage almost a third as big again as that in Bosra, but its ruinous state makes estimating seating capacity difficult, as many of the blocks have been taken away for building works elsewhere in the town. The theatre is perhaps best appreciated from a distance rather than close up, though the scant remains are hardly impressive from whatever angle you view them.

The formidable **citadel** of Apamea, **Qalaat Mudiq**, occupies a spectacular position, overlooking the Orontes Valley on one side and the desert on the other. A fort was first established on this hill in Seleucid times; later on it became an Arab bulwark against the Crusaders, who captured many of the castles on the western side of the valley and were in fact in control of this castle between 1106 and 1149. Inside the walls there is no reminder of the former fortress, but instead a small village with its own stores, stalls and a small mosque, outside of which hustlers will sell "antiques", coins and other artefacts supposedly found around the ruins. The main reason for coming up here, however, is the fantastic view over to the ruins from the entrance to the citadel.

The museum

Hard by the modern main road, the **museum** (daily except Tues 9am–6pm; S£200) occupies an eighteenth-century Turkish *caravanserai*, which was used by trading convoys as a warehouse and rest place. Housed in the dark, cavernous rooms which line the courtyard, the artefacts from Apamea and nearby Roman settlements mostly date from between 230 and 370 AD.

The mosaic set into the ground as you enter the building depicts *Socrates and the Sages,* with the philosopher surrounded by his followers in a composition that's strongly reminiscent of typical portrayals of Christ and his disciples. Look out also for the two bulky, functional sarcophagi nearby, which were found in the same tomb and date from around 230; the first one you come to is that of a former legionary and has an inscription dedicated by his wife. Further on is another wonderfully preserved mosaic, measuring over 7m in length, entitled *The Judgement of the Nereides*. Found in the eastern cathedral it depicts a competition, judged by Poseidon (fourth figure from right), who has declared Cassiopeia (nude figure, third from left) to be the most beautiful maiden.

Qalaat Burzey

Beyond Apamea the marshy but fertile **Ghab depression** opens up around the Orontes River; scorchingly hot in summer, the valley is crossed by a dense network of minor roads, with principal roads running north—south on either side. Dramatically situated on a steep bluff, **Qalaat Burzey** (also Mazra or Barzuya) is the principal site of archeological interest here, 34km northwest of Apamea,but is only really worth visiting if you've rented your own transport in Homs, as public transport options are severely limited. To reach the castle take the main road which runs along the western edge of the valley from Misyaf towards Jish Shughur; 2.5km north of the village of Jooreen the road skirts a small artificial lake, and from here you must walk along a track and then scramble up a steep boulder-strewn slope to the ruins, just visible from the road.

The castle remnants lie scattered across a barren hillside, with magnificent views over the Orontes valley to the east. In Seleucid times a castle stood here protecting the route between Latakia and Apamea, though what can be seen today dates from the eleventh century when the Crusaders occupied the site. In 1188 Saladin took the castle after a series of fierce raids against its apparently impregnable walls. The main entrance to the castle, where its defensive strength was concentrated, would have been through the western wall. The widespread ruins are fairly insubstantial, but it's possible to pick out the watchtower overlooking the valley, two levels of fortification, a large chapel and the rectangular keep, which is an Arab construction.

Misyaf and around

Numerous microbuses ply the forty-kilometre route west from Hama to **MISYAF**, a fairly dull junction town which nevertheless contains the best preserved of the **Assassin castles** (see box below). The initial view of the castle as you descend the road from Hama is the finest, especially in the early morning when it rises fairytale-like out of the mist. The mess of stonework used in its construction reflects both the poor quality of Assassin work and the fact that this site has been fortified since Hellenistic times; the Classical masonry used in the walls suggests the existence of a nearby Roman settlement from which building materials were pilfered. The Assassins took over the fortress in 1140, as one of a network of sites

---

THE ASSASSINS

The **Assassins** (*Hashashin*) are a Shi'ite Muslim sect who earned their popular nickname, probably in the eleventh century, by their reputed use of hashish to prepare themselves for attack. This reputation, however, is recorded only in travellers' tales (most famously Marco Polo), and not in any native Islamic source, and probably only serves to illustrate outsiders' long-term bewilderment at the motives and beliefs of the secret sect. The central element of their beliefs is, in fact, a devotion to the eighth-century Shi'ite leader **Ismael**, though the sect hold certain tenets that predate even Mohammed, such as the idea that good and evil are both a natural part of a world whose creator may himself be separate from God. Man therefore contains both good and evil, as well as an element of the divine, access to which the Assassins claim to possess – and which was supposedly revealed to novices through the use of hashish.

The first recorded references to the sect date to the period of political and religious fragmentation in the late eleventh century, when they were essentially a terrorist group in Persia, based around a small territorial holding that emerged upon the death of the Fatimid Caliph Mustansir in 1094. In the twelfth century the Assassins began to expand their influence into Syria basing themselves at the castle of **Misyaf**, which they acquired in 1140. The sect then undertook a policy of killing anyone, Muslim or Christian, who might threaten their independence, whence the term "assassin", brought back to Europe by the Crusaders, derives its present meaning. The Assassins were particularly active between 1163 and 1193 under the leadership of **Rashid al-Din Sinan**, who was dubbed the "Old Man of the Mountains" by the Crusaders. In 1176 Sinan even dared to make an attempt on the life of the orthodox Sunni leader Saladin, who was laying siege to Misyaf. The story goes that Saladin was awoken by nightmares to find on his bed a poisoned dagger and a foreboding verse which seemed to have been left by Sinan himself. Duly frightened, Saladin made a hasty retreat, asking for Sinan's pardon and promising to call off his campaign against the Assassins.

The sect's strength diminished during the late twelfth century as the Sunnis extended control from Damascus and Aleppo, and much of their coherence was lost in 1260 with the sacking of their Persian headquarters in Alamut by the Mongols. In the early 1270s Sultan Baibars put down an Assassin revolt and placed their castles under Mameluke governors, effectively destroying their political identity and reducing them to a harmless minority. The sect's members sought refuge in the mountains where they have lived until modern times. During the last century many settled around the desert town of Salamiyeh, though the largest remaining group is in India and Pakistan.

they established to protect their presence in the mountains, after they had fled persecution by orthodox Sunni regimes in Damascus and Aleppo. The plan of the castle is fairly conventional with a central keep enveloped by an outer wall with square bastions, further protected by the steep rocky slopes below. A visit won't last long as it's quite a small place, but tourists here are rare and the guardian may decide to make a fuss of you, plying you with tea and dusty posters.

Deir Soleib

The small, unassuming village of **DEIR SOLEIB** plays dispassionate host to a couple of fascinating **Byzantine churches**, fairly well preserved and not dissimilar to those found in the Dead Cities around Aleppo. No buses run all the way to the village, which lies 4km east of Misyaf, south of the main road to Hama, so ask a microbus driver travelling back to Hama to drop you at the turning and then walk or hitch the last 4km; bear in mind when returning that buses along the main road dry up around 2pm. Alternatively, simply negotiate a price with a taxi driver in Misyaf. Just before you reach Deir Soleib you'll come upon the first church, dated stylistically to the sixth century, though the building is largely undecorated except for the occasional carved cross. The walls and the semi-domed apse which protrudes from the rear of the church are still intact, and you can make out a cross-shaped font in the baptistery off the southern end of the narthex and a mausoleum with three sarcophagi to the south of the church. Internally the church, though a three-aisled basilica in form, is almost square; a gallery reserved for women would have once ran along the upper levels of the side aisles. The second Byzantine church can be found 2km southeast of the village, reachable only on foot. Dated by an inscription above the central portal to 604–5 AD, it's much more ruinous than the first, but its setting, a jumble of masonry surrounded by stillness, is absorbing.

Qalaat Shmaimis

Rising out of the desert with breathtaking aplomb atop the summit of a steep volcanic cone, 20km southeast of Hama, are the remains of the thirteenth-century Ayyubid fortification **Qalaat Shmaimis**. The castle is set at least a kilometre back from the road, and the scramble up to it is a strenuous one, so you may want to consider coming here either by taxi or as part of a tour organized by one of Hama's hotels, rather than by simply hopping off one of the many buses that plod along the road to Salamiyeh. As the drawbridge has disappeared, you'll need gripping footwear to get up the slippery slope and inside the castle. Once there, as so often the case in Syria, the remains offer nothing but a disappointing jumble of masonry. However, the views from the ramparts, across the windswept plains and over towards distant grey hills, are predictably superb, and it's the breezy and utterly silent remoteness of the place which grabs the imagination most.

Qasr ibn Warden and Anderin

The remarkable desert fortress complex of **Qasr ibn Warden**, 62km northeast of Hama, is one of the most flamboyant Byzantine constructions in Syria. It was completed in 565 AD, the last year of the reign of Emperor Justinian who had attempted to restore to the empire much of the land lost in the east since Rome's heyday in the second century. In order to secure the conquests of his military commander Belisarius against the Persians, he constructed a series of fortifications along the

Euphrates. Unlike formidable Halebiye (see p.221) and Resafe (see p.219), however, Qasr ibn Warden displays a fey extravagance, which actually has much more in common with the architecture of Constantinople, including the distinctive brick and basalt banding of the imperial capital. Rather than meeting the Persian threat head on, this settlement was probably designed more to monitor the Bedouin and to serve as the residence of some important military commander – possibly even Belisarius himself, who died one year after its completion.

The key must be obtained from the genial guardian of the site, who lives in the house closest to it, marked "Maison de la Mission National". The centrepiece of the complex is the **palace**, entered through a broad vaulted hall. Beyond are a series of rooms to the left and right, mainly residential quarters and ceremonial rooms, and a stairway leading to the second-floor dormitory area, where you can look down onto the courtyard and the restored stables at the far end. The **church** next to the palace also still impresses. The staircase on its northwest side leads to an upper storey, probably reserved for women according to Byzantine tradition. Unusually tall, the church was built with pointed rather than semicircular main arches, with its dome – long since collapsed – raised slightly awkwardly on a drum. These moderately eccentric features, together with the general clumsiness of the carvings, have led to speculation that the architect was not from Constantinople but rather a local imperfectly imitating the forms of the capital, which had recently been copied in Damascus. The last building in the complex is a **military barracks**, 100m to the south of the palace, which at one time would have been the largest building of the three, though nothing much remains of it today.

It's best to arrange your own **transport** in Hama to get to Qasr ibn Warden, though buses from the small eastern station near the Great Mosque in Hama run as far as the dusty town of Al-Hamra. To cover the last 16km from there, you'll have to negotiate with one of the local taxi drivers – it's a small place so it won't take long for you to get noticed.

Anderin

No buses, or indeed road, reach out to **Anderin**, 25km beyond Qasr ibn Warden, so if you don't have a car you'll have to pay someone to take you there, either from Hama or Al-Hamra. The last 3km or so is along a bumpy desert track, making progress slow and your driver increasingly unhappy as he ponders the damage being done to the underside of his vehicle. Once there, you'll find that Anderin, though an extensive site, dating back to at least the second century AD, offers nothing but a mass of ancient rubble emerging from the landscape, making a trip barely worthwhile anyway. Little is discernible apart from a Byzantine church and barracks, though at one time this would have been a settlement of some significance with a further nine churches. However, the town was built largely of mud-brick and has almost entirely disintegrated, the more substantial stonework having been pilfered, even within the last couple of decades.

Isriya

The third-century AD Roman temple at **ISRIYA** can be reached in about ninety minutes from Salamiyeh via a new paved road that continues on across the desert to Resafe (p.219), though no buses run along here. Alternatively, there is an unmetalled desert track from Anderin, but you would need four-wheel drive and a guide for this journey.

A Roman town was built here at the crossroads of two trading routes which ran from Resafe to Salamiyeh and from Qinnesrin to Palmyra. The settlement boasted a citadel as testament to its defensive importance, but today the white limestone **temple** stands alone on the citadel mound. The eastern doorway of the stocky building contains impressively elaborate decoration, similar to and contemporary with examples at Baalbek in Lebanon. A staircase in the masonry to the right of the doorway will take you up to the former level of the terrace. The improvised Bedouin graveyard situated in front of the temple lends the place a curious air of sanctity, but the most remarkable aspect of Isriya is its sheer remoteness – this must be one of the loneliest outposts of Syrian archeology.

travel details

Trains

Hama to: Aleppo (approx 1 daily; 2hr 30min); Damascus (1 daily; 4hr 30min); Homs (1 daily; 1hr 15min).

Homs to: Aleppo (approx 1 daily; 3hr 45min); Damascus (1 daily; 3hr 15min); Hama (1 daily; 1hr 15min).

Local buses and microbuses

Hama: frequent services to Aleppo (2hr 30min); Damascus (4hr); Al-Hamra (40min); Homs (1hr); Maarat al-Numan (1hr); Misyaf (35min); Salamiyeh (30min); Skailbeyeh (40min).

Homs: frequent services to Aleppo (3hr 30min); Crac des Chevaliers (1hr 15min); Damascus (3hr); Hama (1hr); Tartous (2hr).

Karnak buses

Hama to: Aleppo (4 daily; 1hr); Damascus (4 daily; 3hr); Homs (4 daily; 1hr).

Homs to: Aleppo (2 daily; 2hr); Damascus (3 daily; 2hr); Hama (2 daily; 50min); Latakia (2 daily; 3hr); Palmyra (1 daily; 2hr 30min); Tartous (2 daily; 1hr).

Pullman buses

Pullman buses **from Hama** cover the same routes as Karnak, plus Latakia (4hr); Qamishli (8hr); Raqqa (4hr); and Tartous (2hr). **From Homs**, Pullman buses run to the same destinations as Karnak.

CHAPTER FOUR

THE COAST AND THE MOUNTAINS

S yria's coastline will win few admirers. For most of its length, the beaches are strewn with liberal quantities of garbage, and the air is muggy and hazy in summer, chilly and damp in winter. Even worse, in many places the sea is filthy, with the stench of sewage never far from the nostrils. Things get better in the two main towns of this region, **Tartous**, which boasts a reasonably intact old quarter, and **Latakia**, with a cosmopolitan, European air about it that's unique in Syria. If it's **beaches** you're after, you'll have to head north of Latakia before you can find anywhere decent or safe to swim; but if you're on the lookout for history, you'll find it dotted all along the coast, encompassing remains from the Bronze Age to the Middle Ages – and usually cheek-by-jowl with modern beach resorts, oil refineries or military zones. Undoubtedly the principal draw is just north of Latakia at **Ugarit**, where you can see the remains of a city which rose to prominence around 3000 BC and whose scribes and civil servants had a hand in inventing what was probably the world's first written alphabet. You can see scant Roman remains at **Jableh**, south of Latakia, and Phoenician ones at **Amrit**, near Tartous, although neither is a patch on similar sites up in the mountains or in other parts of the country. The Crusaders, whose castles are a major attraction in the mountains, have left their mark in the old city and cathedral at Tartous, on the nearby island of **Arwad**, and further north along the coast at **Qalaat Marqab**.

It's in the rugged **Jebel al-Sariya**, the extension of the Anti-Lebanon range which rises up behind the coastal plain, that you'll find most of the points of inter-est in this region. These mountains have the strongest regional identity in Syria: their climate, scenery and wildlife are different from everywhere else in the coun-try, more akin to upland areas of Greece or Cyprus. Winters are cold and wet, with snow likely in January and February, and chilly, rainy days the norm until the end of April. In the summer it's generally cool and cloudy; while the rest of

---

ACCOMMODATION PRICE CODES

In this book, all hotels have been categorized according to the **price codes** out-lined below. They represent the minimum you can expect to pay for a **double room** in each hotel; for further details, see p.31.

① under S£300/US$7.50
② S£300–600/US$7.50–15
③ S£600–1000/US$15–25
④ S£1000–1400/US$25–35

⑤ US$35–50/S£1400–2000
⑥ US$50–90/S£2000–3600
⑦ US$90–130/S£3600–5200
⑧ US$130 and over/S£5200 and over

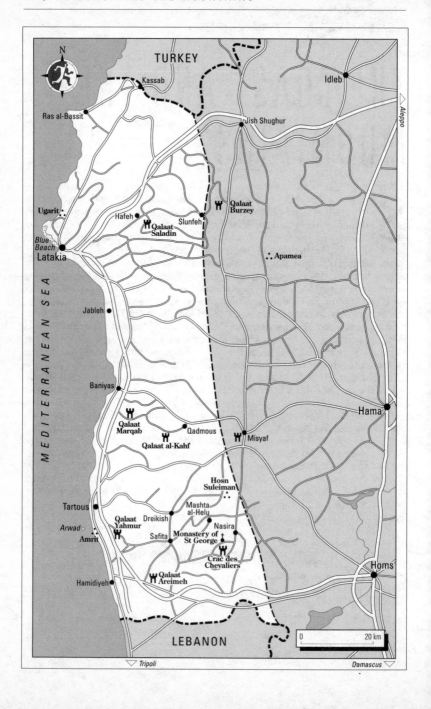

the country gradually wilts under months of drought, the mountains often experience short, heavy thunderstorms, particularly in the early evenings. The scenery tends to be grassy limestone moorland in the south, with villages hidden by steep bluffs and overlooked by ruined castles, but as you go further north you'll encounter forests of spruce and pine, and valleys dotted with churches and stone-built farmhouses. The people of the mountains are initially more reserved than city- or desert-dwellers and, though Arabic-speaking, have traditionally been regarded with mistrust by other Syrians, partly because many of them follow the Christian or Alawite faiths.

Undoubtedly the major draw in the mountains is the **Crac des Chevaliers**, the magnificent Crusader fortress built during the twelfth century to protect the vital upland route linking Tartous with Homs. Now a regular stop for tour buses, which rumble up here from Damascus or, increasingly, from cruise ships docked at Tartous, the Crac shouldn't be missed, but after seeing it you'll probably want a taste of some of the other, less visited sites. The Greek Orthodox **Monastery of St George** lies very close to the Crac, and in the same area is **Safita**, a modern town which boasts the imposing keep of the Crusaders' **White Castle**. Higher up in the mountains, and difficult to reach with or without your own transport, you'll find the remains of an ancient Roman temple at **Hosn Suleiman**, a site of worship (of a variety of deities) for centuries which is impressively situated amidst desolate moorland scenery. In the north of the region the Crusaders established another base at **Qalaat Saladin**, taken in 1188 by the Muslim general whose name it bears, and now an impressive ruin, dramatically surrounded by woods and steep valleys.

With **accommodation** possibilities in the mountains rather limited, you'll most likely find yourself staying in Tartous or Latakia and daytripping inland from there. Both towns are easily reachable by road from Damascus and Aleppo, but away from the coast **public transport** becomes limited and sporadic, and you'll find yourself relying on slow, irregular buses or whatever transport locals can provide. The more you venture off the beaten track, the more interest and curiosity – and therefore offers of help – you will attract. With patience and perseverance you can reach all the places in this chapter without your own wheels, although you might find yourself having to fork out hefty wads of cash to locals if you want to reach some of the more obscure places; good humour and a sure sense of how much you are willing to spend on transport are necessary prerequisites for negotiating lifts in this way. If this doesn't appeal but you still want to see more than the Crac des Chevaliers, then seriously consider **renting a car**, either in Latakia or, planning ahead, in Damascus, Homs or Aleppo – this is the region in Syria where you'll find it most worthwhile, although the lack of good maps and inadequate signposting will pose problems for drivers. Perhaps the most disappointing aspect of the mountains is the lack of opportunity for **hiking** – there are no recognized paths or trails, and no maps to let you guide yourself, so you'll most likely end up walking along roads between villages.

Tartous and around

The charming small fishing town and former Crusader stronghold of **TARTOUS** is now Syria's second most important port after Latakia – although you will probably see nothing of the docks, which are located a fair distance to the north of the city. As far as visitors are concerned, Tartous is principally a pleasant base for

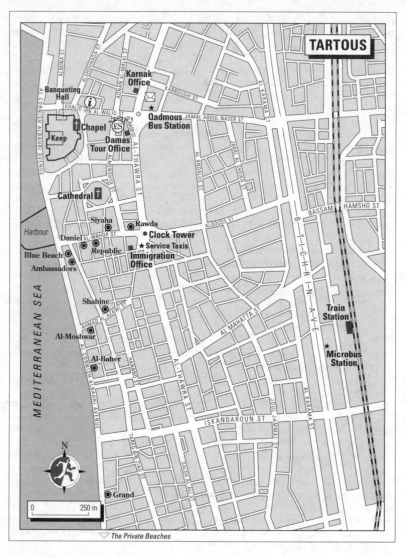

TARTOUS

Banqueting Hall

Karnak Office

Chapel

Keep

Damas Tour Office

Qadmous Bus Station

Cathedral

Siyaha

Rawda

Clock Tower

Daniel

Service Taxis

Republic

Immigration Office

Blue Beach

Ambassadors

Shahine

Al-Moshwar

Al-Baher

Harbour

MEDITERRANEAN SEA

Train Station

Microbus Station

ISKANDAROUN ST

N

0   250 m

Grand

▽ *The Private Beaches*

excursions to the Phoenician remains at **Amrit** and over to the island of **Arwad**, as well as up to the Crac des Chevaliers and other, lesser monuments in the mountains. It's an unhurried place, centred around an attractive harbour from where the boats to Arwad leave. The former Crusader **cathedral** (now a museum) and the nearby **Old City** are definitely worth looking round, but the litter-strewn beach and string of scrawny fish restaurants along the waterfront are likely only to dampen your enthusiasm for the place.

Some history

Tartous was founded by the Phoenician colony on Arwad and remained an important settlement through Hellenistic and Roman times. It became a major Christian stronghold, and during the fourth century a chapel was built here which is claimed to be the first dedicated to the Virgin. An earthquake in 487 largely destroyed the chapel but left its altar miraculously unscathed; this was later incorporated into a cathedral built by the Crusaders in 1123 which became a popular pilgrimage site. In 1152 control of Tartous passed to the Knights Templars, who extensively fortified the town, transforming it into their most significant base after their headquarters in Acre. The Templar garrison was forced to blockade itself in the castle keep in 1188 when Saladin's forces raided and destroyed much of the town (including the cathedral), but their final defence held strong and Tartous remained in Crusader hands until their very last days on the mainland in 1291. The Templars clung onto Arwad for eleven more years before a final withdrawal to Cyprus.

The cathedral

The **cathedral** has a flat, expressionless facade – the result of a solidly defensive reconstruction following its mauling at the hands of Saladin's troops – and the best that can be said of the early Gothic three-aisled interior is that it's grim but impressive. Following the Crusaders' departure from Syria, the building served a variety of purposes: in 1697 Henry Maundrell reported that it had become a cattle shed, filled knee-deep with excrement, while in the nineteenth century it was put to use as a mosque, before being commandeered by the Turkish army during World War I. In the mandate era the cathedral was substantially restored, and it now houses a sporadically interesting, if poorly laid out, **museum** (daily except Tues: April–Sept 9am–6pm; Oct–March 9am–4pm; S£200). Most noteworthy among the exhibits are some marble sarcophagi from Amrit and an 800 BC black stone carving of the god Baal; coins, costumes and fragments from all periods and in no discernible order make up the rest of the display, with only a handful of faded French labels to assist those who don't read Arabic.

The city walls

In Crusader times the **walled city** of Tartous formed a large rectangle, its western facade lapped by the sea and its other three sides protected by a deep ditch filled with sea water. Little remains of these outer fortifications apart from a small, square tower marking their southwestern corner, by the harbour at the end of Al-Wahda Street.

In the northwest corner of the city was a fortified **inner compound** protecting a banqueting hall, a chapel and a keep. Today a small square stands in its courtyard, though exploring the tight surrounding streets is difficult due to the confusing incursion of shabby modern dwellings. Little remains of the great hall to the north of the square, where the knights would have met and deliberated, though the chapel in the northwestern corner is far easier to recognize. The **keep**, where the Crusaders holed themselves up while Saladin was busy razing the town, occupies the western side, but its forbiddingly dark interior is usually kept locked. The western face of the keep would have met the sea directly in

Crusader times and from the modern-day road that runs past it you can see a small postern gate in its sloping wall; this was probably the exit used by the Templars on their final retreat from the mainland to Arwad.

The beaches

Tartous's **seafront**, which is promenaded for a couple of kilometres heading south from the harbour, is ideal for a relaxing stroll while you watch families at play on the beach or follow the progress of the small boats which bob out to the tiny island of Arwad. The succession of colourful stalls selling all the regular seaside accessories, and numerous cafés, restaurants and ice-cream parlours provide the place with a distinct holiday atmosphere. However, despite the antics of the locals, the polluted sea is not fit for swimming, and the **beach**, which stretches south from the harbour up to and beyond the ruins of Amrit, is in its northern part relentlessly filthy and litter-strewn – it's often a lot more pleasant to walk along the road than along the sand (which should on no account be done in bare feet). A couple of kilometres south from the Old City cleanliness improves slightly, as the beaches here are privately owned and allied to the nearby holiday-home complexes (it's possible to rent one of the grubby **chalets** for around S£500). You will be approached for money if you use these beaches but if you're just walking along simply shrug and feign ignorance.

Practicalities

With usually only one passenger train a week travelling in either direction up the coast the centrally located **train station** is unlikely to be of much use to you. The **microbus station** for all destinations in the mountains, as well as Homs, Latakia and Damascus, is a short walk from the centre on 6 Tichrin Avenue. Qadmous are the **Pullman** kings in these parts; they've got their own handy terminal on Jamal Abdul Naser Street, with frequent timetabled services to and from Aleppo, Baniyas, Damascus, Homs and Latakia. Damas Tour have an office on Al-Naser Street but only serve Damascus and Latakia. **Karnak**, on Al-Thawra Street, offer less frequent services on the same routes as Qadmous, and have a daily departure to Beirut via Tripoli. **Service taxis** hang around the clocktower on Al-Thawra Street, and also do the run into Lebanon (as well as Damascus, Homs and Latakia), but they're far more expensive.

The **tourist office** (daily except Fri 8am–2pm) is on Khalid ibn al-Walid Street, just to the north of the old city; as usual they're very nice people, but unable to provide you with anything beyond free hand-out maps.

Efficient **exchange** service is offered at the Commercial Bank of Syria on Khalid ibn al-Walid Street (daily except Fri 8am–1pm). The **immigration office** is just off Al-Wahda Street, by the clocktower and identified by a decrepit sentry box outside (daily except Fri 8am–2pm). The **post office** (daily except Fri 8am–8pm) is on Al-Thawra Street, opposite the Karnak office; telephone services are also available (daily except Fri 8am–10pm). If you need a **pharmacy** try Al-Iman opposite the *Daniel Hotel* on Al-Wahda Street.

Accommodation

Most of the **cheap hotels** are situated near the harbour on Al-Wahda Street. The best is the *Daniel* (☎043/220 582; ②), which is often full. The state of the rooms here varies dramatically from the clean to the downright grotty; most have a private shower room though on no account take a room without a fan in summer. Breakfast is available. The *Republic* (☎043/222 580; ①) almost next door has reasonably clean doubles if unappetizing showers. Further east down the street are the very basic *Siyaha* (☎043/221 763; ②), where you can get a bed in a shared room for S£100, and the small and poky *Rawda* (①). There are a couple more unnamed budget options around the corner on Al-Thawra Street and Al-Salhieh Street for anyone really down on their luck.

A number of decent **moderate hotels** line the seafront. Just along from the *Daniel* are two very similar establishments offering basic but clean sea-facing rooms with balcony and private bath; the *Blue Beach* (☎043/222 746; ③) is very friendly and slightly better value than the *Ambassadors* (☎043/220 183; ④) next door. About 200m south of these is the *Al-Moshwar* (④), not a bad choice though rather haphazardly run; eager staff are prepared to lower their inflated prices dramatically here. The *Shahine* (☎043/221 703, fax 315 002; ⑤), just down Ahmad al-Azawi Street, has a selection of very spruce if somewhat overpriced rooms – they're certainly not as special as the price might imply, though the place is often full. The *Al-Baher* (☎043/221 687; ③) is a lot cheaper for similar sort of quality, and they're ready to drop their prices by a third in response to some tactical indecisiveness at reception. Finally comes the *Grand Hotel* (☎043/225 475; ⑤) whose plush foyer is about as grand as you'll get in Tartous, though the place generally has an air of having seen better days.

Eating and drinking

The *Grand* and *Shahine* hotels both have very decent **restaurants** with varied Western menus, or there are a cluster of places down by the harbour, none of which can be especially recommended; **fish** is inevitably available in all of them though it's very rarely appetizing. Otherwise it's just the usual choice of chicken or kebab plus side dishes for about S£200 (fish would be about S£100 more). For something cheap and **Western** head to the pizza bar opposite the *Shahine Hotel*; next door is a good ice-cream parlour. There are a few restaurants along the southern beaches which serve the usual Syrian cuisine for slightly inflated prices, although they're quite nice places to chill out by the sea.

Arwad

Of the many Syrians who come to Tartous for a beach holiday, the majority make the journey over to **ARWAD**, the small island that rises invitingly on the horizon 3km off the coast. As long as it's not too rough, small vessels crammed with families and picnic baskets ply the route from the small harbour in Tartous throughout the day, a journey of about twenty minutes. You pay for your trip only when you leave Arwad, at the ticket booth by the harbour entrance there (S£20 return).

It's quite easy to romanticize Arwad, to talk of its interesting, traffic-free narrow lanes that wind up to the remains of its Crusader fort, of the sight of small boats and fishermen repairing their nets along the harbourfront. However, it's very difficult to ignore the island's more unsavoury side: the stinking rubbish lying piled up everywhere; too many people crowded into too small a space; the recent proliferation of ugly, faceless concrete buildings; the shamelessly polluted sea and slime-covered beaches. All this is a great shame, as you get the feeling that – if they tried – the Syrian authorities could make Arwad a really pleasant place. Although it's something of a "holiday island" there are no seaside facilities here at all, and no hotels or good restaurants either, just a bunch of really tacky eateries and juice stalls along the harbourfront. When you've had enough, boats ferry people back to the mainland until sunset – be sure not to get stranded.

Tacky though it may be today, the island has an illustrious and ancient **history**, encompassing Phoenician and Crusader settlement. Arwad is mentioned in the Bible: Genesis 10:18 records that the original settlers were descendants of Canaan (a grandson of Noah). During Phoenician times Arwad was a prosperous maritime state (the name derives from the Phoenician word for "refuge"), but the Romans, who took control in 64 BC, didn't really take much notice of the place, although St Paul is said to have visited the island on his journey to Rome. Arwad was the last Frankish settlement in the Middle East to fall to the Muslims; the mainland Crusader strongholds of Acre and Tartous itself had fallen in 1291, but the soldiers in Arwad grimly held on until 1302 when they finally retreated to Cyprus – and the history of the Crusades in the Middle East came to a decisive end. The **Crusader fort** (daily except Tues 9am–4pm; S£200) at the highest point of the island remains Arwad's main point of interest. That's not saying much, however, as all you get for the entry charge is a look around a poor museum and the chance to clamber over some crumbling fortifications – though the view over the rooftops across to Tartous is a fine one.

Amrit

AMRIT, 8km south of Tartous, was founded by the Amorites some time in the third millennium BC and developed by the **Phoenicians** as a religious centre to complement their settlement on Arwad. It's virtual abandonment during the early second century BC has meant the rare survival of Phoenician ruins without extensive remodelling by later generations. Set in a largely deserted agricultural area, with the sea glistening in the background, the peaceful remains may well induce you to stay longer than you expected.

The most important monument is a **temple** dating to the late fourth century BC, an early and considerably less elaborate antecedent of the Temple of Bel in Palmyra. It consists of a large court cut out of the rock, in the centre of which is a well-preserved *cella* where the image of the resident god Melqart would have been placed. The court was flooded by a local spring (a feature unique to this site) whose supposed healing properties are the most likely explanation for the existence of the temple. This sacred pool was surrounded on three sides by a colonnaded arcade which has been recently reconstructed. Traces of a **stadium** can be seen across the choked river from the top of the unexplored *tell* next to the temple, though the only way to get a closer look is back via the road.

Situated on a small ridge 700m south of the temple are a couple of tall cylindrical funerary monuments, known as the **spindles**, standing atop small burial chambers; a torch would be useful for a closer look round. The larger spindle has four battered lion sculptures around its base, a Persian influence which, along with the Greek and Egyptian styles found at the site, illustrates the Phoenicians' susceptibility to outside influences through their extensive trading links. There are many other monuments, mausoleums and burial chambers in the vicinity, but as the area is partially a military zone it would be wise not to be too tactless in your wanderings and photography. The best example, signposted on the main road 1km south of the spindles, is a huge two-storeyed cube-shaped **mausoleum**, once topped by a pyramid, and mysteriously known as the *Burj al-Bezzaq* (Snail Tower). It contains two burial chambers and undoubtedly belonged to one of Amrit's most important families. Most impressive are the colossal blocks of stone used in its construction. To get there, follow the signposted tarmac road off the main highway until it curves left, when you should take the dirt track which goes straight ahead; the monument can be seen down at the end of a small path heading through the trees to your right.

To get to Amrit take the Hamidiyeh **microbus** from Tartous, making sure the driver knows where you want to get off. From where you'll be dropped off, you can see the temple, a signposted two-kilometre walk away. Getting back, simply flag down any bus heading back into town along the coast, or you could walk it along the beach in a couple of hours. A rusted sign has, for many years, been announcing the impending arrival of a luxury beach resort along here, but there's scant evidence that it's going to happen in the foreseeable future.

Inland from Tartous

Inland from the industrial sprawl of modern Tartous the mountains begin, often shrouded in mist or low cloud whilst the town languishes in the sun on the coastal plain. If Arwad and Amrit disappointed you, then excursions further afield from Tartous certainly won't. The uplands here are cool and green, with villages built of stone on hillside terraces and clustering around dirt tracks which are barely motorable. Some of the settlements you'll pass through seem barely touched by the twentieth century, their streets occupied by ragged children – tending equally ragged goats and chickens – who stop and stare whenever a stranger appears.

The Crusaders were immediately attracted to a landscape such as this: sparsely settled, simple to farm and easy to defend and establish command of. They built some of their most enduring architectural monuments here, supreme among them the impregnable fortress of **Crac des Chevaliers**. Nowhere else in the mountains is as commercialized or popular as the Crac, though **Safita**, where you can see the remains of the **White Castle**, is busy turning itself into something of a mountain retreat for the well-heeled. The Roman temple at **Hosn Suleiman**, the area's other highlight, is interesting to clamber round and wonderfully situated amongst some desolate scenery.

Only a limited number of **buses** grind along the twisting upland roads, making forward planning essential. Hitching or paying for lifts may be a necessity, but it is highly unlikely that you will ever get stuck anywhere. Safita is the main public transport hub in the mountains, and it would be easy to combine a trip to its White Castle with a visit to Hosn Suleiman, possibly taking in Qalaat Yahmur on the way back. Although there are no direct buses between the two, it would also just about be possible to visit the Crac des Chevaliers and Safita in one day (ignoring Hosn Suleiman), but it probably makes more sense to do separate day-trips from Tartous. Tartous is by far the best base for exploring this part of the country: there are **accommodation** possibilities at Safita, the Crac des Chevaliers and by the Monastery of St George but they're recommended principally for those with their own transport.

After Jerusalem was taken on the First Crusade many knights headed off home, leaving at most only five thousand men to defend their conquests. The superior Frankish armour and horses, combined with the disunity of their Muslim opponents, had made the conquests relatively easy, but with such small numbers left behind any losses suffered meant heavy losses. As reinforcements tended only to trickle in, it was evident that the gains could only be held with a network of imposing **fortifications**. Many of these castles remained in Crusader hands for up to a hundred and fifty years, as the majority of the local populace seems to have accepted the **feudal order** that was imposed upon them, and the invaders did not bother to threaten the major Muslim population centres.

The Crusaders had some natural allies in the Christian Maronite community and in the Shi'ite Assassins who were the enemies of the Sunni regime, but the invading Europeans also made efforts not to offend local sensibilities; the coins struck by the Venetians even bore an Arabic inscription. Local people were obvious beneficiaries of the **trade** and caravan traffic stimulated by the European invasion, and the feudal system brought with it remarkably equitable and cheap taxation and justice. The Crusaders even took some pains to put something positive into the community by building orphanages and hospitals. Ibn Gubayr, a traveller writing just before the Battle of Hattin in 1187 (quoted in Robert Feddens' *Syria and Lebanon*), jealously described the lands controlled by the Franks: "Allah preserve us from such a temptation! The Franks allow them to keep half of the harvest and limit themselves to the imposition of a poll tax of one dinar and five kirats. Apart from this they only levy a small tax on timber. The Muslims are proprietors of their own houses and run them as they wish . . . one of the chief tragedies of the Muslims is that they have to complain of the injustices of their own rulers, whereas they cannot but praise the behaviour of the Franks, their natural enemies. May Allah soon put an end to this state of affairs!"

The Crac des Chevaliers

The **CRAC DES CHEVALIERS** (daily: summer 9am–7pm; winter 9am–5pm; S£200) is quite simply an essential stop for anybody travelling in Syria. Set on a high, wind-swept ledge above a rocky valley, with superlative views across the mountains in every direction, you won't find a better-preserved Crusader castle anywhere – it's still as formidable now as it must have been the day the Knights Hospitallers surrendered it in the thirteenth century. Even for those with only a passing historical interest, a visit is unlikely to disappoint.

Some history
Archeological evidence suggests that the site may have been occupied by the **Egyptians** during their struggle for dominance in Syria with the Hittites, which culminated in the Battle of Kadesh around 1285 BC. It was still a prime defensive location when the **Crusaders** arrived on the scene in the early twelfth century. The **Knights Hospitallers** gained control of the castle in 1144, completely rebuilding the place and fortifying it so well that it survived two major Arab assaults in the late twelfth century. However, during the thirteenth century the Crusader presence in the Holy Land thinned out considerably, leaving the Crac increasingly isolated and occupied by a garrison of only two hundred men (it

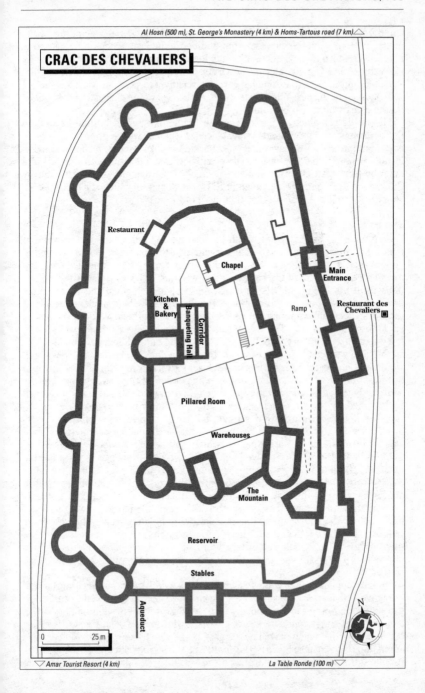

Al Hosn (500 m), St. George's Monastery (4 km) & Homs-Tartous road (7 km)

CRAC DES CHEVALIERS

Restaurant

Chapel

Main
Entrance

Kitchen
&
Bakery

Corridor

Banqueting Hall

Restaurant des
Chevaliers

Ramp

Pillared Room

Warehouses

The
Mountain

Reservoir

Stables

Aqueduct

0   25 m

N

Amar Tourist Resort (4 km)

La Table Ronde (100 m)

could house four thousand). In 1271 **Sultan Baibars** began a siege of the castle, managing to breach the outer wall but finding the inner defences solidly impregnable. To resolve the stalemate he sent a forged letter into the castle, supposedly from the Grand Commander of the Order in Tripoli, urging surrender, and the depleted and dejected Hospitaller garrison hastily accepted the sultan's offer of safe passage to the sea. Within twenty years the rest of the Crusader possessions on the coast would also be gone.

The castle remained in use during the Mameluke period but as the foreign threat disappeared its strategic importance lessened. A village grew up inside the castle, and in 1909 T.E. Lawrence reported that the regional governor was living in the keep, and that the castle had recently "withstood a siege on the part of a neighbouring district with complete success". The villagers were turfed out by the French Antiquities Department in 1934 who declared, with just a hint of Gallic superiority, that the Crac was "a monument of France".

The castle

Before entering the castle it's worth completing a circuit of the **outer walls** to gain a full appreciation of its defences, and also to wind your way onto the hill behind that provides the classic Crac photo opportunity. The south side was the most vulnerable point of the castle; a ditch was dug to try to isolate the fortifications from the ridge and it is here that the walls are thickest and towers most tightly grouped. Despite these efforts, this is where Baibars managed to break through, successfully mining one of the towers; the southern wall you see now is an Arab reconstruction. The **aqueduct** (which looks like a bridge) would have fed water into the reservoir between the inner and outer defences.

You enter the castle on the east side through a dark, steep passageway which would in Crusader days have boasted at least four gateways. Before passing into the heart of the castle make a clockwise inspection of the next line of defence. The sickly green stagnant water in the **reservoir**, which would once have been replenished by the aqueduct, stands at the bottom of what Baibars' besieging forces called **the mountain** – a huge, tall stone slope some 25m thick at its base. Why exactly it was built has been the subject of some debate: possibly it was a buttress against earthquakes (which had severely damaged the site in 1157 and 1170), or it might have been constructed to prevent any form of mining (though as it stands on solid rock mining was hardly an option). Another theory suggests that it could have been used to produce a smooth surface to prevent scaling – T.E. Lawrence attempted to climb it in 1909 and got only halfway up, and this without people throwing rocks and boiling fat down onto his head. On the south side of the moat is a long, unsupported arched chamber that probably functioned as **stables**, Arab work completed on the rebuilding of the southern outer wall. From here you can complete the circuit – carefully avoiding the litter strewn across the yard – arriving once again at the entrance ramp to the castle interior.

Directly opposite you'll come to a graceful thirteenth-century **corridor**, its roof attractively divided into seven vaulted bays, whose delicately carved Gothic doorways and windows fit incongruously with the Crac's fiercely solid military architecture. A Latin inscription here reads, "Grace, wisdom and beauty you may enjoy, but beware pride which may alone tarnish all the rest." From here two doorways admit you to an austere **banqueting hall**, a century older but still Gothic in style. Behind this is a long arced **chamber**, which would once have been filled with the castle's stocks and provisions, and would also have housed the kitchen and bakery; you can work out the remains of the oven, more than 5m in diameter, on the floor. The **pillared room** to the south of the courtyard may have been the refectory, and remains of oil jars can be seen in the warehouses beyond it. Back on the courtyard is a twelfth-century **chapel**, a simple construction with little Christian decoration save some traces of painted rosettes on the north wall. After the Crusaders left, this was converted into a mosque, of which the *minbar*, or pulpit, can still be seen.

Climb the staircase by the chapel up to the **northern ramparts**, where one of the towers contains an overpriced **restaurant** that also sells souvenirs. On a clear day you may be able to spot the tall keep of the White Castle in Safita (see p.156), which gave the Crusader garrison here a quick communication system on to the coast. Finally, you can cross the court over to the **southern ramparts** that sit above "the mountain". The towers here provided the accommodation quarters for the most important of the knights; being the tallest parts of the castle they provide the most breathtaking views.

Practicalities

The only direct **microbus** to the Crac des Chevaliers is the frequent service from Homs (1hr 30min), but it's easy enough to get there from Tartous in about an hour and a half: take one of the frequent Homs-bound microbuses and ask to be left off at the Crac turn-off on the motorway, where you can pick up the Homs–Crac microbus. Remember to ask for **Qalaat al-Hosn**, the local name for the Crac; Al-Hosn is the name of the village immediately below the castle. (On the motorway from Tartous towards Homs, you'll pass after 25km another, signposted Crusader fortification, **Qalaat Areimeh**; however, though the views from the ramparts are good, the remains are disappointing and the trip only recommended for those with their own transport or prepared for a stiff walk.) The microbus service back towards Homs from the Crac dries up mid-afternoon, but taxi and microbus drivers tend to hang around the castle entrance all day, and the *Restaurant des Chevaliers* situated right in front of the castle entrance can get hold of a taxi for you if you're desperate.

The *Des Chevaliers* and *La Table Ronde*, 200m up the hill beyond the main entrance, both rustle up **food**, though it's not very inspiring – the standard Syrian fare of kebab or chicken and chips. The latter is also the only place to **stay** in the village itself (☎031/734 280), with basic rooms available (②) or a spot to pitch your tent (S£200). Signposted 4km beyond the castle is the *Amar Tourist Resort* (☎031/733 203; ⑤), a luxury choice with restaurant and summer-only pool. Otherwise, if you have your own transport, you could stay at one of a number of options near the Monastery of St George.

The Monastery of St George

The Greek Orthodox **Monastery of St George** (daily 9am–8pm; free), founded in the sixth century, is a relatively easy addition to sightseeing at the Crac, though the building itself will take up little of your time. It's a working monastery, built mostly during the last hundred years, with only a few medieval parts still intact. The peaceful chapel in the first courtyard to your right as you enter dates to 1857; descend into the lower courtyard for a look at a more interesting thirteenth-century one, recently restored after flooding, whose solemn interior features a remarkable 300-year-old ebony iconostasis made in Aleppo. This chapel might be locked but wait around for someone to open it for you. No **microbuses** run the 4km between the Crac and the monastery, so you'll have to negotiate with a **taxi** or microbus driver at the castle entrance (about S£100). To get back to Tartous from the monastery, either hitch or walk twenty minutes back along the way you came to the main road which heads off to Nasira, where you can pick up a microbus towards Homs; then get off at the Homs–Tartous highway and catch another microbus to Tartous from there.

This is quite a picturesque area, and the road to the monastery has a number of good **hotels** along it. The clean and friendly *Al-Khoudr* (☎031/730 245; ④) is virtually next door, and a little beyond this is the very plush *Al-Wadi* (☎031/730 456, fax 730 399; ⑥), one of Syria's best luxury hotels, where all rooms have TV, telephone and fridge, and bars, restaurants, tennis courts and a swimming pool are thrown in for good measure. The *Al-Naaim* (☎031/735 422; ③) is a decent (and more decently priced) choice, but next along, the *Al-Riad* is now only a restaurant, though you can camp here for an extortionate US$6.

Safita and Qalaat Yahmur

Numerous microbuses ply the road from Tartous to the burgeoning hill-town of **SAFITA** (45min), signposted across the mountains by its distinctive **keep**, all that remains today of the **White Castle** of the Templars. For a town standing seemingly aloof in such peaceful mountain scenery, Safita has a maddeningly impatient and claustrophobic air; its narrow streets are choked with busy shoppers and relentlessly noisy traffic, making progress slow and wearing. Any one of the steep, winding alleys from the main road will lead you up to the keep, which maintains irregular opening hours but is generally shut in the early afternoon; try asking around for the key at the adjacent restaurant if necessary. A Crusader fortification was originally built here in 1112, but it was destroyed by Nur al-Din in 1171 and what you see today dates from the early thirteenth century. In 1271 the Templar garrison was ordered by the Master of the Order in Tartous to evacuate the castle on the approach of Baibars; this action effectively isolated the Crac des Chevaliers which fell only two months later.

Upon entry to the keep it's slightly surprising to find inside a fully functional **church**, dedicated to St Michael and serving the town's Greek Orthodox community; the windows of the church were originally firing slits. The entrance fee to the keep is a donation in one of the boxes provided. A narrow stairway leads up to a spacious room where the garrison would have been housed, with a further set of stairs taking you up to the crenellated terrace and some fine sweeping views; from here communication was made with other castles via signal fires. Just to the east of the keep is one of the castle's original gateways and part of the thirteenth-century wall.

Practicalities

Safita acts as a traffic hub for the mountains, and from its tiny **microbus** station, located 100m down the hill from the small central roundabout, you can venture on to Mashta al-Helu, Hosn Suleiman and Homs. To get here **from the Crac des Chevaliers**, catch a Homs microbus back to the Homs–Tartous motorway, where you can hail a Homs–Safita microbus (total journey time about 1hr 15min).

Among **hotels**, the *Safita Cham Palace* (☎043/525 980; ⑧), off the western end of the main street, is the luxury chain's least opulent, though still out of the budget of most independent travellers. A ten-minute walk east of the mini-roundabout near the bus station on Ali Yehia Street is a signposted but unnamed hotel (☎043/221 932; ③) which has reasonable rooms. If you need something to eat, head for the **restaurant** next to the keep which serves standard Middle Eastern fare at not too outrageous prices and boasts great hillside views.

Qalaat Yahmur

Any journey between Tartous and Safita could be easily broken with a visit to the undoubtedly minor but well-wearing **Qalaat Yahmur**, 10km southeast of Tartous, an interesting complement to the larger fortifications in the mountains. The small, stocky castle lies a short 2km from the main road in the village of Beit Shalluf. What you see today is a twelfth-century Crusader reconstruction of a Byzantine fortification and consists of a stubby square tower surrounded by a very well-preserved outer wall. The castle is now given over to the housing of animals, but it's OK to nudge past them for a view into the interior. The upper storey of the tower can be reached via an external stairway; two watchtowers stand at the southeast and northwest corners of the outer wall, both Arab additions.

Mashta al-Helu

Nestling in the southern mountains is the resort of **MASHTA AL-HELU**, 18km northeast of Safita though signposted from just about everywhere. It's got a number of fair **restaurants**, overlooking some sweeping mountain scenery, and numerous ice-cream stores in the centre of town, but it lacks any real character and hardly justifies a special trip – the only thing to see is a small **cave complex** (S£25) 3km outside of town and accessible by local taxi. There is one **hotel**, the four-star *Masta al-Helu Resort* (☎043/584 000, fax 584 060; ⑥), a luxury residence with tennis courts, a swimming pool, restaurants and coffee shops. They also do car rental, but it's best to arrange this in advance at the hotel's office in downtown Damascus (☎011/222 6508), located next to the *Fardoss Tower Hotel*.

DREIKISH, 7km north of Safita, is a name that will probably be familiar to you as it's plastered across the labels of most bottles of mineral water in Syria, but though the place is styled by local literature as another mountain retreat, it holds even less allure than Mashta al-Helu and isn't worth the time of day.

Hosn Suleiman

You can approach **HOSN SULEIMAN**, a ruined **temple** situated within a sheltered natural amphitheatre in the mountains, via a direct if infrequent **bus** service northeast from Safita (40min); buses back dry up around midday so bear this in mind when planning your day's schedule. This wild and rocky location, with its gigantic half-collapsed ruins set impressively against the scenery, was a site for cult worship for thousands of years. From around 2000 BC the Canaanites were worshipping their god Baotocecian Baal here (the patron of the Phoenicians at Arwad), and later the site became a cult centre for the followers of Zeus Baotocecian, a hybrid of Baal and his Greek equivalent, Zeus. The Roman temple, the remains of which can be seen today, was probably built between the middle of the first century AD and the end of the second. Worship of various pagan cults took place here well into the fourth century, by which time Christianity had been firmly adopted as the religion of the Roman Empire.

The temple consists of a large rectangular building, built from huge blocks up to ten metres in length, enclosing a central raised area (the cella) which housed the altar, now little more than a tumbled mass of masonry and boulders. There are impressive entrances, one in each wall, the most elaborate of which is the northern gateway, where carved figures of lions can still be seen. On the eastern gate an inscription in Greek, dated to 171 AD, records the dedication of the temple by local people, who had collected the funds needed to build it. If you cross the road you can see the scant remains of a monastery (*al-Deir*), believed to have been a separate temple adapted later on for use as a Christian convent and basilica.

The coast between Tartous and Latakia

Frequent buses and microbuses bowl along the motorway from Tartous to Latakia, 80km north, taking you past a series of dull towns, sprawling industrial complexes and intensive farms that are well watered by winter and summer rains. The view from a passing vehicle is not enticing, but there is scope to break your journey and get away from the road if you want to. **Baniyas**, with its huge oil refinery, gives access to **Qalaat Marqab**, a mountain-top Crusader stronghold, and further on at **Jableh** you can see the remains of a Roman amphitheatre and wander round an attractive fishing harbour before pushing on. Both places would also be easy to visit on day-trips from either Tartous or Latakia, but the less compelling Ismaili fortress of **Qalaat al-Kahf** is really only worth visiting if you have your own transport.

Qalaat Marqab

From afar **QALAAT MARQAB** (daily except Tues 9am–4pm; S£200) rivals even the Crac with its foreboding presence, and even if, close to, its vastness represents nothing more than an illusion of greatness, with the majority of the site being taken over by a tenacious marrying of rubble and undergrowth, the castle still stands as one of the most formidable examples of Crusader castle-building in Syria. First fortified by the Muslims in 1062, the site passed into Crusader hands in the early twelfth century, though it wasn't until 1186 that the **Knights Hospitallers** came here; they spent the next twenty years or so converting it into one of their major strongholds. Though powerful enough to withstand sieges in 1204 and 1280 (Saladin didn't even attempt to breach it during his 1188 campaign), dwindling manpower and the loss of the Crac in 1271 led in 1285 to the castle's fall; after mining by Baibars' successor Sultan Qalaun resulted in the collapse of the south tower, the beleaguered knights inside surrendered the castle in return for a peaceful escape to Tartous and then Tripoli. The tower was rebuilt under Arab occupation, and the bands of white marble in the stonework observable from outside are a distinctive Mameluke touch. During the Ottoman period the castle was converted into a prison.

The castle's defences were heavily weighted towards its weakest point in the south, which is by far the best-preserved section. The main entrance here leads you into a large hall which takes you between the outer and inner defences; head on to the inner gateway from where stairs lead you into the main **courtyard**. The ramparts here offer the best views over the Mediterranean and the recently industrialized town of Baniyas. The courtyard is mostly lined with storage areas, though opposite is a spacious Gothic **chapel** (declared a cathedral in 1188). South of this are a barracks and the remains of the great hall, built over a massive cistern, and beyond that is the solemnly dark granite keep boasting walls 5m thick. The large area of the castle to the north of the courtyard is badly overgrown and largely ruined, the area having been heavily built over after the Crusaders left. An Arab cemetery and Ottoman governor's palace may be rooted out amongst the mess of rubble.

Occasional **microbuses** wind their way up the six-kilometre road to Marqab from Baniyas bus station, though you could always take a taxi to save time waiting. Buses back dry up in the early afternoon. Approaching by car there is no turn-off from the main highway, so you would have to enter Baniyas, take the old coast road south and head up the mountain from there. In the hills above the highway just before the town, look out for a basalt **watchtower** built at the same time as the castle and designed to protect the coastal road and the important Crusader settlement at Baniyas.

Qalaat al-Kahf

To the southeast of Qalaat Marqab, about 30km away by an almost bewildering trail of winding mountain roads, is the Ismaili fortress of **Qalaat al-Kahf**, sitting on a peaceful ridge between two wild gorges. The road up to the castle is barely good enough for vehicular traffic, and the castle itself is mostly ruin, though it does feature a remarkable entrance passageway inscribed in Arabic and carved from solid rock, which gives the place its name "Castle of the Cave". The fortress was built by a local lord in the early twelfth century and then sold to the Ismailis, one of eight acquisitions the sect made between 1132 and 1140. Baibars finally captured the castle in 1273, and it remained in use until Ottoman times, finally being razed in the early nineteenth century. To **get there** without your own transport the easiest thing to do would be to catch a microbus to the town of Qadmous, 24km east on the main road between Baniyas and Misyaf, and then arrange transport with a local from there, possibly by motorbike (cheaper than a car so bargain accordingly).

Jableh

Travelling between Baniyas and Latakia the only place of note you'll pass is **JABLEH**, a small harbour town located just off the main coastal motorway. Little trace remains of the town's ancient history as an important port under Phoenician, Roman and Byzantine rulers. The centre of Jableh is now dominated by a large modern stadium, next to which stands the **bus station**. To the southwest of this are the remains of a **Roman amphitheatre** (daily except Tues 9am–2pm; S£100), much of it overgrown and falling down. The first eleven rows of seating are well preserved, their yellow stone glinting in the sun, and it's now undergoing slow restoration work by archeologists. Nearby is a mosque, built on the site of a church dating from Byzantine times, containing the **shrine of Ibrahim ben Adham**, a local mystic and Islamic saint who died in 778. Heading over to the waterfront, you'll find two small **harbours** for fishing boats, the older of which is thought to have been cut into the rock by the Phoenicians. You can smoke a quiet *nargileh* or get something to **eat** while taking in the attractive views from a couple of cafés on the clifftops.

Latakia and around

Although there's very little to see in Latakia itself, it's an excellent base for seeing the surrounding area. There's a busy, breezy feel to the town, which boasts a good variety of hotels and restaurants, and excellent transport connections. It's easy to head out to the nearby historical sites, foremost among which are the former Phoenician city of **Ugarit**, a short distance north along the coast, and the Crusader castle **Qalaat Saladin**. And if you've grown weary of looking at beaches along the coast smothered in garbage, then take heart – the **Blue Beach**, just north of the city, is the cleanest in Syria, although you'll have to pay for the pleasure of using it, while the black beaches at **Ras al-Bassit** are impressively located and easily accessible from Latakia.

Latakia

Syria's fourth largest town and the country's principal port, **LATAKIA** comes as a pleasant surprise after the drabness of most of the rest of the coast. It's a thoroughly modern place, prosperous and cosmopolitan, with a lively student presence and a diverse cultural and sporting life. The wide boulevards lined with palm trees, the bustling street cafés and restaurants, and the shops brimming with designer labels (even if they are fakes imported from Turkey) give the place a distinctly European feeling.

Some history

Though there is evidence to suggest continuous settlement here stretching back to at least 1000 BC, Latakia only came to prominence in the wake of Alexander the Great's conquests, when it was transformed into a major city of the **Seleucid** empire. Renamed in honour of Laodicea, the mother of Alexander's general Seleucus I Nicator, it developed into an important port, usurping Arwad's previous dominance and becoming the main supplier of wine to the Hellenistic world. The town was even briefly declared capital of Syria in the late second century AD by Septimius Severus, though that role soon reverted to Antioch. Devastating earthquakes in 494 and 555 badly damaged Latakia, but it was rebuilt by Justinian before being seized by the invading Arab army in 638. After capture by the Crusaders in the autumn of 1097, the town oscillated between Muslim and Christian control for nearly a century until it was decisively retaken by Saladin in 1188. Latakia benefitted from a small but influential Venetian trading colony from 1229 until 1436, but after their expulsion the town settled on a long path of decline. By the end of the nineteenth century it was no more than a minor fishing village with a population in the region of six thousand; in 1876 Baedaeker described its "squalid, poverty-stricken appearance". The town's fortunes were revived during the mandate era when the French made it capital of their new **Alawite** state and with the formal creation of Lebanon and the handing back of the Hatay region to Turkey, Latakia suddenly found itself in the role of modern-day Syria's major **port** – the new government therefore having little choice but to expand and develop the city.

Arrival and information

Pullman and Karnak **buses** use the new terminal just beyond the **train station** on Abdel Qader al-Housayni Avenue, where all the major companies have their

Herbs and spices in the Damascus souks

Prayer mats in the courtyard of the Umayyad Mosque, Damascus

Colonnade in the Roman city of Shahba

Umayyad Mosque, Damascus

Story-teller in the Nofara Café, Damascus

The cardo maximus at Apamea

The Roman theatre at Bosra

Norias (medieval waterwheels) on the Orontes at Hama

The Crac des Chevaliers

Blue Beach near Latakia

Fishing boats on the island of Arwad

Smoking a water pipe on a wall at Arwad

The narrow-gauge train along the Barada Valley

offices. From here, a taxi is the best option into the centre, around the western end of 14 Ramadan Avenue. Qadmous services from Baniyas, Homs and Tartous arrive at a station located behind the *Haroun Hotel* on Place Al-Joumhouria – again a taxi ride from the centre. The station for local buses and microbuses is a little more in the heart of things on Al-Jalaa Street, within walking distance of most hotels. The **airport** is 25km south of the city, near Jableh; taxis to the city cost around S£300.

The **tourist office** (daily except Fri 8am–7pm) is on the eastern end of 14 Ramadan Avenue, opposite the *Riviera Hotel*; a free city map and a friendly chat are the only reasons for coming here.

Accommodation

Most of the city's **hotels** congregate around the western end of 14 Ramadan Avenue; cheapies to avoid on the avenue itself include the *Afamia* and the *Ferdos*. The very cheapest places are in the noisy area just to the north of the mosque here, and apart from the *Latakia* (see below) have little to differentiate them. Latakia's luxury hotels are located not in the city centre but on Blue Beach, 8km to the north.

INEXPENSIVE

Al-Atlal, at the port end of Yousef al-Azmah St (☎041/236 121). Its quiet location away from the city centre, friendly owner and reasonably clean rooms make this one of the better budget options. ②.

Ebla, tucked away, and signposted, directly behind the *Riyadh* on 14 Ramadan Ave. A selection of claustrophobic rooms (with paintwork in varying states of undress), clustered around a small, but charmless, courtyard. ②.

Ishbilia, Omar bin al-Khattab Ave (☎041/222 864). A reasonable selection of rooms located high enough up to neutralize some of the traffic noise, though the showers are dingy. Prices seem open to negotiation, but bargain hard. ②.

Kaoukab al-Chark, 14 Ramadan Ave (☎041/238 452). Reasonable if basic rooms; you pay extra for an en-suite bathroom. ②.

Latakia, on the second floor of a building on Arwad St, off Yousef al-Azmah St, north of the mosque. The best of numerous similar cheapies next to the mosque (beware the wake-up call). A variety of rooms are available, some with shower and toilet, and the English-speaking owner is prepared to bargain. ①.

An-Nahhas, Ibrahim Hanano St (☎041/238 030). A relaxed and friendly place, though slightly grotty and in a noisy area. ②.

Ramsis, Ibrahim Hanano St (☎041/238 058). A pretty good deal, with fairly clean rooms and an owner who speaks basic French. ①.

Al-Zahran, 14 Ramadan Ave (☎041/425 128). A noisy location, though don't be put off by the grubby entrance as inside are a number of acceptably clean rooms with balcony and bath. ①.

MODERATE

Haroun, Place Al-Joumhouria (☎041/427 140). A bit dull but probably the best value for its price. Very clean rooms all have a bath, TV and fridge. ④.

New Omar Khayam, Al-Jalaa St, near the microbus station, right next to the stadium (☎041/228 219). A recent addition to the Latakia hotel scene and quite a bright little place. French spoken at the desk. ⑤.

Al-Nour, 14 Ramadan Ave (☎041/423 980). Acceptably clean if uninspiring selection of rooms without TV or fridge. Overpriced for what you get, and the management don't seem especially keen to have your custom. ④.

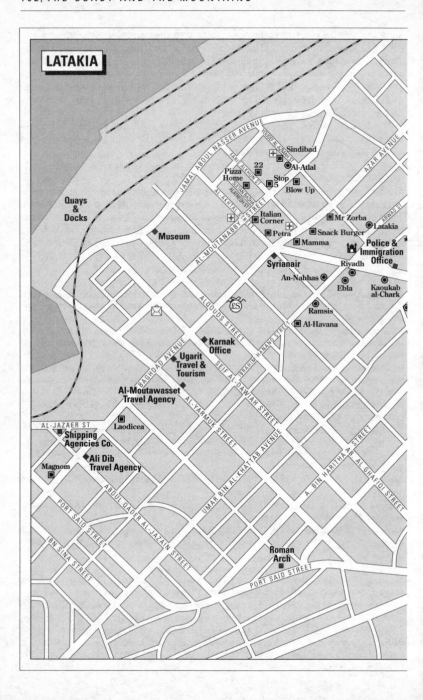

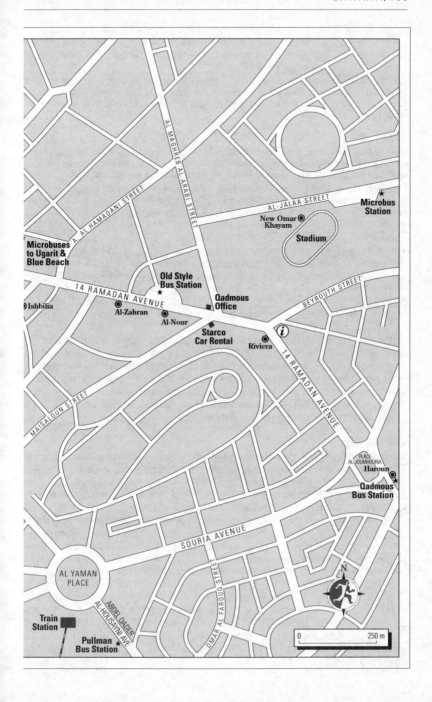

Riviera, 14 Ramadan Ave (☎041/421 803, fax 418 287). One step into the beautifully air-conditioned reception area tells you that this is the best place to be in downtown Latakia, if you have the money. The staff are all professional and friendly, and speak very good English; rooms are all equipped with TV and fridge. ⑤.

Riyadh, 14 Ramadan Ave (☎041/239 778). A clean and comfortable option with the possibility of either a balcony at the front or a quieter room at the back. En-suite shower rooms tend to be a little cramped. It's a little overpriced, though wavering at the reception area can generally knock a few dollars off. ④.

EXPENSIVE

Cote d'Azur de Cham, Blue Beach (☎041/228 691). A resort in itself with its own private beach, swimming pool, mini-golf and tennis courts. The rooms are essentially self-contained apartments with kitchenettes, and there are all the usual bars and restaurants. ⑦.

Meridien Hotel, Blue Beach (☎041/229 000). Also has a private beach, which non-guests must pay to use, with swimming pool, restaurants, bars, tennis courts and even, in summer, all-night karaoke on the beach at *Piano Bar II*. ⑦.

The City

The city's **museum** (daily except Tues 8am–2pm; S£200), on Jamal Abdul Nasser Avenue, is housed in an old Ottoman khan which served as the Alawite governor's residence during the French mandate. It's not especially good value, but there are some interesting examples of pottery, glassware and inscribed clay tablets from nearby Ugarit, and the exhibits have been thoughtfully labelled in English. The final room features an incongruous selection of contemporary paintings which won't detain you.

A rare surviving testament to Latakia's ancient past (which is featured on the sides of the city's taxis) is the four-sided **Roman gateway**, or *tetraporticus*, on Port Said Street in the southern part of the city. The sturdy, and highly unusual, near-cubic shape, ensured its survival through the several major earthquakes which devasted much of the old settlement. Dating to the late second century, this would have marked the eastern end of the ancient Roman city; occasional Classical columns litter the surrounding streets.

The beaches

The road north out of the city centre towards Ugarit passes after about 8km the *Cham Cote d'Azur Hotel* complex, situated at the landward end of the Ras ibn Hani promontory. Here non-guests can pay S£500 to use the hotel's private beach, go swimming, waterskiing and windsurfing in crystal clear blue water, or just lounge under the palms; the place goes under the name of **Blue Beach** and the scene could be anywhere on the Mediterranean, but the sands are spotless and the water completely clean. Further up the road running west along the promontory is the *Meridien Hotel*, slightly less of an eyesore and on a less crowded part of Blue Beach, which is nonetheless private, charging the same as the *Cham* for similar facilities. People using these two private beaches tend to be mostly Europeans (who come here because it's warmer than back home) and Arabs from the Persian Gulf area (who come because it's cooler), and you're unlikely to meet any Syrians.

The couple of kilometres of Blue Beach running up to the *Cham Cote d'Azur* are occupied by holiday complexes, where getting onto the sand is a lot cheaper: you pay around S£50 at one of numerous turnstiles. This stretch tends to be a lot livelier and untidier than the hotel beaches, and on Fridays it can be claustrophobically busy.

Most **microbuses** heading out from Latakia to Ugarit pass the stretch of beach in front of the holiday complexes and stop outside the *Cham Cote d'Azur* complex; you will probably have to walk from here if you want to get to the *Meridien* (20min along the road).

Eating and drinking

Latakia offers a good selection of inexpensive **restaurants**, although it can at times feel as if the city is hell-bent on offering the ultimate pizza challenge. None of the cheap *felafel* and chicken haunts at the western end of 14 Ramadan Avenue have been listed below; there's nothing much to choose between them – just roll up and choose the one which looks cleanest. For some good stand-up Western fast food head for either *Snack Burger* or *Mr Zorba* which are located just off Azar Avenue, to the north of the *Mamma* restaurant.

Most of the choices listed below are on or near Al-Moutanabby Street, and nowhere else does Syria's young population seem so evident; watch them, decked out in smart Western clothes, as they self-consciously preen themselves over an early evening ice cream. You can eat a main course at any of the places listed below for under S£300, and usually much less; many of the restaurants listed also double up as **bars**.

Blow Up, Al-Moutanabby St. Standard Syrian fare in relaxed ambience with a decent bar. First-floor window seats available for people-watchers.

Al-Havana, Ibrahim Hanano St. A bright spot with friendly staff and an absorbing view over a busy inner-city square. You can come here just to chill out over a beer if you want; its musical selection only confirms the ubiquity of the Spice Girls.

Italian Corner, Al-Moutanabby St. Reasonably priced and popular place, but the pizzas are a bit too fluffy and short on toppings. A small selection of chicken and steak dishes also available, plus full bar.

Laodicea, Baghdad Ave. Despite the shiny appearance, a pretty standard Syrian restaurant serving uninspiring fare at a relaxed pace.

Magnom, at the southern end of Baghdad Ave. Decent, cheap place serving a limited menu of Western fast food (pizzas, burgers, lasagne), cheekily announced by a familiar-looking yellow "M" sign.

Mamma, Azar Ave. Good pizza/hamburger joint for a quick sit-down meal, though slightly cramped.

Petra, Al-Akhtal St. Luminous decor on the theme of Greek mythology provides the pleasing background to some very tasty eats. A good selection of Western and Arabic food, including the usual Italian dishes so popular in the city, and a full bar available.

Pizza Home, Sultan Basha Alatresh St. Cheap and cheerful pizza joint.

Sindibad, Yousef al-Azmah St. Intimate little place located next to the *Al-Atlal Hotel*.

Stop 5, Al-Moutanabby St. Serves the best pizza in town, as well as a limited number of other Western dishes. Intimate place with efficient service and an English menu; European beer available.

22, Faris Alkhun St. Another good pizza-oriented sit-down place, where your ale comes in a genuine beer-mug. The decor is nautically themed, though the serviettes bear the logo of Syrianair.

Listings

Airline Syrianair are on Baghdad Ave; there are two flights a week from Latakia airport (both Fri), one to Damascus (S£600) and one to Cairo (US$180).

Bus departures For most long-distance journeys (including Antakya in Turkey) use the Karnak and Pullman bus station on Abdel Qader al-Housayni Ave. The major companies have offices here; Qadmous also have an office on 14 Ramadan Ave and a separate station for their services to Baniyas, Homs and Tartous on Place Al-Joumhouria, behind the *Haroun Hotel*. The company located next door to the Qadmous office on 14 Ramadan Ave operates services to Turkey and Lebanon. Karnak, which serves Aleppo, Damascus (via Tartous and Homs) and Beirut, has its office just off Baghdad Ave in the centre of town. Unless you're really counting the pounds, you can safely ignore the clapped-out station at the eastern end of 14 Ramadan Ave which has old-style buses serving Aleppo and Damascus, not renowned for their comfort or air conditioning (fares are about half the price of the Pullman services). For most local destinations head for the local bus and microbus station on Al-Jalaa St; however, micros for Ugarit, via Blue Beach, leave from behind the school on 14 Ramadan Ave.

Car rental Ugarit Travel and Tourism on Baghdad Ave is a Europcar agent. Starco (☎041/416 502) is a local car rental company situated at the eastern end of 14 Ramadan Ave opposite the Qadmous bus company office. Otherwise try the luxury hotels.

Exchange The Commercial Bank of Syria (daily except Fri 8.30am–1.30pm) is on Baghdad Ave; the exchange booth has a separate entrance all to itself and is very efficient. Their branch in the *Meridien* on Blue Beach has longer hours and is open on Fridays (daily 8am–2pm & 5–8pm).

Ferries In the past ferries have run from Latakia out to Volos in mainland Greece via Cyprus and Crete, and also down to Alexandria via Beirut, but at the time of writing all of these were in abeyance. For the latest information ask at the office (presently shut) marked "shipping agencies company" on Al-Jazaer Ave or at the nearby Ali Dib travel agency on Abdul Qader al-Jazain St. If you find that it's still impossible to leave Syria by sea, you could pick up one of the regular service taxis for Beirut and sail from there instead; transit visas for Lebanon are available at the border, and you'll be able to find plenty of ferries to Egypt, Cyprus and Greece once in Beirut.

Flight agents Numerous travel agents on Baghdad St and around the main shopping district can book flights. Examples include Al-Moutawasset on Al-Yarmuk St which deals with Air France, Alitalia, Royal Jordanian and Turkish Airlines, and Ali Dib, on Abdul Qader al-Jazain St, which acts for KLM, Lufthansa and Qantas.

Immigration office Situated on the second floor of the police station on 14 Ramadan Ave opposite the mosque (daily except Fri 8am–2pm). Service here can be extremely slow and frustrating. There's a photographer's just behind the police station for those requiring photos for their visa extension.

Pharmacies There are two situated opposite each other at the western end of 14 Ramadan St and a couple more nearby at the northern end of Ibrahim Hanano St.

Photography Numerous shops on Baghdad Ave sell Kodak or Fuji film and offer developing services.

Post office The main branch is on Seif al-Dawiah St (daily 8am–11pm) and offers fax and telephone facilities.

Service taxis For the run down to Tripoli and Beirut in Lebanon, service taxis depart from outside the *Kaoukab al-Chark Hotel* on 14 Ramadan Ave.

Ugarit

The area stretching along the coast to the immediate north of Latakia is very fertile, with richly productive orchards hidden behind high cypress trees. About 16km along stands the site of **UGARIT** (Ras Shamra in Arabic; daily: summer 9am–6pm; winter 9am–4pm; S£200), once the most important settlement on this stretch of the Mediterranean, and the place where one of the first alphabets was devised. The site is usually pretty busy by Syrian standards, being close to Latakia and the nearby resort hotels, but it's easy to reach and worth looking round for an hour or so. There are frequent **microbuses** from behind the school on 14 Ramadan Avenue in Latakia to the site (stopping outside the entrance), or you could take a taxi.

THE UGARIT ALPHABET

It is debatable whether the **Ugarit alphabet** actually is, as claimed, the world's first alphabet – Crete, Cyprus and Egypt lay similar claims – but it's certainly one of the very earliest examples. The alphabet discovered on tablets here consists of thirty letters, in sequence and pronounciation similar to modern Arabic, and containing some Arabic words which are still in use. Devised between 1400 and 1300 BC when Ugarit was at the height of its power as a trading and mercantile centre, the alphabet is formed using triangles and stalks arranged at different angles and in different combinations to make up individual letters; there are no vowels, and no accents.

The nature of what was found on the tablets varies from the ethereal to the mundane. A will written using the alphabet declares: "Starting from today, I, Yaremano, give up all my properties to my wife Baydawe, and two sons, Yataleeno and Yanhamo. If one of my sons treats his mother meanly, he must pay five hundred pieces of silver to the king. Beyond that, he should take off his shirt, leave it on the door handle, and go out into the street. But the son who treats his mother with respect and consideration, will be given all her property." Sayings and thoughts found on tablets include advice such as "Do not tell your wife where you hide your money" and "A life with no light does not deserve less than death". Other documents of a less personalized nature consist of royal and political correspondence (indicating a high level of administrative efficiency) and extensive lists of the goods which passed through the town.

On some tablets were written myths and religious texts. One tells the story of Kart, a king who had no son and who departed for faraway places looking for a woman who would bear children for him. Another story tells of Akhaat, the son of King Daniel; one day the boy was eaten by eagles and, as a result, all the plants in the world suddenly died. The tablets also include the first known musical text, which has rhythm and short notes. It was deciphered and played by a musicologist at Berkeley University in the 1970s, who declared it to "sound very familiar to us, and to be part of the international musical heritage".

Some history

The site of Ugarit was discovered in 1928 after a local farmer's plough hit a large piece of masonry buried in the soil; he contacted the French colonial authorities, whose archeologists began excavating the area the following year. What the farmer had found were the remains of one of the most powerful and wealthy cities in the Middle East, an important trading and government centre which had lain abandoned and uninhabited since a disastrous fire, caused by Philistine raiders, destroyed the place in 1180 BC. After the fire, the site had been gradually covered by soil and silt, becoming indistinguishable from the fertile land along the rest of the coastal plain.

Ugarit was first settled in the Neolithic period – very roughly, around 7000 BC – and rose to prominence around 3000 BC when it traded extensively with Cyprus and Mesopotamia. One of the finds the French archeologists made was a shipment of a thousand perfume flasks from Cyprus, unearthed from a city warehouse and believed to date from this time. The Temple of Baal was famous over the whole of the Near East, and records show that priests received offerings from as far away as Egypt; Baal was considered to be the son of the god El, creator of the universe and the source of all wisdom, the god of storms, rains and hills and the prime figure mentioned in the mythical texts found at Ugarit. The city's most important feature for today's archeologists and historians, however, was the palace library, where in 1948 clay tablets were unearthed covered in one of the earliest known alphabets. The tablets, now in museums as far apart as Aleppo and New York, contain mythical and religious texts, plus more mundane inventories of goods received at the port and customs duties paid, and have provided invaluable evidence concerning the history of language and writing.

The site

Ugarit's fascination lies more in its age and history than in what's left to see there. Being far older than the Roman sites in Syria, the settlement has far less still standing, and to the uninitiated the waist-high pieces of stone wall enclosing extensive areas of rooms, with narrow streets separating the buildings, won't mean very much. It's well worth buying a detailed plan of the site at the ticket office and trying to listen in on any guided tours which might be taking place.

There are only a couple of areas of the site where you can make out the remnants of specific structures. The **Royal Palace** (late fourteenth to thirteenth century BC) forms the largest collection of buildings, consisting of over ninety rambling rooms and six courtyards, which you enter through the original (and still very well-preserved) gateway to the city, located to the immediate right of the path up from the ticket office. At one time the palace was the largest and most opulent in western Asia, including courtyard fountains, burial chambers and even a piped water and sewerage system, its grandeur reflecting the wealth of the city itself.

At the highest point of the site, to the northeast of the palace, you can see the foundations of the **temples** dedicated to Baal and to Dagon, the god of the underworld, although it's hard to discern anything much of interest. Between the two temples in the former house of the high priest, many chants and other religious texts written on stone tablets were found by archeologists. As you look around you'll see numerous **wells and water courses**; water played an important part in funeral rites here, and it was believed that the dead had to have water near them.

Ugarit was a port town and the sea once came right up to its walls; after it was abandoned the harbour silted up and the Mediterranean retreated, leaving a dry area of scrub between the site and the sea. The blue water can be glimpsed through the trees from the ruins, but you can't get down to the sea at this point as the area is occupied by the military.

Qalaat Saladin

In 1909 T.E. Lawrence visited the Middle East as an undergraduate researching a thesis on medieval architecture, and declared **QALAAT SALADIN** to be "probably the finest example of military architecture in Syria"; the castle has not survived as well as Crac des Chevaliers and lacks the foreboding presence of Qalaat Marqab, but a visit will leave few feeling shortchanged.

The Phoenicians first fortified this site in the first millennium BC, but what you see today largely dates to the twelfth century, courtesy of the Crusaders. However, the castle only ever occupied – rather than commanded – the ridge it's built on, and in July 1188 Saladin easily breached the vulnerable walls of the lower court; the overstretched garrison within surrendered without much of a fight. For historians, Qalaat Saladin is interesting as it provides a good example of an early Crusader fortification which was not reworked by the Templars or Hospitallers,

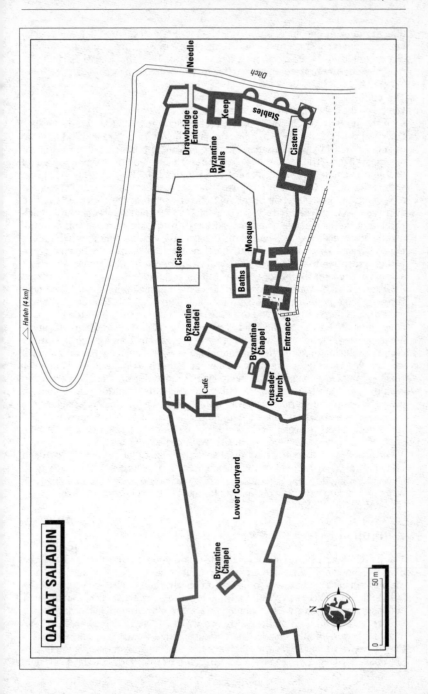

QALAAT SALADIN

△ Hafeh (4 km)

Needle

Ditch

Keep

Drawbridge
Entrance

Stables

Byzantine
Walls

Cistern

Cistern

Mosque

Baths

Byzantine
Citadel

Byzantine
Chapel

Crusader
Church

Entrance

Café

Lower Courtyard

Byzantine
Chapel

N

0   50 m

though under Arab control it underwent a number of facelifts: the lower terrace became home to a small town while remains of a mosque, palace and bathhouse can be found in the castle proper. It was only in 1957 that Qalaat Saladin was renamed after its Arab conqueror; previously it was known as **Saone**.

The castle

Lawrence described as "the most sensational thing in castle building" he had ever seen the massive **ditch** cut from the rock which provides the castle's eastern defence. Most of the ditch-digging was probably done in Byzantine times and then finished off by the Crusaders, leaving only an improbably tall stone **needle** to support a drawbridge. The castle **entrance** is located up the steps at the end of this unique ravine (daily except Tues 10am–6pm; S£200).

Immediately to your right on leaving the ticket office are two well-preserved **towers**; in the lower section of the first one are some of the stone balls hurled over the castle walls by Saladin's troops in 1188. Beyond the second is a courtyard, with the formidable, two-storeyed **keep** (with walls over 5m thick) in the middle of its eastern side. South of the keep are the castle's pillared stables and a huge cistern – now home to a skittish colony of birds – while the former **drawbridge entrance** to the castle is just to the north, where a look down the sheer sides is not recommended for vertigo sufferers.

Heading back towards the centre of the castle you can't miss another awesome Crusader **cistern** along the north wall, some 32m long and 10m deep. A short walk west of here will bring you to a **café** situated where the upper terrace looks down upon the lower one; the latter is permanently choked in undergrowth, making progress slow, but you can venture across it to a small, suffocated **Byzantine chapel**. Returning to the café and continuing eastwards you'll pass, on your left, the jumbled remains of the main **Crusader church**, behind which is another small Byzantine chapel and the badly ruined inner segment of the **Byzantine citadel** – difficult to climb up to and not particularly rewarding once you get there. Opposite the entrance gateway where you came into the castle stands the main evidence of Arab inhabitation of the site: a late thirteenth-century **mosque** and a twelfth-century palace complex featuring some recently restored **baths** – note the attractive stalactited carving above the palace entrance gate.

Local **buses** or **microbuses** from Latakia will only take you as far as Hafeh (40min) where, at the end of the village, is a sign in English directing you to Qalaat Saladin, 4km south: either walk, hitch or look out for enterprising locals who often run up and down on their motorbikes offering lifts to weary foreigners for anything up to S£100.

Slunfeh

Many microbuses from Latakia to Hafeh continue on 15km to **SLUNFEH**, the most welcoming of Syria's mountain resorts. It's a popular day-trip for locals and the busy main street is awash with restaurants and cheap eateries, though there's little to do here except stroll through the town, appreciate the cool mountain air and enjoy the dramatic views. Should you wish to **stay**, the pricey *Slunfeh Grand* (☎041/750 606; ⑥), right in the centre of town on Alsayed al-Raeis Street, is comfortable though slightly basic – and curiously only the wedding suite has a TV. Fifty metres away, on Fayel Mansour Street, is a much simpler establishment simply labelled "hotel" (②). The frequent **microbuses** from Latakia (1hr) via Hafeh, and occasional microbuses from Aleppo, all pass along the main street by the *Slunfeh Grand*.

Kassab and Ras al-Bassit

The stretch of mountainous coastline between Latakia and the Turkish border forms one of the most surprising, and attractive, landscapes in Syria. Here you'll find gorse-covered slopes dotted with stone farmhouses and tiny churches, and deep ravines and valleys carpeted with forests of pine and spruce. Most of the inhabitants are poor farmers, surviving on the limited agricultural potential of the land, or urban rich, whose gated and guarded villas line many of the roads leading towards the sea.

KASSAB is the principal town in the region, an attractive place situated in a bowl in the mountains about ninety minutes by road north of Latakia. It's more like a hill town in Greece or Sicily than a typical Middle Eastern settlement; indeed, you'll see far more churches than mosques here, while many of the inhabitants speak Turkish as their first language. There's nothing specific to see, but it's pleasant to wander round, taking in the views across the hills and enjoying the cool, clean air. During late August the town's population swells from 3000 to around 30,000, as Syrians flock here to escape the summer heat and many locals rent out their rooms and houses. For foreigners wishing to **stay**, the best bets are a short walk up the hill from the main square and crossroads: the *Al-Rawda* (☎041/711 008; ③) and the nearby *Amira* (☎041/711 007; ②), which both provide decent, clean rooms though the latter is open May–November only.

From the dusty crossroads in the centre of Kassab, where buses from Latakia stop, a road heads over the hills to **RAS AL-BASSIT**, where you'll find black sand beaches running north along the rugged coastline towards the Turkish border. The road twists and turns, then crosses over a low pass before dropping down to a long valley and finally heading to the sea. If you have your own transport, it'll be hard to resist eating at one of the cheap hotel restaurants with viewing terraces along the mountain road, and if you do you'll probably find yourself joined by groups of well-to-do families who live in the white-washed villas nearby. The **beaches** themselves are relatively litter-free and impressively situated against the mighty backdrop of Mount Casius just over the Turkish border, whose summit was held sacred by both the Phoenicians and the Greeks. The southern stretch of beach is the most developed, lined with numerous chalets, restaurants, cafés, tablefootball tents and even some basic video-game arcades. There is one **hotel** here, the *Bassat Tourist* (☎041/429 668; ⑤), which has decent rooms and its own restaurant and swimming pool, but is slightly overpriced. Bare chalets along the beach and main road cost in the region of S£1000 a night.

Microbuses between Latakia and Kassab are fairly frequent, certainly in summer when the last one back leaves at around 8pm. There is, however, only one scheduled departure from Kassab down to the beaches (at 10am; 30min), so you may well have to hire a taxi to take you down there (S£300 would be a fair price though the driver will probably attempt to charge you more). Direct microbuses between Latakia and Ras al-Bassit (not routed via Kassab) are very frequent in summer (50min), less so out of season. Just before entering Kassab the road from Latakia swings past a **border post**, where you can ask the bus to stop if you want to cross over into Turkey – be warned, however, that there's not much traffic on the Turkish side. Nor are there any buses from Kassab into Turkey so all in all it's probably easier simply to catch a direct service from the Pullman station in Latakia.

travel details

Trains

CFS claims to operate two trains per day (one of them overnight) between Damascus and Latakia (7hr), via Tartous (6hr). In reality, you'll probably find the service is reduced to one train per week (or none at all). Check at the Hedjaz Station in Damascus for current details. Four daily departures between Latakia and Aleppo are also scheduled (3hr 30min) – again, more likely to be one a week in reality.

Local buses and microbuses

Latakia, frequent services to: Baniyas (1hr); Hafeh (40min); Jableh (30min); Kassab (1hr 15min); Ras al-Bassit (50min); Slunfeh (1hr); Tartous (1hr 30min); Ugarit (20min).

Safita, frequent services to: Dreikish (20min); Homs (1hr 30min); Hosn Suleiman (40min); Mashta al-Helu (30min); Tartous (45min).

Tartous, frequent services to: Amrit (15min); Baniyas (30min); Damascus (5hr); Homs (2hr); Jableh (1hr); Latakia (1hr 30min); Safita (45min).

Karnak buses

Latakia to: Aleppo (2 daily; 4hr); Beirut (1 daily; 9hr); Damascus (2 daily; 5hr); Homs (2 daily; 2hr 30min); Tartous (2 daily; 1hr); Tripoli (1 daily; 5hr).

Tartous to: Aleppo (2 daily; 5hr); Beirut (1 daily; 8hr); Damascus (2 daily; 4hr); Homs (2 daily; 1hr 30min); Latakia (2 daily; 1hr); Tripoli (1 daily; 4hr).

Pullman buses

Pullman buses from Latakia run frequently to all the same destinations as Karnak, and also to Antakya in Turkey. From Tartous Pullman buses depart frequently to the same locations as Karnak, apart from Beirut and Tripoli.

Domestic flights

Syrianair flies once a week (currently Fri mornings) from Damascus to Latakia and back. Journey time is 1hr; the fare is S£600.

CHAPTER FIVE

ALEPPO AND AROUND

Aleppo is the sort of place that's hard to dislike. Instantly more appealing than Damascus, with none of the brutal concrete architecture or abandoned building sites which beset the capital, it's a relaxed, comparatively green and uncluttered city where it's worth kicking back for a few days, at the very least. There are road, rail and air connections with the rest of Syria, and north into Turkey, and the hotels and restaurants are at least equal to those of Damascus in terms of both quality and variety – and, unfortunately, price.

Aleppo's long and eventful history has bequeathed it an impressive array of ancient monuments, crowned by the largely medieval **citadel** and the fabulous **Great Mosque**. Evidence of long and close **ties with Europe** can be seen in the wide avenues and extensive, fountain-strewn parklands of the New City, which in summer provide a cool haven from the clamour of the warren-like souks. Two thousand years of trading history have given the city a cosmopolitan air which Damascus significantly lacks: many of the cheap hotels are occupied by itinerant buyers and sellers from Turkey, Armenia and Russia, who noisily display their wares at bus stations, in the souks and on the street, and there's a high proportion of Armenian, Kurdish and Turkish immigrants, who own many of the restaurants, hotels and market stalls in the city centre. There's also a significant **Christian minority**, many of whom still live in the medieval **Jdeide Quarter** and worship in its ancient churches. Another distinctive Aleppo landmark, the **Baron Hotel**, has been owned and run for over fifty years by a woman from the English Lake District and is a unique reminder of the city's colonial past and European outlook.

In the parched, empty scrubland beyond the fertile depression to which Aleppo owes its existence are the so-called **Dead Cities**. The weed-infested ruins of these Roman and Byzantine settlements crop up at astonishingly regular intervals across northwestern Syria, and are easily visited on day-trips from Aleppo. Pre-eminent among them is the complex surrounding the **Church of St Simeon**, commemorating the mystic saint who spent nearly forty years sitting on top of a stone pillar. Such was Simeon's notoriety that pilgrims once travelled here from as far afield as England just to get a look at him from the base of his pillar; now it's bus-loads of tourists who form the curious, picking over the sad remains of the pillar – reduced to a stump by all the pilgrims chipping away at it – and wondering what all the fuss was about. It's also worth making time for the more homely Dead Cities **around Maarat al-Numan**: the taverns, baths, churches and ordinary houses of these small provincial towns are remarkably well preserved and usually completely deserted save for passing shepherds.

The other highlights around Aleppo are the ruins of the third-century BC town of **Cyrrhus**, up near the Turkish border, and **Ebla**, a five-thousand-year-old city state whose remains can be seen submerged in a windy *tell* just off the main Aleppo–Damascus highway.

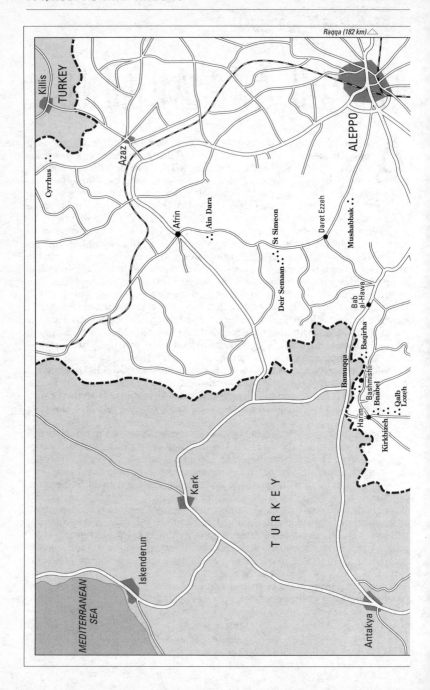

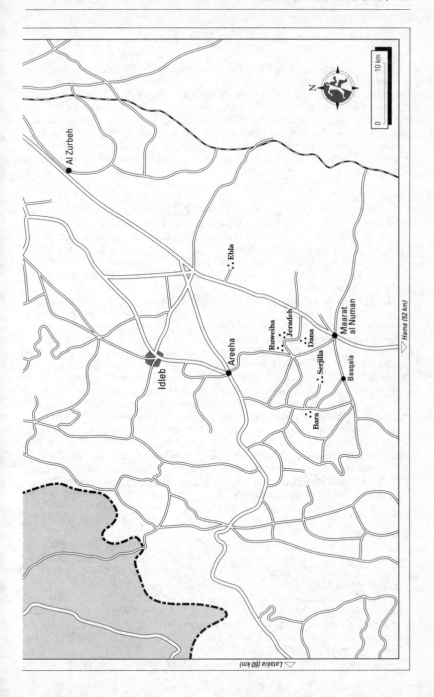

ALEPPO

One of the attractions of **ALEPPO** is its manageability: the centre of town falls into very distinct areas, and once you've got the basic layout clear, finding your way around is very easy. The first district you'll see is the **New City**, where all of Aleppo's hotels, restaurants, banks and other useful facilities, such as the post office and airline offices, are situated. **Baron Street** is at the heart of this district and will be your first point of reference when you arrive. All but one of the city's bus stations can be found in the southern part of the New City, and on its northern fringes, beyond the spacious **city park**, you'll find the train station. The New City is devoid of any specific sights, however, save the **National Museum**, which gives a comprehensive and well-organized perspective on the ancient history of northern Syria.

To the east of the bus stations are the **souks** of the old city, a huge area of covered markets and open **khans**, the trading and customs houses of Ottoman times which are still used as arenas for frantic buying and selling. The souks hide a number of tiny mosques, their entrances lost amongst the stalls; not easily missed, though, either in terms of size or of compelling interest, is the **Great Mosque**, one of the largest mosques in the world, situated in the centre of this teeming market area.

Emerging from the eastern end of the souks you'll come across the **citadel**, the defensive and administrative heart of medieval Aleppo whose distinctive ramparts and formidable, towered gateway will probably be already familiar to you through posters and photographs (for a sneak preview, look on the back of a S£100 note). Although the rooms of the tower have been splendidly restored to give some flavour of the city's wealth during the Middle Ages, there's not actually an awful lot to see in the citadel, and its most alluring aspect is the view over the whole of Aleppo that you get from the upper walls. The area south of the citadel consists of streets lined with artisans' workshops, mosques and madrasas, and is a good place to head for if the tourist crowds in the souks and citadel become wearing.

The **Jdeide Quarter** to the northwest of the citadel is home to Aleppo's Christian community, where you'll find churches belonging to the major sects, in addition to the fascinating **Museum of Popular Tradition**. If the churches are locked and the museum doesn't grab your attention, it's still well worth exploring this district, as it's another good place to escape the crowds: most of the streets are quiet, traffic-free lanes, narrow and twisting, with tall, shuttered houses whose upper floors often overhang the street to give welcome shade.

Some history

Aleppo's past rivals that of Damascus in terms of scope and complexity, and like the capital, though with less justification, it claims to be the oldest inhabited settlement on earth. The earliest mentions of the city are recorded on stone tablets found at Mari, on the Syrian Euphrates, which date from around 2000 BC. From this time onwards Aleppo was the capital of a succession of prosperous city states, governed by the Amorites, the Hittites (after the Battle of Kadesh in 1285 BC), the Assyrians, the Persians and, after 333 BC, by the Seleucid dynasty, founded by one of Alexander the Great's generals, who named the city **Beroia**. Virtually nothing remains of these settlements, nor of later Roman and Byzantine occupation, although history records a visit in the fourth century by **St Helena**, mother of

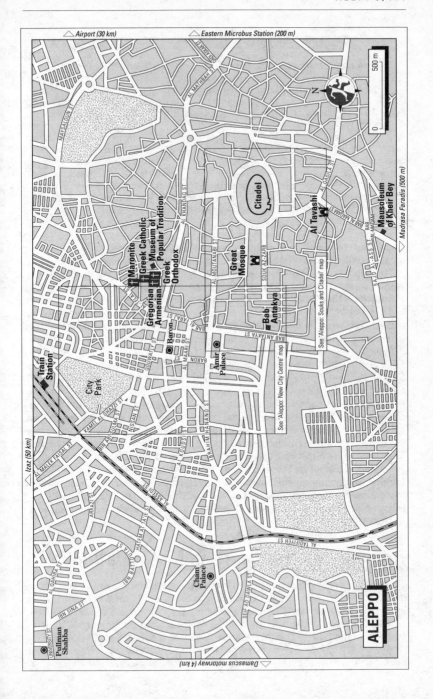

△ Airport (30 km)   △ Eastern Microbus Station (200 m)

500 m

N

Citadel

Al Tavashi

Mausoleum
of Kheir Bey

Madrasa Faradis (500 m) ▷

Maronite
Greek Catholic
Museum of
Popular Tradition
Greek
Orthodox

Great
Mosque

Gregorian
Armenian

Baron

Bab
Antakya

See 'Aleppo: Souks and Citadel' map

Train
Station

City
Park

Amir
Palace

See 'Aleppo: New City Centre' map

△ Izaz (50 km)

Cham
Palace

Pullman
Shahba

ALEPPO

▽ Damascus motorway (4 km)

CROSSING THE BORDER FROM TURKEY

If you're entering Syria overland **from Turkey**, Aleppo is likely to be the first place you come to. Several buses a day run direct from the *otogar* in **Antakya** to Aleppo, costing around US$13 and taking four hours, though delays at the border can make this longer. A cheaper (and possibly quicker) option on this route might be to take a *dolmus* from Antakya to Reyhanli, then hitch or take a taxi to the border, where a Syrian microbus should be waiting to take you on to Aleppo. If you want to enter Syria via **Gaziantep**, you'll probably need to take a taxi to the border, cross it on foot, and then pick up another taxi to Aleppo; the whole journey should take about 3–4 hours and cost around US$30. If this seems too much, check if the infrequent Gaziantep–Aleppo bus is running, or just use a taxi between Killis and the Turkish border post, then again from the Syrian border post to Azaz, where you can pick up an Aleppo-bound microbus. Every week there's a direct train from Istanbul to Aleppo, which takes two days and a night.

Constantine the Great, in honour of whom was founded a Christian cathedral (later turned into the Madrasa Halawiye) adjacent to the site of the present Great Mosque.

The importance of the city grew after the Arab invasion of Syria during the seventh century. The Great Mosque was built by the Umayyad dynasty, and the city was fortified anew, allowing it to repel two attempts at capture by the Crusaders, in 1098 and 1124. By the 1180s the victorious Saladin considered Aleppo important enough to make his son **Al-Zaher Ghazi** city governor, and it was he who extensively rebuilt the citadel, which became the cornerstone of Aleppo's defences.

The later Middle Ages saw renewed prosperity for traders, as the city became a natural stopping place on the main overland routes from the Mediterranean to China. By 1800 Aleppo was the largest city in Syria, with sizable Kurdish, Armenian, Jewish and Christian communities, but the development of new sea routes to the Far East led to a gradual decline in fortunes. In 1939 **Iskenderun**, for centuries the natural seaport for Aleppo, was ceded by France to Turkey, and the redrawing of the Turkish–Syrian border less than 40km from the city meant that much of its hinterland was cut off. However, Aleppo's international outlook continued unabated by the decline in trade: it was the terminus for the Orient Express in the 1930s, with railway carriages in the main train station proudly advertising Paris as their final destination, and the French colonial administration laid out tree-lined streets and a spacious, leafy city park in the manner of European capitals.

Arrival, city transport and information

Chances are that you'll **arrive** in the city by **bus**, in which case you'll have to work out exactly which bus station you're going to finish up in (see p.210): there are at least eight bus terminals in Aleppo (including the city bus station), but the good news is that seven of them are right in the centre of town, within easy walking distance of all the hotels. The exception is the eastern bus station, 3km east of the centre, which you'll arrive at if you've entered the city by ordinary bus or microbus from the northeast of the country (principally Raqqa and Deir ez-Zur);

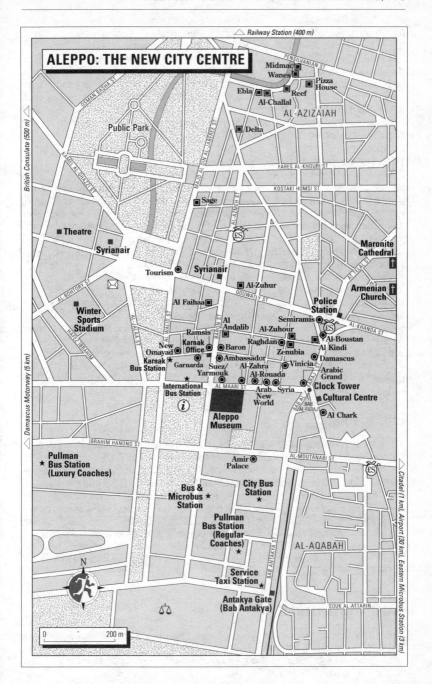

△ *Railway Station (400 m)*

ALEPPO: THE NEW CITY CENTRE

PENSILVANIAN ST
OSMAN BASHA ST
Midmac
Wanes
Pizza House
Ebla
Reef
Al-Challal
AL-AZIZAIAH
Public Park
Delta
FARES AL-KHOURI ST
KOSTAKI HOMSI ST
Sage
Maronite Cathedral †
Theatre
Syrianair
Armenian Church †
Tourism
Syrianair
Al-Zuhur
QOUWATLY ST
Police Station
Winter Sports Stadium
Al Faihaa
Semiramis
AL-KHANDA ST
Al Andalib
Al-Zuhour
Al-Boustan
Ramsis
Raghdan
Al Kindi
New Omayad
Karnak Office
Baron
Zenubia
Damascus
Karnak Bus Station
Garnarda
Ambassador
Vinicia
Arabic Grand
Suez/ Yarmouk
Al-Zahra
Clock Tower
International Bus Station
Al-Rouada
Cultural Centre
AL MAARI ST
Arab Syria
New World
BAB AL-FARAJ
Aleppo Museum
Al Chark
AL-MOUTANABTI ST
Amir Palace
Pullman Bus Station (Luxury Coaches)
IBRAHIM HANONO ST
City Bus Station
Bus & Microbus Station
Pullman Bus Station (Regular Coaches)
AL-AQABAH
Service Taxi Station
SOUK AL-ATTARIN
Antakya Gate (Bab Antakya)
N
0   200 m

British Consulate (500 m) ◁
◁ Damascus Motorway (5 km)
Citadel (1 km), Airport (30 km), Eastern Microbus Station (3 km) ▷

from there, you could catch a city bus to the local bus station, south of Baron Street behind the *Amir Palace Hotel*, or a taxi to your hotel.

The **airport** is 30km east of the centre along the road to Raqqa; there's a dedicated bus which will get you to the New City, dropping you off outside the Karnak and international bus stations, with departures from the airport every thirty minutes (S£10). From the **train station**, it's a fifteen-minute walk across the city park to the main area of hotels along Baron Street; note however that the daily train from Damascus usually gets into Aleppo at around 11pm – not the most convenient of times to start hunting for accommodation.

City transport

You're unlikely to feel much of a need to use the crowded **microbuses** or the smoke-belching, jam-packed blue or orange **buses** which form the bulk of Aleppo's city transport. As usual, there's no published or posted indication of routes or timetables, so you'll just have to ask for help from locals (who'll think you're mad for wanting to go anywhere by bus); tickets are purchased on the bus. Located directly behind the *Amir Palace Hotel* south of Baron Street, the city bus station is a chaotic, bewildering place, strewn with wind-blown rubbish of all descriptions.

You're much more likely to resort to your own two feet, or to **taxis**, for getting around. You can hail these yellow, often clapped-out American-built limousines anywhere, and you shouldn't have to pay more than S£40 for a ride across town – although you're asking to be charged over the odds if your journey starts or finishes at one of the big hotels. Ask the driver to use the meter, though often you'll be told that it's broken or out of date, in which you'll need to agree on a fare before you set out. Some of the taxis are actually shared **service taxis**, which run set routes, picking up and dropping off people as they go; they're difficult to distinguish from the normal taxis, apart from the fact that they're often carrying a carload of passengers instead of people in ones or twos.

Information

The staff in the **tourist office**, located in a pavilion opposite the museum in the New City, are unusually helpful and knowledgeable (daily except Fri 8.30am–3pm). You can hire English-speaking **guides** here for S£1200 per day, and pick up a useful free **map** of Aleppo. Much better, however, is the city map on the fold-out Freytag-Berndt *Road Map: Syria*, which you should be able to buy in the **bookshop** at the *Amir Palace Hotel* close by. This is the principal source of English-language books and maps in the city, selling novels, guidebooks and coffee-table tomes about Syrian art, architecture and cooking. Either the bookshop or the tourist office should be able to give you information on festivals and other **events** in the city. The *Syria Times* is also a good source of info on Aleppo events, but can be difficult to find; try the newsstands on Baron Street or the *Amir Palace* bookshop.

Accommodation

There's no shortage of **hotels** in Aleppo, covering the full price and quality range, and they're rarely full; what's more, looking around for somewhere to stay is easy, as most are concentrated in the area around Baron Street and Bab al-Faraj (the former location of a city gate, now marked by an ugly turn-of-the-century clock-tower). Prices are, however, higher than in other parts of Syria (with the exception of Damascus), and Aleppo's role as a trading centre might mean that you find noisy sessions between sellers (often Russians and Armenians) and buyers actually taking place in your hotel, at all hours of the day and night. Street noise can be a problem too, especially in cheaper places.

Rock-bottom dosshouses can be found along Al-Maari Street, roads leading off it and around the clocktower by Bab al-Faraj (at the eastern end of this street), many of them located in the upper floors of apartment blocks. Some of these places are intolerably unhygienic and unsafe, with bedbugs and superior types of armour-plated insect life coming as standard. Prices start from as little as S£175 for a night in a single room, although you'll be hard pressed to find anything other than doubles or triples available in most establishments, the former going for around S£200 and upwards. We've earmarked the best of a pretty bad bunch below. In all these hotels (and even some of the slightly more expensive ones), a little haggling might reduce the price, particularly if you're staying for a few nights.

A notch further up and you're usually paying US$25–50 for a double room (US$20–40 for a single) in a **mid-range hotel**. Apart from the *Al-Boustan*, slightly to the east by Bab al-Faraj, all these hotels are located on Baron Street or roads immediately leading from it, often above airline offices or travel agencies. Most of these hotels will require payment in US$, in cash or travellers' cheques; none take credit cards but with a bit of persuasion they'll probably take Syrian pounds instead, depending on the mood of the desk staff.

Finally, the **top-of-the-range** big boys include the *Amir Palace*, close to Baron Street, and two five-star establishments a taxi ride from the centre, out in the western suburbs close to the university.

Budget

Arabic Grand, Bab al-Faraj (☎021/211 375). Prime but noisy location by the clocktower intersection. Singles, doubles and triples available. ②.

Al-Chark, 50m southeast of Bab al-Faraj (☎021/239 122). Cleaner and quieter than others at this price around the clocktower. Doubles without bath (no singles available). ②.

Damascus, Bab al-Faraj (☎021/210 786). Rock-bottom prices in a noisy location overlooking the clocktower intersection. Basic but bearable for a night or two. ①.

Al-Raouda, Al-Maari St (no phone). Cheap, basic hotel, with doubles only; separate bathrooms on both floors. ①.

Syria, Al-Maari St (☎021/219 760). Better than many in this street, at about the same price. ①.

ACCOMMODATION PRICE CODES

In this book, all hotels have been categorized according to the **price codes** outlined below. They represent the minimum you can expect to pay for a **double room** in each hotel; for further details, see p.31.

① under S£300/US$7.50	⑤ US$35–50/S£1400–2000
② S£300–600/US$7.50–15	⑥ US$50–90/S£2000–3600
③ S£600–1000/US$15–25	⑦ US$90–130/S£3600–5200
④ S£1000–1400/US$25–35	⑧ US$130 and over/S£5200 and over

Vinicia, Bab al-Faraj (☎021/238 558 or 239 909). Better and slightly more expensive than others around the clocktower. Rooms are decent and have fridges. ③.

Yarmouk, Al-Maari St (☎021/217 510 or 227 990). Popular hotel, and very good for its price; praised by many budget travellers, and fills up quickly as a result. Choice of doubles/singles with/without bath. ②.

Al-Zahra, just off Al-Maari St (no phone). Acceptably clean option; occupies the floor below and uses the same lift as the *Assia Hotel*, which cannot be recommended. ②.

Mid-range

Ambassador, Baron St (☎021/211 833). Cheaper mid-range option: no air con in rooms, and no breakfast available. Singles, doubles and triples available. ③.

THE BARON HOTEL

Since its opening in 1909 the **Baron** has been the most famous and talked-about hotel in Syria, although nowadays its fame rests solely on its illustrious list of former guests, and has little to do with the rather sorry condition which currently besets the place. At the time of writing, the hotel is still managed by **Coco Masloumian**, a direct descendant of one of the founders, two brothers who, like many of their kinsfolk in the 1890s, fled the Turkish pogrom in Armenia and sought refuge in Aleppo. The brothers decided to open a hotel in what was then the chic European part of town, not far from the railway station (where part of the Orient Express terminated) and with a terrace overlooking a marsh, where game could be easily shot for the hotel's dinner table. Incorporating the best of Oriental hospitality and European standards of luxury, the hotel's reputation quickly spread, and its guest list grew to include Kemal Ataturk, Theodore Roosevelt, Lady Louis Mountbatten, the aviators Charles Lindbergh and Amy Johnson, the writer Agatha Christie and her archeologist husband Sir Max Mallowan (many of whose finds are now on display in the archeological museum), and, most famously of all, T.E. Lawrence (of Arabia), a copy of whose bill can be seen in the lounge. Coco Masloumian's English wife Sally, who still manages the hotel, married him just after World War II when she was a nurse working in Aleppo; she, like the hotel itself, is one of the few remaining links that Syria has with its colonial past.

Ninety years after its opening, some of the Baron's original colonial charm still remains – although none of its famed luxury. Rooms are airy but bare and shabby, with plumbing that has a mind of its own and beds and furniture which have seen better days. You can no longer shoot game from the terrace, as the former marsh has long since been drained and built over, but sipping a cool beer whilst people-watching the busiest street in Aleppo will no doubt compensate. Although modern office buildings now rather dwarf the humble *Baron*, the hotel remains the most distinctive building on the street.

The hotel's **bar** is by far its most noted feature nowadays, a meeting point for travellers and expats, who sink with ease into the faded armchairs and read back copies of *Time* magazine or gather on the terrace in the cool of summer evenings – when the ancient French thermometers pinned to the wall indicate that the temperature has at last dropped to something bearable. You'll find lots of people drink here just to savour the atmosphere, secretly glad that they're not actually staying – although the place is usually booked solid, with many guests asking to be put up in Lawrence of Arabia's old room (he actually occupied several during his many stays). If you do decide to stay, then be prepared for plenty of noise from the street outside, in addition to night-time rumblings from the pipes and perhaps even the sounds of Agatha Christie's typewriter, as her ghost rewrites *Murder on the Orient Express* in the room she used as her study.

Baron, Baron St (☎021/210 880, fax 218 164). Legendary hotel which is a tourist sight in itself (see box), but tales abound of shabby rooms and antiquated plumbing; a lot of guests seem to spend their time sitting around the (very convivial) downstairs bar, slagging the place off. It's overpriced for rooms without shower or bath, but you should still book in advance. ④.

Al-Boustan, Bab al-Faraj (☎021/217 104 or 217 456). Located just north of the clocktower, this is a small, well-appointed and fairly priced hotel. ④.

Garnarda, just off Baron St (☎021/224 458). Clean, spacious rooms in another well-priced mid-range option. ④.

New Omayad, on a side street between Baron and Al-Walid streets (☎021/214 202). Good rooms with air con in a quiet location, away from traffic noise. ⑤.

Ramsis, Baron St (☎021/216 700). Located opposite *Baron Hotel*, the plush foyer is there to make you forget how shabby the rooms are. Rather overpriced for what it is, though the rate includes breakfast. ⑤.

Tourism, Al-Walid St (☎021/210 156, fax 219 956). Superior to the other mid-range options in terms of facilities on offer, and size and comfort of rooms. A bit soulless but if you want a centrally located, well-appointed hotel and can't quite afford the *Amir Palace*, this is the place to head for. ⑤.

Expensive

Amir Palace, Ibrahim Hanono St/Al-Raies Square (☎021/214 800, fax 215 710). Luxury high-rise, with TV, central air conditioning and all mod cons, located just south of Baron St and across a main road from the museum. Cheaper and more central than the other luxury-class hotels. ⑦.

Chahba Cham Palace, Al-Koudsi St (☎021/249 801, fax 229 334). Huge place with an outdoor pool, tennis courts, fitness centre, sauna, beauty parlour, business centre, shops, disco, and several restaurants and bars; comfortable rooms have satellite TV and central air conditioning. Stay here long enough, however, and you'll probably find the inconvenient location, the bland sheen and impersonal service rather wearing. ⑧.

Pullman Shahba, University St (☎021/667 200, fax 667 213). Smaller, less impersonal and better value than the *Cham Palace*. There's an outdoor pool, a café/snack bar, two restaurants, and all rooms have TV and central air conditioning. ⑦.

The New City and the National Museum

Although the city's main hotels, restaurants, shops, transport and business facilities are found in the New City, the **National Museum of Aleppo** is the only specific tourist sight here. Other than that, the pleasant **city park** is worth spending some time in, especially on warm afternoons or during the early evening in midsummer: it's a shady area of paths, greenery and fountains, laid out in the late 1940s like a Paris park, with refreshment stalls and a children's pleasure park thrown in for good measure. The place is unique in Syria, where urban greenery is something of a rarity, and beats hands-down any of the scruffy public parks in Damascus. Late in the day the park is the arena for Aleppo's Mediterranean-style *passegiata*, when families dressed to the nines wander the paths and sit by the fountains, consuming copious amounts of ice cream.

The National Museum of Aleppo

Housed in a purpose-built pavilion around an open courtyard, the **National Museum** (daily except Tues 9am–6pm; S£200) chronicles the history of Aleppo

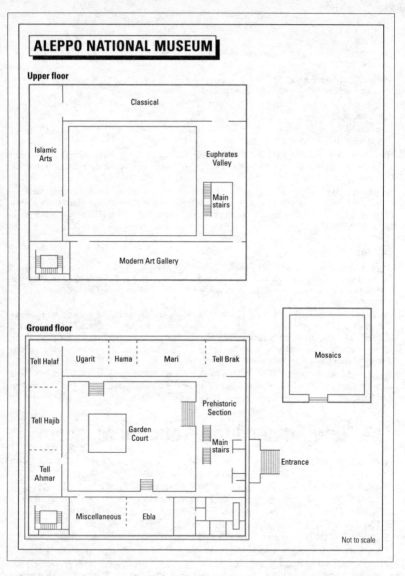

ALEPPO NATIONAL MUSEUM

Upper floor

- Classical
- Islamic Arts
- Euphrates Valley
- Main stairs
- Modern Art Gallery

Ground floor

- Tell Halaf
- Ugarit
- Hama
- Mari
- Tell Brak
- Mosaics
- Tell Hajib
- Prehistoric Section
- Garden Court
- Main stairs
- Tell Ahmar
- Entrance
- Miscellaneous
- Ebla

Not to scale

and northern Syria from earliest times to the Ottoman era, its main displays being archeological finds from various sites in the Gezira in northeastern Syria. The collection is well set out in airy rooms and reasonably well labelled, with a detailed guidebook available at the entrance if you want more info than we've given here. A visit is especially rewarding if you've already been to the sites from which the majority of the finds come (such as Mari, Ugarit and Ebla).

Ground floor

You enter the museum building past some bemused-looking statues fashioned from black basalt which were unearthed from Tell Halaf in northeastern Syria; three thousand years old they may be, but their gormless, eye-popping expressions render them an unintentionally amusing introduction to the museum. To the right of the ticket desk is a room designed for a mosaic collection, which, when it is finally installed, promises to be one of the museum's highlights. After the entrance hall you should turn right, and follow an anticlockwise direction around the central courtyard to get the intended chronological perspective of the ground floor.

•**Prehistoric section**. In the first room you can see figurines that probably represent the mother goddess, stone tools and pieces of pottery found in a 1990 dig at Tell Kashashuk in the northeast; the small clay balls in case 2 were used as slingshot in catapults. The most interesting find in this section is a burial urn from Tell al-Abr on the Euphrates which contained the skeleton of a two-year-old child, thought to have been killed by a flint weapon that was found with the bones. In the same display case, the six-pointed "Star of David" on the ceramic pieces, which were fashioned some three thousand years before the birth of King David, indicates the ancient lineage of this symbol.

•**Tell Brak**. Most of the pieces in this room were unearthed in the 1930s by the British archeologist Sir Max Mallowan, husband of Agatha Christie, at Tell Brak and other sites in northeastern Syria (see also p.231). Mallowan gave a lot of the best finds to the British Museum in London, and what grabs the attention most here are the necklaces fashioned from beads of different shapes and materials and the stone tablets written in cuneiform script, all of which date from around 3000 BC.

•**Mari**. The most interesting exhibit from this Bronze Age (c.1700 BC) site is the Golden Lion, made from (now oxidized) bronze, with its sad, benign eyes. The two life-size statues in this section are of a ruler of Mari, Prince Ishtup-Ilum, found in the main throne room of the palace, and of a spring goddess holding a vase, whose ox-horns were a common symbol of divinity in the ancient East.

•**Hama**. The finds from the region surrounding Hama go back to around 1000 BC, including, in the first case, a minute statuette of gilded bronze, depicting a bearded deity with ox-horns sitting on his throne. Other cases contain ceramic pieces and the like, and against one wall you can see two lions which guarded the citadel in Hama around 800 BC.

•**Ugarit**. The most significant discovery made at Ugarit, a major Bronze Age trading centre on the coast near Latakia, was the temple archives, dating from around 1200 BC and written in what is believed to be the world's first alphabet; the language used by the scribes and merchants in Ugarit was Akkadian, at that time the principal language of diplomacy and trade in the eastern Mediterranean. You can see some of the tablets in one case, and in others a variety of secretarial paraphernalia, such as cylinder seals, weights and the like.

•**Tell Halaf, Tell Hajib and Tell Ahmar**. Excavated by German archeologists in the 1930s, many of the Tell Halaf finds were taken to Berlin but were destroyed in allied bombing raids in World War II. As you enter the room, two enormous statues of seated women greet you, dating from around 1000 BC and thought to represent members of the Halaf ruling dynasty; between them is part of the facade of what must have been a glorious temple palace, featuring a winged sun-disc being transported by mythical figures, one of which is half-man, half-bull. Further on, the most important Iron Age finds from Tell Hajib are intricate, clearly Egyptian-inspired ivory carvings, inlaid with precious stones and decorated with coloured glaze. In one design you can see the birth of the Egyptian god Horus, who sits on top of a lotus flower. Close by are paintings which once adorned the royal palace at Tell Ahmar, completed around 850 BC and clearly the reflection of an egomaniacal regime: we see the king scorning vanquished leaders, holding receptions and communing with humble-looking deities. In the rooms that follow the Tell Ahmar display, there's little of immediate interest, except perhaps some stone tablets from Ebla, and pottery pieces from Al-Ansari, a Bronze Age settlement very close to Aleppo.

Upper floor

The collections on the upper floor do not fit in with the chronological ordering of the ground floor and, on the whole, are not as absorbing.

•**Euphrates Valley**. There's little labelling in English in the first of the upstairs rooms, which contains mainly plans and finds from early sites along the Euphrates. Most of these settlements flourished during the fourth and third millennia BC, their livelihood based on river trade with Babylonia and other, more important Euphrates settlements further downstream. The designs – of clay figurines, bronze and stone vessels, and animal sculptures – are fairly unsophisticated and pale in comparison with some of the beautiful finds from later settlements downstairs.

•**Classical section**. The most interesting of the upstairs galleries is that devoted to finds from Roman-era sites in Syria, particularly Palmyra. Coins, statuary, glass and bronze objects and mosaics are on display, but most prominent here is a tombstone found at Manbij, 90km east of Aleppo: the sculpture is of an elegant, seated woman, with a Greek inscription carved into the stone which reads simply and poignantly, "Rest in peace, Marta".

•**Islamic arts**. Only a tiny hint is given here of the richness of Islamic art fashioned in Syria from the eighth century onwards. The gold and silver coins produced by successive Arab dynasties are very fine, and the astrolabe in the corner also stands out – a fussy, mathematically complex device consisting of a myriad of globes and rings, used by early medieval scholars for determining the altitude of stars and planets. In the centre of the room, a model of the old city of Aleppo, with walls and gates, markets and mosques appearing as they were in medieval times, is probably the single most interesting exhibit of the upstairs galleries.

•**Modern art gallery**. This ever-changing (but mostly awful) selection of paintings gives you something of a feel for Syrian modern art; you probably won't come away from this room thinking you want to see any more of it.

The souks and the Great Mosque

The area of town between the *Amir Palace Hotel* and the citadel is taken up by the **souks**, which for many travellers are the principal attraction of Aleppo. Dark, noisy and crowded with animals, traders and shoppers, the souks form one of the largest areas of covered market anywhere in the world, a labyrinthine network of passages broken only by the open courtyards of mosques and by the quadrangles of medieval **khans**, the combined inns and warehouses used by merchants in

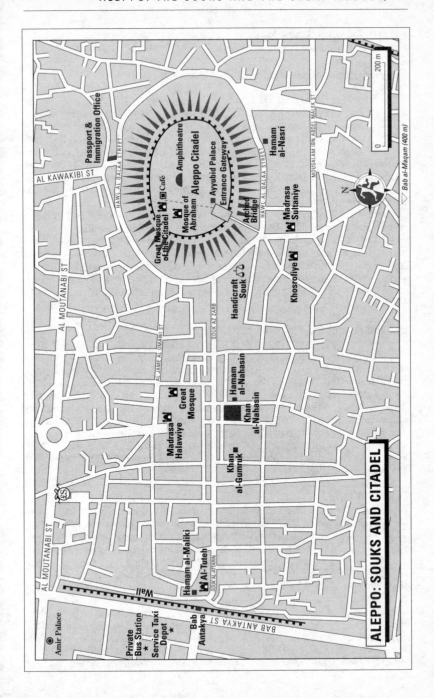

ALEPPO: SOUKS AND CITADEL

Amir Palace

Private Bus Station

Service Taxi Depot

Bab Antakya

Hamam al-Maliki

Al-Tuteh

SOUK AL-ATTARIN

BAB ANTAKYA ST

Wall

Khan al-Gumruk

Madrasa Halawiye

Great Mosque

AL JAME AL OMAWI ST

Hamam al-Nahasin

Khan al-Nahasin

AL MOUTANABI ST

AL MOUTANABI ST

AL KAWAKIBI ST

Passport & Immigration Office

HAWL AL QALAA STREET

Great Mosque of the Citadel

Café

Mosque of Abraham

Amphitheatre

Aleppo Citadel

Ayyubid Palace

Entrance Gateway

Arched Bridge

Hamam al-Nasri

HAWL AL QALAA STREET

MOUSALAM IBN ABDEL MALEK ST

Madrasa Sultaniye

Khosrofiye

Handicraft Souk

SOUK AZ ZARB

N

0   200 m

▽ *Bab al-Maqam (400 m)*

Ottoman days. The **Great Mosque**, which lies in the northern part of the souk area, is an unmissable haven of glacial calm after the bustle of the markets.

The souks

An incredible array of goods is sold in the souks, ranging from whole, fresh animal carcasses (with entrails available in a separate bag), to jewellery, fabrics, clothing, ornaments, shoes, nuts, spices and household goods. Whether you want a packet of washing powder or a genuine antique *nargileh*, this is the place to come. The souks are divided into sectors, with traders in each zone selling one particular thing, which makes shopping and shopping around easy. There is little pressure to buy from the traders, most of whom talk genially on mobile phones while drinking endless tiny cups of strong, sweet tea, which you may be offered yourself in the course of your discussions over what's on offer. Don't forget to bargain fiercely for what you want – often you can get the price down to a half of what is originally suggested, and with so many traders selling much the same sort of thing, arriving at a fair price is always easy. The souks **open** from about 10am to 5pm, and virtually all traders close up on a Friday (you can still walk through the passageways at any time). If it's souvenirs and handicrafts you're after – inlaid backgammon boards, ornate copperware and the like – you're better off looking for it in the designated **handicrafts souk** to the south of the citadel (see p.193).

Bab Antakya and the city ramparts

The best way to get your bearings is to spend a little time walking up and down the main street (Souk al-Attarin–Souk az-Zarb), an ancient highway aligned west–east through the middle of the souks. It's wider than other passageways and starts at the **Bab Antakya**, the old medieval gateway located southeast of the *Amir Palace*, across the road from the service taxi depot. This is the former Antioch Gate into the old city and is thought to stand on the site of a Roman triumphal arch. Now it's the setting for several small forges, where metalworkers sweat all day over hot anvils and raging ovens. Just beyond the gate a flight of stone steps leads up to the left and onto the old city **ramparts**, from where there are good views across the New City; you'll find the **Hamam al-Maliki** halfway up the steps (see p.198).

Souk al-Attarin

Head back down the steps from the ramparts and you're into **Souk al-Attarin**, the western portion of the main drag through the souks. After a couple of twists, which take the road around the **Al-Tuteh Mosque**, supposedly constructed from pieces of the old Roman triumphal arch (and usually closed), the street becomes completely straight and plunges into darkness. The arched roof, pierced by regular holes through which sunlight streams and rain cascades, covers an alleyway along which stallholders sell meat fresh from animal carcasses whilst donkeys nuzzle away at bags of discarded entrails. It's a fascinating place, although the stench of gently rotting meat and the rivulets of blood trickling across the cobbles can be quite gagging, and vegetarians might care to take a different route into the souks. Beyond the meat souk are stalls selling pots and pans and other kitchenware, followed by clothing and material stalls, the nuts, spices and coffee souks, and then more fabric sellers, with everything on offer from mass-import materials from the Far East to locally woven, intricately patterned textiles which you can buy off the roll.

Khan al-Gumruk and Khan al-Nahasin

Just beyond the meat souk, 400m from Bab Antakya, and below a high dome in the ceiling punctured by four windows, a huge set of oak doors on the right side of the street marks the entrance to the **Khan al-Gumruk** (labelled in English). After passing through a stumpy, dark tunnel you emerge in the spacious court-yard of this former Ottoman customs house, laid out in the usual khan style, with stables and warehouses on the ground floor, and living accommodation above, reached by the upstairs gallery. In the sixteenth century this was the headquar-ters for the English and Dutch consulates and trade missions, a self-contained and inward-looking diplomatic sanctum whose design itself reduced contact between European traders and their Muslim counterparts. The Europeans were not allowed out of the building at night, for reasons of their own safety, and although some hunted or played sport in the surrounding countryside (or even made a pil-grimage to Jerusalem), by all accounts the merchants led a fairly restricted and isolated life, often drinking away their boredom in the khan's own ale house. The English trade mission, founded by Elizabeth I in 1581, closed in 1791, and since then the building has been used by souk traders, who operate in far less cramped surroundings than their colleagues along the covered lanes. You can use the smaller doors to gain access on Fridays, when the place is eerily empty and silent, save for stray cats sunning themselves on the stones and chasing wind-blown pieces of loose fabric left by careless traders.

Beyond the entrance to the khan is the gold and jewellery souk (with a left turn to the Great Mosque – see p.190), and an intersection, at which a right turn will bring you to the **Hamam al-Nahasin**, a bathhouse dating from the thir-teenth century where you can still sweat away in the hot room, or come under the skilled care of a masseur. Dead opposite is the entrance to the **Khan al-Nahasin**, where footwear is sold among the archways and raised galleries of the former residence of the Venetian consul. It's a welcome arena of sunshine, but the architecture (spoiled by accretions through the ages) is nothing special – although the Belgian consul, whose residence this now is, probably finds it quite pleasant.

Souk az-Zarb

Back on the main west–east lane, which becomes the **Souk az-Zarb** beyond the intersection, you'll find further stalls selling materials and household goods and, continuing east, traders who'll flog you a *kafir* or a Moroccan fez. By now you're getting closer to the citadel and what's on offer is more tourist-orientated. The street finally emerges, after a short graded uphill section, on Hawl al-Qalaa, the road at the foot of the citadel mound.

Unless you're heading straight for the citadel, the best thing to do now is to turn around and go back the way you came, this time diving off from Souk az-Zarb or Al-Attarin into the narrower, mercifully donkey-free lanes to the sides. You'll encounter more khans (none of them particularly special) and tiny mosques (most of which are hidden from view and/or locked), but more importantly you'll find yet more things on offer, sold by traders as willing to practise their English on you as they are to sell you their wares. Don't be surprised if you end up buy-ing something you never actually wanted, from a trader who says he's been to

London and asks you how Arsenal are doing: after you've been immersed in these tunnels for a few hours, you'll realize that the off-beat comes as standard in the Aleppo souks.

The Great Mosque

The **Great** (or **Umayyad**) **Mosque** was founded in 715 AD by Caliph al-Walid I, and probably completed by his brother Caliph Suleiman within two years, thus following hard on the heels of, and attempting to emulate, the other great Umayyad foundation, the Great Mosque in Damascus. Earthquakes, fires and bouts of rebuilding, however, mean that what you see today dates mostly from medieval times. There are entrances on all four sides, from the souks on the south and east, from a public square on the north, and from a small lane on the west side (leading up from the intersection 20m beyond the Khan al-Gumruk), which is the **entrance for non-Muslims**. It's best not to visit during prayer times (or any time on a Friday), although you're unlikely to be asked to leave if you do show up then. For most of the time the mosque is an airy retreat from the rest of Aleppo, almost hermetically sealed by solid medieval stonework from the noise and clamour of the city.

Once inside you'll find that the mosque's architecture is curiously artless, grandiose without being in any way beautiful or graceful, the proliferation of green neon strips almost an apology for the general plainness of the overall design. The courtyard is hot and devoid of shade, and in summer people generally linger among the cool colonnades which run along three sides, worshipping, sleeping, talking or sitting in family groups. A distinguishing feature of the long, narrow **prayer hall** is a reliquary, draped with beautifully embroidered cloth, which is said to contain the head of Zacharias, the father of John the Baptist.

More appealing architecturally than any of this is the square **minaret**, one of the finest in Syria, which was built as a free-standing construction to a height of 47m by the Seljuk Turks in 1092. Each side is adorned with attractive wooden carvings, kufic script and inlaid stonework, with none of the panels identical to any other. The earthquakes which have regularly beset Aleppo through the ages have caused the tower to lean visibly from the vertical.

The Madrasa Halawiye

Opposite the tourist entrance to the mosque is a shabby building which, more than any other in Aleppo, reflects the city's varied history. Formerly the theological school attached to the Great Mosque, the **Madrasa Halawiye** is entered by a flight of stone steps leading down to a shady courtyard, which is lined with the former cells of students. Most of the doors and windows have been boarded up, and guttering, electric wiring and random foliage spills out of the crumbling walls everywhere you look. The interior of the prayer hall, however, is in a much better state of repair, entered through a wooden door straight ahead of you; the place is often locked, but if a tour group shows up or there's a custodian present, you'll probably get a look in.

The building stands on the site of the **Cathedral of St Helena**, founded in the sixth century in honour of the mother of Emperor Constantine; by all accounts it was a glorious Byzantine basilica, but all that's left of it are the six columns with ornate capitals, supporting the dome of the left *iwan* in a semicircular arrangement. It was only in 1124, after four centuries of co-existence with the Great

Mosque built in its garden, that the cathedral was commandeered by the Muslim ruler of Aleppo and turned into a madrasa, in response to the thoughtless wrecking of Islamic monuments by the besieging Crusader army.

The citadel and south Aleppo

As well as being the most distinctive feature of Aleppo's skyline, the **citadel** is the city's major historic monument, with a regular stream of tour buses disgorging their loads outside the main entrance from early morning onwards. It's a disappointing place in some ways, spoilt both by thoughtless restoration work and by shameful neglect; the rooms in the entrance gateway are magnificent, but after you've left them and entered the citadel mound proper, it's only the dramatic views over Aleppo from the ramparts which are really memorable. A stroll away from the citadel, among the mosques and dusty artisans' quarters of **south Aleppo**, is in many ways more rewarding, if only because it covers an absorbing part of the modern city which many visitors overlook.

The citadel

Not surprisingly, the small, steep-sided mound on which the citadel sits has been in use for defensive purposes since Bronze Age times (around 1600 BC); less obviously, the hill has also been accorded religious significance over the centuries, and it's thought that both the Greeks and the Romans worshipped various gods here in addition to using the site as an army base. Most of what you see of the defences now is the result of rebuilding and strengthening by a series of rulers between 1150 and 1400, whose efforts were hampered by the repeated adverse attention of Crusader and Mongol armies. During the later Middle Ages the city began to grow around the citadel mound, somewhat nullifying its defensive role, and the Mamelukes developed the place as a showpiece royal palace, turning the tower bastions into magnificent state rooms but doing next to nothing with the area inside the old walls.

What remains today (daily except Tues 9am–4pm; S£200, additional charge for cameras and camcorders) falls into two separate parts: in the formidable entrance gateway you'll find a succession of restored rooms, linked by passages and stairways, which formed the Mameluke palace; beyond that, on the open summit of the mound, you'll find two mosques, plus a ramshackle collection of remains of the various fortifications which once stood here.

The entrance gateway

The only way into the citadel is across a fine stone **arched bridge** which straddles the (now dry) moat. Beyond lies the **entrance gateway**, a spectacularly formidable feat of early medieval engineering, built across several storeys. After coping with missiles being thrown from the upper storeys, potential invaders would have had to negotiate the twists and sudden darkness of the passageway which curls around inside the gateway. Small wonder, then, that the citadel in its present form was never successfully captured. After 1400, when the threat of Mongol invasion was severely reduced, the gateway took on much more of a ceremonial function, and the interior was altered accordingly. To see the rooms used as a palace by the Mameluke rulers, you need to turn right after crossing the bridge, pass through the first set of huge steel doors, and then follow the passageway as it swings abruptly left; ahead of you is a door set at the top of a short flight of steps. Beyond the door you'll pass through several dull halls (once domestic quarters, kitchens and an armoury, and now left bare) before reaching the grandiose **throne room**, the centrepiece of the royal palace. Extravagantly restored, the main feature of the room is the ornate wooden ceiling, carved with profuse geometric shapes and patterns to wonderfully luxuriant effect.

The citadel mound

Beyond the main gateway, the flat, windy summit of the citadel mound is crossed by a central, paved and stepped path which runs to the café by the north wall. Much of the summit is a weed-infested jumble of half-excavated ruins, worth little more than a casual glance.

On the right, as you emerge from the passage through the gateway, you'll see what remains of the **Ayyubid palace**, built in 1230 but destroyed by later Mongol invasions (which prompted the building of the much more solid defences you've just walked through). The fourteenth-century palace baths have undergone recent restoration, but apart from that all you can make sense of here is a maze of former courtyards and rooms.

Further along the path, on the left, there's rather more that's worth looking at in the **Mosque of Abraham**, dated to 1167 and probably founded by the Muslim commander Nur al-Din. Abraham, who is especially revered by Muslims, as well as by Christians and Jews, because of his adoption of one supreme God, is thought to have stayed and worshipped at this spot on one of his frequent journeys across the desert; the site is also thought to have been a resting place of the head of John the Baptist (which eventually finished up in the Umayyad Mosque in Damascus). The building is rather plain and austere, as is the **Great Mosque of the Citadel** a little further on – although the latter has a certain serene beauty, its cloistered courtyard and trees providing some relief from the starkness of the rest of the citadel. Built in 1214 by the Ayyubids, it's a small, sombre but well-proportioned affair, with a plain, square-towered minaret standing not far away, overlooking the citadel's northern walls.

The small **café**, next to the Great Mosque of the Citadel in what remains of a nineteenth-century Ottoman barracks, provides the greatest attraction of the top part of the citadel, as it commands a stunning view over the domes, minarets, walled courtyards and rooftop gardens of central Aleppo. From the café you can follow the **citadel walls** around the mound, though in some places they've crumbled almost to nothing. In the eastern part of the summit, the modern open-air **amphitheatre** has no historical right to be here, but it's impressively used for occasional shows – in the summer of 1996, for example, it was the setting for a performance of Purcell's opera *Dido and Aeneas*.

South from the citadel

There's little specific to see in the area to the south of the citadel, and many of the Islamic monuments covered in this section are locked for most of the time. Nevertheless, an hour's walk from the citadel entrance gets you right away from the tour groups, into an area of Aleppo which still retains many ancient touches, though you'll have to look for them carefully, along backstreets and behind houses and shops.

The formidable entrance to the Aleppo citadel

The Armenian Patriarch and Assad side by side at the Armenian Church, Aleppo

Coppersmith near the Aleppo souk

Qalaat Saladin

St Simeon's Basilica, with the stumpy remnants of his pillar

The Euphrates River glimpsed through a Roman arch at Halebiye

Bedouin woman with hay-laden horse at Serjilla, near Aleppo

Ruins at Serjilla

Along the banks of the Euphrates

Harvesting wheat in northeastern Syria

Roman monumental gateway, Palmyra

The desert near Palmyra

Hamam al-Nasri and the handicrafts souk

You'll find several **cafés** opposite the entrance to the citadel, serving coffee, tea and soft drinks to weary tourists. Close by to the east, the **Hamam al-Nasri** is the best-appointed baths in Syria, spruced up in 1985 by the government with the specific aim of luring in tourists, and their presumed fistfuls of dollars. It's not the most authentic hamam experience, and it carries a comparatively hefty price tag, but for the uninitiated this may be the best place for an introduction to the complex business of having a Turkish bath; details of these baths, and of others in Aleppo which are more used to seeing Syrians rather than visitors, are given in the "Listings" section on p.198.

Behind the cafés the **handicrafts souk** is another tourism initiative by the Syrian government, a bright and airy L-shaped hall where copperware, fancy footwear and textiles, weaved and brocaded rugs, inlaid wooden backgammon and chess boards, musical instruments (mainly of the drumming and strumming kind) and brightly coloured earthenware are on sale. If you're looking for souvenirs, this is the place to come; the choice is better, though prices are higher, than in the main area of the souks, where you'll spend much more time looking for exactly what you want.

South to the Bab al-Maqam

Immediately south of the handicrafts souk is the **Khosrofiye Mosque**, a high-walled building with a spacious courtyard. The oldest Ottoman mosque in Aleppo, it was built in 1537 by Sinan who went on to become the most famous architect of imperial Istanbul. The five domes above the portico and the tall, slender minaret are very Turkish in appearance. Opposite the mosque stands the **Madrasa Sultaniye**, a religious school built in the early thirteenth century, with a particularly fine *mihrab* in the prayer hall (though it's usually locked); also in this building is the tomb of Sultan Al-Zaher Ghazi, a son of Saladin and governor of Aleppo, who founded the mosque and initiated much of the fortification work on the citadel.

Continuing due south on the road running between the mosque and the madrasa, you soon reach an intersection where you should veer left (southeast) down a road lined with shops and workshops. The next road junction is surrounded by all manner of small metal forges and meat shops, with the usual hanging carcasses outside. Here you need to turn right (ask for Bab al-Maqam), along a road which gradually becomes more residential, with narrow dusty lanes leading off into a district dense with low-rise dwellings and stalls. On the right after about 100m, you'll pass the sixteenth-century **Al-Tavashi Mosque**, its facade lined with slender columns (and its door usually firmly shut). Ten minutes later you'll reach **Bab al-Maqam**, one of the original gates into the city, a solid stone structure whose fifteenth-century arches now provide shade for traders and animals.

From the Bab al-Maqam to the Madrasa Faradis

Immediately beyond Bab al-Maqam is a small, busy intersection, clogged with traffic and donkey carts laden with produce for the markets which line the surrounding streets. You need to cross over the main east–west drag here (Sajd al-Ass Street) and take the road which runs diagonally right from the intersection, heading southwest. On the left after 40m is the sixteenth-century **Mausoleum of Kheir Bey**, a plain, domed building whose patron was in fact buried in Cairo, posted there on diplomatic business after this, his intended tomb, had been completed.

After 300m the road forks; take the right-hand fork, which runs straight through the middle of a large cemetery, and after 200m or so turn left following the south side of the cemetery wall. This lane is unmarked, running between the gravestones on the left and walled buildings on the right. It looks as though it leads nowhere, but after 100m you'll reach the **Madrasa Faradis**, founded by the widow of governor Al-Zaher Ghazi in 1234 and considered by many to be the most beautiful of all Aleppo's mosques. Entered through a small door on the right, the cool central courtyard, whose shallow pool reflects the domes and sky, is lined with arcades supported by ancient columns; inside everything displays a restrained simplicity and charm, especially the main prayer niche which is richly inlaid with marble.

The Jdeide Quarter

Lying northwest of the citadel and east of Baron Street, the **Jdeide Quarter** is a fascinating warren of serpentine, traffic-free lanes, lined with large medieval houses which overhang the streets on the upper floors. It's the traditional home of Aleppo's large Christian community, and although there are only a few specific sights to aim for, it's a wonderful area to wander round, particularly during the afternoons when all is shady, shuttered and silent. This is a private world, of closed doors and high stone walls enclosing hidden courtyards, where even walking down the deserted streets can seem intrusive. Things are different on Sunday mornings, however, when, to the accompaniment of pealing church bells, clergymen scurry along the lanes with cassocks billowing, hurrying past well-to-do families making their sedate way to church. Few of the streets carry names or are marked on maps, and it's easy – perhaps even preferable – to get pleasantly lost; before immersing yourself completely in the maze of narrow passageways, however, you should at least make an effort to find the **Greek Orthodox** and **Armenian** churches, plus the **Museum of Popular Tradition**, which constitute the main sights of the area.

The churches

There are several ways of approaching the Jdeide Quarter, but the easiest is to follow Al-Telal Street from the New City, a pedestrianized thoroughfare which leads northeast from the city's main police station (itself just north of the clocktower). The street is lively and modern, lined with pharmacies, clothes shops, photo processing labs and stores selling electrical gear and tapes. When the pedestrian zone finishes, take the street on the right to a pleasant square, where you'll see the **Maronite church** facing you, with the smaller **Greek Catholic church** to your right. Both are late nineteenth-century constructions and neither is particularly interesting, with uninspiring stonework – and firmly closed doors.

From this attractive square, turn right (south) along a narrow lane which twists and turns a number of times, bringing you to a T-junction where you should again turn right. A short distance along this road, on the right-hand side, you'll find the **Greek Orthodox church** which – unlike most of the district's other churches – usually keeps its doors open and is worth looking round. Built in the 1860s, it has an ornate, if rather fussy iconostasis, and a shady, leafy courtyard, containing the grave of a former Russian diplomat. A little further on along the same street is the late medieval **Gregorian Armenian church**, its decorations including fifteenth-century paintings, carvings and icons.

The Museum of Popular Tradition

Heading back (east) along the street from the Armenian church, and passing the T-junction and the lane you emerged from earlier, you'll come to the Syrian Catholic church on the left (usually closed), beyond which (again on the left) you'll find the **Museum of Popular Tradition** (daily except Tues 8am–2pm; S£200).

The Christian community of Aleppo has traditionally comprised wealthy business families, who built for themselves large, ornate and distinctly private dwellings, architecturally and socially shutting themselves away from the rest of the city. Some still remain private houses; others have been converted into schools and ecclesiastical residences, their intricate wooden decorations and inlay work firmly barred from public view; two have recently been renovated and turned into rather swish restaurants (see p.196). The house known as **Beit Ajiqbash**, built in 1757, is one of the few which is open to public view, and it's the architecture which captures the attention as much as the museum which now occupies the building. The central courtyard, planted with trees and cooled by a splashing fountain, is a delight, while around it in the main living rooms, you'll see some wonderfully preserved wooden wall panels and ceilings, meticulously carved and painted, and richly inlaid eighteenth-century chairs and tables. The other parts of the museum are disappointing, consisting of hackneyed displays of clothing, weapons and the like that seem quite out of place here – though it's worth persevering for the views across Aleppo from the upstairs windows.

Eating, drinking and entertainment

There's an excellent variety of restaurants in Aleppo, from greasy chicken-and-kebab stalls to classy joints set up in restored eighteenth-century houses. Enjoy the diversity while it lasts – if you're heading off into the sticks next, particularly east, the food options quickly become much more limited. There are fewer options for drinking; the city centre abounds in cavernous coffee bars, but the only places you'll find selling alcohol are the restaurants in Al-Aziziah, upmarket hotels and dodgy nightclubs.

Restaurants

It's very easy to group **restaurant** types according to area: as a rule, you'll find the cheapest places are around Baron Street, with the mid-range and Western-orientated options in Al-Aziziah, east of the city park; the most luxurious restaurants the city has to offer are in the Jdeide Quarter to the east, and in the smartest hotels in the university district to the west.

In the listings below the restaurants have been categorized as cheap (under S£200 for a main meal), moderate (S£200–400) or expensive (over S£400). All the restaurants recommended in Al-Aziziah serve alcohol unless otherwise stated.

Baron Street and around

Al-Andalib, Baron St, next to *Baron Hotel*. Very pleasant rooftop restaurant overlooking Baron St, serving chicken, kebabs, chips and salad, but not much else. Cheap.

Al-Faihaa, just off Baron St, near junction with Qouwatly St. Spotless *felafel* joint. Cheap.

Al-Kindi, just off Bab al-Faraj. Long, narrow restaurant with efficient service and very filling portions. There's a counter at the far end where you can choose sweet pastries and the like for dessert. Slightly more upmarket than others in this area. Cheap.

Zenubia, just off Bab al-Faraj. Good, intimate kebab house. Cheap.

Al-Zuhour, just off Bab al-Faraj. Large, basic, breezy but welcoming restaurant, where the tasty shish kebab comes with barbecued onions and tomato, and there's plenty of bread and salad. Cheap.

Al-Zuhur, Qouwatly St, near junction with Baron St. Tiny kebab-and-hamburger joint in a pedestrian mall, surrounded by other similar places. Cheap.

Al-Aziziah

Al-Challal, on road linking Al-Jaberee St with Pensilvaniah St. Elegant, good-value restaurant with terrace. Extensive menu of *mezze* and main dishes, served by very friendly Kurdish waiters. Mid-range.

Delta, on northwards extension of Yousef al-Azmeh St. Bland, defiantly could-be-anywhere place, decked out in shiny chrome with soft-playing muzak to accompany your international or Syrian food; filling if unadventurous. Mid-range.

Ebla, on road linking Al-Jaberee St with Pensilvaniah St. The most modestly priced establishment in this quarter, with an excellent range of food that includes starters, desserts, European dishes and lots of affordable Syrian dishes to try out. Cheap.

Midmac, just off road linking Al-Jaberee St with Pensilvaniah St. Rip-off of Macdonalds, but the shady terrace and nice interior decor make this a more elegant establishment than its Western near-namesake. Kebab, chicken, steak, veal, pizza, spaghetti and of course burgers and fries are all on offer, with lots of varieties of ice cream for afters. No alcohol. Mid-range.

Pizza House. Imitator of the similarly named Western chain, set back a little from the other restaurants in this district on a side road. Excellent variety of pizzas and soft drinks, but not much else. Cheap.

Reef, on road linking Al-Jaberee St with Pensilvaniah St. Extensive menu with European food and beer; tables spill out onto a canopy-covered pavement terrace. Mid-range.

Sage, Al-Jaberee St. Swish-looking place that's much less expensive than you might judge from the outside; the Syrian and international food is good, though the choice is limited. Cheap.

Wanes, on road linking Al-Jaberee St with Pensilvaniah St. The favourite eating place of Aleppo's expat community. European-orientated, with pleasant food at slightly inflated prices. Mid-range.

The Jdeide and university quarters

Pullman Shahba Hotel, University St. This top-class hotel over in the university quarter boasts a pricey, but very good Italian restaurant – the only one in Aleppo.

Sissi House. Beautifully furnished restaurant in the Jdeide Quarter, where the food is good – traditional Syrian dishes, with not much change out of S£700 for a meal for two without wine – though not quite as good as the ambience might suggest. The building was once the elegant home of a wealthy Christian family, and has been restored accordingly to good effect. To get there, head for the Maronite cathedral (for directions see p.194) and follow the long, straight passage which runs along the northern (left-hand) wall of the building. Expensive.

Yasmeen House. Also in the Jdeide Quarter, this restaurant includes an outdoor section, along the terraces and in the courtyard of an eighteenth-century residence. The cuisine is exclusively Syrian, with enticing *mezze* and main courses that you choose from a folder of photographs, proffered by well-informed, English-speaking waiters. To get there, it's best to take the tiny lane leading south from the square outside the Maronite cathedral (see p.194), and ring or knock on the back door; the front entrance is close to the Museum of Popular Tradition (you'll have to ask around from there for directions). Expensive.

Bars and cafés

All over the centre of Aleppo, particularly along Al-Maari Street and Baron Street, and around the clocktower, there are big **coffee houses** where you can sit and drink nothing but coffee until the early hours of the morning. The clientele is almost exclusively male; women are likely to find these places uncomfortable, particularly if they go there alone. Usual activities are talking, playing cards or backgammon, or just puffing on a *nargileh* and watching the world go by. On the ground floor of the *Amir Palace Hotel* on Ibrahim Hanono Street is a sit-down **café** and snack bar which sells Western-style coffee, plus sandwiches, pizzas, cakes and the like; the prices are rather steep but this is the place to come to if you're homesick for Western snack food.

There are no stand-alone **bars** in Aleppo, and if you want something alcoholic but don't fancy paying to get into one of the sleazy nightclubs, you'll have to go to a hotel. The most popular hangout in Aleppo, both with tourists and resident Westerners, is the ground floor and terrace bar in the *Baron Hotel* (see p.183); the armchairs have seen better days but are comfy, and the decor hasn't changed much since the 1950s, but the inflated prices keep all but the most well-heeled Syrians away. The tables out on the terrace provide a great opportunity for people-watching Baron Street, but there's little shade and on summer afternoons you'll prefer to be inside. The *Amir Palace* has a bland downstairs bar, but this is where you'll find probably the best range of drinks on offer in the city.

Entertainment and nightlife

Aleppo goes to bed quite early, and by midnight most of the activity is centred on the sleazy **nightclubs** along Baron and Qouwatly streets. It's hard to recommend any of these places, but you'll find them soon enough if you want to – just follow the flashing neon, and be prepared to part with about S£400 for an evening of belly-dancing and the like. The alcohol flows quite freely, and most of these joints are a magnet for prostitutes and their pimps, who manage the brothels next door.

If you're after something a little more edifying, there are two **theatres** in the city: an open-air amphitheatre on top of the citadel mound, and a more conventional indoor performance venue on 17 April Street, just west of the main post office. To find out what's on, try to pick up a copy of the *Syria Times*, ask at the tourist office or, more reliably, visit the venues themselves.

There are at least a dozen **cinemas** in Aleppo, all of them along Al-Azmeh Street (the northern extension of Baron Street), Qouwatly Street or around the clocktower. Most show an endless diet of Jackie Chan films and other martial-arts pap, but occasionally more interesting stuff turns up – anything from 1970s Michael Caine movies to recent European and American arthouse and mainstream works. Almost everything is subtitled in Arabic and French, so there's usually something around with an English soundtrack that's worth seeing. Prices are extremely low (about S£30), but the cinemas are fleapits, with lousy projection and sound quality, and an audience which normally insists on talking throughout the film. The posters pinned up outside and in the lobbies indicate what's showing that day; films sometimes change on a daily basis.

Listings

Airlines The following all have offices at the southern end of Baron St: Air France (☎021/210 306); British Airways (☎021/210 624); Gulf Air (☎021/212 522); KLM (☎021/211 074); Lufthansa (☎021/223 005); Saudi Arabian Airlines (☎021/214 114); THY Turkish Airlines (☎021/245 955). Syrianair also has a Baron St office (☎021/220 501), but their main office is up by the southwestern corner of the park, immediately north of the post office (☎021/234 946 or 238 256; daily 8.30am–5.30pm, until 2.30pm Fri). Most airlines take most major credit cards; Syrianair takes only American Express or cash.

Airport bus Leaves from outside the international/Karnak bus station for the 40min journey (S£10).

Car rental Some travel agencies along Baron St offer car-with-driver rental for S£3500 per day upwards. To rent a self-drive car, contact the Europcar desk (☎021/212 0624) at the *Pullman Shahba Hotel* on University St in western Aleppo.

Car repair At Mitsubishi Service, a block southeast of the *Baron Hotel*, on a road running parallel with Baron St (☎021/221 673), most western models are catered for. There's also a string of car repair shops along the eastern end of Al-Koudsi St.

Consulates The UK is the only English-speaking country with diplomatic representation in Aleppo. The consulate (☎021/680 502 or 680 503) is on the corner of Abu Firas al-Hamadani St and Muhammad Said al-Zaim St, due west of the train station; look for the Palmyra Languages Centre next door (large signs).

Emergency services Police ☎112; ambulance ☎110; fire ☎113; traffic police ☎115. The main police station is on the major intersection 200m north of the clocktower.

Exchange Branch no.1 of the Commercial Bank of Syria is on Al-Moutanabi St, on the right as you walk east from the *Amir Palace Hotel* (daily except Fri 8.30am–noon); they change cash and travellers' cheques, as does the branch on the east side of Al-Azmeh St (the northern extension of Baron St), which is open until 1pm (but likewise closed Fri). The exchange booth on the clocktower roundabout (corner of Bab al-Faraj and Qouwatly St) is open daily 8am–8pm, but only changes cash. All these places will exchange Turkish lira and most other Western and Middle Eastern currencies.

Hamams Designed for tourists, the Al-Nasri opposite the entrance to the citadel is the best-appointed in Syria. Open for women Mon, Thurs & Sat 9am–5pm; men Mon, Thurs & Sat 5pm–midnight, plus all day Tues, Wed, Fri & Sun; prices start at S£365 for use of all the rooms. Locals use the Hamam al-Nahasin opposite the Khan al-Nahasin in the souk, and the Hamam al-Maliki by Bab Antakya (turn left up the steps after coming through the gate from Bab Antakya St); prices are much cheaper but times vary on a regular basis.

Hospital The University Hospital is 5km west of the city centre at the north end of Haoul Albaldeh St.

Music Dozens of tiny stalls lining the western end of Qouwatly St, in particular, sell cassettes of Arabic and Turkish music, or you can buy bootleg cassettes of virtually anything from the small boys who spread their wares out on mats on Baron St during the evenings.

Pharmacies At the corner of Qouwatly St and the pedestrianized Al-Telal St are two excellent pharmacies.

Post office Aleppo's main post office is at the north end of Al-Jalaa St, opposite the southern rim of the city park – you can't miss the huge transmission mast on the roof. Daily 8am–8pm, closes at noon on Fridays; post, phone telex and fax services.

Swimming There's a huge, modern indoor swimming pool in a building called Grand House, just up from the *Pullman Shahba Hotel* on University St, west of the city centre; open for men Thurs 10am–2pm & 3–6pm, women Mon 10am–2pm & 3–6pm, & Fri 10am–2pm, families Sat & Sun 10am–2pm & 3–6pm (S£50). The *Pullman Shahba* and *Chahba Cham Palace* hotels will let non-residents use their outdoor pools for S£500 per day.

AROUND ALEPPO

It would take a week or more to visit all the historical sites around Aleppo, but for most people two or three days will be rewarding enough. Renting a car in Aleppo is recommended, as public transport is unreliable, even if distances are short. Whether or not you have a vehicle, the most sensible way to see the region is on a series of day-trips from the city.

From the constant offers of taxi drivers and travel agency touts in downtown Aleppo, you'd think that the **Church of St Simeon** was the only place worth visiting from the city. It's true that this ruined church and the pilgrimage complex that surrounds it is a compelling excursion, but you'd be missing out on a lot if you made it the only place in the area that you saw. The St Simeon complex is just one of a huge number of so-called **Dead Cities** around Aleppo, ruined Roman-Byzantine settlements dating from a century or so either side of 500 AD; we've described in detail only a handful of the most interesting and accessible in this section, but there are dozens of other more remote and decaying sites to keep serious ruin buffs happy, especially around Maarat al-Numan.

The section that follows has been divided into three parts, kicking off with the most popular and accessible clutch of ruins, which lie to the **northwest of Aleppo**. In addition to the St Simeon complex, you'll find the remains of a Roman

THE DEAD CITIES

It is remarkable that the barren limestone hills that stretch from Aleppo to the Turkish border could even support a population; that the extensive remains left to us here are easily the best-preserved relics of the Byzantine world is extraordinary. The so-called **Dead Cities** consist of an estimated 780 towns, villages and monastic settlements in what was once the hinterland of **Antioch** (present-day Antakya in Turkey), the most important city of the Roman and Byzantine Middle East.

Many of the sites originated in the first centuries after Christ as the country estates or summer resorts of the wealthier citizens of Antioch. Settlements slowly grew up to house the farmers who cultivated the hardy land, and a monastic boom from the middle of the fourth century to the end of the sixth century led to the construction of sixty monasteries in the region. The area was a wealthy one, its prosperity founded upon the production of **oil** from olive orchards and **wine**, and their export, through Antioch, to the rest of the Byzantine world. However, the devastating economic effects of successive wars led to the slow abandonment of the settlements: the struggle between the Byzantines and the Sasanian Persians in the sixth and early seventh centuries saw the destruction of many of the settlements and their orchards, and during the Persian occupation of Antioch, all international trade through the town ceased; then, once the Arabs had taken over the city later in the seventh century, the Byzantines imposed a trading boycott on their old possessions. The resulting political insecurity and economic hardship forced the peasants who occupied the Dead Cities back to self-sufficiency on the more cultivatable plain of Amuq, to the northeast of Antioch. The area was largely abandoned by the tenth century, and has only very recently been in any way repopulated. However, as the Byzantine settlements had to be constructed almost entirely from the rugged local limestone, due to the lack of woodland in the area, they have survived, largely undisturbed, in great numbers and often in an astonishing state of preservation.

temple at Ain Dara, and Cyrrhus, a former Roman city right on the Turkish border. The few sites to the **west of Aleppo**, more difficult to reach and generally in a much poorer state of preservation, are really only of specialist interest. To the **southwest of Aleppo** is the major Bronze Age dig at Ebla, and the remote, surprisingly intact Dead Cities around Maarat al-Numan, of which Serjilla, in particular, and Ruweiha are the most interesting.

Northwest of Aleppo

Most visitors to Aleppo will find themselves making a trek out to the remains of the monumental **Church of St Simeon**, erected in the fifth century to revere the famous pillar-sitting ascetic. Less interesting destinations are the messy Roman ruins at **Cyrrhus**, up by the Turkish border, and the recently restored tenth-century BC temple complex at **Ain Dara**, remarkable more for its age than for any aesthetic impact. Attempting to visit all three in one day without your own transport would be stretching things too far; better to tackle Cyrrhus as a morning trip from Aleppo, and then combine Ain Dara and St Simeon in one long day.

Cyrrhus

The dramatic location of the ruins at **CYRRHUS**, set against the backdrop of the Turkish mountains, goes some way towards compensating for their relatively paltry condition. Founded around 300 BC to cement Seleucid control of the region, the settlement was taken over by the Romans and then refortified by Justinian in the sixth century. Cyrrhus was occupied briefly by the Crusaders five hundred years later, but disappeared from the pages of history soon afterwards.

The only way to get to Cyrrhus without a car is to take a **microbus** from the Baron Street local bus station in Aleppo to the village of Azaz, 51km north, and then bargain with a taxi driver to cover the last 28km; arrange a return fare, as not much traffic heads up the rough road and hitching would be problematic. On the way your driver will have to negotiate a couple of interesting Roman humpback **bridges** – they still serve their original purpose but, with no sides, steep slopes and narrow runways, crossing them can be hair-raising.

Approaching the site you'll pass, just outside the south gate, a hexagonal Roman **tower tomb** dating to the third century, the lower floor of which houses the tomb of the Muslim prophet Uri, giving the site its local name Nabi Uri. About 200m after entering through the south gate, you'll come to the **theatre**, originally larger than Bosra's and partially restored by the French during the 1950s; the seating embedded into the hillside is quite well preserved but there's no trace of the free-standing upper tier, and the rest is largely a jumble of masonry, the stage wall having collapsed during an earthquake. The scant remains of the citadel crowns the hill above the theatre; it's worth stumbling through the undergrowth only for the terrific views on a clear day across to the Turkish mountains. In the northern part of town is a large but badly ruined basilica, while the complex is surrounded by bare Byzantine walls, which follow the line of the Hellenistic defences.

The St Simeon complex

The **St Simeon complex** is the most popular and rewarding day-trip from Aleppo; you can't fail to be taken aback by the scale of the project which, together with the finesse of the carving's produces one of the most awesome remains in the country. The object of all this architectural attention, Simeon, joined the community of monks in the settlement of **Telanissos** – present-day **Deir Semaan** – in the early fifth century; following his death in 459, his remarkable life was commemorated by this huge church complex, built between 476 and 491 on the hill above Telanissos and consisting of four separate basilicas in the form of a cross, centred around the pillar on which he spent most of his time on earth. At the time it was the largest church in the world, and the hill had to be extended artificially to accommodate the western basilica. Telanissos became almost entirely given over to the housing of pilgrims visiting the church, and in the early sixth century a *via sacra* was built leading up from the village – though today entry to the church is via the **ticket office** on the eastern side of the hill (daily: summer 10am–6pm; winter 9am–4pm; S£200). The hastily built **wall** that surrounds the church is a tenth-century Byzantine fortification, hence the site's local name, **Qalaat Semaan**.

SAINT SIMEON

Simeon was born the son of a shepherd in the region of Antioch around 390, and following a revelatory dream joined the monastic community at Telanissos some time around 410–412, spending the rest of his life here. His asceticism soon manifested itself in some unusual behaviour: wearing spiked girdles which drew blood, and in summer burying himself in the ground up to his chin. From this he progressed to chaining himself to a rock in the middle of a roofless enclosure on the hill next to the village. His conduct naturally provoked much attention, and soon people were coming from miles around to witness his piety, seek advice and ask for miracles. To prevent the laying on of hands, Simeon took to standing on top of a **pillar**, at first 3m high, but later extended to 6, 11 and finally 18m; a railing around the top prevented him from falling off in his sleep. As the pillar height grew so did Simeon's reputation, and he began to attract pilgrims from as far away as Britain and France; he was dubbed **Simeon Stylites**, from the Greek for pillar (*stylos*).

From his perch Simeon preached twice daily to warn of earthly things and speak of the heavenly joys to come, and he diligently took time to answer every question asked of him, even giving the Byzantine emperor some advice on doctrinal disputes. However, he resolutely refused to let women into his sight, even cold-shouldering his mother; one woman who dared breach this rule was said to have dropped dead on the spot. Simeon used to pray while bending his body, arms outstretched, so that his head touched his toes, like a human hinge. He did this repeatedly, and to pass the time the pilgrims below would keep count; on one occasion Simeon had completed over 1200 of these manoeuvres before the counter gave up.

Simeon died in 459, at the end of a remarkable 38-year stint on top of his pillar. Six hundred imperial troops immediately swooped in and took his body away for burial in Antioch (it was later moved to Constantinople). His life and example spawned many imitators, the best known being **St Daniel** (409–93) in Constantinople, and **St Simeon Stylites the Younger** (517–92) who lived on a mountain on the outskirts of Antioch.

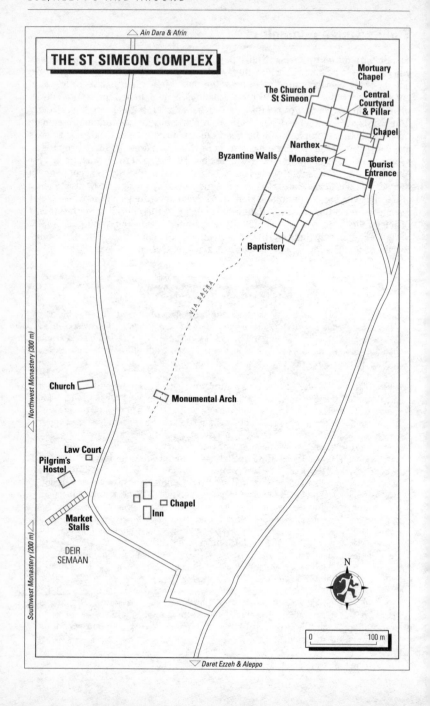

THE ST SIMEON COMPLEX

Ain Dara & Afrin

Mortuary Chapel

The Church of St Simeon

Central Courtyard & Pillar

Chapel

Byzantine Walls

Narthex

Monastery

Tourist Entrance

Baptistery

VIA SACRA

Church

Monumental Arch

Law Court

Pilgrim's Hostel

Market Stalls

Chapel

Inn

DEIR SEMAAN

Northwest Monastery (300 m)

Southwest Monastery (200 m)

N

0   100 m

Daret Ezzeh & Aleppo

Despite the fame of the place, getting to St Simeon by **public transport** could be a lot easier. Microbuses from the Baron Street station in Aleppo to the nearest village, **Daret Ezzeh**, are frequent and take an hour, but once there you'll probably have to negotiate with a microbus or taxi driver to take you the final 8km, as microbuses heading north are very infrequent. If you're using your own transport from Aleppo, you might consider making a stop at the goat-filled basilica church at **Mushabbak**, visible 1km south of the highway, 5km before you reach Daret Ezzeh. Dating to the late fifth century, it was probably built to serve pilgrims on their way out to St Simeon; it's not as stunning visually as many of the Dead City sites, but its state of preservation, up to roof level, is remarkable.

Qalaat Semaan

It's best to head first up the hill to the church complex, **Qalaat Semaan**. From the ticket office ascend the ridge, where you'll see on your right the **church**, announced by its glorious **narthex**, and on your left the more modest baptistery. The church's triple-arched entrance is one of the most dauntingly impressive sights in the country, not only in terms of scale but also for its decoration, with each arch topped by a triangle and beautifully ornamented; note particularly the acanthus leaves carved as if swaying in the breeze, a floral decoration that originated here and spread throughout the Byzantine empire. On entering, it becomes plain that each of the four basilicas is big enough to be a major church in its own right. The bare limestone lends the place an austere dignity, though when it was built the interiors would have been plastered and painted, and the floors decorated with multicoloured paving, traces of which can still be made out through the dust and dirt.

The south, west and north basilicas were never used for religious services, only for the assembly and organization of pilgrims, the major ceremonies taking place in the **east basilica**, which is larger than the other three and bent slightly off axis to orientate it towards true east. Its interior columns were lost during the sixteenth and seventeenth centuries when the building was occupied by local aristocracy, but the attractive floral decoration on the apse has survived. The **western basilica**, on top of its artificial terrace, is the most ruinous of the four, though it compensates with a mighty view down onto the confusing remains of Deir Semaan, and across the Afrin valley that stretches lazily beyond.

The four basilicas meet at a **courtyard**, at the centre of which is all that remains of Simeon's **pillar**. It's a slightly bizarre sight, a plain block of stone – the rest having been whittled down over the centuries by souvenir-hunters – sitting in pride of place among the magnificent ruined arches. Streams of tourists merrily ascend the block, wave at each other, get their picture taken and then jump off, their elevated moment of asceticism having passed. The square courtyard was converted into an octagon by the creation of four corner exedras, and the effect of the huge arches and intricate decoration is one of opulence and grandeur – this is where you feel the full force of imperial patronage that backed the project. The original domed wooden roof over the courtyard collapsed during an earthquake in 528 and was not replaced.

Just beyond the north basilica, within the Byzantine walls, are the remains of a small **mortuary chapel**, its lower level carved out of rock. The U-shaped building forming a courtyard with the church's southeastern walls is a **monastery** that was used to house the resident and visiting clergy (non-clerics would have been accommodated down in Deir Semaan). Note the small chapel which would probably have been used for the daily services in the complex – the east basilica being employed only on Sundays and feast days. Now return to the path – in fact the final stage of the *via sacra* which led up from Deir Semaan – which culminates in the great south narthex. Head on to the **baptistery**, 200m away, a square building cunningly concealing an octagonal interior which would originally have been topped by a wooden roof. Mass baptisms for converts would have taken place here at the semicircular font (still surviving) before entry to the church.

Deir Semaan

An agricultural settlement was founded at **Deir Semaan** (then Telanissos) some time in the first centuries after Christ, followed at the beginning of the fifth century by a monastic community. Simeon's antics on the hill above soon transformed the village into a pilgrimage centre, a role which was cemented with the construction of the church complex after his death in the late fifth century. Of the **via sacra** which links the village to the church, the most obvious remnant is an arch halfway up the hill which has undergone some recent reconstruction. The village continued to serve the pilgrimage trade until it died out in the twelfth century.

Deir Semaan covers an extensive area, though the incursion of a modern-day village, built from and among the ruins, makes discerning the ancient constructions difficult – indeed much of a visit comprises trampling around people's back gardens and over their improvised fences. Plans have been in place for around thirty years to relocate the villagers before the ancient ruins become completely obliterated, but the will to carry them out seems lacking. The site is always open, so ignore the cheeky young shepherds who attempt to charge entrance fees to the old buildings where they tend their sheep.

On the west side of the modern road, near the bottom of the *via sacra*, stands a **church** whose western facade is largely intact, though it's a modest building worth only brief exploration. About 100m south of this, again by the road, is the ruin of a **law court**, behind which are the remains of a **pilgrim's hostel** (or *pandocheion*) and eleven **market stalls** strung along the town's old east–west axis. Around 200m southwest of these, the fairly intact **southwest monastery**, consisting of three colonnaded buildings and a large chapel grouped around a courtyard, would have housed pilgrims as well as resident monks. Another remarkably preserved complex, the **northwest monastery**, 150m north, also comprises a number of accommodation blocks and a church. The most remarkable ruin at Deir Semaan, however, is the huge two-storeyed pilgrims' **inn** east of the modern road at the base of the hill; this was the major *pandocheion* in the village and much of the impressive building still survives. A bridge behind leads to a terrace cut from the rock, beyond which is a **chapel**, half-hewn from the rock, containing a number of burial niches.

Ain Dara

The sizeable mound of **Ain Dara** which rises out of the fertile plain 17km north of Deir Semaan conceals a history stretching from the fourth millennium BC through to the sixteenth century. The most obvious reminder of this is a tenth-century BC Hittite temple, atop a hillock about 400m west of the road across cultivated fields, which was recently restored by a team from Japan and is now a somewhat incongruous mixture of ancient masonry, concrete and scaffolding;

elsewhere on the site, you may feel slightly short-changed as so little of any consequence remains standing.

Microbuses from Deir Semaan to Afrin, via Ain Dara, are very infrequent, so if you're coming this way, you would be advised to pick up any traffic passing, paying the driver appropriately for his trouble. The microbus **from Aleppo** to Afrin does not run via Deir Semaan, but rather does the loop along the main road that runs past the turn-off for Azaz – making it just about possible to combine visits to Cyrrhus (see p.200) and Ain Dara in one day. To get to Ain Dara from Afrin take another microbus from the small station for the final 10km south.

Only a small area of the *tell* has been extensively excavated, with most of the attention focusing on the **temple complex**. On the pathway to its entrance can be found a couple of huge stone lions – it is thought that the temple may have been devoted to Ishtar, a goddess of fertility, often symbolized by lions. The paved courtyard in front of the temple features a well and basin used for ritual handwashing before entering the precinct. Imprinted on two large limestone blocks in the doorway to the precinct are giant footsteps; theories abound as to their significance, the most likely being that they signify the presence of a god. Before going through also check out the winged sphinxes and lion figures that decorate the walls and guard the entrance, some of which are in surprisingly good condition; inside, however, the small antechamber and main cella are badly worn and evoke little.

West to Harim and Qalb Lozeh

The ancient sites due west of Aleppo, along the road to and beyond fortress-crowned Harim, are really recommended for ruin buffs and car drivers only: what little there is to see lies scattered and neglected, with nothing that lives up to the St Simeon complex in aesthetic or historical significance; microbuses run as far as Harim, but if you want to continue to the impressive church of Qalb Lozeh, you'll have to bargain with taxi drivers. If you're determined to press on, however, you'll need at least a day to see everywhere here, plenty of water and food because there are few shops of any kind around, and your passport, as Harim is right on the Turkish border.

Driving west from Aleppo along the road towards Bab al-Hawa, you'll pass after about 40km – just before the turn-off up to Daret Ezzeh – a remarkably preserved stretch of second-century **Roman road** marching 1200m into the distance. Most of the Roman roads that criss-crossed the whole of Syria have long since disappeared, but this stretch was built more solidly than most in order to accommodate a steep slope, and was restored during the French mandate.

Head south off the main road 5km beyond the Daret Ezzeh turn-off, before reaching Bab al-Hawa, to Sarmada. Two kilometres west of Sarmada you'll pass, embedded in the hillside on your right about 400m from the road, the **Monastery of St Daniel**, which dates to the late sixth century and thus the last phase of the monastic blossoming of the Dead Cities. Just 4km beyond this is the turn-off to **BAQIRHA**, signposted in English. A well-preserved Roman temple, dedicated to Zeus, stands on the southern edge of the site here, consisting of a cella preceded by one surviving column of an originally four-columned portico; the monumental gateway also survives, dated by inscription to 161. Down the hill are the jumbled remains of a Byzantine town, where two early sixth-century churches can be identified from the chaos, of which the western one once formed part of a monastery.

Continuing west along the road towards Harim, you'll find, just beyond the village of Bashmishli, the ruins of **BAMUQQA** scattered amongst an oak grove which provides plenty of shelter on a hot day. Seventeen farmhouses and a small church litter the site; the prominent two-storeyed farmhouse would have belonged to the landowner and probably dates from the first century AD, thus making it one of the earliest buildings in the Dead Cities. The house is filled with fuel lamps and has something of a sacred air to it, as it holds the tomb of a local Alawite saint; an underground burial chamber 100m to the south of the house probably marks the burial spot of the original tenant. The other dwellings at Bamuqqa testify to the expansion of smallholdings in the fourth century, while the church dates even later, to a few decades before the Muslim invasion.

HARIM is a pleasant provincial town dating back to Byzantine times, which is crowned by an Ayyubid **castle**, built in response to the Crusader threat in the late twelfth century. The conical sides of the castle mound were pared down and paved with smooth stone to prevent scaling, and the whole structure was then surrounded by a moat. The inside of the castle is disappointingly ruined, but it's free to get in and from the ramparts you have fine views over the town, which is a little more colourful than most, the locals having painted their houses in pastel shades in preference to the dull concrete tones which characterize most Syrian towns.

From Harim, head due south for nearly 5km, via some unremarkable ruins at Bnabel and the more substantial Byzantine settlement of Kirkbizeh, to **QALB LOZEH**, whose **church** is one of the best-preserved and most attractive ecclesiastical monuments in Syria. It was built around 460, probably as a stopping point for pilgrims on the way to view St Simeon's pillar, and is an important architectural survival: it's the earliest Syrian example of a Roman basilica on a monumental scale, while the lavish semicircular entrance arch with its three-storeyed flanking towers is a direct precursor to the grand Romanesque cathedrals of medieval Europe. The original wooden roof of the nave has long since collapsed, though some of the stone slates from the roofs of the two side aisles survive; these would have been flat to allow light into the church from the windows above the nave. The projection of the apse beyond the basic rectangular form of the building was also a new idea, and remarkably its semi-domed roof and intricate decoration have survived intact.

Southwest from Aleppo

To the southwest of Aleppo, accessible from the major highway to Hama and Damascus, are the least visited desert sites in this area of Syria. The easiest to get to by public transport is **Ebla**, a Bronze Age settlement interesting more for its antiquity than for the little you can see there today. Finds from the site are displayed in a good museum in the largest town hereabouts, **Idleb**, which also boasts a hotel. Further south, the Roman-Byzantine sites to the west and north of **Maarat al-Numan** are remote and practically deserted; little effort has been made to restore them, yet the state of repair of the buildings in **Serjilla**, in particular, is remarkable. It's best to visit these Dead Cities with your own transport, but even then the poor state of the roads, the lack of signposting and the fact that there are so many similar-looking sites out here make getting around difficult and time-consuming.

Idleb

Only fifty minutes by road from Aleppo, there's not a great deal to be said for **IDLEB**, although if you have your own transport, you could at a pinch use it as a base for exploring the ancient sites in this area. The central *Grand Hotel* (☎023/221 137; ④) on Al-Malky Street offers decent **rooms** and an attached **restaurant**, and there's a bank and a post office on either side of the hotel; note however that the tourist office marked on town maps on Al-Jalaa Street has closed down.

Idleb also boasts a surprisingly good **museum** (daily except Tues 9am–4pm; S£200) on Al-Thawra Square on the way into town from Aleppo. It starts unpromisingly with a folklore collection, an array of dead birds around a fountain and some mediocre paintings, before perking up with a fine selection of Roman-Byzantine gold and silver coins. Upstairs the Ebla collection is a very worthwhile accompaniment to the site (see below): all the exhibits are well illustrated and explained in English, and there is even a reconstruction of a royal archive room. A final section of the museum exhibits displays from various local *tell*s.

Ebla

Unless you know a lot about archeology, or have an unusually vivid imagination, you won't find much to appreciate at the important Bronze Age site of **EBLA** (Ibla), though its location amidst scorching, flat and often very windy desert plains is certainly compelling. The site lies 45km south of Aleppo off the main highway to Hama and Damascus; any local bus or microbus driver will drop you at the turning on the highway, and from there it's a walk of thirty minutes or so east along a road that runs through a dusty desert village, with a number of bee-hive houses built of dried mud bricks. At the fork in the road beyond the village, 3km from the highway, a modern brick building serves as **site ticket office** (the site is open at all times, and the entrance fee of S£100 is collected during the ticket office's irregular opening hours), café and small **museum** – best visited after looking round the remains to put what you've seen into some sort of context. This is as far as drivers can get, but the site itself is a little further on along the road, just over the brow of a small hill.

Ebla was a powerful and agriculturally rich city state which rose to prominence in the centuries leading up to 2400 BC. By 1600 BC, however, the city had been destroyed by Hittite forces, although a settlement of some sort persisted here – in 1450 BC the Egyptian Pharaoh Thutmose III recorded on a monument at Karnak that the Egyptian army marched through Ebla on its way to the Euphrates, and nearly three thousand years later the first Crusader army passed by and recorded that the place had changed its name to Mardic. Since 1964 Ebla has been excavated by an Italian team, and in winter there may be someone at the archeologists' office who can guide you around the remains. The most important find has been fifteen thousand **clay tablets**, recording aspects of the economy and administration of the city, which have been shipped off to museums in Aleppo and Damascus and are slowly being deciphered and translated.

Approaching the site from the northwest from the ticket office, the first thing you'll come to is the ring-shaped **outer mound**, which gives a good impression of the huge scale of the city; thirty thousand people once lived within these walls, which were pierced by four monumental gateways, of which the best preserved is on the southwestern side. Most of the excavations have taken place around the site of the **Royal Palace** on the central citadel (signs will point you towards "Palace G"), revealing residential areas and underground burial chambers; most clearly discernible is a stairway leading down into what was once a huge audience chamber.

The Dead Cities around Maarat al-Numan

The Dead Cities to the southwest of Aleppo are centred around a modern market town, **Maarat al-Numan**, 20km south of Ebla on the main highway and exactly halfway between Aleppo and Hama, making either a good base from which to visit this area. There are dozens of ruined Roman-Byzantine sites all over the surrounding countryside, of which the three described in this section – **Bara**, **Serjilla** and **Ruweiha** – are the most interesting and the easiest to get to. You'll see further ruins set against the skyline in whatever direction you look, many of them wholly deserted and inaccessible by motorized transport.

Maarat itself is easy to get to by public **transport**, as most buses travelling between Aleppo and Hama will stop there. However, to get beyond Maarat, the only option for those without a car is to negotiate with taxi drivers at the bus terminal or main square in the town, or with any willing vehicle owners. Distances are too far to make walking a viable option, and the lack of traffic in the desert here makes hitchhiking difficult – and even potentially dangerous, if you end up getting stranded. If you're driving yourself, beware the lack of signposting and the poor roads, and be prepared to take a few wrong turnings in places.

Maarat al-Numan

MAARAT AL-NUMAN is a dusty, sprawling, unattractive place, centred on an east–west main street. At the eastern end of the street, just up from the **bus terminal** and facing a square, stands a sturdily built Ottoman **khan**, supposedly the largest in Syria, which now houses a good collection of Byzantine **mosaics** (daily except Tues 9am–4pm; S£200). Unearthed from village sites around Maarat, the mosaics once adorned the houses of the local rich; the best preserved, and most finely executed, shows Romulus and Remus and dates from 511 AD. The museum was opened in 1987 and, not surprisingly, sports a garish mosaic of Assad above the entrance.

If you've got a little time to spare you might want to take a quick look at the town's other historical monuments. On the main square north of the museum, the **Grand Mosque** is a solid, unremarkable building, with a particularly elegant minaret dating from 1170. Constructed after the original fell down during an earthquake, the tower was designed by the architect to rival the minaret of Aleppo's Great Mosque. If you follow the street north from the square for about 800m you'll find all that remains of the **citadel** – really little more than a mound and a few boulders, its sorry state the result of centuries of pilfering of the original stonework to use as building material in the rest of the town.

Bara (al-Kafr)

Heading west from Maarat, you'll reach after 10km Basqala, where you should take a road which heads north for 5km to **BARA**. Here the modern village of al-Kafr and the ruins seem almost to grow into each other, with the villagers using parts of the ancient site for olive and citrus orchards. In the late fifth century Bara was an important religious centre, and there are remains here of at least five churches. The major focus of the ruins are two **pyramid tombs**, which are obvious from the village; a tarmac road runs past the first, the larger of the two. The tombs are excellently preserved, and carry restrained Classical carvings with the Christian "chi-rho" symbol visible in many parts of the design. From here it's interesting to scramble around the substantial but haphazard remains of churches and ordinary houses that surround the tombs.

The large building which stands alone on a slight rise to the southwest of the pyramid tombs, reached along a confusing network of metalled roads, is a former monastery, **Deir Sobat**, whose walls are very well preserved (parts of it have been recently reconstructed).

Serjilla

From Bara a road runs east, climbing slightly into more barren terrain. The insubstantial ruins of **Bauda**, scattered along the right-hand side of the road after 4km, include another pyramid tomb. After another 3km the road terminates in a shallow bowl at lonely **SERJILLA**, a beautifully preserved Roman provincial town and one of the most absorbing ancient sites in Syria. Smaller and more manageable than Palmyra or Apamea, Serjilla has no grand colonnaded avenues or ostentatious amphitheatres; there are simply modest town houses, a tavern, public baths and a small parish church, which are now used for shelter by herds of goats.

Near where the road ends, on the left, the **necropolis** area contains a large stone sarcophagus, while down the hill are the remains of the **public baths**, small in scale but beautifully intact. Beyond the baths, the **tavern** would have been an unremarkable building in its day, but now, with its perfectly preserved two storeys and its frontage marked by a double portico of three columns on each level, it is recognized as one of the most perfectly preserved Roman buildings of any type, anywhere. There's a small triple-naved **church** just above the tavern, which dates from around 370 AD or earlier, and was enlarged several times. One of the rooms off the church contained three sarcophagi, thought to be those of local church or civic dignitaries, which have since been removed. Many other buildings run on beyond this central cluster, the former residential areas of the town gradually giving way to desert; on the horizon, other Dead Cities can be seen, which can be approached simply by walking to them across the plains.

Ruweiha

Ruweiha lies 12km north of Maarat al-Numan along the back roads, the route there taking you past several less interesting Dead Cities. Four kilometres north of town along the main highway to Aleppo, turn left and after another 3km you'll pass the ruins of **Dana**. Here you'll notice a recently reconstructed pyramidal-roofed tomb, which is dated by inscription to 324 AD, the year that Emperor Constantine made Christianity the official religion of the Roman Empire. About 500m to the north of these remains, reachable only on foot, stands **Qasr al-Banat**, a well-preserved three-storey building thought to be a former monastery, with its associated (and much more ruinous) church close by. The road leading north from Dana then brings you, after about 3km, to the scattered remains of **Jeradeh**, of which the most obvious survivor is a sixth-century, six-storey tower.

Turn left at the road junction at Jeradeh and you'll reach **RUWEIHA** after 2km. Set in a desolate landscape, the ruined buildings of this extensive site are used by settled Bedouin as dwellings, with the spaces between the houses given over to rudimentary cultivation of figs and watermelons. Look out for the fifth-century **columned basilica**, close to the road and fairly easy to distinguish amidst the piles of overturned boulders; nearby an odd structure supported on eight columns might have once been a tower lived in by a recluse. Thereafter the most obvious place to aim for, though a long way back from the road, is the **Church of Bissos**, one of the largest churches in northern Syria. Although much of the building has collapsed, many of the arches spanning the nave remain so it's easy to appreciate the size of the original building. The domed tomb nearby is that of Bissos, the church's benefactor, who may have been a local priest or bishop.

travel details

Trains

Train times bear little relation to what's published in the *Thomas Cook Overseas Timetable*, and if you want to leave the city by train you really have no option but to go to the station and ask about the current situation.

Aleppo to: Damascus (daily; 6hr); Deir ez-Zur (weekly; 4hr); Hama (daily; 2hr 15min); Homs (daily; 4hr 15 min); Istanbul (weekly; 36hr); Latakia (weekly; 3hr 30min); Raqqa (weekly; 2hr 15min); Qamishli (weekly; 6–7hr); Tartous (weekly; 2hr 30min).

Buses

There are seven bus depots in Aleppo (including the city bus station – see p.178), and which one you use depends on where you want to go and how you want to travel. Six of the depots are within easy walking distance of Baron Street, and four of them are located right next door to one another, which can make things a bit confusing. The locations of the six central depots are marked on the map on p.179, that of the eastern bus depot on p.177.

Local buses and microbuses to destinations north, west and south of Aleppo

This depot is located immediately west of the city bus station, on the street which forms the southerly extension of Baron Street. You buy tickets at the windows in the cavernous entrance hall, or on the bus itself; keep asking for the destination you want and eventually you'll be shown the right bus. As a guide, it costs a mere S£60 to travel to Damascus, taking 6hr – an uncomfortable amount of time to spend in one of these vehicles. Other destinations include: Afrin (1hr 15min); Azaz (1hr); Daret Ezzeh (1hr); Hama (2hr); Harim (1hr 15min); Homs (3hr); Idleb (50min); Latakia (4hr); Maarat al-Numan (1hr).

Local buses and microbuses to destinations in northeastern Syria

This depot is located 3km east of the centre, beyond the citadel, at the northeastern end of Qadi Askar St. Destinations include Deir ez-Zur (7hr) and Raqqa (4hr); change at Raqqa for services to Qamishli and Hassakeh.

Pullman buses

Out on Ibrahim Hanono Street is the station for **luxury Pullman buses**, with services in ultra-modern, air-conditioned vehicles to destinations all over Syria. Shopping around the various windows for what you want is easy; booking in advance is possible but not really necessary. Frequent departures to Damascus (5–6hr; S£150), via Hama (1hr) and Homs (2hr), with less frequent services to Deir ez-Zur (4hr), Latakia (4hr), Qamishli (5–6hr), Raqqa (3hr) and Tartous (5hr).

Immediately south of the city bus station (behind the line of low-rise apartment buildings) you can catch **cheaper Pullman buses** for similar destinations all over Syria; some companies also offer routes to Beirut and Tripoli (Lebanon). Vehicles are older than the luxury Pullman buses described above (though generally comfortable enough, with TV and some sort of air conditioning), but fares are about a third less; frequencies and journey durations are about the same. The depot is clean and well organized, with a good sit-down café on the left as you enter. Shop around at the windows for destinations and times you want; as a guide, most companies charge S£90 to Damascus and S£250 to Beirut.

Karnak buses

The hassle-free Karnak bus office is on Baron Street (daily 7am–8pm), and their buses leave from the area behind the office. As a guide, services to Damascus (4 daily; 5hr) cost S£130, to Amman (1 daily; 9hr) S£430 and to Beirut (3 daily; 7hr) S£250. Other destinations covered are: Deir ez-Zur (1 daily; 4hr); Hama (4 daily; 1hr); Homs (2 daily; 2hr); Latakia (2 daily; 4hr); Tartous (2 daily; 5hr).

Private international buses

Offices around a square immediately west of the southern end of Baron Street run coaches to destinations in Turkey, Saudi Arabia, Jordan, Lebanon and Egypt. The place is less hectic than other bus stations in Aleppo, and it's easy to shop around for what you want. Buses are usually modern and comfortable, but it might be a good idea to ask to look at the vehicle before you part with your money. A through fare to Istanbul, for example, is around S£1200, with a change of bus likely in Antakya (total journey time 24hr), while heading in the opposite direction at least one company

offers services to Riyadh (S£1200) and Cairo (S£1000). You can also buy through tickets (with at least one change, in Istanbul) to Bucharest (S£3500), Sofia (S£1700) and even Moscow (S£8000).

Service taxis

For long-distance journeys from Aleppo, these congregate across the road from the Bab Antakya. You will be besieged by touts as soon as you walk up, with fares to Damascus offered at S£500 per person and to Beirut for S£600 per person; other destinations covered include Homs and Hama.

Planes

From Aleppo, Syrianair flies 2 or 3 times daily to Damascus; twice weekly to Abu Dhabi, Berlin, Kuwait, Rome and Stockholm; and once weekly to Athens, Cairo, Dubai, Frankfurt, Istanbul, Jeddah and Sharjah.

CHAPTER SIX

THE EUPHRATES VALLEY AND THE NORTHEAST

The history of Syria east of Aleppo is dominated by the Euphrates, the longest river in western Asia and the region's life-blood. Its valley cuts a luxurious green swathe through the desert, supporting the principal towns of Raqqa and Deir ez-Zur in the same way that it once allowed a succession of ancient city states to thrive. Apart from the riverside restaurant and excellent new museum in Deir, however, these modern settlements have limited appeal in themselves, although they both offer a reasonable selection of hotels, allowing you to use them as bases for excursions out to the astonishing variety of archeological sites along the valley. At least getting around between the main towns is fairly easy: bus links are good from Deir ez-Zur to Damascus (via Palmyra) and from Raqqa to Aleppo, and frequent microbuses and Pullmans buzz along the main road beside the river.

The wealth of evidence of human occupation in this region ranges from the era of the first settlers on this part of the Fertile Crescent to the time of Saladin's campaigns during the Middle Ages. From Raqqa you can travel west to **Qalaat Jaber**, a medieval castle perched above **Lake Assad**, the huge reservoir created by damming the Euphrates at **Ath-Thawra**, and to **Resafe**, an ancient walled city situated amid barren desert. In the opposite direction lie the Roman remains at **Halebiye** and **Zalebiye**, two former fortress towns which face each other across the river between Raqqa and Deir ez-Zur. Undoubtedly easier to get to and more interesting are the sites between Deir ez-Zur and the Iraqi border: from Deir you can trav-

---

ACCOMMODATION PRICE CODES

In this book, all hotels have been categorized according to the **price codes** outlined below. They represent the minimum you can expect to pay for a **double room** in each hotel; for further details, see p.31.

① under S£300/US$7.50
② S£300–600/US$7.50–15
③ S£600–1000/US$15–25
④ S£1000–1400/US$25–35

⑤ US$35–50/S£1400–2000
⑥ US$50–90/S£2000–3600
⑦ US$90–130/S£3600–5200
⑧ US$130 and over/S£5200 and over

THE EUPHRATES RIVER

The **Euphrates**, along with the Tigris, forms the eastern part of the Fertile Crescent, the great arc of cultivation stretching all the way from the Jordan and Orontes rivers in the west (see the box on p.121). At various times the Babylonians, Sumerians, Assyrians and early Muslims strove for control of the rivers, and the legendary wealth and power of the state of Mesopotamia, the "land between the rivers" (in modern Iraq), derived from the trade and agricultural advantages brought by the Tigris and Euphrates. Other great cities supported by the two rivers included the Sumerian cities of Ur, Uruk (biblical Erech), Lagash and Nippur, founded from 5000 BC onwards. Later on, Babylon (on the Euphrates) and Nineveh (on the Tigris) became great and glorious capitals, and tradition also locates the Garden of Eden in Mesopotamia. Less important and powerful were the ancient cities that grew up along what is now the Syrian part of the Euphrates, the largest of which were Mari and Dura Europos, both now located close to the point where the river enters Iraq.

The name of the Euphrates (in Arabic *Nahr al-Furat*) is always linked in history with that of the **Tigris** (*Nahr Dijlah*), which flows parallel to it through Iraq. The two merge in a huge swamp in southeastern Iraq, the Shatt al-Arab – though by that time most of the Euphrates' water has already been used for farming or has simply evaporated away – and eventually drain into the Persian Gulf. The Tigris, which touches Syria but does not flow through it, is a shorter but commercially more important river, because its channel is deeper; the important Iraqi ports and cities of Mosul, Basra and Baghdad line its banks. Until such time as Iraq may be open to tourists, the ruins of the cities along the Syrian part of the Euphrates are the only reminders of the rivers' ancient civilizations that can be easily visited today.

Control of the waters of the Euphrates is still a matter of bitter contention between the states through which the river passes. For many years Turkey, Syria and Iraq have argued about how this vital commodity should be distributed, disagreements which occasionally threaten to spill over into armed conflict. In the 1980s, the Syrians blamed the frequent failures of electricity supplies across the country on Turkish activities further upstream on the Euphrates, which interrupted (unintentionally or otherwise) the flow of water to the hydroelectric turbines on their dam at **Ath-Thawra**. Built in the 1960s and supporting **Lake Assad**, one of the largest lakes in the Middle East, the dam has allowed the Euphrates to be controlled and its water used for extensive agriculture along the banks. It is this narrow strip of farmland along the river which comprises the most obvious feature of the region for travellers: a humid streak of settlement that cuts through the otherwise parched landscape, buzzing with the activity of cultivators and tractors, with the chugging of diesel-engine irrigation pumps rarely out of earshot.

el out to the remains of **Mari**, first settled over five thousand years ago, the ruined medieval castle of **Qalaat Rahba** and the ancient Roman city of **Dura Europos**.

Northeastern Syria, beyond the Euphrates, is one of the homelands of the **Kurds**, one of the world's largest ethnic groups to which history has denied a political homeland. Syria's Kurdish minority is small and somewhat less persecuted than those of neighbouring Turkey and Iraq (see the box on p.230); nonetheless, the area has long been seen as being naturally hostile to Assad, and if you travel here the likelihood is that you'll find plenty of people willing to talk politics with you. The northeast, however, is rather devoid of attractions for visitors; you'll see numerous *tell*s – mounds which mark the sites of long-buried

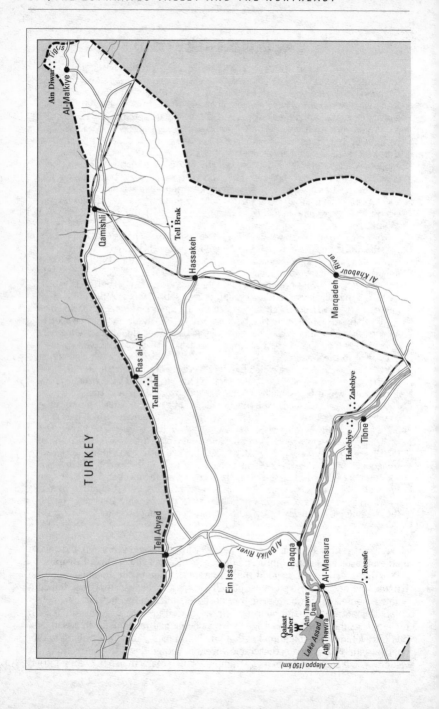

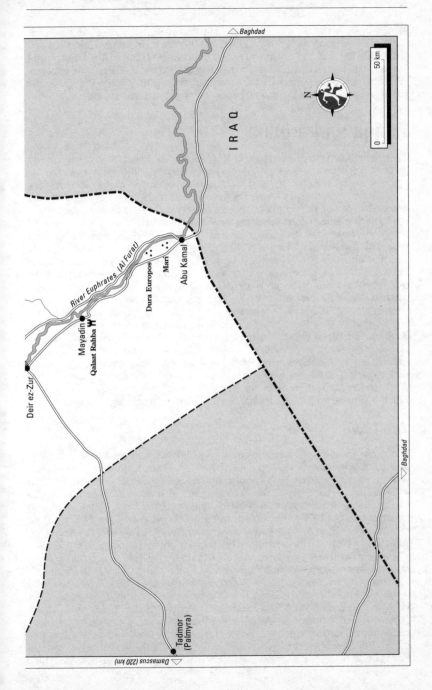

former cities – but they are uninteresting except to the initiated archeologist. Most of the area consists of flat desert, and the two main towns, **Hassakeh** and **Qamishli**, are dull and unattractive. The impressive bridge at **Ain Diwar**, right in the northeastern corner of the country on the Turkish border, is the only specific sight in this part of Syria; it takes some getting to, but if you make it you can't fail to be impressed by the magnificent scenery of the Tigris valley.

Raqqa and around

There's nothing very inspiring about **RAQQA**, the first place of any real size you come to if you're travelling east by road from Aleppo. Although it was once the summer capital of Abbassid-ruled Syria, next to nothing of Raqqa's former glory remains, and nowadays it's a busy market town and transport interchange and not much else. Although you get occasional glimpses of the river from the Aleppo road, the first time you get to see the Euphrates properly is as you cross the road bridge just before the town. Here the river is a series of sluggish, braiding channels, with families picnicking and children playing and bathing from the muddy beaches which line the banks and islands. The centre of town is immediately beyond the bridge; orientation is easy, as the central square is marked by a clock-tower (which chimes like an electronic version of Big Ben), and by the huge masts on top of the post office, visible from beyond the town's limits.

The choice of hotels and restaurants is fairly poor for a town of this size but if you have your own transport, you could easily spend two or three days using Raqqa as a base to visit the medieval fortress of **Qalaat Jaber**, perched on a promontory above Lake Assad, and the ancient cities of **Halebiye** and **Resafe**, to the east and west of town respectively. You'll face problems, however, if you don't have a car: local buses from Raqqa cover only parts of the routes to these sites, so you'll have to shell out for taxis or lifts, try your hand at hitching on largely traffic-free roads, or be prepared to trudge long distances on foot along the desert roads.

The Town

Raqqa was founded in Hellenistic times, possibly by Alexander the Great himself, and in the Byzantine era was developed into an important fortress on the front line with the Persian empire. In 772 Raqqa was completely rebuilt as a second capital to control northeast Syria by the Abbasid caliph Al-Mansur, who provided it with the horseshoe-shaped walls (once lined with a hundred towers) that survive in small part today. In 1258 the town was razed by Mongol invaders and fell into ruin; after slumbering for centuries it was only revived following the construction of the Ath-Thawra Dam and its elevation to the status of provincial capital in the 1960s.

The best place to see what remains of the Abbasid walls is at the partially reconstructed southeastern corner of the old city by the sturdy brick **Bab Baghdad**, the only surviving town gate, which dates to the twelfth century. Follow the walls north from here for about 200m (try to ignore the stench from the improvised rubbish tip), and on the left will appear the **Palace of the Maidens** (*Qasr al-Banat*), a ninth-century residence centred around a small courtyard with four *iwan*s and a fountain, which has survived relatively well, though the site is inhabited by annoyingly excitable dogs and pesky kids. To the northwest of here up Saif al-Daula Street is the largely ruinous, if expansive, **Great Mosque** (or Friday

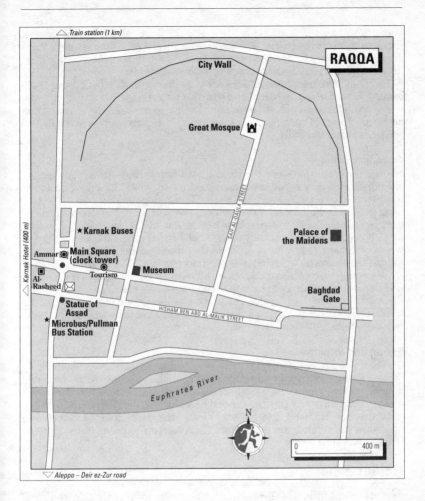

Mosque), originally dating to the late eighth century, though rebuilt by Nur al-Din in 1165–6; the tower and standing colonnade date from this reconstruction, but they're all that remain of a building that was once 100m square with eleven towers. On the way back to the main square is a small, dishevelled **museum** (daily except Tues: summer 9am–6pm; winter 9am–4pm; S£200) displaying a range of unexciting and unlabelled remains; it's not really worth the entry charge, though the custodian is open to bargaining.

Practicalities

Arriving by **microbus** or **Pullman bus**, you're likely to be dropped off at the main bus station, south of the clocktower; the **Karnak** bus station is immediately north of the main square. It's an easy walk from either terminal to any of the hotels. If you arrived by **train** from Damascus or Qamishli, you'll probably want to take a taxi from the station, which is 2km northeast of the town centre; if there aren't any taxis or you decide to walk, then come out of the station, turn left and keep going, and you'll eventually end up at the clocktower.

The **post and telephone offices** are next door to each other on the clock-tower square. There's no **bank** here, so arrive with enough money for your stay; and you can forget any ideas you might have had of renting a car or booking an air ticket. The road running north from the main square is where you'll find all the usual shops and stalls.

Accommodation

Right in the centre you'll find two basic but OK **hotels**, with shared showers: the *Ammar* immediately north of the main clocktower (☎022/222 612; ②), and the *Tourism* to the east (③) where you get a TV and fridge in your room. The best hotel in town is the *Karnak*, a strange establishment located in a residential district, ten minutes' walk from the town centre. Run by the government bus company, it carries nostalgic echoes of state-run hotels in the old Eastern Europe, with a cavernous, tatty lobby, indifferent staff and the curious feeling that no one ever actually stays here. The hotel is overpriced (☎022/232 265; ④), but for your money you get a comfy, carpeted room, efficient air conditioning, a fridge, a TV and the impression that you have the run of the whole place. To get there, take the road from the Assad statue below the clocktower, walking away from the direction he's facing, and you'll find that the road curves round to the right, before you reach the hotel on the left.

Eating and drinking

The best place to **eat** is at the *Karnak Hotel*, although their choice is decidedly limited: an ingeniously improvised spaghetti consists of a plate of pasta, a separate helping of lamb pieces and a bottle of tomato ketchup. Around the clocktower, among some fairly ordinary chicken-and-kebab places, the *Al-Rasheed* has a better ambience – but not necessarily better food – than most. It's set back behind a children's playground, and the outdoor terrace seems to be populated more by straggly cats than diners.

Qalaat Jaber

Just off the main Raqqa–Aleppo road, Ath-Thawra town is an ugly, confusing place, built to accommodate workers on the dam and then given over to those whose houses were drowned as Lake Assad filled. The only reason for coming here is to continue on to **Qalaat Jaber** (daily except Tues 9am–4pm; S£200), 30km northwest of town along a road that passes right over the dam itself. However, the castle is difficult to get to without your own transport: you'll have to take one of the frequent buses from Raqqa to Ath-Thawra, and there take a taxi (S£350) to complete the journey.

Qalaat Jaber is impressively situated on a rocky promontory lapped by the shores of the lake, though once it overlooked the Euphrates valley from on high, guarding an important crossing point on the river. The first records of a castle here date from 1087; it was taken by the Crusaders in 1104 but remained in Frankish hands for less than fifty years. In the late twelfth century, and then again in the fourteenth, it was refortified as an Arab stronghold, surrounded by massive

---

LAKE ASSAD

Lake Assad is an artificial creation which resulted from the damming of the River Euphrates in the 1960s. The turbines in the **Ath-Thawra Dam** now provide the bulk of Syria's electricity, and the control of the river's flow has been a boon to agriculture across the entire region. Less pleased than the farmers and the government were the inhabitants of the villages upstream of the dam, which were flooded as the lake filled; hundreds of people were forcibly rehoused in the ugly town of **Ath-Thawra**, at the lake's southern end.

Also flooded by the reservoir were numerous ancient monuments: many were documented by UNESCO archeologists before the waters rose, and some were moved, Abu Simbel-style, up to higher ground. In the centre of Ath-Thawra, for example, is a 27-metre-high minaret, originally attached to a mosque in the village of Maskana. Also moved to a position at the north end of the lake was the tomb of Suleiman Shah, one of the first Ottoman Sultans, who drowned in the Euphrates near Qalaat Jaber. Although the Turks were kicked out of Syria at the end of World War I, they had a clause inserted in the Treaty of Versailles stipulating that a small garrison of Turkish troops should guard the tomb, an arrangement which continues to this day.

---

outer defensive walls. The only break in these defences was an arched **entrance gateway**, which today is the most impressive part of the structure. It's pleasant to stroll around the walls, enjoying the good views across the lake, but a lot of the place is rubble and ruin. The interior of the castle is mostly bare apart from an isolated brick minaret, and recent crude restoration work seems to have involved not much more than pouring concrete into gaps in the medieval brickwork.

A lot of Syrians come here to swim or fish in the lake, the castle forming an impressive backdrop to the narrow beaches along the lakeshore. The area gets busy on Fridays but is virtually deserted for the rest of the week; a small **refreshment** place next to the castle entrance serves soft drinks and a limited range of snacks.

Resafe

RESAFE is one of Syria's most characterful desert ruins, a city half-buried in sand whose glistening gypsum walls and astonishingly grand cathedral appear to rise out of the ground in the middle of nowhere. As no **buses** run to Resafe, you will have to either negotiate with a taxi driver in Raqqa, or catch a microbus to the village of Al-Mansura, which stands at the turning off the main Aleppo road, and hitch or arrange a lift from there. For those with their own transport, the paved road has recently been extended across the desert from Hama via Isriya and Salamiyeh, though it's a long, hard drive.

The town's origins go far back – it's even mentioned in the Old Testament, as Receph in II Kings and Isaiah – though it remained a minor caravan settlement between Palmyra and the Euphrates until after the fall of Dura Europos in 256, when it was fortified by the emperor Diocletian in response to the Sasanian threat. In 305 a Christian Roman soldier named **Sergius** was martyred here for refusing to sacrifice to Jupiter, in a brutal manner that attracted much attention: he was made to walk from the Euphrates to Resafe in shoes pierced with sharpened nails, and then had a hole ripped through his tongue and a rope passed

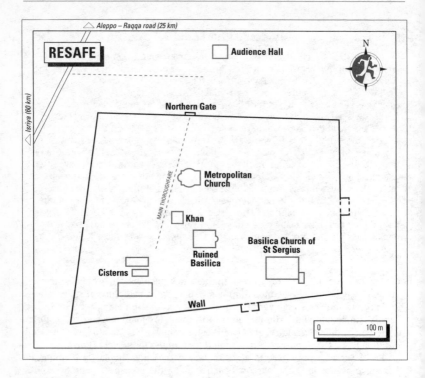

through by which he was led to his place of execution. Soon after his death Resafe became a site of pilgrimage and steadily grew, eventually being renamed **Sergiopolis**. During the sixth century a large basilica was constructed to cope with the pilgrims and the city walls were rebuilt. Nevertheless, the town fell to the Persians early in the next century, thus weakening Byzantine control of the region and paving the way for the successful Arab invasion. A sacking by Abbasid troops in 750, combined with a devastating earthquake in the late eighth century, shattered the city, though it continued to house a small Christian population right up until the thirteenth century.

The site

Just outside the northern walls and the entrance to the city is a late sixth-century **audience hall** that once belonged to Al-Mundhir, the chieftain of a Christian Arab tribe who patrolled the desert between Palmyra and the Euphrates for the Byzantines. The building, however, is presently under restoration, drifting sand having done a good preservation job over the centuries.

Similarly well-preserved is the city's **northern gate**, not only a fine piece of workmanship but also an impressive defensive construction; originally there would have been an outer gateway and a hallway in front of the gate, but this superstructure has not survived. From inside the gate you can climb up and walk along the upper gallery, built to allow defenders quick and easy access around the **walls**. The northern walls are by far the best preserved and allow you to get your bearings with an overview of the site, though admittedly it's largely empty: most of the buildings were constructed of mud and have disintegrated over the centuries. Only a small area of the huge site has been excavated, and many of the holes in the sand are said to be the result of more informal diggings by the local Bedouin, busy looking for hidden treasure.

Following the main thoroughfare from the northern gate for about 100m, you'll come to the ruinous **metropolitan church** which dates to the 520s. A number of sarcophagi belonging to bishops have been found here, leading to the conclusion that this would have been the episcopal church of Resafe, as distinct from the pilgrimage churches you come across later. The church's design is interesting in that it's an ambitious example, only slightly later than the similar Bosra cathedral, of an attempt to construct a square-planned building with a domed roof. Another 100m will bring you to the jumbled remains of a Byzantine **khan**, and 100m beyond this is the first of the city's huge **cisterns**; signs in Arabic point out the dangers of standing too near the edge of these massive constructions, which would have contained enough water to supply the population for up to two years.

East of the cisterns is a badly ruined late fifth-century **basilica**, thought to have contained the grave of St Sergius before it was carted off to Constantinople. Though unimpressive today, it would at one time have been nearly as big as the last church in the site: commonly known as the **Basilica Church of St Sergius**, but officially renamed the Basilica of the Holy Cross in 1977 following the discovery of a dedicatory inscription, this grand edifice was built in the 550s to accommodate the increasing numbers of pilgrims to Resafe. The leaping arches which divide the side aisles from the nave still provide an opulent effect, and in recent years the well-preserved inner walls have been partially reconstructed, but there is no evidence now of the fine stone carvings and colourful mosaics for which the church was once famed.

Halebiye and Zalebiye

The twin Roman fortresses of **Halebiye** and **Zalebiye** face each other across the Euphrates at a rather desolate spot midway between Raqqa and Deir ez-Zur. There's nothing much to see at Zalebiye, on the north bank, but Halebiye is interesting, comprising a series of well-preserved walls, fortifications and former barracks which rise above the river on a gentle hillside; a rickety modern bridge links the two sites. There are two ways of approaching by **public transport**, neither of them easy. On the south bank of the river, frequent microbuses and buses along the Raqqa–Deir ez-Zur road will drop you off at Tibne, but from there you'll have to resort to lifts from locals, or a stiff two-hour walk along the desert road, to get to Halebiye. Fewer buses and microbuses run along the road on the north bank of the river from Raqqa to Deir ez-Zur, but it's only a thirty-minute walk to Zalebiye from the turning where you're dropped off. Don't let the fact that there's a train station at Zalebiye on the Raqqa–Deir ez-Zur line excite you – it's only 2km from the site, but trains are as infrequent as a blue moon.

Halebiye

Halebiye was founded in around 265 AD by Zenobia, the rebel leader of the Palmyrenes (see the box on p.242), but most of what you can see today is the result of refortification three hundred years later by the emperor Justinian, who made the settlement one of the key forts along Byzantium's eastern flank.

Justinian was particularly keen to secure Byzantine rule in Syria, which by that time was a Christian stronghold, but Halebiye was unable to resist capture by the Persians in 610 AD. The fortifications were used a little during the first years of Arab rule in Syria, but earthquake damage took its toll and eventually it was abandoned to the desert foxes and itinerant shepherds. The site (open at all hours; no entrance fee) is bleak, usually deserted and very impressive, particularly as the sun sets, throwing shadows over the stark hills and casting a warm glow over the stones and the river. You can make some sense of the place by studying the plan by the main **entrance gate**: the banks of the Euphrates are lined with walls and other defences, which also spread up the hillside, where they are punctuated by massive square bastions and, on the north side, by the **praetorium**, which housed the troops. Overlooking it all, and a fair clamber uphill across fallen pieces of masonry, is the **citadel**, the only part of the site used by the Arabs (as a look-out post); not surprisingly, the view from there is particularly stunning.

Zalebiye

If your curiosity isn't satisfied by Halebiye, continue on the road from Tibne along the south bank of the river, where you can see scant remains of Roman rock-cut tombs and funerary towers dotting the hillside. Crossing the Euphrates by an uncertain wooden bridge and turning right along a bumpy track will bring you to the fortress of **Zalebiye** (a testing walk of up to 2hr in total from Halebiye). Its history mirrors that of Halebiye, but it's far smaller and the ruins are much more scattered and indistinct.

Deir ez-Zur and around

Much more attractive than Raqqa, with a good range of facilities, hotels and restaurants, **DEIR EZ-ZUR** is the most appealing base for travellers on the Syrian Euphrates. There's a distinctly oriental feel about the place, with its chaotic confusion of traffic, bicycles and animals, and its colourful, pungent markets. Gliding incongruously through all this are the sleek stretch limos of oil executives from the Persian Gulf, come to do business with Al-Furat, the Syrian state oil company: in 1984 extensive **oil fields** were found around Deir ez-Zur, which by 1994 were producing 600,000 barrels a day, earning Syria over US$2 billion a year in exports – a minuscule amount compared to the Gulf states, but a major boon for a poor country like Syria. Apart from the unusually good archeological museum, there's nothing much to do in Deir itself except sit on the terrace at the riverside restaurant, or join the locals for a swim by diving off the nearby pedestrian suspension bridge. It's all very laid-back and unhurried – this is one of the hottest places in Syria during the summer – and makes a good place to stay for two or three nights, travelling out by day to the fortresses of Halebiye and Zalebiye to the northwest, and the ancient remains of Mari and Dura Europos to the southeast.

Opened in 1996, Deir's **archeological museum**, a one-kilometre walk west of the central 8 Azar Square(daily except Tues 9am–6pm; S£200), is one of Syria's very best: well-laid-out and thoughtfully presented with some excellent reconstructions, including some prehistoric housing and even a Mari temple. Everything is labelled, intelligently and in great detail, in English. The exhibits mostly cover the period up to 636 AD, with particularly good sections on nearby Mari and Dura Europos, and the various local *tell*s. Well worth spending a couple

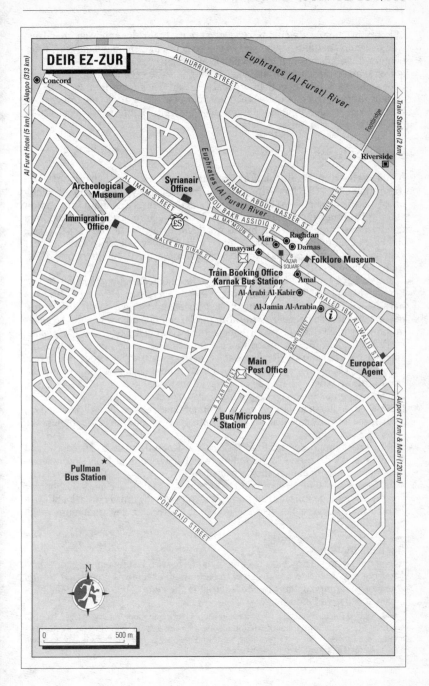

of hours in, the place would be perfect were it not for the annoying attendants who insist on shuffling behind you as you walk around, sighing loudly and dropping unsubtle hints as to their inability to afford a packet of cigarettes.

Deir's other museum, on the main square, is far less compelling, housing an odds-and-sods **folklore collection** (daily except Tues 9am–1pm; S£100). The curator will take you on a quite breathless tour of exhibits that range from papier-mâché camels and Bedouin dummies to cigarette lighters, wicker baskets, cracked teapots and busted watches.

Practicalities

If you **arrive** at the **train station** 2km out on the northern outskirts of town, there should be a CFS bus waiting for you, ready to take you to the train booking office, one block northwest of 8 Azar Square in the centre. The **main bus station** and the **Pullman terminal** are both south of the centre, a short taxi ride from the downtown hotels; **Karnak buses** will deposit you outside the Karnak office, right next door to the train booking office. If you fly in, you'll arrive at the **airport** 7km southeast of town, linked to the Syrianair office on Alaam Street in the centre by an airline bus.

You can get your bearings in town from the main central intersection, 8 Azar Square, around which you'll find most of the places to stay. Heading north from here, you'll come to the pedestrian suspension bridge across the Euphrates, beyond which is an open-air **swimming pool** if you don't fancy joining the locals in the river itself. East of 8 Azar Square (turn right just past the *Ugarit* restaurant) is a useless **tourist office** (open erratic hours), while immediately to the southeast are the **souks**. Heading west from the square will get you to the **bank**, where you'll spend an age changing your cash or travellers' cheques, and the **immigration office**, where you can spend even longer getting your visa extended; both operate morning hours (roughly 8.30am–12.30pm, closed Fri), but these seem to fluctuate largely on the whim of their staff. The large and modern **main post office** (daily 8am–8pm, Fri until 1pm) is south towards the bus stations on 8 Azar Street.

When it's time to **depart** from Deir ez-Zur, **Karnak** buses to Damascus and Palmyra, and **CFS buses** to the station (which leave an hour before train departures) operate from outside their adjacent offices (see above); the offices can be a little tricky to find on foot, situated at the far end of a closed-in shopping arcade, with no identification in English. If you want to **rent a car**, ask at the *Al-Furat Hotel*, where a Peugeot 205 will cost US$40 per day (minimum rental period 3 days).

Accommodation

Accommodation is fairly easy to come by in Deir, with **hotels** catering for everyone from impoverished backpackers to Kuwaiti oil executives. You'll find several cheap or mid-range options to choose from in the centre, but heading upmarket means heading out of town a way.

Amal, Khaled Ibn al-Walid St. This place had such a bad reputation that it was forced to shut down by the Syrian tourist board when the souk area was rebuilt. Still closed for refurbishment at the time of writing, it's gleaming white and yellow exterior suggests it may be worth a look; history has witnessed greater turnarounds.

Al-Arabi Al-Kabir, Khaled Ibn al-Walid St (☎051/222 070). Brighter and slightly more expensive than the other cheapies in town, with clean rooms but uninviting ablutions. ②.

Concord, Al Hurriya St (☎051/225 411, fax 224 272). New hotel in the northwestern suburbs of town, a taxi ride from the centre. Cheaper than the *Al-Furat Cham* and by far the better option: smaller, friendlier and much closer to the town centre. There's a bar, a restaurant and a pool. ⑦.

Damas, Abou Bakr Assiddiq St (☎051/221 481). Basic but acceptable hotel overlooking an arm of the Euphrates, and one of the better cheapies. Beds in shared rooms available for S£100. ②.

Al-Furat Cham Palace, 5km west of the town centre along the main road to Raqqa (☎051/225 418). Built for oil executives and tour groups, this is one of the most characterless hotels of the Cham Palace chain. Facilities include two restaurants, two bars, a large outdoor pool, a fitness centre, and tennis and squash courts, but if this is the sort of luxury you're looking for you're probably better off at the *Concord*. ⑧.

Al-Jamia al-Arabia, Grand St, off Khaled Ibn al-Walid St (☎051/221 371). Reasonably clean premises, though the ablutions are gloomy. The English-speaking owner will lower his prices at the drop of a hat. ②.

Mari, a block north of Al-Ma'moun St (☎051/224 340). Larger and newer hotel than the *Raghdan*, and slightly less expensive, but not as good value; rooms and showers are clean, but it's all rather soulless. ④.

Omayyad, Al-Imam St. Bare, relatively clean, budget option, where the friendly owner speaks some English. ②.

Raghdan, Khaled Ibn al-Walid St (☎051/222 053). Definitely the best mid-range option, a quiet hotel just north of the centre with air conditioning and spacious rooms. ⑤.

Eating and drinking

There's precious little variety among the cheap **restaurants** in town, consisting mainly of chicken-and-kebab places around the central square. Most visitors seem to end up at the restaurant by the Euphrates at least once; again, you're probably in trouble if you don't like kebab, chicken, salad or chips (about S£200 per person), but the relaxing setting is unbeatable, especially in the afternoon. After dusk, however, the mozzies begin to emerge, and it might be best to head away from the river to the rooftop restaurant of the *Mari Hotel*, which offers slightly more choice at a slightly higher price. The charmless restaurant in the *Al-Furat Hotel* offers an all-you-can-eat buffet in the evening for S£500.

Qalaat Rahba

Worth a stop, if time permits, on the way to Dura Europos and Mari are the ruins of **Qalaat Rahba**, which stand 2km south of the village of Mayadin, itself 44km southeast of Deir on the road towards the Iraqi border. Buses from Deir stop in the centre of the village, from where it's a manageable walk along a desert track to the castle. The castle had only a short military career: it was built by Nur al-Din in the mid-twelfth century as part of his Syrian unification strategy, but fell out of use during the Mongol invasions of the late thirteenth and fourteenth centuries. The remains are impressively poised from afar and, with quite a good portion of the inner fabric surviving, including a well-preserved central keep, the effect is not entirely diminished when you take a look up close. There are also some glorious sweeping views across the desert from the ramparts.

Dura Europos

The initial sighting of the walls of **DURA EUROPOS** across the parched desert plain from the main road raises expectations like no other site in Syria and, although little remains within the walls above foundation level, the expansive ruins (open at all times; S£200 if there's a custodian present) lend themselves to a relaxed appreciation. The historical importance of Dura only came to light in 1920 when British soldiers digging trenches here came across some wonderfully preserved **wall paintings**; previously the place had been dismissed as an unremarkable Arab fortification. The site was initially excavated in 1922–3 by a French team, but the more significant work was done by a Franco-American effort of 1928–37, written up by one of the American directors Clark Hopkins in an excellent book called *The Discovery of Dura Europos* (see p.271).

Unfortunately for visitors, Dura Europos is most famed for monuments which have been taken away from the site. The Dura **synagogue** is now one of the most celebrated exhibits in the National Museum in Damascus (see p.80), but there was also great excitement at the discovery here of a **chapel**, dated to 231 and thus the world's earliest identified site of Christian worship. Like the synagogue, the walls of the chapel were adorned with paintings, depicting Christ's miracles, and

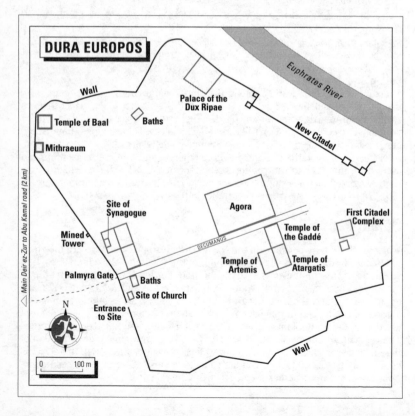

DURA EUROPOS

Wall

Temple of Baal

Mithraeum

Palace of the Dux Ripae

Baths

Euphrates River

New Citadel

Main Deir ez-Zur to Abu Kamal road (2 km)

Site of Synagogue

Mined Tower

Palmyra Gate

Baths

Site of Church

Entrance to Site

N

DECUMANUS

Agora

Temple of Artemis

Temple of the Gaddé

Temple of Atargatis

First Citadel Complex

Wall

0   100 m

a stone basin was also found inside, believed to have been used as a font; all of this was transported wholesale to Yale University during the 1930s.

Buses to Dura Europos from the main bus station in Deir ez-Zur are very frequent, passing the entrance to the site after about ninety minutes. The same buses head on to Mari and can be flagged down on the main road.

Some history

Dura Europos was established around 290 BC to defend the route between Apamea and Seleucia-on-the-Tigris, two major Seleucid military bases. From 113 BC the town came under the influence of the Parthians, while the Romans established themselves just to the northeast at Circesium; their mutual economic interests along the Euphrates were recognized by a treaty signed in 20 BC. In 164 AD the Romans took over the town, establishing a major garrison and embarking upon a substantial building programme. However, Dura's demise was a sudden one: in 256 the Sasanian Persians captured the town, and decided to destroy it and banish the inhabitants, rather than occupy the site, thus leaving the chaotic region without a substantial stronghold for centuries to follow.

The site

Entry to the city is no longer through the main western gateway, the imposing **Palmyra Gate**, which consists of two bastions, linked by a passageway over the arch, and is believed to date to around 17 BC and the days of Parthian rule. Instead you gain access to the site through a gap in the wall about 50m to the right – look out for the armed ticket-seller parading around on his motorbike. The site of the third-century **chapel**, now at Yale, is by this entrance, but there's little to see. The **synagogue** was situated between the first and second towers to the north of the gate, where you can just about work out its pillared courtyard. Ironically, the synagogue owes its remarkable state of preservation to the **siege** by the Sasanians in 256, which led to the final downfall of the town: anticipating the siege, the defenders of Dura piled huge amounts of sand and gravel against the town walls in an effort to prevent them from being collapsed by mining; all the buildings closest to the walls were also filled with sand, thus preserving their interiors. However, the Sasanians, undeterred by the strengthening of the walls, succeeded in mining the second tower from the Palmyra Gate, under the protection of a ramp; archeologists have found skeletons in the mine bearing coinage from 256. Timbers supporting the roof of the mine would have been burned, causing it, and the tower above, to collapse; the attackers would then have rushed over the wall via the ramp and short ladders, and Dura must have fallen quickly thereafter, as there is no evidence of major fighting in the town proper.

It's best now to walk into the town along the **decumanus**, originally colonnaded, that leads from the Palmyra Gate. To the left after 300m is the site of the Hellenistic **agora**, the main marketplace around which would have been grouped the main civic institutions; in the Parthian era bazaar buildings were built on the open space, which today is a slightly confusing mess of foundation-level walls. To the right of the decumanus at this point lies the **Temple of Artemis** which dates back to Seleucid times, though it was modified by the Parthians; consisting of a simple entrance altar and cella, it would have been the most important pagan temple from Hellenistic to Roman times. Next to this are a couple more **temples**, one dating to 31–2 AD dedicated to the Syrian goddess Atargatis, the other serving two Palmyrene gods known as the Gaddé and dating to the mid-second century AD.

The decumanus eventually collapses into a *wadi*. On the hill to your right at this point, the **first citadel complex** was constructed by the Greeks as a residence for the chief magistrate. It probably remained in use as a residence, for the civil governor of the town, after the construction of a **new citadel** in the early second century, the ruins of which stand across the *wadi* alongside the Euphrates. Over the centuries the river has eroded most of this second complex away, and today only the western face survives with its three gates; the view across the river from the top is the best thing about the place.

Further along the river bank are the remains of the **palace of the Dux Ripae**, built for the commander of the Roman garrison during the heavy militarization of Dura against potential Sasanian attack in the early third century; two courtyards and the remains of an arcaded corridor overlooking the river can just about be made out. Unusually, the rest of the Roman military camp was situated within the main town, between here and the western walls, taking up nearly a quarter of the settlement. This was almost a self-contained colony with its own baths and temples, including the first-century AD **Temple of Baal** at the angle of the walls, where British troops discovered the frescoes (now held in Damascus) that alerted the world to the importance of the site. To the south of this, the early third-century **Mithraeum** was dedicated to the Persian god Mithras, who was especially popular with the Roman legions.

Mari

Sweltering on the bleak, featureless plains near the Iraqi border, **MARI** is the most significant Mesopotamian site that can still be visited (no set hours; S£200 if there's a custodian present). It was first occupied around 2900 BC, but its most famous ruler was **Zimrilim** (1775–1760 BC), who endowed the city with its major monuments, only for them to be destroyed during the sacking of the city by the Babylonians in 1759 BC. Despite the site's importance and age, there isn't actually all that much here to grab the eye, although the intimacy and manageability of the remains are appealing.The site lies just off the main road, 10km north of the dull border town of Abu Kamal; **buses and microbuses** from Deir ez-Zur (2hr) and Abu Kamal (30min) stop by the short track over to the ruins, which are well signposted. By the entrance to the site is a small tent-like **café**, which shelters the occasional tour-bus groups from the heat of the sun; if you come here independently you're likely to have the whole site to yourself.

The site

Mari has attracted the attention of archeologists, mostly French, since 1933, and investigations at the site are still going on. The most important part of the city is the **Royal Palace**, now protected from rain by a modern roof: Zimrilim used the wealth accrued through trade to build this vast residence, which had over three hundred rooms and covered an area measuring 200m by 120m. To get some idea of the scale of the place, wander round the excavated rooms which are grouped around two central courtyards and defended by five-metre-thick walls. Elsewhere on the site are five temples and the foundations of a **ziggurat**, a pyramidal tower built in many Mesopotamian towns, which would once have been surmounted by a temple. Chunks of pottery poke out of the dust here and there, discarded by archeologists as they worked on the site, but most of the important finds are in Damascus, Aleppo or the Louvre in Paris. These include the **state archives**,

RELATIONS BETWEEN IRAQ AND SYRIA

Relations between Syria and its larger, oil-rich neighbour to the east have always been somewhat strained. Saddam Hussein and President Assad come from rival wings of the socialist Ba'ath Party, and have been at ideological loggerheads since the 1970s. By the time war broke out between Iraq and Iran in 1980 (over disputed oil fields at the head of the Persian Gulf), it was inevitable that Assad would voice support for Iran. This resulted in Iraq and Syria breaking off diplomatic and trading ties, and the only land crossing between the two countries, at **Abu Kamal**, was sealed to all traffic. Things might have got better in 1988 with the ending of the Iran–Iraq War, but instead, two years later, they worsened with Saddam's invasion of Kuwait: Syria gave full support to the UN coalition against Iraq, and even sent troops to assist in "Operation Desert Storm" in early 1991.

Since then, however, the situation has been gradually thawing. UN sanctions against Iraq allowed Saddam's regime to sell $2 billion worth of oil to other countries in exchange for food and medical supplies. Syria, needful of oil and with an efficient food industry, saw a role for itself in fulfilling this "oil-for-food" deal. In the first six months of 1997 Syrian companies won contracts worth $20 million to supply Iraq with permitted food and medicines, and in May of that year the border at Abu Kamal was opened for the first time in fifteen years. By August the UN had declared the border at Abu Kamal a legal point of entry for goods to Iraq. The border is still closed to all but carefully controlled trade and diplomatic traffic, but there are definite signs that the two countries are on the way to re-establishing full ties. Meanwhile, a populist advance was made in the summer of 1997 when Iraqi singers Kazem al-Saher and Elias Khodr gave live concerts in Damascus, attended by hundreds of their Syrian fans who, up to then, had only been able to hear them on tape.

which consist of 15,000 stone tablets detailing the household accounts of the Royal Palace and the administrative records of the kingdom.

The Northeast

The area of Syria to the northeast of the Euphrates is little visited by tourists. Prosperous city states grew up here in ancient times, evidenced by the numerous small *tell*s emerging from the plains, which have been picked over extensively by archeologists but are of no real interest to the uninitiated. The only true sight is at **Ain Diwar**, where the arch of a former Roman bridge is surrounded by the fabulous scenery of the Tigris valley. You'll need perseverance and time to get there, or indeed anywhere in this region, as distances are long and public transport rather poor. It takes at least six hours by road, for example, to travel from Deir ez-Zur to **Qamishli**, the largest town in the region and a pleasant jumping-off point for Ain Diwar.

Hassakeh

HASSAKEH, the northeast's second town, is a charmless modern settlement, 180km north of Deir ez-Zur, with absolutely nothing of interest. However, if for some reason you need to break your journey here and want somewhere to stay, head for the centre of town and ask for the *Ugarit* (☎052/222 002; ②), near the clocktower by the souks, which turns out to be one of the best budget **hotels** in

THE KURDS

Of the one million **Kurds** living in Syria, the vast majority are divided between Aleppo, and the towns and villages of northeastern Syria. Little is known about the history of this ethnic group: it is thought they were originally a nomadic people in central Asia, who came to settle in the mountain territories of what is now eastern Turkey and northern Iran. Although there are about twenty million Kurds in the Middle East today, spread through a contiguous region covering Syria, Turkey, Iraq, Iran and parts of the former USSR, they have never been grouped in a state of their own; problems faced by those campaigning for a **united Kurdistan** are that Kurds speak four languages (all of which have their roots in Farsi, the language of modern Iran), are divided in religious loyalty between Sunni and Shi'a Islam, and are traditionally organized into powerful and rival clans.

In **Turkey and Iraq**, which have much larger Kurdish populations than Syria, the Kurds are seen as a serious threat to internal stability. Saddam Hussein used poison gas to wipe out many Kurdish villages in the mountains of northern Iraq, which he assumed to be significant areas of dissent against his Ba'ath Arab regime, and in Turkey the terrorist group the **PKK** has been fighting for an independent, Marxist Kurdish state in the southeast of the country since 1978. The Ankara government has accused Syrian Kurds (and the Syrian government) of harbouring many PKK members, who use the northern part of Syria as a base for incursions into southeastern Turkey, an accusation fiercely denied by Syria.

In **Syria** the Kurds are seen as less of a threat than in Turkey and Iraq, mainly because there are fewer of them and because many have abandoned traditional Kurdish territories in the northeast to live in Aleppo or even Damascus. Nevertheless, any show of Kurdish solidarity is treated as a form of dissent against the government: in their August 1997 report on Syria, for example, Amnesty International alleged that thirteen Syrian Kurds were arrested in February and March of that year after they illegally celebrated *Nawruz*, the Kurdish New Year festival, in the province of Aleppo.

Syria. Each room (including the singles) is immaculately clean and features a TV and fridge, and the owner is even willing to bring his prices down. It's unlikely, but if the *Ugarit* is full, the *Al-Fursan* (☎052/220 272; ②), round the corner, is the best of the rest of the cheapies – on all accounts overlook the *Ramsis* (☎052/221 026; ②), right under the clocktower. The town's most expensive hotel is the *Al-Sanabel* (☎052/224 283; ④) on Qouwatli Street, to the south of the clocktower, though it's not that much better than the *Ugarit*. Plenty of reasonable **restaurants** congregate on Fares al-Khouri Street; try *Pizza Rami* if you want a change from chicken or kebab.

All **buses** use the depot in the north of town; note that there are no direct services from Raqqa. The **bank** and **post office** are both in the centre of town on Jamal Abdel Nasser Street.

Qamishli and around

It's the presence of the frontier with Turkey, only 1km from the centre, which is the most obvious feature of **QAMISHLI**, with Kurds, Turks and Syrians seeming to mingle in almost equal numbers. There's nothing to see in the town itself, but you'll probably end up spending a night here as you press on elsewhere; transport connections by road, air and rail are the best in the region, and if you've time to spare it's well worth making the effort to travel out to the bridge at **Ain Diwar**.

You're likely to arrive at one of two **bus stations**, both of which are a fair distance from the centre. Hassakeh and Deir ez-Zur microbuses use a terminal southwest of the centre, which is just within walking distance, but you'll need a taxi if you arrive at the main terminal, 4km east from the centre, where coach services from Aleppo and Damascus, and microbuses from Raqqa, terminate. It should be quite easy to flag down a passing microbus on the main road outside the **train station**, which is in the northeastern outskirts of Qamishli on the way to Al-Malkiye. The **airport** is 3km out on the road to Hassakeh, and again you'll need a taxi or passing microbus to get you into the centre.

Hotels in Qamishli are all at the eastern end of the main drag, which becomes the road out to Al-Malkiye and the train station. The *Chahba* (☎053/420 874; ②)

TELL BRAK AND AGATHA CHRISTIE

The area of Syria northeast of the Euphrates has more than its fair share of **tells** – "the rubbish heaps of history", as Robert Tewdwr Moss memorably dubbed them in *Cleopatra's Wedding Present* – and sometimes you can see four or five of these bald, sun-scorched mounds rising above the horizon at any one time, breaking the monotony of the otherwise flat horizon. They are of no interest to the casual visitor: unless a dig is actively in progress all you'll see is bare rock. For archeologists, however, no *tell* has revealed more than **Tell Brak**, which you can see clearly from the Hassakeh–Qamishli road, at the village of the same name.

Tell Brak was excavated extensively in the late 1930s by the archeologist **Sir Max Mallowan**, and further digs have taken place periodically since then. Mallowan's most famous discovery was the remains of the **Eye Temple**, dating from around 3000 BC and named after the the the hundreds of offerings he unearthed, all of them idols depicted with one enormous eye. Teams of British archeologists have also discovered remains of a **Mitannian Palace** (c.1500 BC) and the **Akkadian Fortress**, built on the site a mere two thousand years ago. More recent still is a nearby **Byzantine fort**, whose outline, invisible at ground level, was picked up by French aerial surveys in the 1920s.

Mallowan was married to the British writer of detective fiction **Agatha Christie**, who accompanied him on many of his digs in what is now Jordan, Turkey and Syria during the 1930s. She tells of her travels in Syria in an unusual little book entitled *Come, Tell Me How You Live*, first published in 1946 and reprinted in a number of editions since. Renting the bat-infested house of a local sheikh, she let her husband get on with the spadework at Tell Brak while she tended the sick and catalogued the finds. Villagers were offered *baksheesh* on top of their regular pay for any objects they unearthed; at one point, in their haste to acquire still more *baksheesh*, the men dug so furiously that part of the pit collapsed on top of them, killing a number and sending the rest off in flight across the desert. But the next day, she records somewhat insensitively, those same men were back, digging enthusiastically and seemingly with "no care for their lives at all. . . They were laughing about the deaths and making dumb show of the whole thing this morning during the work! Max says death isn't really important out here." Her curiosity about all aspects of Syrian life, however, is infectious: in her epilogue to the "inconsequent chronicle" she admits that she loves "that gentle fertile country and its simple people, who know how to laugh and enjoy life . . . who have dignity, good manners, and a great sense of humour, and to whom death is not terrible. *Inshallah*," she announces as a hopeful conclusion, "I shall go there again, and [I hope] the things that I loved shall not have perished from this earth."

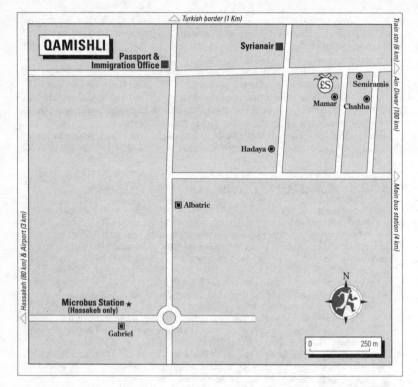

is a dreadful place, dingy and cramped, and accessed through a covered area of workshops. Only slightly more expensive but much better value is the *Mamar* (②), on a side street running south from the main road, with clean rooms, air conditioning and TV. Located on the main road between these two, the *Semiramis* (☎053/421 185; ③) is easily the best hotel in Qamishli, where visiting oil executives stay in cavernous doubles with fan, air conditioning and TV. The other hotel which quotes its prices in dollars is the *Hadaya* (☎053/420 141; ②), but it's somewhat overpriced for clean but very basic rooms.

Along the main street are various kebab-and-chicken **restaurants**, but if you want something different, head for the *Gabriel Restaurant*, opposite the Hassakeh microbus terminal, which is open for pizzas and other meals from about 8.30pm

---

TRAVELLING INTO TURKEY: A WARNING

You can cross into Turkey at three border posts in this region – most conveniently at **Qamishli**, but also at **Ras al-Ain** and **Tell Abyad**, further west. However, travelling in southeastern Turkey is, at the moment, a risky venture. The uprising by the Kurdish separatist group the PKK has involved shootouts, curfews, a heavy military presence and kidnappings of foreign tourists. For further information, see the latest edition of *The Rough Guide to Turkey*.

onwards and has a very pleasant outdoor terrace. On the way there you'll pass the much cheaper *Albatric* where you can gorge on hamburgers or pizzas with fries at any time of the day or evening. The **immigration office** by the statue of Assad opens every morning except Friday for visa extensions, and there's a **Syrianair office** just north of the main street.

Ain Diwar

The Tigris River doesn't actually flow through Syria, but for a short distance it forms part of the frontier with Turkey. At **Ain Diwar** on this stretch, one arch of a bridge built originally by the Romans remains. The site is remote and heavily militarized, being so close to Turkey and Iraq, and not surprisingly, it takes time and expense (not to mention luck) to get there; but the effort is worth it, for the stunning location as much as the arch itself.

Taxis from Qamishli, which congregate outside the *Chahba Hotel* at the western end of the main street, will get you to the bridge and back comfortably in a morning (S£1500 or less). If you don't want to spend this much, take a **bus** to Al-Malkiye, the nearest town of any size to Ain Diwar, and pick up a taxi there for S£350 or so. The road beyond Al-Malkiye ends just beyond the village of Ain Diwar at a **police station** overlooking the Tigris valley. The policemen here are friendly and helpful, having nothing to do all day but stare through their binoculars at Turkey, and treat visitors with interest and respect. You can't see the bridge from the police station, but you can see the river, forming a stately curve cut through the hills, and on a clear day it's possible to see beyond Turkey to the mountains in northwestern Iran – one of the most exciting views anywhere in Syria.

To get to the bridge itself, right down in the valley, you'll have to travel in a police four-wheel-drive vehicle or, at least, carry on in your own vehicle with a police escort. Beware, however, that the track down to the bridge crosses many irrigation streams and ditches so will be impassable if it's rained recently. Surrounded by marsh and rushes, the solitary **arch** is a sturdy affair, constructed from basalt and inlaid on one side with sandstone panels depicting the signs of the zodiac. The Roman camp of **Bezabda** once stood on this side of the river, and the bridge was built to give access to Roman-occupied Anatolia. There's no way of crossing the Tigris here now, but you can hear the steady bumping and rolling of Turkish trucks as they bounce over the potholes on the other side of the river – the only thing, apart from the cicadas, which disturbs the peace of the location.

travel details

Trains
One weekly overnight from Qamishli to Damascus (14hr) via Hassakeh (1hr), Deir ez-Zur (3hr), Raqqa (4hr), and Aleppo (7hr); first-class sleepers available.

Buses and microbuses
Deir ez-Zur to: Abu Kamal (frequent; 2hr 30min) via Mayadin (1hr), Dura Europos (90min) and Mari (2hr); Aleppo (frequent; 5hr); Damascus (frequent; 6hr); Palmyra (frequent; 3hr); Qamishli (3–4 per day; 5hr).

Hassakeh to: Deir ez-Zur (2–3 per day; 4hr); Qamishli (frequent; 1hr).

Qamishli to: Aleppo (2–3 daily; 5hr); Damascus (2–3 per day; 10hr); Al-Malkiye (2 daily; 2hr).

Raqqa to: Aleppo (frequent; 3hr); Deir ez-Zur (frequent; 2hr); Qamishli (2–3 per day; 4hr).

Flights
Deir ez-Zur to: Damascus (2 weekly; 1hr); Kuwait (1 weekly; 2hr 40min).

Qamishli to: Damascus (3 weekly; 1hr).

CHAPTER SEVEN

PALMYRA AND THE DESERT

T he main Damascus–Aleppo highway roughly marks the division between the green, mountainous western part of Syria and the vast **desert** of the southeast, which stretches into Iraq and Jordan. However, this is not the desert of popular imagination, with endless rolling sand dunes as are found in Arabia or the Sahara; nor does this part of Syria boast the spectacular

---

▬ TRAVELLING IN DESERT REGIONS – SOME ADVICE ▬

Although volcanic ridges break the surface here and there (most notably around Palmyra), the Syrian desert is otherwise just a scorched void. In other words, the **scenery** is nothing special, and if you want the opportunity to go trekking in the desert you're in the wrong place – the Jordanian desert (particularly around Wadi Rum) is vastly more attractive. Similarly, you're unlikely to want to **drive off-road**. The main desert highways linking Damascus and Homs with Palmyra and Deir ez-Zur are busy roads, travelled by plenty of trucks, buses, army vehicles and private cars, and fuel and food stops are fairly regularly spaced. Disappearing off at frequent intervals are desert tracks, little more than wheel-ruts cut into the dust which mostly lead off to remote Bedouin settlements. Following these twisting, multibranching tracks is highly inadvisable: there are no adequate **maps**, and no signs or points of reference to orientate you, and in no time at all you'll be simply (and seriously) lost. The only occasion on which you'll need to use them is if you decide to travel out from Palmyra to **Qasr al-Heir al-Sharqi**, but this is too dangerous to attempt on your own, and we recommend you hire a car with a driver in Palmyra.

If you're **driving yourself on the main highways**, there are several points to bear in mind. Always take spare supplies of water and fuel, and be prepared for frequent police **checkpoints**. Traffic moves fast on these highways, overtaking aggressively, and often makes no use of headlights at night. Gaping potholes can be a problem: regular drivers on the routes seem to know where the main ones are, but to the uninitiated they appear out of the blue without much warning, so check the **spare tyre** before you set out and keep a steady hold on the wheel. In addition, look out for animals, either in groups or singly, which are usually being herded by children. There is plenty of passing army and police traffic should you need help or have an accident.

The **Bedouin** are incredibly hospitable and will come to the assistance of anyone in trouble. Their black tents are very distinctive and, if you chance upon a Bedouin camp (except in Palmyra where they see lots of visitors), it is highly probable that you will be invited in to take tea with them or have a meal. Be warned, though, that most Bedouin keep semi-wild dogs, which have no respect for their masters' traditions of hospitality.

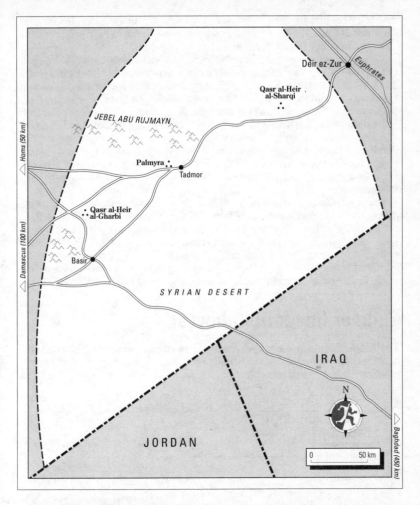

scenery of the Jordanian desert. Instead the Syrian desert consists for the most part of flat, rocky and seemingly infinite plains, where the glare of the sun, the intensity of the heat and the sheer emptiness are extraordinary to witness.

It is surprising that any human habitation could survive in such desolate surroundings, and it is tempting to romanticize – as much of Arab mythology does – both the landscape and the people who make this astonishing environment their home. Dotting the desert scene are the black goat-hair tents of the **Bedouin** (see the box on p.248), nomadic herders who drive their camels, sheep and goats from place to place in search of grazing land as they have done for millennia, their lifestyle little affected by the twentieth century save perhaps for a few modern cooking utensils and beat-up Nissan trucks. A few tiny villages on the main roads and tracks – ramshackle collections of crude concrete-box houses and traditional mud-brick beehive dwellings – break up the monotony of the plains, but for large stretches of the seven-hour road journey from Damascus to Deir ez-Zur there is no evidence of any human activity.

No settlement can be established in such an area without a regular supply of water; at a site just over 200km northeast of Damascus, a last geological fold in the Anti-Lebanon range creates the right conditions for a spring, reliable enough to support ancient **Palmyra** (and its modern adjunct **Tadmor**). For many, a visit to this ruined city which emerges from the desert beside an oasis of palm trees is the highlight of a visit to Syria, and there's no denying, despite the rising swell of tourism in Palmyra, that it remains one of the most exotic and absorbing destinations in the Middle East. Travelling to, staying in and looking round Palmyra is very straightforward, the only drawbacks being the considerable distances you'll find yourself covering on foot around the site, and, in summer, the dust, flies and intense heat.

The emphasis on Palmyra in this chapter is unavoidable: the only other points of interest in the Syrian desert are the fortress of **Qasr al-Heir al-Sharqi** (Qasr al-Heir East), well worth a visit if you've got some spare time and plenty of spare cash, and the fringe sites to the east of Hama (covered in Chapter 3). If you had visions of hiking or driving through the desert to visit long-forgotten sites in the middle of nowhere, then forget it; in most of this region, the only permanent signs of life you'll find are cement works, oil installations and army camps.

Tadmor (modern Palmyra)

TADMOR, the modern service town on the northeast side of the Palmyra ruins, takes its name from the ancient Semitic settlement on this site. Its characterless buildings line streets arranged in a rigidly obsessive grid pattern and, apart from

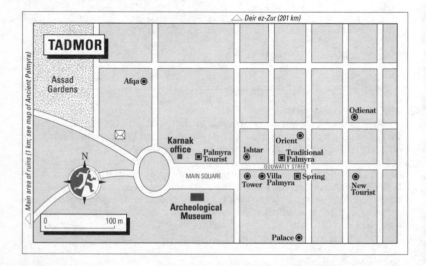

the buzz of hotels and kitsch tourist shops along the west end of Qouwatly Street, it's a sleepy place, knocked dead on summer afternoons by the stultifying heat (and consequent siesta). All the facilities you'll need whilst visiting Palmyra are here, and thankfully nothing is more than a twenty-minute walk away from the main area of the ruins. The only specific sight in the modern town is the **museum**, conveniently situated right on the main square. As for the **oasis** to which the settlement owes its existence, the only evidence you'll see is the mass of trees in the hollow between Tadmor and the Temple of Bel. (Water used to gush out of the ground at the Eqfa spring, located next to the *Cham Palace Hotel*, but it dried up in 1994.)

Arrival and information

All **buses and microbuses** (see p.251 for details of services to and from Tadmor) will drop you off in the main square, outside the archeological museum and within comfortable walking distance of all hotels but the *Cham Palace*. The **tourist office** is situated on the road out to the ruins (Mon–Thurs, Sat & Sun 8am–2pm & 5–8pm, Fri 8am–2pm), but it's difficult to know how they could be of much use to you. The modern **post office** to the west of the main square (daily except Fri 8am–2pm) is simple to use, and there's 24-hour access to the card-operated phones outside. Beware, however, that there's no bank in Tadmor, so you'll either have to plan ahead and come with enough cash for the duration of your stay, or persuade the *Cham Palace Hotel* to change cash or cheques for you (at a lousy exchange rate). The *Cham Palace* will let non-guests use their **swimming pool** for S£300, but much better is the pool filled straight from a spring, located amidst cool oasis greenery opposite the tourist office.

Accommodation

With tourist numbers in Palmyra mushrooming, there's a wide choice of **hotels**, and fierce competition keeps prices down and availability up. New hotels of every category are appearing every year, and the list below is only a selection.

If you choose a hotel right on Qouwatly Street, try to get a room at the back – noise from the road can be a nuisance at night. Air conditioning is not as vital here as elsewhere as it gets quite chilly at night, although you may be glad of a cool retreat in the middle of the day. In winter it can get cold and you'll need a room that's adequately heated.

ACCOMMODATION PRICE CODES

In this book, all hotels have been categorized according to the **price codes** outlined below. They represent the minimum you can expect to pay for a **double room** in each hotel; for further details, see p.31.

① under S£300/US$7.50	⑤ US$35–50/S£1400–2000
② S£300–600/US$7.50–15	⑥ US$50–90/S£2000–3600
③ S£600–1000/US$15–25	⑦ US$90–130/S£3600–5200
④ S£1000–1400/US$25–35	⑧ US$130 and over/S£5200 and over

Budget

Afqa, one block north of the post office (☎031/910 386). Poorly lit, rather dingy hotel which is at least away from the street noise. One of the cheapest places in town, and the price includes breakfast. ②.

Ishtar, Qouwatly St (☎031/913 073, fax 913 260). One of the best-value and most conveniently situated hotels in Tadmor, with clean rooms and genial owners, though street noise can be a problem. ③.

New Tourist Hotel, Qouwatly St (☎031/910 333). Old hotel with cramped and dingy rooms that catch a lot of street noise. Until recently it was the only budget lodging in Tadmor, and was consequently something of a backpackers' meeting place; you can still exchange views with other travellers via their polyglot noticeboard, but nowadays you can do a lot better than this for somewhere cheap to stay. ②.

Mid-range

Odienat, one block north of Qouwatly St (☎031/912 058). OK place in a quiet location, with private bathrooms but no air con. ④.

Orient, one block north of Qouwatly St (☎031/910 131, fax 910 700). Clean, functional rooms in a good-value, modern hotel on a quiet street. ③.

Palace, one block south of Qouwatly St (☎031/911 707). Good, quiet hotel with nicely appointed rooms. ④.

Tower, Qouwatly St (☎031/220 116). Good-value hotel with clean, en-suite rooms and a lounge on the first floor. ④.

Upmarket

Cham Palace, 3km from Tadmor, beyond the ruins, on the Damascus road (☎031 912 231, fax 912 245). Low-rise, 250-room bunker emerging from the greenery of the surrounding oasis, where guests can enjoy the use of the Oasis Disco, tennis courts and swimming pool – or they can simply cool off in their marble-floored bathrooms. Bedouin visits, sightseeing tours and transport to the Arab Castle at sundown are all laid on. ⑦.

Villa Palmyra, Qouwatly Street (☎031/910 156, fax 912 554). The only upmarket hotel in the centre of Tadmor, where modern rooms come with TV, minibar and air con as standard. There's a bar in the lobby and a restaurant on the top floor. ⑤.

Zenobia (☎031/910 167, fax 912 407). A smaller, much more attractive (not to mention cheaper) hotel than the *Cham Palace*, located amid the ruins with a cool outdoor bar and terrace restaurant. ⑥.

The Palmyra Archeological Museum

The **Palmyra Archeological Museum** on the main square (daily except Tues: April–Sept 8am–1pm & 4–6pm; Oct–March 8am–1pm & 2–4pm, except Ramadan 8am–3pm; S£200) was established in 1961 to house those finds from the ruins which hadn't already found their way to museums in Damascus or Europe. Its collections of **funerary and religious art** (to the left of the main entrance hall) are particularly absorbing, featuring huge late second- and third-century AD statues which once adorned the tombs of wealthy Palmyrenes and which provide ample demonstration of their opulent lifestyle. The brightly coloured patterns of the men's costumes and the intricate designs of the women's headbands and jewellery have been astonishingly well preserved. In poorer nick are some of the dead Palmyrenes themselves, who lie in glass cabinets surrounded by the embroidery and stonework found in their graves.

In the rooms to the right of the main entrance hall are the collections of **ceramics and mosaics** found in private houses in the city. The most notable mosaic,

Achilles at Skyros (c.270 AD), depicts Achilles flirting with the daughters of the king of Skyros. Also in this section are an excellent model of how the Temple of Bel originally looked, and an interesting guide (in French only) to the Palmyrene alphabet.

Eating and drinking

The best **restaurants** are in the upmarket hotels, most of which also have **bars**, but there are also a number of cheaper, more basic eating places catering to the passing tourist trade, where prices are generally slightly higher (and the food slightly better) than in similar establishments elsewhere in the country.

Al-Nakhil, in the *Cham Palace Hotel*. International cuisine, including pasta, smoked salmon, meat dishes and fruit desserts. A meal for two with wine will leave you little change from S£1000 – not particularly good value and the unappetizing view from the window is of a dusty carpark.

Palmyra Tourist Restaurant, on the main square. Everybody seems to end up here at some time or other, whether they have just emerged from the museum or are waiting for a bus. It's good value, despite being an obvious tourist trap: the choice is limited, but the food is good and the spacious, shady terrace is cool and attractive in summer.

Spring Restaurant, Qouwatly St. Kebabs, chicken and chips, along with sandwiches and desserts such as yoghurt, are served in this backpackers' favourite, situated close to all the cheap hotels.

Tourist Oasis Restaurant, next door to the tourist office. Nothing special at all – the usual kebab, chicken, chips and beer – and the flies are a nuisance.

Traditional Palmyra Restaurant, Qouwatly St. A good breakfast venue, and a cheap option for any meal, interestingly decorated with copious (and spurious) ornaments and kitsch, serving Syrian, Lebanese and Turkish dishes.

Villa Palmyra Hotel. The top-floor restaurant of this plush hotel on the main street serves an evening three-course buffet for S£400, not including drinks – pricey, but the food is excellent, and the service attentive.

Zenobia Hotel. At the hotel's attractive outdoor terrace restaurant, you can enjoy a leisurely dinner as the sun goes down over the ruins and the air cools surprisingly quickly. Column capitals are used for tables, and a meal for two (undistinguished Arab or Western food, with beer) will cost around S£600.

TADMOR PRISON

Though one can wax lyrical about Palmyra's romantic ruins and idyllic location, the town that abuts it has a more unsavoury side, playing host to Syria's largest and most notorious prison. It's a holding place predominantly for political prisoners, and though these are mostly Islamic extremists, military dissidents and members of the secular opposition are also incarcerated here. Tadmor is a name that has struck fear since the late 1970s: tales of torture, mutilation, isolation and imprisonment without trial or even reason have been widely documented, though by far the most infamous episode in the prison's history occurred on June 27, 1980 when, in retaliation for an attempt by the Muslim Brotherhood on President Assad's life, a special unit allegedly shot dead a thousand prisoners in their cells. The Syrian authorities do not allow international observers into the prison, but reports from ex-internees tell of typical cells of 5m by 20m holding up to seventy prisoners – the figure rising to two hundred in the aftermath of the 1982 Muslim Brotherhood uprising. In the most crowded cells inmates would have to sleep either in shifts or by crouching on the floor. The extremities of heat and cold in Palmyra make life in Tadmor prison especially harsh, with only four thin blankets issued to each inmate to serve as both mattress and cover.

Ancient Palmyra

If you've approached Tadmor from Damascus, you'll already have a fair impression of the general layout and size of the ruins, as the road sweeps past the Temple of Bel and the monumental gateway before entering the modern settlement. Ancient **PALMYRA** covers a huge area, which most people will have to visit on foot, probably over the course of several separate visits. It's a good idea to get a perspective on the history and the layout of the site before setting out; despite it being no more than a twenty-minute walk from the hotels in the centre of Tadmor to the main area of ruins, you need to plan your visit carefully if you want to make the most of the place. You're free to wander around the bulk of the ruins at any time, but the Temple of Bel has specific opening hours, and you'll have to hitch up with an official tour if you want to see inside the funerary towers.

At the very least, you'll need a day to see Palmyra – and several if you want to do the place justice. In summer, early morning and late afternoon are the best times for sightseeing; your impression of the place will be somewhat compromised if you end up trudging round the ruins in the hottest part of the day, so spending the afternoon under a tree or in a café is a good plan of action. Wear a hat around the ruins – there's precious little shade – and take some drink with you, rather than paying over the odds for cans and bottles sold by the hawkers, who tend to congregate around the monumental arch and the tetrapylon. Small boys from local Bedouin families who live around the site of Diocletian's Camp make an enterprising busi-

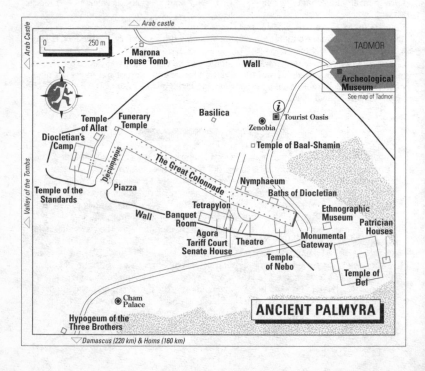

ness of selling cups of tea to thirsty visitors in that part of the site. At any time of year, the light on the pale stones can be blinding, so take a pair of sunglasses – which will also protect your eyes from the dust and sand that are frequently blown around by the desert winds. In winter, be prepared for rain, or even snow.

It's easiest to think of the site as falling into four distinct parts: the **Temple of Bel** was the religious centre of the Roman city and still gives a good impression of its former magnificence, despite being altered through subsequent use as part of the Arab fortifications; the **great colonnade** links the Temple of Bel with Diocletian's Camp, and along its length are the remains of the theatre, the agora, temples and other Roman buildings; dotting the hills to the southwest of the city are dozens of underground and tower **tombs**; and lastly there's the **Arab castle**, which gives a great overview of the site.

Some history

Since earliest times, nomads have recognized the attractions of the **springs** at Palmyra, and there is evidence that Neolithic man settled and farmed the land around the Eqfa spring. Records dating from around 1800 BC found at Mari on the Euphrates refer to a desert fort at **Tadmor**, the first written evidence of the city's existence (its name meant "guard post"). For at least two millennia the city was little more than the seat of a minor desert chief, forever in the shadow of Petra, the wealthy Nabatean capital in what is now the Jordanian desert, which was better positioned to be the western focus of trade routes across the desert to the interior of Asia.

When the Roman emperor Trajan annexed the kingdom of Petra in 106 AD, however, the fortunes of Palmyra suddenly began to look up: Antioch (modern Antakya in southern Turkey) emerged as the centre of Roman power along the eastern Mediterranean coast, and the treasures found in the increasingly prosperous and powerful kingdom of Parthia to the east of the Euphrates caught the attention of the Romans. Trade routes between Antioch and Parthia were established, and Palmyra, which lay between the two, quickly emerged as the most important **caravan city** of the western desert.

Virtually all of what you see today in Palmyra dates from a comparatively short period of its history – the second and third centuries AD. Within thirty years of the fall of Petra, slaves, dried foods, spices, silk, ebony, incense, ivory, jewels and glassware were being traded through Palmyra, and its **merchants** began to flaunt their individual and collective wealth, endowing the town with grandiose monuments, temples and palaces, designed to show visitors how rich they were; many of them achieved an immortality of sorts by erecting statues of themselves on the columns lining the main streets. One particularly wealthy merchant, named **Male Agrippa**, obviously thought that there wasn't much point in all this flamboyance unless someone important came to look at it, and in 129 he personally paid for a state visit of the Roman emperor Hadrian to the city – after which it was briefly renamed **Palmyra Hadriana**. Not content with imperial patronage, Male Agrippa later funded the virtual rebuilding of the city's most famous monument, the vast **Temple of Bel**. Yet despite the sudden rise of a wealthy merchant class, Palmyrene society remained largely tribal and agricultural rather than urban, its power and wealth enjoyed only by a privileged few.

Palmyra had been nominally incorporated into the Roman province of Syria during the reign of Nero (54–68 AD), and throughout the second century the Romans maintained a small garrison in the city, but their political influence was limited; the Palmyrenes were wealthy enough to be able to guard their independence from Rome jealously. In 224, however, the Parthian dynasty in Persia was replaced by the **Sasanians**, who were hungrier for territorial gains than their predecessors and began to threaten Roman rule in Syria. This upset the delicate balance of power in the area, and in 273 the Romans under Emperor Aurelian sacked Palmyra (after it had been held for a while by the legendary **Queen Zenobia** – see the box) and brought it under direct control. By 300 Emperor Diocletian, alert

QUEEN ZENOBIA

Zenobia is one of the most fascinating and controversial figures in the ancient history of Syria, a reputedly beautiful Arab queen who dared to defy the Romans, and whose strength and courage provide inspiration to sentiments of Arab and Syrian nationalism to this day. She rose to prominence as the wife of **Odenathus**, who ruled Palmyra from 252 AD. Recognizing the increased threat the Romans felt from the Persian Sasanian dynasty, Odenathus took great pains to curry favour with his imperial overlords, and led campaigns against the Sasanians on behalf of Rome. However, in 267 he was murdered, leaving his charismatic and powerful wife to rule Palmyra as regent on behalf of their young son, Wahballat.

Immediately, Zenobia began to seek greater independence from Rome. Under her, Palmyrene armies captured Bosra and campaigned as far away as Turkey and Egypt, apparently as part of her designs on ruling the eastern part of the Roman Empire from Palmyra, under the title Augusta, leaving the western half under Roman control. Not surprisingly, the Roman emperor **Aurelian** had other ideas, and launched a campaign against the Palmyrenes, defeating them at Emesa (Homs) in 272 and pressing on to attack and occupy Palmyra itself. Zenobia fled the city eastwards on a camel, probably planning to reach Persia to seek the support of the Sasanians for a campaign against Aurelian, but was captured by Roman forces as she tried to cross the Euphrates. Palmyra was formally surrendered to Aurelian, and after a revolt there in 273, the Romans sacked the place, burning, destroying and murdering at random. Zenobia was taken to Rome in chains, and was shown off as a vanquished ruler who had dared to challenge Roman authority. Contemporary reports say that she suffered the humiliation of being paraded through the streets in a full victory cortege that included elephants and gladiators. Zenobia was then imprisoned in the city, and seems to have met an untimely death at the hands of the Roman authorities.

Always a formidable figure of Arab legend, in 1997 Zenobia was the subject of a 22-part **Syrian TV series**, *Al-Abadid* ("Anarchy"), which was watched by millions of people throughout the Arab world, and which portrayed Zenobia's struggle against the Romans as a metaphor for Syria's contemporary defiance of Israel. Part of the series was shot in Palmyra, and the central role was played by Raghda, one of the most beautiful and famous Arab film stars. One of the aims of the TV series was to end disputes about Zenobia's ethnic origins: with Israel cast as the imperialist aggressor of modern times, the frequent assertions that Zenobia was herself Jewish have proved rather galling to those anxious to promote her as an icon for anti-Zionist sentiment. The TV series therefore took great pains to point out her Arab identity, but there has never been any real proof that she was Jewish, her most likely ancestors being Cleopatra and the Greek rulers of Egypt. In a similar political vein, the reason for Zenobia's defeat according to the TV version was disunity amongst her followers – a plea for a united Arab stance against Israel, which, despite the popularity of the series across the Middle East from Abu Dhabi to Beirut, seems highly unlikely to materialize.

to the continued military threat from the east, had established a huge fortified camp in Palmyra and strengthened the walls, transforming the city from an ostentatious showpiece into a military stronghold. Under the Sasanians, Persia was a military threat rather than a source of trading riches, and decline set in at Palmyra which, by the time the emperor Justinian refortified the walls in the sixth century, had rendered the city a virtual ruin.

In the twelfth century there was a brief revival of interest in the city, when the Mamelukes refortified the walls of the Temple of Bel and constructed the **Arab castle** on a prominent site overlooking the city, much of which by then had crumbled to nothing. In Ottoman times the site was finally abandoned to the desert winds, visited only by sheltering nomads – and also by some of the very first **European tourists**, among them Englishmen Wood and Dawkins, who published *The Ruins of Palmyra* in 1753. Their engravings of designs found in the ruins influenced the Neo-Classical architectural movement in Britain, and several eighteenth-century stately homes (such as Blair Castle and Drayton House) boast Palmyra-style ceilings and cornices.

The Temple of Bel and around

The vast **Temple of Bel** (daily: summer 8am–1pm & 4–6pm; winter 8am–4pm; S£200) is by far the best preserved (or reconstructed) of the city's monuments and the site's main focal point – fittingly, as Bel (a Babylonian pronunciation of Baal, meaning "master") was the supreme deity of the Palmyrenes, equated with the Greek god Zeus. Its cella was built in 32 AD to replace a Hellenistic temple, which itself was constructed on a sacred *tell* dating back to the Bronze Age (2200–1500 BC); the last phase of building took place in the late second century when the monumental entrance gateway was added.

Before going inside, take a look at the curious patchwork **walls**, their haphazard assortment of stonework being the result both of numerous reconstructions following earthquakes, and of the twelfth-century reinforcement when the main entrance gateway was turned into a keep, and the cella into a mosque. The **ticket office** is to the left of the gateway and has a good selection of guidebooks; personal guides, who hang around outside or at the ticket office, will ask for S£200, though they can easily be bargained down to S£150 if you've dressed down for the occasion.

The courtyard

The temple **courtyard** housed a small town until the French removed it in 1929. In 1876 Baedeker reported that the settlement inside the temple consisted "of about fifty huts, partly built with fragments of columns and ancient materials, and arranged in long lanes . . . the traveller may enter the houses and mount upon the roofs without scruple, the wives and families of the peasantry being much less shy than the ladies in towns"; modern-day guides will point with pride to the former location of their family's house. The compound is surrounded by occasional **pillars**, used to support a wooden roof which gives the site a much greater sense of enclosure. The centrepiece is the huge cella reached via a broad flight of stairs, but to your right as you approach you'll see a **ritual pool** for the washing of hands and knives used at the **sacrificial altar** opposite – note the **passageway** for the unlucky camels, cattle and sheep that leads up to it from next to the ticket office. In front of the altar are the scant remains of a long **banquet hall**.

The cella

The **cella** was the holiest part of the temple, accessible only to the priests, where, besides Bel, Yarhibol (a solar god) and Aglibol (a lunar god) were worshipped. Its soaring entrance **portal** was reconstructed by the French, and none too well at that as it narrows visibly at the top. To the right of the portal are some interesting carved **cross beams** with traces of their original colouring, which would once have supported the peristyle ceiling; depictions on the stonework include a temple with a fruit-laden altar and Aglibol, identified by the crescent moon at his shoulder, a combat between some divinities and the forces of evil and, on the second beam, a procession featuring a camel and some veiled women.

As you walk into the cella you'll notice that the **entrance** is slightly off-centre; the original entry point was to the south, but the building was reorientated to accommodate two shrines. This arrangement concurred with Semitic tradition, and was used in the Temple of Jerusalem; the northern shrine would have been the holier of the two, with the southern one probably used to hold a portable statue of Bel used in ritual processions. The ceiling of the cella would originally have been made, like that of the courtyard, of Lebanese cedar. In the walls note the holes in the joints between the blocks of stone: bronze would have been used to fasten the blocks together but most of it has been greedily removed over the centuries; only at base level has some been left to strengthen the walls against potential earthquakes. Faint **frescoes** on the interior walls recall the Byzantine era, when the temple was converted into a church; in the twelfth century it was turned into a mosque, and a **mihrab** was added on the south wall – a function which persisted right up until the clearing of the temple interior in 1929. The roof of the **northern shrine** consists of a single stone, carved with images of the seven planetary divinities, with Jupiter in the middle, encircled by the signs of the zodiac. On the lintel is a very worn but identifiable eagle with wings outspread which represents the god Bel. The **southern shrine** is simpler but still marvellously decorated, if defiantly sooty, it having been used as a home over the course of the centuries. Some sacrifices would probably have taken place on the roof, but the staircases that led up there from beside the shrines are now too unsafe to climb.

The back of the cella is its most photogenic side, with columns reconstructed by the French antiquites department in 1938. Just behind the cella are some recently excavated remains of the previous **Hellenistic temple**, while in the northeastern corner of the courtyard you can ascend some steps for a view over the oasis of olives and palm trees (unfortunately it's all private land if you were thinking of going for a wander there).

The patrician houses and the ethnographic museum

Behind the temple are the remains of a couple of **patrician houses**, dating to the third century; you can make out the plan of a series of rooms grouped around central courtyards, but the most interesting aspects of the houses, the mosaics, have been moved to the Palmyra Archeological Museum.

The **ethnographic museum** (daily except Tues 9am–1pm; S£200), to the northwest of the temple, houses a reasonable collection of Bedouin and local traditional costume, all labelled in English, inside a late nineteenth-century Ottoman governor's residence, which during the French mandate was used as a military prison.

Along the great colonnade

The **great colonnade** which forms the main axis of Palmyra is not a straight line but changes direction twice on its 1200-metre journey, once at the wedge-shaped triple-arched **monumental gateway** that bends the street round towards the Temple of Bel entrance, and then again at the tetrapylon further west. The gateway was built in the early third century and is richly adorned with carved acorns, grapes, palm trees and oak leaves. Souvenir sellers congregate here, as well as camel-ride touts, with whom you could negotiate a ride out into the desert visiting a nearby Bedouin tent for some tea. Just beyond the gateway are the low remains of the late first-century **Temple of Nebo** (a Mesopotamian god of oracles and wisdom, equated with Apollo), the construction of which was largely funded by the Elahbel family who built the best-preserved of Palmyra's tower tombs. Only the temple podium, with a cella faced by an outdoor altar, and the surrounding column bases survive, however; note that the colonnade extends only around three sides of the courtyard because the northern end of the temple was sliced off to accommodate the shops that lined the main street.

This eastern end is the best-preserved section of the colonnaded main axis, though most of the **columns** along the street have been re-erected this century. You can still see the column brackets which would have held the statuary of civic notables, largely officials, military men and businessmen; many of the inscriptions are still legible though the busts have all gone. Back in 1876 Baedeker reported that there were numerous busts available for the traveller to buy, though he suggested that "not more than 30–40 [piastres] should be paid" as they were "generally of rude execution".

Opposite the Temple of Nebo, four tall Egyptian red-granite columns form the entrance to the **Baths of Diocletian**, which date from the reconstruction of Palmyra in the early fourth century following Zenobia's defeat – though a bath complex had probably been situated here for about a century previous to this. The identifiable octagonal room was the dressing room; its paving stones are original and in the centre of the room is a drain, but beyond this there is little to aid the imagination as no walls survive.

Around the theatre and the tetrapylon

A short walk west along the axis will bring you to the second-century **theatre**, which was buried in sand until the 1950s. The lower seats have since been restored and the stage facade partly reconstructed, though there would have originally been another two storeys on the facade and higher levels of seating, probably constructed out of wood. The building has been dated to early in the second century, before this part of the great colonnade, and may well have dictated the main street's change in direction at this point – though the theatre probably lost its changing rooms behind the stage in the process.

At the back of the theatre are the remains of the **senate house**, the debating arena for the city's governing body, a small, strangely shaped building that was partially amputated during the construction of the street around the theatre. To the south of the senate house is a large courtyard area known as the **tariff court**, after the discovery here of a five-metre-long inscribed stone (transported to St Petersburg in 1901), which set out a decree of 137 AD listing the Palmyrene tax arrangements for goods entering or leaving the city. West of here, the early second-century **agora** is surrounded on all sides by a portico, which would at one time have been bordered by up to two hundred bracketed columns; the slots on the walls suggest that space on the columns ran out at some stage. At the south-western corner is a small **banquet room** with some bare remains of benches around the walls.

Back on the main axis, head for the **tetrapylon**, a grouping of four sets of four columns marking a slight bend in the road and the intersection of a cross street; impressive centrepiece to the ruins though it is, only one of the columns is original, the rest having been reconstructed in concrete. Just to the east of this are the pitiful remains of a **nymphaeum**, a public water fountain.

To Diocletian's Camp

The stretch of the main street to the west of the tetrapylon is the oldest part, dating from the early second century, and has only partially been excavated. At the far end stands a late second-century **funerary temple** – basically an elaborate temple tomb – which has recently been restored with a large quantity of concrete (and not much subtlety); there's a crypt underneath, but you can't at present get in.

From here head on into **Diocletian's Camp**, essentially a city within a city established by the emperor about thirty years after Aurelian's destruction of Palmyra in 273 (before this the Roman garrison had its camp near the site of the Palmyra Archeological Museum). If you head south from the funerary temple down the broad decumanus for 300m and then turn westwards down another columned avenue, you will pass the pitiful remains of a second tetrapylon before arriving at the sloping monumental stairway that heralds the **Temple of the Standards**; for a good view back over the site, ascend a winding staircase to the inner shrine for the Roman legion's standards. Just to the northeast of this you'll see the scant remains – a doorway and a few columns – of the second-century **Temple of Allat**; a fierce-looking early first-century AD lion found here has been reconstructed and now stands in front of the Palmyra Archeological Museum. The decumanus ends at an oval piazza, an unusual feature in Roman town planning (the only other example is at Jerash in Jordan). This would have opened out behind the southern gate to the city, which was the main entrance leading in from Damascus – probably the reason the decumanus is wider than the main colonnaded axis.

Around the Temple of Baal-Shamin

If you're returning to Tadmor from Diocletian's Camp and the great colonnade, you can easily take in the interesting ruins which lie near (and partially under) the *Zenobia Hotel*. The best preserved is the **Temple of Baal-Shamin**, who as "lord of the heavens", and thus of fertilizing rain, was naturally an important god in Roman Syria, often equated with the Greek god Zeus. Though the temple dates to 17 AD, its main focal point, the cella, was added in 130, and owes its remarkable state of preservation to its conversion into a church during the Byzantine period, when the entrance doorway was moved to the west. In the 1950s a Swiss team carefully restored the cella to its original form, and today it is not only one of the most intact monuments on the site but one of the few to have been fully excavated; on the ground to the north and south of the cella you can work out the form of two colonnaded courtyards.

About 150m west of the temple, six columns but not much else identify the remains of a sixth-century Christian **basilica**. Apart from this, little of the area north of the great colonnade has been excavated from beneath the dust and sand that has accumulated over the centuries. The well-preserved northern **wall** of the settlement dates from Diocletian's fortification of Palmyra, but was reinforced by Emperor Justinian in the sixth century; by the northern gate are the remains of a military barracks.

The tombs

Two basic types of tomb are found in Palmyra, **tower tombs** and **hypogea** (underground chambers). The tower tombs are older, dating back perhaps as far as Hellenistic times, though the latest was built in 128 AD and they were used for burials up until the third century. Dated hypogea range from 81 to 251 AD, but some tower tombs also have underground chambers, a transitional phase. The tombs are found in two areas, the Valley of the Tombs on the south side of Diocletian's Camp, and the southwest necropolis by the Damascus road. Although it's possible to wander round the more decrepit tower tombs by yourself, the only way to get inside the fascinating reconstructed tombs is on one of the highly recommended official **tours** that leave from outside the Palmyra Archeological Museum (which include the Temple of Bel as an optional extra). At present the tours, which last an hour or so, leave at 8.30am, 10am, 11.30am and 4.30pm; buy your ticket (S£100) at the window just outside the museum entrance which has full details posted up in English. The only drawback is that the quality of guide can vary dramatically: you could just get a local with basic English earning some extra money, or a university lecturer topping up his government salary in his vacation.

The Valley of the Tombs

The **Valley of the Tombs** stretches back for about 1km behind Diocletian's Camp, a bleak place where the tombs range from ruinous stacks to extremely well-preserved edifices which you'll need to join a tour to see. Many of the hypogea are still waiting to be discovered, having been buried in a tenth-century earthquake, while many others have collapsed and been raided in the intervening centuries. The most obviously photogenic batch of tower tombs lie in a row on the hill opposite Diocletian's Camp. Unfortunately none of these are included on the official tour, though you can peek through the bars into the prominent and impressive **Tower Tomb of Iamliku**, on the right of the grouping, which has undergone some restoration; dating to 83 AD, this would have had the capacity for up to two hundred burials.

You can head on west along the valley path for about 500m beyond this, passing an enticing selection of tombs, some merely rubble and others plain but well-preserved examples which you can climb inside and explore. By far the largest and most intact is the **Tower Tomb of Elahbel**, which stands four storeys high and would have had room for no fewer than three hundred incumbents (a hypogeum lies underneath, but entry is not possible). The family of Elahbel was one of the most important in the city, largely responsible for the construction of the Temple of Nebo, and their position is reflected in the splendour of this tomb, which was constructed, according to the inscription above the entrance, in 103 AD. The iron grill door replaces what would originally have been two massive stone ones hewn from the quarries to the north of the city. Inside, traces of the original colouring indicate how rich the decoration would have been; grand pilasters stretch to the ceiling, and remarkably dignified busts representing deceased family members look down upon you from all angles – it is refreshing to see these for once in situ, rather than ripped out of context in the corner of some anodyne museum. A narrow staircase leads up to the roof, which affords a fine view back over the valley.

The southwest necropolis

In the **southwest necropolis**, just beyond the *Cham Palace Hotel* by the main road to Damascus, the tower tombs are unremarkable but there is an astonishing underground chamber, the **Hypogeum of the Three Brothers**. Dating to the second century and restored in 1947, it's accessible on the museum-run tour. An inscription in Aramaic above the entrance records the names of the brothers and the fact that some of the 360-body capacity was later sold off to other families. The stone doors and the frescoes inside are all original, with the three brothers represented inside circular frames at the end of the main corridor. Other paintings deal with the theme of the soul overcoming death, including Ganymede being raised by the eagle of Zeus (on the ceiling), and Achilles achieving immortality in battle, after throwing off the women's clothes used by his mother to hide him with the daughters of Lycomedes, the king of Skyros. The right wing of the hypogeum

---

THE BEDOUIN

The **Bedouin** – whose name derives from the Arabic for "desert wanderers" – live in the deserts of Syria, Iraq and Jordan, and in all the countries of the Arabian peninsula and North Africa. Once a race fiercely adherent to ancient nomadic traditions and tribal loyalties, many Bedouin have now resettled (either under compulsion or voluntarily) in permanent desert communities and large cities. Some, however, are still traditional desert-dwellers, living in makeshift goat-skin tents and tending their herds of goats or sheep – even if many have abandoned camels for pick-up trucks. Back in the days of mass, overland trans-Asiatic trade, the Bedouin held positions of importance as suppliers of pack animals to the caravan merchants, and patrolled trade routes giving guidance and military protection to the convoys as they crossed the dangerous terrain from oasis to oasis. Now, the Bedouin have lost much of their former political strength, but while city-dwelling Arabs have a reputation for looking down on them, many in the same breath will celebrate the Bedouin's status as legendary Arab heroes.

Tribal loyalty is the bedrock of true Bedouin nomadic communities. A complex web of relationships attaches every Bedouin to an extended family: the *fakhida* is a network of cousins, down to the fifth generation; a *fakhd* is made up of several of these groupings, and forms part of a tribe, each member of which, in theory, shares one common ancestor. Tribal connections are expressed in Bedouin **dress**: the male headdress, known as the *ghutra*, is a large square of cotton, coloured according to the traditions of each individual tribe and folded around the head to give protection from heat, dust and flies. Most Bedouin men and boys also wear a loose-fitting, ankle-length gown called a *thawb*, made of cotton and usually coloured white, grey or black, which buttons up at the neck like a nightshirt. Women wear long-sleeved dresses or gowns, sometimes multicoloured, but occasionally black. Their hair is concealed, and sometimes kohl, a black cosmetic, is rubbed around the eyes to keep out the glare of the sun; intricate designs may be painted onto other exposed parts of their skin. As in cities, veils are often, but not always, worn over the face. In the desert, women are much less visible than men and may retreat

contains the sarcophagi of the three brothers; in the left wing is a funerary monument to Male, the most important of them, who died in 142 AD.

The Arab castle

The **Arab castle** (*Qalaat ibn Maan*) was built on top of a precipitous volcanic cone a thousand years after the ruins over which it presides. There are no fixed opening times and entry charge: technically it's free, and open in the morning and then in the late afternoon until dusk, but these arrangements depend largely on the custodian at the main gate who may ask for some *baksheesh*.

To **get there** by car follow the road from the roundabout in Tadmor, which winds itself up the hill from behind. Alternatively it takes about forty minutes to walk from the roundabout: the path that branches off the road by the Marona house tomb is steep but obvious and affords a number of irresistible backward glances over the site. If you're walking you'll pass a number of funerary monuments, most of them pretty ruinous, though it is worth pausing at the **Marona house tomb**, a solid square building constructed as a mausoleum for the family of a wealthy Palmyrene merchant in the early third century. It was converted later

into their own private tents when strangers approach – whilst the men of the community welcome the visitor hospitably.

Nowadays, most Bedouin herd goats or sheep, driving them – with dogs, donkeys, camels, assorted family members and Nissan pick-ups – from place to place in search of pasture. Camel herders are rare, though groups of these rather ragged beasts can still be seen from the desert roads and tracks; they are much more common further south in the Arabian deserts and the Sahara. Occasionally, the Bedouin will hunt desert animals and, if the soil is good enough, cultivate a few crops. Traditional Bedouin **meals** comprise a communal bowl of rice, cooked by the women but eaten first by the men, followed by endless small cups of coffee, flavoured with cardamom. To suit their surroundings the traditional washing ceremony before prayers may be performed with sand rather than water.

Bedouin **hospitality** – to fellow tribespeople, Arabs and foreigners – is famous, a tradition of looking after any stranger who emerges from the desert that stems from the harshness of the environment. For centuries it's been the subject of comment by Middle Eastern travellers, and nowadays many tour groups are given the opportunity to "take tea with the Bedouin"; in Palmyra children approach independent visitors with similar offers, which are more likely to be an authentic experience, although *baksheesh* will be expected. Out in the desert, the Bedouin often hold the keys to places such as the fort at Qasr al-Heir al-Sharqi, and tea will be offered as a matter of course; in remote desert regions, visitors who happen across a Bedouin settlement will find the hospitality they are given almost overwhelming. If you are invited into a tent remember to remove your shoes upon entering. In general Bedouin men will not sit or shake hands with women, though female visitors from the West will be made welcome. You will probably be offered a shot of bitter black coffee followed by sweet, sickly tea and possibly some food. Conversation begins with obligatory questions concerning marriage and may progress onto such diverse topics as sex, football and death depending on the quality of your host's English, or indeed your Arabic – a greeting at least in the local tongue would go down very well.

into a house, thus destroying the internal plan, but was rebuilt by the Department of Antiquities in 1946. The building is alternatively known as the "palace of the serpent" because of the carving of a snake to be found on the southwestern pilaster, though generally the decorative style is restrained.

The date of the first fortification on the volcanic cone is unclear, though it seems likely that a castle was built here in the twelfth century. What is certain is that in the early seventeenth century a Lebanese emir, Fakhr al-Din, built the present edifice to secure his control of this part of the Syrian desert. His plan, however, to provide a territorial bulwark against encroaching Ottoman power, failed dismally: he himself was captured by the Ottomans in 1635 and was later executed in Istanbul. The castle was abandoned thereafter, and is now in a poor state of repair – when you get up here you'll probably be disappointed both by the crude restoration work that's been done in places, and by the fact that there really isn't much to see inside the walls. But in truth, the main attraction is not the castle itself but the **view** from its ramparts, encompassing the ancient ruins, the oasis and the modern town on one side, and the rocky spine of the Jebel al-Tadmoria on the other, all of it fringed by the grey desert, flecked with the characteristic black tents of the Bedouin. The best time to come up is when the sun is setting over the arid hills to the west, a crowded, camera-clicking occasion but one which is not easily forgotten.

Qasr al-Heir al-Sharqi

It takes time, patience and expense to reach **QASR AL-HEIR AL-SHARQI** (Qasr al-Heir East), but once you've got there it's hard not to be impressed by the ancient splendour of the setting, with the bright orange walls of the ruins rising out of the wretched desert plains. The drama of the scene goes a long way towards making up for what are, close to, some fairly disappointing remains – certainly they don't compare favourably with the ruins of Resafe (see p.219), which has a similar ambience and is at least accessible by road.

The only sensible way of **getting there** (at least until the proposed tarmac road is built) is to hire a driver in Palmyra: not only is the thirty-kilometre desert track from the main highway extremely confusing (there are dozens of similar tracks made by the Bedouin and no signposts), but in wet weather you will need four-wheel drive to avoid the risk of getting stuck in the mud. Ask around outside the entrance to the museum, where drivers congregate to take people out to Palmyra's tombs, or ask at your hotel; S£2000 seems to be the average price. You could also ask around the touts by the monumental triple archway who will do the trip for S£1500; the reliability of their vehicles may be open to question, though four-wheel drive is only really essential after rainfall. Often in summer drivers will want to make an early start to avoid the heat of the day, so expect a 6am or 7am pick-up, arriving back at midday. In any case remember to take plenty of water with you as you won't find any on the way. For anyone with only a little time to spend in Syria, it would be possible to drive from Qasr al-Heir al-Sharqi all the way across the desert to Resafe – but you will end up paying through the nose for this.

The original purpose for the complex, which was constructed around 700, is open to speculation; probably the Umayyads built it to consolidate their control of the region in the face of local tribal wars, also developing the site as a caravan stop between Syria and Mesopotamia. The place was finally abandoned in the thirteenth century, probably as a result of the Mongol invasions. A sibling castle, **Qasr al-Heir al-Gharbi** (Qasr al-Heir West), 110km west of Palmyra, has a similar history, but what's left there now is very disappointing and not worth the effort of a visit; its most interesting feature was the grand gateway that now forms the entrance to the National Museum in Damascus (see p.78).

About 5km before reaching the site you'll see remains of the **outer walls** of the settlement, whose circumference would have stretched some 18km; within them would have been a huge garden area, as well as a civilian town and the castle buildings that survive today. Once at the **main site** you'll find two buildings facing each other, the smaller and better preserved of which is thought to have served as a **khan**, though it probably also had a military function as the walls are 2m thick and there is only one entrance. The key is available from a local Bedouin; the interior is a disappointing mess of rubble, though it's possible to climb up the walls at various points. Between the buildings stands a **minaret** which, if contemporary with the other buildings, is the third oldest in Islam; however, its construction remains something of a mystery and it may have started life as a watchtower, as there is no mosque for it to be attached to.

The **western building**, some six times larger than the eastern one, is essentially a mini-town with an identifiable grid pattern of streets, in the centre of which is a small square and a cistern. Though the interior is largely ruinous, parts of a mosque survive in the southeastern corner, and it's clear that the rest of the site was filled with residential and administrative buildings. Outside and about 50m to the north of the minaret are the remains of some **baths**.

travel details

The only way of getting to **Tadmor** on public transport is by **bus**. The state bus company **Karnak** operates between Tadmor and the following towns (their Tadmor office is on the main square, and buses stop outside it): Damascus (4 daily; 3hr); Deir ez-Zur (7 daily; 3hr); Hassakeh (1 daily; 5hr); Homs (2 daily; 2hr); Qamishli (1 daily; 6hr). **Pullman** companies include Al-Furat which has an office in the *Spring Restaurant* and runs services to Damascus and Deir ez-Zur in well-appointed, modern coaches, for a little more than the Karnak fares. **Microbuses** and other **local buses** will get you to Homs, Damascus and Deir ez-Zur in somewhat less comfort, and can be picked up on the main square.

PART THREE

THE

CONTEXTS

THE
HISTORICAL
FRAMEWORK

Juxtaposing Mediterranean, Anatolian and Arabian cultures, modern Syria is the political descendant of a bewildering succession of independent city states and of long periods of control by external imperial powers; what follows is only the barest outline of events, from prehistoric times to the present-day rule of President Assad.

PREHISTORIC TIMES

Man's first permanent settlements were established along the **Euphrates River** around twelve thousand years ago. This is where crops were first planted, and where wild animals were first domesticated and managed; villages grew up where the soil was fertile and the supply of water most abundant. The mastery of food production led eventually to surpluses, which in turn allowed the possibility of specialization, and then trade between individuals and settlements.

It is thought that Aleppo, Damascus and Hama all have their origins in the **Neolithic period**. Each claims to be the oldest continually inhabited settlement on earth, though the archeological investigation necessary to substantiate their claims is obviously impractical. Among Syria's numerous *tell*s – artificial mounds formed by the accumulated debris of centuries of occupation – the most interesting

Neolithic site for the non-specialist is at **Ugarit**; tools imported from Suphan Dagh in eastern Turkey dating back to the eighth millennium BC have been found here, suggesting that trade was sophisticated even at this early stage. Furthermore, a style of pottery known as "Halaf pottery", dating to the sixth millennium BC and originating from **Tell Halaf** in northeast Syria, has been found all over northern Syria and Iraq, testifying to the spread of some kind of homogenous culture over a wide area. The Bedouin still lead lives not too dissimilar to that of the prehistoric herdsmen, while the distinctive **beehive huts** found in northern Syria, and particularly in the area east of Hama, have their counterparts in the round houses of the Neolithic period from roughly the same areas, which were developed as man moved away from caves and rock shelters out into the open.

THE BRONZE AGE (3000–1200 BC)

The development of trade saw the rise of wealthy mercantile centres at **Ugarit**, **Mari** and **Ebla**, which developed into powerful city states with commercial contacts as far away as Egypt, Cyprus and Mesopotamia. Around 2000 BC, however, the established pattern of trade was disturbed by the influx of the **Amorites**, a Semitic people (belonging to a language group of which Hebrew and Arabic are modern-day descendants) from the Syrian desert. In the nineteenth and eighteenth centuries, a number of major Amorite city states emerged: Mari in particular enjoyed great prosperity, and the kingdom of Yamkhad (Aleppo) became the main power in the north, taking over Ebla's old trade. Around 1759 BC Mari was razed by another Semitic people, the Babylonians, under Hammurabi, but Yamkhad and the other Amorite kingdoms in the north of Syria managed to resist the Babylonian threat and developed substantial trading links with the east.

During the fifteenth and fourteenth centuries BC Syria became a battleground between three major powers, the Egyptians, the Hittites and the Mitanni. Based in the northeast around the Khabur River, the **Mitanni** were a non-Semitic people of obscure origin, but were eventually absorbed by the Hittites in the late fourteenth century through a series of marriage alliances. Indo-Europeans in origin, the **Hittites**, based to the northwest, had ended Babylonian rule around 1595 BC. **Egypt** had been developing trading links with the Syrian coastal cities, which gave access to the inland wood necessary for shipbuilding, since the twentieth century BC. By the end of the fourteenth century the Egyptians felt ready to square up to the Hittites, who had by this time extended their influence as far south as Damascus. The decisive battle was fought in 1285 BC at **Kadesh** (present-day Tell Nebi Mend, near Homs) and saw Ramses II ambushed by the Hittite cavalry and lucky to escape with his life (see box on p.125).

The coastal region remained largely untroubled during the conflict between the Egyptians, the Hittites and the Mitanni, allowing **Ugarit**, **Jableh** and **Arwad** to prosper as trading centres, whose wealth allowed them to maintain a large measure of independence from the main powers. The Semitic Canaanites, who had settled on the Mediterranean coast around 2000 BC, were probably the first people to develop a form of writing that used letters rather than words or syllables. The alphabet consisted of thirty letters, similar to modern Arabic in sequence and pronunciation, and indeed the language contained some words which are still in use today.

THE IRON AGE (1200–333 BC)

Around 1200 BC Hittite dominance was brought to an end by the aggressive migration of the **Sea Peoples**, a coalition of tribes from around the Aegean who are thought to have variously ended up in Palestine, Anatolia and Sardinia. The coastal cities were razed, including Ugarit, but they subsequently revived under the **Phoenicians**, whose massive expansion of sea trade led to the creation of over fifty colonies around the Mediterranean and the spread of the Phoenician script (developed from its Canaanite predecessor).

Out of the chaos created by the passing of the Sea Peoples, the **Arameans**, a Bedouin people of Semitic origin, migrated into central and northern Syria. Their language, Aramaic, took hold across a wide region of the Middle East, and a thousand years later was being spoken by Jesus; it still survives in certain isolated villages today, most notably Maalula near Damascus. Around 1000 BC, the north of Syria was absorbed by the **Assyrians**, based in northern Mesopotamia, who adopted the Aramaic language and its Neo-Phoenician script. In 612 BC, in turn, the Assyrian capital Nineveh was cap-

tured by the **Babylonians**, who took over their prosperous western possessions; this was the time of the legendary palaces and hanging gardens of Babylon. Babylon fell in 539 BC to the **Persians**, who rapidly took over the whole of the Middle East and Asia Minor.

THE HELLENISTIC PERIOD (333–64 BC)

The Persians' dominance of Asia Minor and incursions into Greece eventually provoked a Greek expeditionary force led by **Alexander the Great**. The struggle was decided over a series of battles in 333 BC, the greatest at Issus in southern Turkey. Eventually Alexander managed to march his army all the way down the Syrian coast, ending up in Egypt and founding the port of Alexandria. When he died aged 33 in 323 BC in Babylon, he had created an empire bigger even than the Persians', which changed the whole orientation of the region; Syria, save the coast, had until then had been essentially eastward-looking, but now it looked westwards for its government and ideas, while the West became susceptible to influence, especially religious ideas, from the East.

On his death Alexander's new empire was divided between his two most able generals: Ptolemy took over Egypt, southern Lebanon and southern Syria (including Damascus), while Seleucus took northern Syria, Mesopotamia and Asia Minor. Antioch (modern-day Antakya in Turkey) became the capital of the **Seleucid empire**, and **Apamea** was founded as a military headquarters; to these and other cities were given the characteristic Hellenistic grid street-plan which to varying degrees survives today. Yet Greek manpower in the Seleucid empire was never more than fifty thousand, and perforce the city states were allowed to retain a large measure of independence. In 198 BC the Seleucids took over southern Syria but within a hundred years, as their lack of numbers began to tell, the empire began to crumble: the Arabic Nabateans took Bosra and Damascus, while the Parthians made inroads into the eastern empire and the Armenians sniffed around in the north.

THE ROMAN PERIOD (64 BC–395 AD)

After their conquest of Greece the **Romans** took an increasing interest in the Seleucid empire, and in 64 BC the Roman legate Pompey invaded and formally created the Roman province of Syria, with its capital at Antioch, which was to become the third most important imperial city after Rome and Alexandria. Damascus was brought under direct Roman rule in the early part of the first century AD, and in 92–3 Palestine was also integrated.

The Roman period saw Syria, which benefitted as middleman in the east–west trade in luxuries, flourishing economically; the country also became a major area of cultivation, grain and wine being its specialities. Many roads were built and new settlements sprang up, particularly in the hinterland of Antioch (the Dead Cities) and the Hauran. In 106 the annexation of the Hauran was completed by creating the province of Arabia to the south of Damascus with **Bosra** as its capital; Bosra and Qanawat were then extensively replanned. Syria in turn had its influence on Rome. In 187 Septimius Severus, a Libyan general in the Roman army, married Julia Domna, a high priest's daughter from Emesa (Homs). Soon afterwards he became emperor, and upon his death Julia became effective ruler in Rome behind her son Caracalla; the line produced two further emperors, Elagabalus and Alexander Severus. In the mid-third century Philip the Arab, from Shahba, briefly ruled the Roman Empire.

The main threat to the Romans came from the **Parthians** to the east, who by the late second century had become a major source of concern. **Dura Europos** was reinforced and **Palmyra** was taken under direct rule. In 224 the Sasanians took over Persia from the Parthians and in 256 they captured Dura Europos, four years later capturing the emperor Valerian himself at Edessa in southeastern Turkey. Valerian was subsequently tortured and killed, leaving the Romans happy to enlist any local help they could; they turned to Odenathus, the Palmyrene prince, who campaigned deep into Sasanian territory. He was killed in 266 but his wife **Zenobia** had even greater glory in mind, declaring herself a Roman empress, sending forces to Egypt and attacking Antioch. Emperor Aurelian had no choice but to confront Zenobia head on, forcing her to flee Antioch and defeating her army in battle just outside Homs in 272. Back in Palmyra, she was forced to flee the city when Aurelian placed it under siege, and was finally captured on her way to the Euphrates and sent

to Rome a prisoner; after a further revolt in 273 Palmyra itself was razed.

Emperor Constantine gave official recognition to **Christianity** in 313, though Syria, and especially Antioch, had been a strongly Christian region since the first-century missions of St Paul. Before 313 Christian churches had merely been adapted houses (as for example at Dura Europos), but during the fourth century they now began to adopt the grandeur of Roman public buildings. In 392 Christianity was declared by the Emperor Theodosius I to be the official religion of the Roman Empire and began to flourish by imperial patronage; pagan temples were either destroyed or adapted for Christian use, and by the fifth century Syria was covered in churches.

THE BYZANTINE PERIOD (395–636)

In 395 the Roman Empire was officially divided into east and west; the western half fell to Germanic invaders in 476 but the **Byzantine** eastern half called itself Roman until the fall of Constantinople to the Ottomans in 1453. Despite troubled frontiers and internal church divisions Syria continued to prosper economically; what are known as the Dead Cities thrived on their olive oil exports, the Hauran became intensely cultivated and building projects multiplied. No other area of the Byzantine Empire contains such a wealth of architectural evidence from this period as Syria, with its villages, churches and monastic remains, pride of place going to the basilica devoted to St Simeon, northwest of Aleppo.

During the reign of Justinian (527–65) the empire won back much of the land that had been lost in the west, but the continuing **Sasanian** threat led to a number of defensive projects along the Euphrates, including the fortifications at Resafe and Halebiye. The two sides locked horns in an epic struggle covering the late sixth and early seventh centuries, resulting in a mutual exhaustion that paved the way for a completely new force to emerge in the region.

THE ARAB CONQUEST, THE UMAYYADS AND THE ABBASIDS (636–1097)

On the death in Mecca in 632 of **Mohammed**, who had founded Islam and united the Arabian tribes, his successors went about extending their influence in the area north of the Arabian peninsula. Caliph Omar succeeded in conquering all of present-day Syria, Lebanon, Israel, Jordan and Egypt, with the decisive battle for Syria taking place in 636 at **Yarmouk River**, near present-day Dera (see box on p.100). Under his successor Caliph Othman all of Persia was captured, yet the events following his assassination in 656 led to the first and greatest Islamic division, between the Sunnis and Shi'ites. Othman's natural successor appeared to be Ali, husband of the prophet's daughter Fatima, but he was opposed by the governor of Syria **Moawiya**, who eventually triumphed in 661, founding the **Umayyad dynasty** and moving the capital from southern Iraq to Damascus where his power base lay. The Shi'ites, however, still follow Ali's line, representing about ten percent of all Muslims and found mostly in Iran and the Indian subcontinent.

The Caliphs' rule sat quite easily on the basically Christian population because it rested more on tax incentives than coercion, but the growth of the Islamic faith was slow. Major building projects were embarked on, especially under Khalid Ibn al-Walid (705–15), who was responsible for the Umayyad Mosque in Damascus; the Great Mosque of Aleppo also dates from this period. Military conquests led to Umayyad rule extending far into central Asia, almost to the borders of China and including Afghanistan, Pakistan and the west coast of India. To the west all of north Africa, most of Spain and even southern France came under Arab control.

In 750 the Umayyad line was replaced by the **Abbasids** from Persia who transferred their capital from Damascus to Iraq (Kufa first and then Baghdad after 762). As a consequence Syria fell into a blind spot; the only significant remains in the country from this period are to be found at Raqqa on the Euphrates. With the western possessions neglected, Egypt and then the other North African possessions broke away from Abbasid rule, while revolts in Syria in the mid-ninth century encouraged the spread of Shi'ism. In the mid-tenth century the Abbasid empire fragmented and Syria became a confusing free-for-all, as the Egyptian Fatimids, Seljuk Turks and Byzantines all dipped their fingers in the pot – though none were strong enough to take a firm hold. Sunni and Shi'ite tensions grew, and it is this period of turmoil and uncertainty that the region's confusing religious make-up largely originated, with Shi'ism engendering numerous offshoots. The **Druze** arose out of the teachings of Caliph Hakim of the Fatimid dynasty (see box on p.109), one of many sects thought to have been founded upon a belief in the Caliph's divinity – though only the Druze have survived to the present day. It was also at this time that the Christian **Maronites** (see p.267) holed themselves up in the mountains of Lebanon; tensions between the Druze and Maronites would rumble on for centuries.

Syria's political history at this point can only be related at local level. In the north, first the Hamdanid dynasty (944–1003) then the Bedouin Mirdasid (1023–79) controlled Aleppo, each retaining a large degree of independence from the Seljuk Turks (in theory controlled by the Sunni Abbasid caliphs in Baghdad) and the Byzantines. Meanwhile, the Shi'ite Fatimids held the upper hand in southern Syria. In the late eleventh century however the Seljuks finally gained supremacy in the region, defeating the Byzantines at the battle of Manzikert in 1071, before taking Damascus in 1075 and Jerusalem in 1078.

THE CRUSADES (1097–1260)

The subsequent mass destruction of churches in the Holy Land and ill-treatment of pilgrims by the Seljuks prompted Pope Urban II to call for a **crusade** to reclaim Jerusalem at the Council of Clermont-Ferrand in 1095. In 1097 a 100,000-strong French army arrived in Constantinople and in June 1098, after a nine-month seige, Antioch was taken and Seljuk leadership collapsed. There was little resistance to further conquests and in 1099 Jerusalem was taken. Tartous and Latakia soon fell too, though Tripoli was not taken until 1109 and an assault on Aleppo in 1125 failed. After the Second Crusade in 1148 the defence of most of the inland conquests was left to two autonomous orders of knights, the **Templars** and **Hospitallers**, who, because of their small numbers, relied principally on the forbidding nature of their castles such as Marqab, Saone (Saladin) and Crac des Chevaliers.

The first inroads against the Crusader presence were made by **Zengi**, local ruler of Aleppo (1128–46), and his son **Nur al-Din**, who took Damascus in 1154 and for the first time united Syrian resistance to the Crusaders. His achievements were built upon by his nephew **Saladin**, a Kurd from Iraq who founded the **Ayyubid** dynasty (1176–1260), so called after his family name. By 1186 Saladin had completed the unification of Arab lands from Baghdad to Cairo, and in 1187 he was able to recapture Jerusalem after the decisive battle of Hattin, before sacking Tartous and Latakia and taking Saone after a three-day seige. This in turn provoked the pan-European Third Crusade, which in the 1190s recaptured most of the coastline and secured access for pilgrims to the Holy Sepulchre; in 1227 Jerusalem was handed back by treaty to the Crusaders, though it was retaken by Muslim Turkish invaders in 1244.

THE MAMELUKES (1260–1516)

In 1260 the Ayyubids were replaced in Syria by the Egyptian **Mamelukes**, who under **Baibars** managed to inflict a defeat on a foe far more dangerous than the Europeans. The **Mongols** under Genghis Khan had swept into Persia in 1220, and with the taking of Baghdad in 1258 seemed on the point of overwhelming the whole of Syria and Egypt. However, at the 1260 battle of Ain Jalout in Palestine the Mamelukes decisively halted this progress (though the Mongols were to continue sporadically to wreak havoc, including Tamerlane's destruction of Damascus and much of Syria as late as 1400), and the region breathed a sigh of relief. Baibars now turned his attention to the Crusaders; in 1268 Antioch was taken, then in 1271 Safita and the Crac des Chevaliers. Baibars' successor Qalaun took Marqab in 1285 and Latakia two years later. Tartous was lost in 1291, but a Crusader garrison clung onto Arwad until 1302 – their eventual departure signalled the end of the Crusader presence in the Middle East.

The Mamelukes had been an elite of slave troops of central Asian or Turkish origin, and when they came to power, they drew their court, administration and army leaders all from the same class, with each successive Sultan being specially chosen and reared for the purpose. Their rule was long and stable, and even though their capital was in Cairo, many monuments from this period survive in Aleppo and Damascus, most notably the wealth of mausoleums in the Salihiye district.

THE OTTOMAN PERIOD (1516–1918)

In 1516 the Mamelukes were defeated north of Aleppo by a new Turkish power, the **Ottomans**,

and Syria was once again to be ruled from Constantinople, though this time as a backwater. The Ottoman empire was huge, stretching from the Caucasus to Bosnia, and under Suleiman the Magnificent (1520–66), Serbia, Hungary, Rhodes, Mesopotamia and the whole of North Africa save Morocco was added. As a result, Aleppo was opened up to the West and flourished as the main trading city in the Levant. The role of Damascus in administering and accommodating pilgrims on the annual *hadj* (the ablutions fountain of the Umayyad Mosque is said to mark the midpoint between Istanbul and Mecca) did much to further its economy, as witnessed by the khans and souks built at this time.

Syria was divided into three administrative districts, each governed by a *pasha* responsible to the capital. Yet Ottoman power in the country was not strongly held, with local families often exercising effective power. At the end of the eighteenth century foreign powers, particularly Britain, France and Russia, began to cultivate spheres of influence where they could concentrate their trade. In 1831 Syria was occupied by an Egyptian force, to which the Ottomans and the Western powers reacted by stirring up a Druze rebellion and blockading Beirut with an Anglo-Austrian naval force, forcing an Egyptian evacuation in 1840. According to the Anglo-Ottoman Commercial Convention of 1838, Syria was opened to unrestricted European trade – which largely ruined Syria's embryonic manufacturing industry.

In 1860 the **Druze-Christian troubles** in Lebanon spilt over to Damascus; Muslims invaded the Christian quarter and went on a killing spree for three days, destroying all the principal churches and engulfing an estimated 2500 Christians in the flames. The Turkish chief of police even joined in the killing, luring Christians out of hiding with promises of safety and then shooting them. At the end of the massacre the remaining Christian women were driven naked through the streets and sold to the Bedouin. Europe was horrified and demanded action; the Turkish Sultan responded by ordering the immediate execution of 150 people, including the city's governor and chief of police who were strung up in the streets. Twenty thousand Damascene men were forcibly conscripted into the army and Christian Lebanon was declared to be a separately administered state within the Turkish empire.

Though Syria had to put up with a great deal of inefficiency and corruption from its overwhelmingly indifferent Turkish governors, some important modernizations did occur in the late nineteenth century, such as improvements in civic amenities and sanitation. In 1863 the region's first paved road since Roman times was built to connect Damascus and Beirut. 1894 saw the Beirut–Damascus–Hauran rail link established whilst in 1908 the Hedjaz rail line linked Damascus to Medina.

In the late nineteenth century the **French** made increasing inroads into Syria, after extending considerable loans to the Ottoman authorities; ports were built to open up the Syrian market, much to the detriment of local producers. This led to a certain amount of anti-European and Ottoman feeling among the Arab elite, and at the turn of the twentieth century a number of societies had sprung up in Aleppo, Beirut and Damascus advocating **Syrian independence**.

Widespread Arab nationalism emerged after 1914, when Damascus was made the general headquarters of German and Turkish forces in the Middle East. Feelings against Turkey intensified throughout **World War I**, when Turkish indifference and incompetence aggravated food shortages, leading to the outbreak of a number of serious epidemics and starvation. In 1916 an **Arab revolt** broke out, encouraged by the British, which was immediately answered by the hanging of 21 Arab nationalists on 6 May in Damascus and Beirut. The places of execution are now commemorated as Martyrs' Square in each city, and the anniversary as Martyrs' Day.

THE FRENCH MANDATE (1918–45)

British troops entered Damascus on October 1, 1918 alongside the Arab forces of **Emir Feisal**. The Arabs had been led to believe by the British that the defeat of Turkey would lead to them being granted an Arab state; however, under the secret 1916 **Sykes-Picot treaty** the British had already agreed to a partition of the Middle East with France, and the 1917 **Balfour declaration** had also intimated British support for the creation of a Jewish homeland in the region. An American delegation was sent to Syria and Palestine from the Paris Peace Conference to determine the wishes of the locals, and the ensuing King-Crane report concluded that there was widespread opposition to any foreign mandates being imposed, though there was a feeling for some form of outside assistance provided that it came from America or Britain – though on no account from France. The delegation also strongly recommended the scrapping of the Zionist programme.

On Feisal's return from Paris in May 1919, his supporters immediately organized elections wherever possible; a parliamentary government was even set up, with Feisal being declared **king of Syria**. However at a peace conference in San Remo, Italy, the French and British partition of the Middle East was confirmed, with Britain handed **mandates** over Palestine and Jordan, and France over Lebanon and Syria. In theory the mandates were designed to bring these former Ottoman territories to full independence under the supervision of the great powers as soon as possible; in reality, however, the difference between mandates and colonies was hard to distinguish.

France's initial move was an attempt at divide and rule, with Syria being carved up into three districts and Lebanon being treated as a fourth. Heavy censorship was imposed, presses were confiscated, theatres were closed and the *Service des Renseignements* was set up, precursor of the modern Syrian intelligence service, the Mukhabarat. When confronted with local **resistance** in October 1925 the French bombed Hama, killing over three hundred people. In response to a Druze revolt in the Hauran which spread to Damascus, the French bombarded the capital in October 1925 and February and May 1926; several neighbourhoods, including the Hamidiye Souk, were destroyed, and around three thousand people died.

The continued rebellion, now taking the form of a series of strikes, eventually produced a more conciliatory line from the French: in 1930 a new constitution was drafted, transforming Syria into a parliamentary republic with the French exercising control over foreign affairs and internal security. In 1936, following the British granting of concessions to Egypt and full independence to Iraq, a new left-wing government in France even drafted a treaty providing for Syrian independence, with French consultation on foreign policy. Though this was ratified by the Syrian parliament it was not ratified by the French government before its fall from power, when it was replaced by a more right-wing cabinet anxious to maintain control over its Middle Eastern possessions, especially with the new prospect of oil in the northeast of Syria.

German aggression in Europe led France to cede the **Hatay** region (including Antakya, the old Roman capital of Syria) to Turkey in 1939 in an attempt to ensure Turkish neutrality in the event of any future war. The Hatay had been declared an autonomous state in 1937, and parliamentary elections had been fixed to ensure a Turkish majority, despite being outnumbered by Arabs and Armenians in the region. Syrians are still aggrieved by this chain of events to this day, and maps published in the country depict the Hatay as part of Syria, not Turkey.

Syria's economy stagnated under the French mandate, but at least a modern administrative system was introduced, many roads and public buildings were built and a state education system was founded along with a university in Damascus. Mains water and electricity were introduced to all major Syrian towns, and irrigation and reforestation projects set up; indeed the land under cultivation increased by some fifty percent, while the population rose from two to three-and-a-half million. More selfishly important for today's visitor was the creation of a department of antiquities to preserve and administer the country's architectural heritage; most notable is its work at Apamea, the Crac des Chevaliers and Palmyra.

In 1940 France fell to Germany, and in 1941 Syria was invaded by Allied forces with the mandate being placed under **Free French** control. At the end of the war Syria's and Lebanon's **independence** was finally proclaimed, and the countries were admitted into the United Nations, though French forces did not finally leave Syria until April 1946.

INDEPENDENCE, UNION WITH EGYPT, AND THE RISE OF THE BA'ATH PARTY (1945–71)

In March 1949 the civilian government was overthrown by the army, and by 1954 the **military** was largely controlled by the Ba'ath Party – a socialist organization founded in 1940 on a commitment to a pan-Arab state (*ba'ath* means renaissance) – with support from the Alawite and Druze minorities. During the early 1950s Syria developed close ties with Egypt and the Soviet Union; the United States attempted to destabilize the government by dumping wheat into Italy and Greece, Syria's major export markets, but disclosure of an American plot to install an Iraqi-biased, pro-Western military dictatorship only served to push Syria further into Egypt's arms, leading in February 1958 to a referendum which approved formal union with Egypt and the creation of the **United Arab Republic**.

The new country was to have one president and cabinet but two separate councils ruling Syria and Egypt. In 1959 the National Union, based in Egypt, was declared the only legal political party and in 1960 the first National Assembly was held with four hundred Egyptian and two hundred Syrian delegates. Yet the union's economic policy merely extended inappropriate Egyptian policies to Syria with disastrous consequences, and nationalization and redistribution of private enterprises proved unpopular with Syrian merchants and businessmen. This led in September 1961 to Syria's withdrawal from the UAR. The reforms of the UAR era were rescinded but, beyond this, political infighting produced only stagnation, which in 1963 allowed a **coup** by the military committee of the Ba'ath Party.

Nationalization of banks and insurance companies was immediately reintroduced, and a land law was implemented limiting the size of private holdings. In 1964 a number of the larger industrial firms in Aleppo and Homs were taken under **government ownership**, a new labour law protecting workers' rights was passed and a General Peasants' Union formed. These moves previewed a major restructuring of the economy in 1965, but widespread nationalization provoked demonstrations and rioting in the major cities. This led to a power struggle within the Ba'ath Party between moderates and extremists, won by the latter in February 1966 when General Salah Jadid became president, with the backing of the commander of the air force **Hafez al-Assad**, a member of the Muslim Alawite minority. A command economy was introduced and communists were included in the cabinet; this provoked further demonstrations in 1967, when the regime reacted by using its workers' militia to restore order.

In June 1967, Israel launched the **Six-Day War**, in retaliation for incursions made by Syrian guerrillas in the Golan, Egypt's closure of the Red Sea to Israeli shipping and a mutual defence pact between Egypt and Jordan. Israeli troops, in a lightning pre-emptive military action, captured the West Bank from Jordan, Gaza and the Sinai peninsula from Egypt, and from Syria, the **Golan Heights**. Apart from leaving Syria with a bloody nose, the war severely harmed the country economically, as Israeli air strikes had targeted large factories and the Homs oil refinery. The loss of the Golan Heights was also a massive dent to the regime's prestige, prompting yet more protests through 1968 and 1969, largely organized by Islamic extremists reacting to the perceived atheism of the regime. Extremists and pragmatists – the latter led by Assad – fought for power in the government and, reinforced by the widespread popularity of measures relaxing import restrictions and subsidizing private factories, Assad was able to bring off a **coup** in November 1970.

SYRIA UNDER ASSAD (1971–)

After Assad was sworn in as president of the Syrian Arab Republic in March 1971, small-scale liberalization of the economy allowed him to achieve some form of immediate popularity and stability. Economic ties were strengthened with Lebanon, and Syria benefited from knock-on effects of the rise in oil prices in the early 1970s, with generous economic assistance from Saudi Arabia and Kuwait in particular. Yet during the late 1970s the regime became unpopular for a number of reasons. The government was increasingly regarded as corrupt and Alawite-dominated, the military occupation of much of Lebanon in 1976 following the outbreak of civil war there was proving to be expensive and ill-considered, and the arrival of Lebanese refugees deepened a severe housing crisis. In the forefront of **opposition** were the **Muslim Brotherhood**, a terrorist movement who advocated replacing the regime with a system based on Sunni orthodoxy. They assassinated several major party figures during the late Seventies and early Eighties, and their city-centre bombings killed hundreds of civilians.

Opposition to the regime also encompassed non-violent secular groups and Muslims who were not supporters of the Brotherhood. In March 1980 a one-day national **general strike** was organized by Damascene lawyers and supported by numerous professional associations calling for political reform. Many businesses, schools and universities shut down, while in some cities security forces attempted forcibly to ensure shops remained open, which led to violent clashes in the streets. In the days immediately following, the medical, engineers' and bar association councils were dissolved, and hundreds of activists were arrested. In the same month a hundred demonstrators who had set fire to the Ba'ath Party headquarters in Jirsh Shughur were executed.

From April 1980 to February 1981 **Aleppo** became a major battleground between the government and largely Muslim Brotherhood opposition, and a special prison camp was even set up in the citadel to deal with the insurgents. All in all between one and two thousand people were killed, largely at random, by the security forces in response to attacks on government troops or buildings. Some reports allege that males over the age of fifteen were simply being rounded up, marched to an open space and shot – 83 died like this on August 11 after an attack on a patrol.

On June 27, 1980 around a thousand political prisoners in Tadmor prison were shot dead in response to an **assassination attempt** on President Assad, and on July 7 membership of the Muslim Brotherhood was made punishable by death. The city of **Hama** was one of the major centres of Brotherhood opposition, and in April 1981, in response to the ambush of a security checkpoint on the outskirts of town, government troops at random killed at least 350 men, leaving their bodies in the streets. Opposition continued to ferment, however, and in February 1982 the regime decided to finish it off, deploying thirty thousand troops to flatten Hama after a bout of arrests had erupted into a full-scale rebellion. Thousands died, and a third of the city centre was destroyed in the three-week battle. This uncompromising show of force, combined with the widespread human rights abuses that characterized the ensuing state of emergency, effectively quashed opposition to Assad and secured the future of his regime.

THE ECONOMY

During the early 1980s Syria's **economy** headed into difficulty. Intervention in Lebanon was draining finances, especially after Israel's invasion in 1982, and oil prices fell, hitting not only the small-scale oil industry in Syria but also the subsidies received from more oil-rich Arab neighbours – who were also unhappy at Assad's siding with Iran during the Iran–Iraq war. A

CENSORSHIP

The Assad government has rigidly suppressed books, films and other media which it deems to contain anti-state (or pro-Israel) propaganda. Things are now a lot less paranoid than previously – foreign newspapers and magazines available in Damascus used to be sold with all articles relating to Syria carefully cut out – and the 1990s have seen a definite relaxation in government suppression of information. Satellite TV and fax machines are now legal, though the Internet for the moment remains banned.

BOOKS

The largest publishing houses in Syria are state owned, and the few private ones rely on the government for their licences. Writers tend to be government employees such as translators, editors and teachers, and with their income tied to the state their outlook tends to be conservative. Censorship is rigorous, though fiction tends to be treated more leniently than non-fiction: fiction writers may receive a severe rap on the knuckles, but tend not to be imprisoned for their work, only for any involvement with outlawed political parties – when the poet Shawqi Baghdadi, for example, read out a banned poem at an international conference in Tunis in 1988, his punishment was to be questioned for three days upon his return to Syria. Foreign books about politics and contemporary Syrian or Middle Eastern history are banned, though works of literature or culture are not.

FILM

Film production in Syria dates back to the 1920s, and by the late 1940s a small number of musicals and light comedies were being produced every year, primarily through Lebanese financing and distribution. In 1966 the **National Film Centre** was established as the primary producer of state films, but the presence of a number of talented, individualistic film-makers gave the centre something of a problematic reputation, with films such as Omar Amirallay's *Daily life in a Syrian village* (1974), which portrayed the failure of the Ba'ath agricultural programme. The film was banned, as were five out of the twenty documentary shorts produced by the centre up to 1974, when Assad dismissed the director of the institute, Hamid Merei, replacing him with a more pliable choice. During the 1970s film clubs became important pockets of intellectual resistance to the regime but they were closed down in 1980. At this time most of the talented film-makers went abroad, including Amirally who went to work for French TV, but in the mid-1980s a good new crop of directors emerged. Usama Muhammed's *Stars of the day* in 1988 won first prize at the Valencia film festival, and after impressing many at Cannes won commercial distribution in Spain, France, Germany and Switzerland – though this was before it was ever seen in Syria. The film depicted the moral crisis of a rural family whose members become involved in corrupt city life and, although it was not banned, the film failed to gain distribution within Syria, which amounts to the same thing. All distribution is controlled by the government, but Western commercial films are very rarely censored, and slightly more challenging Western films can be seen fairly readily at the various cultural centres.

Syria has recently become an attractive and cheap production site for many Arab countries, and ironically some of the films and TV serials produced here are far more tightly censored by the Arab Gulf States they're made for than ever by the Syrian authorities.

series of measures to encourage the private sector were followed by further **economic liberalization** in the late 1980s, and approaches were even made to Western financial institutions in an effort to boost investment; in May 1991 Investment Law no. 10 was passed to encourage private and foreign investment in state monopolies. The early 1990s saw a slight economic boom in response, as the negative effects of the collapse of the Soviet Union were leavened by assistance from Kuwait, Saudi Arabia and the United Arab Emirates, in the wake of Syria's support against Iraq during the Gulf War. During the early 1990s revenue from **domestic oil production** peaked at around \$2 billion a year, and there was even talk of establishing private banks and reopening the Damascus stock exchange.

In the mid-1990s growth slowed again: oil revenues receded as prices dropped, worldwide inflation made imports more expensive, and the increasingly erratic electricity supplies damaged internal production. Endemic **corruption** has also been a hindrance, with government licences being awarded more as private favours than for sound economic reasons. The government has made it clear, however, that economic reform will be gradual, to avoid the social and therefore political consequences of a radical change to a full market economy.

YOM KIPPUR AND THE PEACE PROCESS

On October 6, 1973, the Arab states defeated in the Six-Day War launched a major offensive to try to regain their lost territory (the **Yom Kippur War**). There was fierce fighting in the Golan – and Damascus was even threatened for a time – but Israel hung on to its previous gains. Since then, Israel has returned Sinai to Egypt (in 1978 as a result of the Camp David Accord) but has doggedly settled the former Syrian portion of the Golan Heights, much to the anger of Assad, whose government constantly reminds the world of United Nations' calls for Israel to surrender its defeated territory. Yet in recent years Assad's policy towards Israel has moved from one of obstinate opposition towards accepting the possibility of peace, and in 1991 Syria began for the first time to take an active role in the **peace conferences**. As well as demanding the return of the Golan, a fundamental Syrian stance is that there should be Israeli withdrawal from its buffer zone in south Lebanon and a corresponding peace with the Palestinians. Assad seems to accept the principle of a full peace for a full withdrawal, though Israeli talk of open markets and full economic integration worries Damascus and increases the impetus for domestic economic reform – which may in turn provoke greater political openness within Syria.

Aware that Arab strength against Israel can only be manifested through unity, Assad has attempted to engage Israel in regional rather than bilateral talks. This policy was thwarted, however, when Jordan and the PLO signed agreements with Israel in 1994 which paved the way for the creation of an autonomous Palestinian state in the West Bank and Gaza. Assad, ever the pragmatist, remained within the peace process, deciding to play a weakened bargaining hand rather than be excluded altogether. Yet from the Israeli side, it seems that until hardline premier Netanyahu is removed from office the return of the Golan Heights, and thus a peace agreement, is off the cards.

POLITICAL REPRESSION

In the early 1980s Syria was effectively embroiled in a civil war, which brought in its aftermath a state of emergency founded upon widespread and fundamental human rights abuses. To this day, arrest is often based on mere suspicion of subversive sympathies or any kind of link to outlawed political organizations, principally the Muslim Brotherhood, non-official wings of the Ba'ath Party and the Communist Party. People can be arrested without any charge and not given a trial or any legal representation – even on occasions being held in prison long after the imposed sentence has been served. Amnesty International has alleged that torture is used frequently by the Syrian security forces, and that deaths in custody have occurred through torture, suicide or inadequate medical attention. Widespread informers mean that Syrians are ultra-cautious about talking of domestic politics, and it is assumed, rightly or not, that phones are tapped and mail opened. In recent years there have been amnesties – in 1992 when over two thousand political prisoners were released, and in 1995 on Assad's 25th anniversary in power, when another 1200 were set free – yet the pattern of violations remains and an estimated four thousand political prisoners are still inside.

AFTER ASSAD?

Nobody knows who will succeed Assad after his death – and it's certain that nobody could match his towering presence. Assad's eldest son **Bassel**, whose image can still be seen everywhere in the country alongside his father's, was a genuinely popular figure groomed as a natural successor, but he died in a car accident in 1994, driving too fast along the road to Damascus airport heading for a skiing holiday in Europe. Assad's other son **Bashar** was brought back home, and his face is slowly appearing beside those of the president and his late brother, but he seems to lack the character and charisma of either.

Some commentators have maintained that the biggest threat to a peaceful takeover seems to be Assad's brother **Rifaat**, controller of the government forces during the Hama Massacre who attempted to overthrow the president during his recovery from a heart attack in 1984; banished for his sins, he was welcomed back to attend his mother's funeral in 1992. Although Alawite bias has been levelled against the government, some form of tribal dispute is unlikely. The most likely outcome is some form of power struggle within the small elite with which Assad has surrounded himself – who hopefully have a vested interest in avoiding any military confrontation.

RELIGION

Unlike many Arab states Syria does not have an official state religion, though constitutionally the head of state must, in theory at least, be a Muslim. Not only has Assad been keen to avoid religiously contentious issues, but the Syrian government does not even officially recognize the existence of separate ethnic and religious groups within the population.

ISLAM

The Islamic faith was founded by **Mohammed**, who in 609 AD began to hear messages from the archangel Gabriel; these messages and Mohammed's teachings were written down after his death by his followers in the book known as the **Koran**. According to Muslims Mohammed was the last of God's prophets, but they also recognize Jesus and the Old Testament prophets as minor ones (with Christianity being essentially a mistake). The teachings of Mohammed are not thought of as creating a new religion as Allah is considered to be the same God that Christians and Jews worship.

Islam is very much considered a way of life, for which there are five essential tenets known as the "**pillars of faith**": prayer (*salat*) five times daily, called from the minaret of the mosque; a pilgrimage to Mecca, Mohammed's birthplace, at least once in a lifetime (*hadj*); the fast (*sawn*) during Ramadan (see p.40), the ninth month of the Islamic lunar calendar in which the messages were revealed to Mohammed; almsgiving (*zakat*), to build and maintain mosques and to help the poor; and bearing witness (*shahada*) that there is no God other than Allah, with Mohammed being his last prophet.

Prayers are performed at sunset (the Islamic day begins then), after dark, at dawn, midday and in the afternoon; a limited postponement of prayer is allowed under special circumstances such as illness, a journey or war. The call from the minarets at these times is now usually a pre-recorded message: "God is most great. I testify that there is no god but Allah. I testify that Mohammed is his prophet. Come to prayer, come to security. God is great." Before prayer comes ritual **washing** in the ablutions fountain of the mosque courtyard, and shoes are always removed before entering the prayer hall. The worshipper faces Mecca – the **mihrab** in the mosque indicates its direction – and the first chapter of the Koran is then recited: "Praise be to God, Lord of the worlds, the Compassionate, the Merciful, King of the Day of Judgement. Only you do we worship and your aid do we seek. Guide us on the straight path, the path of those on whom you have bestowed your grace, not the path of those who incur your anger, nor of those who go astray." This is then repeated twice with the worshippers in a prostrate position – which symbolizes their status as servants (Islam means "submission") – with the repeated addition of the phrase *Allahu Akbar* (God is most great).

On Friday, the **day of rest**, a sermon is usually delivered by the *imam* at the main midday prayers; visitors cannot enter mosques at this time, and even the Umayyad Mosque in Damascus is closed for prayer. Islam has no one religious leader, or indeed priesthood; the **imam** is roughly equivalent to a Protestant pastor, leading the prayers. Instead the religion concentrates on the individual's personal relationship with God, conducted through prayer and the teachings of the Koran. Indeed it is not necessary or always possible for the worshipper to pray in a mosque, and you may come across men in hotel lobbies prostrate on their prayer mats.

The **hadj** is undertaken by around two million Muslims each year. Theoretically every Muslim adult should visit Mecca as often as is practically possible, as long as the journey and their absence do not bring any hardships to their home. However, for many poorer people the pilgrimage may be a once-in-a-lifetime experience, or even replaced by visits to nearer, lesser shrines; it is even possible for someone to perform the *hadj* by proxy, appointing someone to stand in for them. Returning pilgrims can add the word Hadj to their name if they want, and often in the more basic villages simple scenes will be painted on the wall of the pilgrim's house to show that the inhabitant has been to Mecca.

The **hadj rituals** were established by Mohammed, though today the mass of pilgrims tend not to follow them in strict order. When the pilgrims come within 10km of Mecca they enter a state of holiness known as *ihram* and wrap two white sheets around their bodies. Henceforth, neither hair nor nails may be cut until the pilgrimage is over. In Mecca the pilgims walk seven times around the sacred shrine, the Ka'ba, in the Great Mosque and kiss the Black Stone (Hajar al-Aswad) in the Ka'ba wall. Following this, in between prayers and a ritual reminder of their duties as Muslims, the pilgrims must run seven times between mounts Safa and Marwah and visit the holy places outside Mecca. An animal is then sacrificed to commemorate Abraham's sacrifice and seven stones thrown at the three pillars at Mina (the pillars represent devils). After this the pilgrims heads are shaved. They then return to Mecca to perform a final circling of the Ka'ba before leaving the city.

MUSLIM GROUPS IN SYRIA

Eighty-five percent of Syrians are Muslim, of whom around eighty percent are Sunni, thirteen percent Alawis, with the rest comprising Shia Muslims and the various sects that have sprung from them. The schism between **Sunni** and **Shi'ite** derives from the power struggle between Ali and the Umayyad dynasty of Damascus over the succession of the caliphate. Ali, Caliph from 656 to 661, was assassinated and the caliphate passed to the Umayyad leader Moawiya, who was related to Othman, Ali's predecessor. Those who recognized Moawiya became known as Sunnis, while Shia Muslims only recognize the hereditary successors of Ali. The **Ismailis**, a subsect of the Shia, are followers of an alternative seventh *imam*, and themselves have a further, more extreme subsect, the Assassins (see box on p.139); important in medieval times the Ismailis are now mainly to be found in India and Pakistan, with only small pockets in Syria itself.

The **Alawite** sect, of which President Assad is a member, is a yet more extreme offshoot of the Ismailis. Little is known of the sect as few even of their members learn the tenets of their faith, and they have no prayer houses; founded in the late tenth century, they are considered by some other Muslims to be heretics because they believe in the divinity of Ali.

RELIGIOUS MINORITIES

The **Druze** (see box on p.109) combine Shia and Christian elements; in Syria they live mainly in the Hauran and Golan Heights and are thought to number something over a hundred thousand, though accurate figures are not available.

Christians are thought to account for around ten to thirteen percent of Syria's population, belonging to a wide variety of churches. The Eastern Orthodox Church is represented in three branches: the **Greek Orthodox**, which uses an Arab liturgy, the **Armenian Orthodox**, which uses classical Armenian, and the **Syrian Orthodox**, which uses Syriac, closely related to Aramaic, the language Jesus spoke. The Syrian Orthodox Church claims to be the original church of Antioch, where followers of Jesus were, according to the New Testament, first called Christians but since 1959 the head of the Church, known as the Patriarch of Antioch, has resided in Damascus. The Syrian Orthodox broke away from the main Orthodox family in 451 following a theological dispute over the nature of Christ's divinity at the Council of Chalcedon. Following the establishment of the Jesuits and Capuchins in Aleppo in 1626 a number of Syrian Orthodox communities were united with Rome and became known as **Syrian Catholics**. Throughout the eighteenth century they were heavily persecuted by the Syrian Orthodox Church and it was not until 1782 that a continuous series of Syrian Catholic patriarchs began. The Syrian Catholics also use Syriac, though some services are conducted in Arabic.

All of Syria's Catholic communities come under Rome's jurisdiction. The **Greek Catholics** are the largest group, and are still firmly bound to Byzantine tradition; the diocesan clergy must remain celibate, though priests responsible for rural parishes are allowed to marry. The **Maronites** originated from the teachings of St Maron, a monk who lived near Cyrrhus and died in 433; they are to be found mainly in Lebanon, though there is a sizable community in Aleppo. Small communities of **Roman Catholics** live in Aleppo and in western Syria; in 1987 Rome restored the patriarchate of Jerusalem.

Communities of Armenians have lived in Syria for many centuries, though there was a major influx from Turkey following the attempted genocide at the turn of the last century, when up to a million and a half people perished. The Armenians are overwhelmingly Christian and number over 200,000, most of them based in Aleppo, though there is also a significant community in Damascus. The **Armenian Orthodox Church** uses classical Armenian for its liturgy and is regarded as the guardian of Armenian national identity. It came into being in 301 following the conversion of King Tirdate, thus making Armenia the world's first Christian nation. **Armenian Catholics** also use classical Armenian in their services; they tend mainly to be refugees from the Turkish massacres of 1894–6 and 1915–21, and more than half the members live in Aleppo, though the patriarch resides in Beirut.

BOOKS

There are comparatively few books relating solely to Syria – most of the time the country is included in general books about Middle Eastern history, travel, politics or culture. In the list below, publishers' details for books in print are given in the form "UK publisher; US publisher", where they differ; if books are published in one country only, this follows the publisher's name; "o/p" means out of print – consult a library or specialist secondhand bookseller.

TRAVEL WRITING

Baedeker, *Guide to Syria and Palestine* (o/p). Produced in a number of editions, the oldest being 1876. Interesting from a historical point of view as it was written when present-day Syria was simply part of a crumbling Turkish empire, with fascinating observations on the ruins before the French started restoring them under the mandate – people were still living in the Bel Temple at Palmyra and in the Crac des Chevaliers. Practical information focuses on how to hire horses and camels, and deal with *baksheesh* demands. Contemporary Cook's guides tend to be less personal and comprehensive, but they're quite fun too.

Gertrude Bell, *The Desert and the Sown* (Virago, UK, o/p). An indomitable society woman who indulged her passion for travel, becoming a respected historian, archeologist and linguist; she befriended T.E. Lawrence during their time at the Arab Bureau in World War I and ended up founding Baghdad's National Museum. This book describes her 1905 journey from Jerusalem to Alexandretta but is better on the people she meets than the places she visits.

Johannes Burckhardt, *Travels in Syria and the Holy Land* (o/p). This fascinating account by one of the most important Middle Eastern travellers was originally published in 1822. Burkhardt spent the years 1810–16 wandering the Holy Land dressed as a pilgrim, and is most famous for his underhand discovery of Petra.

Agatha Christie, *Come, Tell Me How You Live* (Fontana, UK, o/p). Christie's husband Sir Max Mallowan excavated many sites in northeastern Syria (most notably Tell Brak) in the 1930s, mostly accompanied by Agatha. This entertaining little book recounts Christie's impressions of the landscape and people of Syria during the mandate era – but says nothing about the history being researched, which absorbed Max but largely bored his wife.

Robin Fedden, *Syria and Lebanon* (John Murray, UK, o/p). First published in 1946, an interesting and readable historical survey covering all the major sites in a broad chronological order. By the same author is the stimulating and well-photographed *Crusader Castles* (John Murray, UK, o/p), written in 1950.

Lieve Joris, *The Gates of Damascus* (Lonely Planet Publications). Account by a Belgian author of a year spent living with a Damascus woman whose husband has been jailed for political crimes. Her depiction of the lives of ordinary Syrians from a woman's perspective is moving, provocative, funny and always perceptive.

Freya Stark, *Letters from Syria* (John Murray, UK, o/p). Series of letters written in the late 1920s, most interesting in their open depiction of the hostility of the locals to the ruling French, particularly in the Hauran which had recently seen a prolonged revolt. See also *Freya Stark in the Levant* (Garnet, UK) by Malise Ruthven, a selection of the estimated fifty thousand photographs Stark took in the Middle East in the early part of this century.

Robert Tewdwr Moss, *Cleopatra's Wedding Present* (Duckworth, UK). Witty and readable account of a gay journalist's travels in Syria during the summer of 1995, finished on the day that its author was murdered in his London flat by an Arab rent-boy. His comments on the landscape and individuals he encounters (particularly the Palestinian ex-commando with whom he falls in love) are wry but discerning.

Colin Thubron, *Mirror to Damascus* (Penguin, UK). Classic travel book written in 1966, a loose, anecdote-ridden chronological guide to the city. Entertaining and thought-provoking, providing many interesting parallels to mull over.

HISTORY

Robert Betts, *The Druze* (Yale University Press). Slightly pompous account of the Druze origins and beliefs, with good sections on the bewilderment that the sect has engendered in the outside world.

Edward Burman, *The Assassins – Holy Killers of Islam* (Crucible, UK, o/p). In-depth look at the sect who were based around Misyaf.

Philip Hitti, *History of Syria* (o/p). Still the classic history, though not the most accessible introduction for the general reader and now nearly fifty years old.

Albert Hourani, *A History of the Arab Peoples* (Faber; Warner). Heavy scholastic work with little directly on Syria, covering the period from the seventh century to the present day. Good on the divergence of Arab Islamic society and culture, and the reassertion of Islamic identity in the late twentieth century.

Philip Khoury, *Syria and the French Mandate* (Tauris, UK; Princeton University Press, US). Valuable contribution to a part of history that French historians have shown little interest in, and Arab ones have been too emotive about. A sequel to his *Urban Notables and Arab Nationalism* (Cambridge University Press, o/p), which explores the birth of Arab nationalism with particular reference to Damascus and the nature of Ottoman rule in Syria – which Khoury asserts was enforced essentially through a local elite.

T.E. Lawrence, *Seven Pillars of Wisdom* (Penguin, UK; Doubleday, US). Lawrence's classic account of the Arab revolt during World War I.

Bernard Lewis, *The Assassins – A Radical Sect in Islam* (Al Saqi, UK; OUP, US). Sensible reading of the sect which dispels a few myths – particularly of the drug-taking.

Peter Mansfield, *A History of the Middle East* (Penguin). Broad general survey covering the period from 1800 to 1990, with little specifically on Syria, though very readable for all that. Written by the former Middle Eastern correspondent of the *Sunday Times*, who also penned *The Arabs* (Penguin).

Abraham Marcus, *The Middle East on the Eve of Modernity* (Columbia University Press). Economic, social and political analysis of Aleppo in the eighteenth century. Not ideal travel reading, but with interesting sections on such diverse topics as literacy, law enforcement and disease.

Steven Runciman, *A History of the Crusades* (Penguin, UK; Cambridge University Press, US). Comprehensive 3-volume work for enthusiasts, pulling no punches on the gossip and gore. Worth comparing with *The Crusades through Arab Eyes* (Al-Saqi) by Lebanese journalist Amin Maalouf, which focuses on the writings of contemporary Arab chroniclers and is slightly shorter.

MODERN SYRIA

Richard Antoun (ed), *Syria: Society, Culture and Polity* (State University of New York Press). Series of stimulating essays, well worth a dip especially for its chapter on women's role in society through the eyes of its female writers.

A.J. Barker, *Arab-Israeli Wars* (Ian Allen, UK, o/p). Israeli-biased illustrated work on the 1948, 1956, 1967 and 1973 wars.

John Devlin, *The Ba'ath Party* (Hoover Institution Press, US, o/p). Useful political work, telling the story of the party from its founding in 1940 to its split in 1966, when the founders were expelled from the country.

Derek Hopwood, *Syria 1945–1986* (Routledge). General historical account.

Moshe Ma'oz, *Assad – the Sphinx of Damascus* (Weidenfeld and Nicholson). Rounded political biography which gives Assad all the personal credit for his achievements, but which ultimately raises more questions than it answers.

Moshe Ma'oz, *Syria and Israel – from War to Peacemaking* (Clarendon). Based on the premise that there can be no full peace in the Middle East without Syria, but unfortunately written with premature optimism during the era of Yitzhak Rabin.

Middle East Watch, *Syria Unmasked* (Yale University Press). A 1991 investigation into human rights violations with particular focus on events leading to the Hama Massacre. Provides a good general perspective of the political situation at the time, though things have thawed slightly since its publication.

Daniel Pipes, *Greater Syria – the History of an Ambition* (Oxford University Press). Interesting history from 1920 to 1988 of Syria's dissatisfaction with the borders imposed on it by the European powers.

David Roberts, *The Ba'ath Party and the Creation of Modern Syria* (Croom Helm, UK, o/p). General work written as a basic introduction to the fluid nature of Ba'ath ideology, by the ex-British ambassador to Damascus.

Patrick Seale, *The Struggle for Syria* (Tauris; Yale University Press). Good account, by a correspondent for the *Observer*, of the political intrigues from independence to the attempt to achieve Arab unity in 1958; most interesting on the Anglo-American-Iraqi attempt to overthrow the Syrian government in 1957. His *Assad: The Struggle for the Middle East* (Tauris), written with interviews with the man himself and many of his most important ministers, gives a useful perspective on Assad's point of view without being an apologist.

Bouthaina Shaaban, *Both Right and Left Handed* (The Women's Press, UK; Indiana University Press, US). Account of the woman's role in modern-day Arab society (including a chapter on Syria), presented through a series of conversations with local women. Documents well the conflict between economic and political freedoms and personal freedom.

ART AND ARCHEOLOGY

Warwick Ball, *Syria – An Historical and Architectural Guide* (Melisende, UK; Infolink, US). Good account, though the unbroken text makes it a bit of a slog and it gives no practical help.

Iain Browning, *Palmyra* (Chatto and Windus, UK, o/p). The best coffee-table book you'll find on Syria, a thorough and interesting appraisal of the site illustrated intelligently with copious photographs.

Ross Burns, *Monuments of Syria* (Tauris; New York University Press). Essential reference book for those who want to explore the sites as thoroughly as they can. Not a travel guide but a hefty gazetteer of sites, so there's no practical information.

Clark Hopkins, *The Discovery of Dura Europos* (Yale University Press, o/p). Fascinating, highly recommended account of the excavation,

guesswork and final unravelling of the site, produced by the American director of the excavations during the 1930s.

Johannes Kalter, *The Arts and Crafts of Syria* (Thames and Hudson). Well-illustrated general work; essential for anyone taking their souvenir-hunting seriously, or seeking a deeper appreciation of the local culture and the meaning of clothes and jewellery in Syrian, and particularly Bedouin, society.

T.E. Lawrence, *Crusader Castles* (OUP, UK; Hippocrene, US). Lawrence's Oxford thesis expanded with a few letters to illustrate his pre-War journeys through East Anglia, Wales, France and the Middle East. It's a slight, overpriced, rather dry book, enlivened by some well-worn quotes and anecdotes and a scent of the man, but had it not been written by Lawrence it would never have seen the light of day.

Paolo Matthiae, *Ebla: an Empire Rediscovered* (Hodder and Stoughton, UK). An exhaustive history of the site.

Essie Sakhai, *Oriental Rugs – a Buyer's Guide* (Parkway, UK; Moyer Bell, US). Have a look at this before entering the Syrian souks if you're serious in your pursuit.

David Talbot Rice, *Islamic Art* (Thames and Hudson). General reference work.

Harvey Weiss (ed), *From Ebla to Damascus* (Washington University Press, US). Series of stimulating archeological essays, printed in the States only and hard to get elsewhere.

ISLAM

A.J. Arberry (trans), *The Koran* (Oxford University Press). The best English-language version.

H.A.R. Gibb, *Islam* (Oxford University Press, o/p). Overview of the historical development of Islam by a professor of Arabic at Oxford and Harvard universities.

SYRIAN POETRY AND FICTION

Ali Ahmad Said (Adonis), *Mirrors* (TR Press, UK, o/p). Short pamphlet of short poems produced in 1976 by the founder of an influential cultural journal *Mawaqif*. No direct political references though an authoritarian shadow hangs over the poet's melancholic drift into desperation.

Hanna Minah, *Al-Wallaah*. Written in 1989 and published in Beirut, this novel set during the French occupation of Syria chronicles the rites of passage of a teenager, torn between his mother's accepting conservatism and his father's critical thinking and political activism which lands him in prison. During the course of the book the hero changes from an ignorant, unquestioning boy into a man who acts and understands the political events surrounding him – and of course he loses his virginity. See also Minah's *Fragments of Memory* (Texas University Press).

LANGUAGE

The combination of harsh, unfamiliar sounds and a seeming mess of scribbles means that most visitors never even attempt to learn Arabic. However, though it's true that a mastery of the language would take many years, it's not too difficult – with the aid of transliteration into Latin script (see p.274) – to pick up a few useful phrases to ease your travels.

Literary Arabic, the ancient language of the Koran, has been formalized today into **Modern Standard Arabic (MSA)**, which is the language that all Arabs understand. Thus newspapers and news broadcasts can be understood from Oman to Morocco. However, different parts of the Arab world have distinct dialects, which have no written form, and Omanis and Moroccans would have problems actually conversing with each other. Helpfully, the **Syrian dialect** is not too far removed from MSA, almost identical to the Jordanian and not too dissimilar to the Egyptian dialect – if you have a smattering of Egyptian Arabic, or a relevant **phrasebook** such as *Egyptian Arabic: A Rough Guide Phrasebook*, you will be able to make yourself understood in Syria.

Syrians place great importance upon **greetings**, civilities and enquiries into each other's health. Always try to greet someone in Arabic before asking them a question, even if the question is in English. Often a greeting will be accompanied by a handshake, though you may be hugged and kissed on both cheeks if your host is especially pleased to see you. The most common greeting is *assalaamu aleikum* (peace be to you). The response, *wa-aleikum assalaam*, reverses the words to mean "to you be peace (also)". *Marhaba* is the other important greeting, being a more simple "hello". One other phrase you will also hear a lot of is *inshallah* meaning "God willing", used as a general answer to anything.

Syrians are also masters of the art of **gesticulation**. One of the most common is an outstretched hand and a flick of the wrist which means "what do you want?"; often taxi drivers will do this at you if they are passing, or you may get this when wandering around a bus station trying to find the right bus. Another common one is raised eyebrows and a slight back-throw of the head which means "no" and is generally taken to be final.

However keen you are to try out your Arabic, you will find that Syrians are even keener to try out their English. Some older Arabs have a knowledge of French from the mandate era, but today English is taught in school. However, most locals will only know a few basic phrases; when waiting at a bus station you may be approached by groups of inquisitive children shouting "what is your name?" at you, but nothing else.

SYRIAN ARABIC

PRONUNCIATION

Below is a very simplified phonetic guide to a few sounds that might cause difficulties, as the complete rules governing prouniciation are too complex to go into here. Just try to speak slowly and clearly, and the locals will be usually more than happy to ignore any of your rough edges. Remember to pronounce everything as transliterated, including for example both consonants in a double consonant – for instance, say "*hom-ma*" for *homma* meaning "they".

aa	as in bad, but lengthened	**gh**	like a growled "r"
ai	as in eye	**'**	signifies a glottal stop, similar to that in regional English when the letter "t" is not pronounced (eg "wa'er" for "water"); but *'a* is a heavy "ah" sound, said from the throat.
ay/ey	as in say		
ee	as in feet		
kh	as in loch		

PRONOUNS

I	*ana*	She	*hayya*
You (singular)	*inta* (masculine)/ *inti* (feminine)	We	*ehna*
		You (plural)	*intoo*
He	*howa*	They	*homma*

BASICS

Yes	*aiwa/na'am*	Excuse me	*an iznak* (to a man)/ *'an iznik* (to a woman)
No	*la*	Sorry	*aasif* (to a man)/ *asfa* (to a woman)
Thank you	*shukran*		
You're welcome	*afwan*	No problem	*mish mushkila*
		God willing	*inshallah*
Please	*min fadlak* (to a man)/ *fadlik* (to a woman)	Nothing	*wallahagga*

GREETINGS AND FAREWELLS

Welcome	*ahlan wa-sahlan*	Good evening	*masa' il-kheer*
(response)	*ahlan bik* (m)/*biki* (f)/ *bikum* (pl)	(response)	*masa' in-nur*
Hello (formal)	*assalaamu aleikum*	How are you?	*kayf halak* (to a man)/ *kayf halik* (to a woman)
(response)	*wa-aleikum assalaam*		
Hi	*marhaba*	I am well, thanks be to God	*qwayyis* (m)/*qwayyisa* (f) *il-hamdu lilla*
(response)	*marhabtein*		
Greetings	*sa'eeda*	Good night	*tisbah* (to a man)/ *tisbahi* (to a woman) *'ala kheer*
Nice to meet you	*fursa sa'eeda*		
Good morning	*sabah il-kheer*		
(response)	*sabah in-nur*	Goodbye	*ma'a salaama*

QUESTIONS AND DIRECTIONS

What is your name?	*ismak* (to a man)/ *ismik* (to a woman) *ey*	hospital	*mustash-fa*
		hotel	*funduq*
My name is...	*ismi...*	museum	*mathaf*
Do you speak...	*titkallim* (to a man)/ *titkallimi* (to a woman)...	passport and immigration office	*maktab il-jawazat wa il-hijra*
Arabic ?	*arabi*	pharmacy	*sayidiyya*
English?	*ingleezi*	police	*shurta*
French?	*fransawi*		
German?	*almanee*	post office	*maktab il-barid*
I speak English	*ana batkallim ingleezi*	restaurant	*mat'am*
I don't speak Arabic	*ana ma-batkallimsh 'arab*	telephone office	*maktab il-telifoon*
I don't understand	*ana mish fahem* (m)/ *fahma* (f)	toilet	*walet*
		tourist office	*maktab as-siyaha*
I understand	*ana fahem* (m)/*fahma* (f)	train station	*mahattat il-atr*
Where are you from?	*min wayn inta*	Left/right/ straight ahead	*shimaal/yimeen/ alatool*
I am...	*ana...*	Near/far	*areeb/ba'eed*
Australian	*ustrali* (m)/*ustraliyya* (f)	How many?	*kam*
American	*amriki* (m)/*amrikiyya* (f)	How many km?	*kam kilometre*
Canadian	*kanadi* (m)/*kanadiyya* (f)		
English	*ingleezi* (m)/*ingleeziyya* (f)	Here/there	*hinna/hinnak*
What does this mean?	*yaani ay*	To/from	*ila/min*
What's that in English?	*yaani ay bil-ingleezi*	East/west	*sharq/gharb*
Where is the...?	*feyn funduq il...*	North/south	*shimal/junub*
airport	*mataar*	When does the bus leave?	*il-autobas yissafir imta*
bank	*bank*	When does the train leave/arrive?	*il-atr yissafir imta/yoosal*
bus station	*mahattat il-bas* (specify *pullman* or *meecro*)	Ticket	*at-tazkarah*
church	*kaneesa*	What time is it?	*issa'a kam*
city centre	*markaz al-medina*	First/last/next	*il-awil/il-akhir/et-tani*
doctor	*duktur*	Not yet	*lissa*

REQUESTS AND SHOPPING

Do you have...?	*fi 'andak* (to a man)/ *'andik* (to a woman)...	Big	*kebir awi*
		Small	*sughayyar awi*
cigarettes	*agayir*	Cheap	*rakhis*
matches	*kibreet*	Expensive	*ghaali*
newspaper	*gurnal*	That's fine	*maashi*
What is this?	*shu hadha*	This/that	*di/da*
How much (is it)?	*bi-kam da*	I don't want	*mish ayyiz* (m)/*ayyza* (f)
It's too expensive	*da ghaali awi*	Open/closed	*maftuuh/musakkar*

SYRIAN ARABIC (cont.)

ACCOMMODATION

Do you have a...?	*fi...*	Can I see it?	*mumkin atfarraj-ha*
room	*ghurfa*	How much is the bill?	*kam il-hasab*
single room	*ghurfa mufrada*	We are leaving today	*ehna musafirin al-yom*
double room	*ghurfa bi sarirayn*	Blanket	*bataniyya*
		Breakfast	*fitar*
Is there...?	*fi...*	Full	*malyaan*
hot water	*mayya sukhna*	Key	*miftah*
a shower	*doush*	Manager	*mudir*
a balcony	*balcona*		
air conditioning	*takyeef hawa*		
a telephone	*telifoon*		

REACTIONS AND SMALL TALK

I don't know	*ana mish 'arif* (m)/ *'arfa* (f)	Don't touch me	*sibnee le wadi*
I am tired/unwell	*ana ta'aban* (m)/ *ta'abana* (f)	Go away	*imshi*
I am sick	*ana marid* (m)/ *marida* (f)	Let's go	*yalla*
I am hungry	*ana gawa'an* (m)/ *gawa'ana* (f)	Help me	*sa iduni*
I am thirsty	*ana 'atshaan* (m)/ *'atshaana* (f)	Slowly	*baranah*
Are you married?	*inta mitgowiz* (to a man)/ *inti mitgowiza* (to a woman)	Enough	*khalas*
		Never mind	*maalesh*
I am (not) married	*ana* (*mish*) *mitgowiz* (m)/ *mitgowiza* (f)	It doesn't matter	*mush muhim*
It's none of your business	*mish shorlak*	There's no problem	*ma feesh mushkila*
		It's not possible	*mish mumkin*

MONEY

Where is a bank?	*feyn il-bank*	British pounds	*ginay sterlini*
I want to change...	*ayyiz* (m)/ *ayyaza* (f) *aghayyar...*	US dollars	*dolar amrikani*
		travellers' cheques	*shikaat siyahiyya*
money	*floos*	Syrian pounds	*giney*

CALENDAR

Minute	*daqiqa*	Later	*bahdeen*	March	*azar*
Hour	*saa*	Saturday	*youm is-sabt*	April	*nisan*
Day	*youm*	Sunday	*youm il-ahad*	May	*ayyar*
Night	*leyla*	Monday	*youm il-itnayn*	June	*huzayran*
Week	*usbu'a*	Tuesday	*youm it-talaata*	July	*tammuz*
Month	*shahr*	Wednesday	*youm il-arb'a*	August	*ab*
Year	*sana*	Thursday	*youm il-khamees*	September	*aylul*
Today	*il-youm*	Friday	*youm il-gum'a*	October	*tishrin il-awal*
Tomorrow	*bukkra*	January	*kanun ath-thani*	November	*tishrin ath-thani*
Yesterday	*imbaarih*	February	*shubat*	December	*kanun il-awal*

NUMBERS AND FRACTIONS

0	sifr	14	arb'atarsha	90	tis'een
1	wahid	15	khamastarsha	100	miyya
2	itnayn	16	sittarsha	101	miyya wa-wahid
3	talaata	17	sab'atarsha	150	miyya wa-khamseen
4	arb'a	18	tamantarsha	200	mitayn
5	khamsa	19	tis'atarsha	300	talaata miyya
6	sitta	20	'ashreen	500	khamsa miyya
7	sab'a	21	wahid wa-'ashreen	1000	alf
8	tamanya	30	talaateen	2000	alfayn
9	tes'a	40	arb'aeen	3000	talaat alaaf
10	'ashara	50	khamseen	4000	arb'at alaaf
11	hidarsha	60	sitteen	1/2	nous
12	itnarsha	70	sab'aeen	1/4	robah
13	talatarsha	80	tamaneen		

GLOSSARY

AGORA Marketplace in a Greek or Roman city.

AIN Spring.

APSE Usually semicircular structure at the eastern end of a church.

BAB Gateway, door.

BAKSHEESH Tip.

BEIT House.

BURJ Tower.

CARAVANSERAI Inn and marketplace for caravans.

CARDO MAXIMUS Main road running usually north–south through a Roman city.

CELLA Sacred chamber housing the image of the worshipped god at the centre of a temple compound.

CRYPTOPORTICUS Dark passage often running beside a colonnaded street.

DECUMANUS East–west street that would cross the *cardo maximus* in a Roman city.

DEIR Monastery.

HADJ Pilgrimage to Mecca.

HAMAM Public Turkish bath.

HAREMLEK Private quarters of an Ottoman residence.

HYPOGEUM Underground tomb.

ICONOSTASIS A screen with icons separating the nave from the chancel in a church.

IWAN Open reception area set off a courtyard.

JEBEL Mountain.

KALYBE Shrine with niches for the display of statues.

KHAN Warehouse/hostel for merchants.

MADRASA Islamic school.

MARISTAN Medieval hospital.

MAYDAN Square.

MIHRAB Niche in a mosque showing the direction of Mecca.

MINARET Tower of a mosque.

MINBAR Mosque pulpit.

MUKHABARAT Secret police.

NARGILEH Water pipe used to smoke tobacco, hubble-bubble.

NORIA Wooden wheel used to lift water from a river.

NYMPHAEUM Public water fountain in a Greek or Roman city with niches for statues.

PASHA Governor of an Ottoman province.

PERISTYLE Roofed, colonnaded corridor.

PLAS Square.

PRAETORIUM Roman governor's residence.

QALAAT Castle.

QASR Palace.

SHARIA Street.

SOUK Market.

TAREE Avenue.

TELL Mound or artificial hill concealing an archeological site.

TETRAPYLON Arrangement of columns and arches marking the intersection of two major Roman roads within a city.

TRICLINIUM Dining room of a Roman dwelling.

VIA SACRA Sacred way.

WADI Valley, dry except during rain.

INDEX

Stay in touch with us!

ROUGH*NEWS* is Rough Guides' free newsletter.
In three issues a year we give you news, travel
issues, music reviews, readers' letters and the
latest dispatches from authors on the road.

I would like to receive ROUGH*NEWS*: please put me on your free mailing list.

NAME . . . .

ADDRESS . . . .

Please clip or photocopy and send to: Rough Guides, 1 Mercer Street, London WC2H 9QJ, England
or Rough Guides, 375 Hudson Street, New York, NY 10014, USA.